Practical Emotional Intelligence

6 Books in 1

Anger Management, Cognitive Behavioral Therapy, Stoicism, Public Speaking, and Self-Discipline

PUBLISHED BY: James W. Williams

© Copyright 2020 - All rights reserved.

The content contained within this book may not be reproduced, duplicated or transmitted without direct written permission from the author or the publisher.

Under no circumstances will any blame or legal responsibility be held against the publisher, or author, for any damages, reparation, or monetary loss due to the information contained within this book. Either directly or indirectly.

Legal Notice:

This book is copyright protected. This book is only for personal use. You cannot amend, distribute, sell, use, quote or paraphrase any part, or the content within this book, without the consent of the author or publisher.

Disclaimer Notice:

Please note the information contained within this document is for educational and entertainment purposes only. All effort has been executed to present accurate, up to date, and reliable, complete information. No warranties of any kind are declared or implied. Readers acknowledge that the author is not engaging in the rendering of legal, financial, medical or professional advice. The content within this book has been derived from various sources. Please consult a licensed professional before attempting any techniques outlined in this book.

By reading this document, the reader agrees that under no circumstances is the author responsible for any losses, direct or indirect, which are incurred as a result of the use of information contained within this document, including, but not limited to, — errors, omissions, or inaccuracies

Table of Contents

Your Free Gift 1

Book #1: Emotional Intelligence 3

Introduction 5

PART 1: Emotional Intelligence: Why are "People Skills" so Important? 7

Day 1: Emotional Intelligence 8

Day 2: Emotions 15

Day 3: Intelligence 19

Day 4: Relationships 23

Day 5: Career 29

Day 6: Leadership 33

Day 7: Shyness 36

Day 8: Self-Esteem 41

Day 9: Social Anxiety 45

Day 10: Coping with Pressure 49

Day 11: Why You Need "People Skills" 53

PART 2: How to Improve Your Emotional Intelligence 56

Day 12: Learn to Deal with Your Feelings 57

Day 13: Think Before You Speak 61

Day 14: Take It on the Chin 64

Day 15: Stand Up for What You Believe In 68

Day 16: Connect 71

Day 17: Reprogram Your Mindset 74

Day 18: Forgive and Get on With Your Life 78

Day 19: Emotional Manipulation 82

Day 20: Step-by-Step Guide to Becoming a Better Listener 86

Day 21: Putting It All Together 90

Closing 96

Book #2: Anger Management 97

PART 1: Anger – A Cry for Help or a Desire to Control? 99

Day 1: What is Anger? 100

Day 2: Signs and Symptoms of Anger 104

Day 3: Why Do I Get Angry? 108

Day 4: Anger in Children 112

Day 5: Anger in Teens 117

Day 6: Anger as Part of Grief 121

Day 7: How Anger Affects Relationships 125

Day 8: Anger in the Workplace 130

Day 9: Anger-Related Disorders 134

Day 10: Anger Across Cultures 138

PART 2: Anger Management 141

Day 11: When Anger Becomes a Problem 142

Day 12: Handling Emotions 147

Day 13: Emotional Intelligence and Anger Management 152

Day 14: Emotional Intelligence 156

Day 15: Mindfulness 160

Day 16: Meditation 165

Day 17: Zen Buddhism and the Importance of Living in the Present 171

Day 18: Inner Peace Techniques for Anger Management 175

Day 19: Cognitive Behavioral Therapy 179

Day 20: Nutrition for Stress Relief 184

Day 21: Putting It All Together 188

Book #3: COGNITIVE BEHAVIORAL THERAPY MADE SIMPLE 193

Introduction 195

Dealing with Overwhelming Emotions 196

Anger 197

Anxiety 198

Depression 199

Negative Thoughts 201

Cognitive Behavioral Therapy 202

Day 1: Get real with your emotions 204

Day 2: Put your feelings to words 207

Day 3: Talk to Someone 210

Day 4: Feel the music 212

Day 5: Take things outside 214

Day 6: Get Physical 216

Day 7: Give Yourself Permission to Heal 217

Day 8: Start Daydreaming Again 219

Day 9: Create a Gratitude List 222

Day 10: Meditate 224

Day 11: Pay Attention to Your Diet 227

DAY 12: Develop Your Own Mantra 230

Day 13: Practice Relaxed Breathing 232

Day 14: Gain Mastery Over Your Emotions 235

Day 15: Step Things Up with New Relaxation Techniques 238

Day 16: Reflect on the Experience 241

Day 17: Focus on the Good 243

Day 18: Uproot the Negative Sources 245

Day 19: Bring Positivity to Others 247

Day 20: Live in the Moment 249

Day 21: Letting it all go 251

Embracing the Brand New You 254

Closing 256

Book #4: Stoicism 257

Introduction 259

Chapter One: Stoicism 101 261

Chapter Two: History of Stoicism 264

Chapter Three: Early Stoicism 267

Chapter Four: Modern Stoicism 270

Chapter Five: The Stoic Logic 273

Chapter Six: General Misconceptions About Stoicism 276

Chapter Seven: toicism in Everyday Living 279

Chapter Eight: The Four Cardinal Virtues of Stoicism 282

Chapter Nine: The Practice of Misfortune 285

Chapter Ten: The Training of Perception 289

Chapter Eleven: Keeping the Balance with Eupatheiai 292

Chapter Twelve: Plato's View 295

Chapter Thirteen: Memento Mori (Remember Death) 298

Chapter Fourteen: Recognizing Limits 301

Chapter Fifteen: Journaling... 304

Chapter Sixteen: Premeditatio Malorum (The Premeditation of Evil) 307

Chapter Seventeen: Amor Fati (Love Fate) 310

Chapter Eighteen: The Power to Enforce Change 313

Chapter Nineteen: Stoicism in Cognitive Behavioral Therapy 315

Chapter Twenty: Stoicism in Pain Management..319

Chapter Twenty-one: Stoicism in Growing Emotional Intelligence.............323

Chapter Twenty-two: Stoic Exercises and Practices to Get You Started 326

Chapter Twenty-three: Taking Ownership of Your Life...................................329

Closing... 332

Book #5: Public Speaking..333

Preface 335

Introduction 336

PART ONE: THE BATTLE WITHIN 339

CHAPTER ONE: The Introvert's Bubble 340

CHAPTER TWO: CROWDED SPACES 346

CHAPTER THREE: BUILDING BLOCKS OF CONFIDENCE 352

CHAPTER FOUR: ELIMINATING OBSTACLES..357

PART TWO: SETTING THE STAGE 363

CHAPTER FIVE: UNDERSTANDING THE WHYS..................................... 364

CHAPTER SIX: CHOOSING YOUR FIGHTS CAREFULLY 370

CHAPTER SEVEN: LOOKING THE PART..377

PART THREE: GOING FOR GOLD 383

CHAPTER EIGHT: THE ART OF PUBLIC SPEAKING............................... 384

CHAPTER NINE: MANAGING YOUR STAGE 390

CHAPTER TEN: THE TOOLS OF THE TRADE 395

CLOSING 399

Book #6: Self-Discipline Mastery **401**

Introduction 403

Chapter 1: The Science of Self-Discipline, Motivation, and Willpower 404

Chapter 2: Shifting Your Mindset 409

Chapter 3: Building Good Habits and Breaking Bad Ones 414

How to Quit Bad Habits 426

How to Practice Delayed Gratification and How to Overcome Temptations 431

Sturgeon's Law and the Pareto Principle 437

Essential Habit #1 – How to Build and Stick to a Workout Plan 438

Essential Habit #2 – Maintain a Healthy Diet 440

Essential Habit #3 – Sleep/Wake Up Early 444

Essential Habit #4 – Work Smart: Eat the Frog 448

Essential Habit #5 – Mindfulness 451

Chapter 4: More Actionable Tips to Build Self-Discipline 459

Chapter 5: Dealing with Burnout the Smart Way 472

Chapter 6 – Discipline Tactics of Navy SEALs and the Spartans 483

Conclusion 490

Thank you! **491**

Your Free Gift

As a way of saying thanks for your purchase, I want to offer you a free bonus E-book called **Bulletproof Confidence Checklist** exclusive to the readers of this book.

To get instant access just tap here, or go to:

https://theartofmastery.com/confidence/

Inside the book, you will discover:

- The science and psychology of shyness & social anxiety
- Simple yet powerful strategies for overcoming social anxiety
- How to become a more confident person by developing these traits
- Traits you must DESTROY if you want to become confident
- Easy techniques you can implement TODAY to keep the conversation flowing
- Confidence checklist to ensure you're on the right path of self-development

Book #1

Emotional Intelligence

The 21-Day Mental Makeover to Master Your Emotions, Improve Your Social Skills, and Achieve Better, Happier Relationships

Introduction

In the fast-changing world, the necessary set of survival skills keeps on changing. While in some situations or during certain periods of human history, physical strength and endurance would have been key to survival, today's "survival" depends on education, IT skills, negotiating skills, knowledge of foreign languages, relationship management, self-awareness, and more.

As we moved from a physical to more social environment, the skills that enable us to survive, successfully cope, and thrive changed to match the world we live in. Our need for physical survival skills gradually diminished, and our need for social survival skills grew.

The global culture is complex and diverse, and it's clear that much more cultural sensitivity is needed both in our everyday lives and, particularly, in the workplace. Most employers are painfully aware that empathy and sensitivity help them get the best out of their teams. This is why self-awareness, social awareness, and self-management skills have become critical for recruitment

Until relatively recently, intelligence has been considered the key to success in life. A high IQ was believed to be the ultimate skill for professional achievement and personal happiness, directly linked to your income, health, and education.

However, over the last fifty years, our understanding of what makes someone successful or happy has changed drastically. We now know that emotional intelligence—the combination of emotions and intellect—is what gives some people an edge over those whose main advantage is a high IQ.

It is now generally accepted that a high IQ is no guarantee of success at any level. It is only when a high intellect is combined with emotional intelligence that it is likely to help you get where you want in life.

Emotional intelligence is about having the ability to nurture and manage your emotions, and to be observant and sensitive to the emotions of others. It's about showing empathy and being willing to participate in the pain or success of others.

Overall, it's a set of skills which not only make you more employable, but also make it easier for you to understand and manage the triggers that can cause certain emotions.

Just like high IQ has been overrated as a requirement for success in life, so were emotions underrated. Most of us have been raised to believe that our actions are guided by our minds, and we are usually unaware of the important role emotions actually play in our lives.

It may sound strange, but emotions guide most of our decisions. We like activities, situations, or people who make us feel good—safe, loved, appreciated, wanted, and so on. We also try to avoid those where we feel threatened in some way—used, unappreciated, belittled, scared, embarrassed, for example.

When you master the art of emotional intelligence, you not only become aware of your feelings, what triggers them, and how best to manage your reactions to them, but you also develop resilience to stress or anxiety triggers.

Emotionally intelligent people know how to deal with difficult situations or people, both at work and at home. By nurturing their self-awareness and self-management, they understand why they feel the way they do, and how to react appropriately in a given situation.

There is plenty of evidence that emotionally intelligent people are generally more successful in life.

Just like knowing when to fight, flight, or freeze can be the difference between life and death, knowing how to act or react under certain circumstances makes a difference between successfully managing a difficult situation, or saying or doing something you may later regret.

The trick with emotional intelligence is to sensitize yourself, so you become more aware of what's going on around you; to start challenging and understanding your reactions and feelings that stand behind them; and to start looking at other people's emotions and behavior from their own point of view.

This step-by-step guide will help you get there in 21 days.

The well-known motivational speaker Leo Buscaglia summed it up beautifully when he said, "Too often we underestimate the power of a touch, a smile, a kind word, a listening ear, an honest compliment, or the smallest act of caring—all of which have the potential to turn a life around."

PART 1

Emotional Intelligence: Why are "People Skills" so Important?

Day 1
Emotional Intelligence

What It is and What It is Not

Emotional intelligence is the ability to recognize, understand, and manage one's own emotions, as well as those of others. An emotionally intelligent person is self-aware and has the ability to tune-in to other people's feelings.

Emotional intelligence revolves around emotional awareness—the ability to identify and name emotions, both yours and the emotions of others. The trick to mastering emotional intelligence is to learn how to create awareness so that over time, you become gradually more and more emotionally intelligent.

The four essential elements of emotional intelligence are:
- Self-awareness
- Self-management
- Social awareness
- Relationship management

Emotional skills not only have to be developed and nurtured, but also constantly improved. To improve these skills, you should continuously work on increasing your self-awareness, as well as learning about nonverbal communication, such as body language, eye contact, touch, and so on.

Another trait necessary for maintaining emotional intelligence is a positive attitude. Being positive about life significantly improves your emotional intelligence, as it helps you resolve conflicts positively so you and those around you can move forward. Sometimes, all it takes for someone to deal with trauma is to talk about it or have someone help them see it from a different angle. Another aspect of emotional intelligence is not to dwell on the negative, but to seek solutions, instead.

So, achieving emotional intelligence is about how well you know and understand yourself, and how much effort you put in to know and understand others.

5 steps to emotional intelligence:

- **Recognize your own emotions**

With some emotions, such as anger or sadness, being able to recognize them for what they are is almost as important as finding a solution to what is troubling you. When you know what you're dealing with (e.g., fear, shame, anger, etc.), you will know how best to manage such a feeling.

- **Recognize the emotions of others**

It's sad how little attention we pay to other people's feelings. Not many people are prepared to listen to others and really try to understand what is troubling them. Besides, as it is often our own words or behavior that made them feel that way—embarrassed, scared, foolish—by ignoring them or their feelings, we are ensuring we don't have to take responsibility for our own actions.

- **Understand different feelings and name them**

When you are envious of someone, is it because you think they have something they don't deserve, or because they managed to get it while you didn't? If you are angry at someone for what they've done to you, could you not be trying to ignore your role in what happened? An essential step in dealing with negative feelings is identifying them and naming them. Only when you know what you're dealing with can you find a solution.

- **Use that information to guide your decision-making and behavior**

Emotionally intelligent people are fully aware of their emotions, understand what triggers them, know how to process them, and can use them in a way that supports rational and responsible decision-making or behavior.

- **Manage emotions in accordance with the circumstances**

The trick of being emotionally intelligent is to know how to manage emotions (yours and other people's), or how to adapt your feelings, behaviors, or words to certain situations. For example, you wouldn't use the same words, facial expression, or body language to cheer someone up as when you are dealing with an outraged person who needs calming down. Adjusting your behavior and words to a specific situation or person, particularly in extreme cases, is crucial for the desired effect to be achieved.

Although many different emotions are necessary for emotional intelligence, the key one needs to have, or develop, is empathy. This is the ability to connect with other people's experiences or feelings. For example, when a friend tells you the drama she went through in court during her divorce proceedings, it's your job to support her with words, body language, and eye contact. You need to listen carefully and participate actively, rather than just sit there, thinking about your own problems. Putting yourself in other people's shoes is about going through whatever is happening to them "with" them, instead of just listening passively.

Many studies show that being willing to help and connect with others on all levels—emotionally, mentally and spiritually—makes emotionally intelligent people generally mentally healthier, more successful at work, and often strong and trusted team leaders. On top of that, they are more popular with their colleagues and business partners, mainly because people appreciate those who care.

Emotional Intelligence is not easy to describe—even psychologists disagree about what it is and how important it is for one's personal or professional development. Emotional intelligence is also easily misunderstood, as many people assume it is a kind of a personality trait, a degree of optimism, or a sign of happiness, calmness, or motivation. Emotional intelligence is NONE of those things.

Perhaps Daniel Goleman, an author and science journalist, described emotional intelligence best when he said that, "In a high-IQ job pool, soft skills like discipline, drive, and empathy mark those who emerge as outstanding."

Why is EI such a Powerful Tool, and How to Make the Most of It

When you understand how high emotional intelligence helps you develop and nurture relationships, both personal and professional, you realize what a powerful tool it is for success in life.

Emotionally intelligent people know how to use both their hearts and minds when dealing with others. Although they are empaths, they know how to prevent others from taking advantage of their kindness and willingness to help, be it their children, aging parents, colleagues, or friends.

Like all kinds of personal development, increasing your emotional intelligence is a lifelong process. However, skills that are not used regularly have a tendency of turning rusty. To make sure this doesn't happen to you, never stop improving your emotional intelligence or polishing your listening and mentoring skills.

<u>4 ways to improve your emotional intelligence:</u>
- **Get to know yourself**

Pay attention to how you react and feel when you receive good news or sad news, when you witness injustice, when you are hurt. Become aware of your own emotions and what triggers them—like certain situations, people or memories.

- **Think twice**

Get into the habit of not reacting immediately, but insead taking a few moments to think about what you're going to say, write, or do. Sometimes, all it takes to avoid a difficult situation is to step back and think. Identifying what triggered a particular emotion, such as anger, envy, fear, or anxiety, is crucial to understanding your emotions and your reaction in certain situations.

- **Analyze yours and other people's feelings**

Never ignore your feelings, no matter how trivial they may seem. Learn to stay with them and figure out why you are feeling the way you do. The answer may not always be what you were hoping for, but that's the only way you'll really get to understand yourself or others.

- **Learn from criticism or mistakes**

It takes maturity and self-confidence not to take criticism personally. Instead of sulking or fuming, think what you could learn from each experience. Try to be as objective as possible—even though in many situations, it may be very difficult.

How IE Helps Your Personal and Professional Development

Emotional intelligence has become a highly sought-after skill. However, while empathy comes naturally to some, others may have to work hard on developing self-awareness and learning how to connect with others.

Emotional intelligence is one of those skills that helps you on almost all levels, and is as important for your professional life as it is for your personal development. Ideally, this should be something you use in your everyday life, both in the boardroom and at home.

Your personal development journey depends partly on where you hope to go in life, but also on your maturity and on the skills you feel you need to develop. As this is a lifelong process, it's never too late to start. The main reason emotional intelligence can help you maximize your potential is that it improves your relationships, which directly boosts your self-confidence and social standing.

<u>4 ways emotional intelligence supports your personal development:</u>

- **Your personal relationships improve**

Being able and willing to understand why your family members, friends, colleagues, or neighbors feel a certain way is a sign that you care enough to help others. Everyone likes those who care.

- **Your confidence soars**

Emotionally intelligent people not only understand emotions, they know how to manage them to make the best of a situation—or at least avoid making it worse. Knowing you can handle any situation automatically makes you feel less anxious, more stable, and more self-confident.

- **You are respected**

Those who find time and energy to listen to other people's problems, try seeing things from their perspective, and offer help or coaching if needed, are usually very popular. They are appreciated, respected, and easily accepted as leaders. Most people prefer talking than listening to others, and they really enjoy being the focus of someone's attention—even if they are not willing to pay that much attention to others, themselves.

- **You develop resilience**

Helping others allows you to boost your own self-awareness and social skills. it also helps you master the art of managing and using your emotions, so you gradually become resilient to stress, as well as more competent in dealing with difficult situations.

4 ways EI can help your professional development:

- **You become popular with colleagues**

Even if they never say it openly, people will appreciate those who are willing to listen to them and who try to understand what they may be going through.

- **You develop good management skills**

Emotionally intelligent people are good managers, which is why this skill is sought-after in the corporate world.

- **You are a good leader**

Being a leader often means leading by example. By dealing with your colleagues and employees in an emotionally-intelligent way, you will be showing them the best way to handle stress, challenges, and other people.

- **You are respected by your business partners**

Emotionally intelligent people are usually excellent negotiators and will be appreciated by friends and respected by competitors.

To boost your professional development with emotional intelligence, you need to focus on developing those skills which are directly linked with the four main elements of emotional intelligence:

- **Self-management**

Learn how to accept, control, express, and use your emotions.

- **Social awareness**

Develop empathy, learn to interpret body language, pay attention to tone of voice and facial expression, and become more involved in your community (try volunteering, or attend meet-ups with people from different social groups).

- **Relationship management**

Collaboration, teamwork, and networking are crucial in most professions. Learn how to develop solid relationships within your organization and with your business partners, and help support others by mentoring or coaching. You should never be too busy or tired to listen to others.

- **Self-awareness**

Continually improve your self-awareness skills by challenging your views, examining how you feel and why, finding out what others think of you and why, owning your mistakes, and considering how your words or actions impact others. All of this will help you understand yourself better. Learn when to get involved and when to step back. If feeling overwhelmed, take a break, rethink, then try again. Never stop polishing your self-awareness skills.

As Satya Nadella, an American business executive from India, said in one of his books, "The energy you create around you is perhaps going to be the most important thing you do. In the long run, EQ trumps IQ. Without being a source of energy for others, very little can be accomplished."

Food for thought:

1) Of the four essential emotional intelligence skills, which ones are you already good at and which ones do you still need to work on? How do you plan to improve the skills you lack?

2) Think of at least two situations where better emotional intelligence skills would have helped you handle the situation more professionally.

3) Create an action plan for how you can apply the principles of emotional intelligence to boost your personal development.

Day 2
Emotions

What is Empathy?

As one of the key elements of emotional intelligence, empathy is the ability to identify with other people's pain, suffering, happiness, success, and so on—the awareness of the feelings and emotions of those around you. Unlike sympathy, which is "feeling for" someone, empathy is "feeling with" someone.

According to emotional intelligence expert Daniel Goleman, empathy revolves around understanding and acceptance.

<u>4 key elements of empathy, according to Daniel Goleman:</u>

- **Understanding others**

To understand, you first of all have to listen carefully. However, most people are not very good listeners, and would rather be listened to. Those who listen with empathy can easily tune into other person's emotions and story, and this makes it easy to see things from their angle. Listening without judging is about using both your heart and head to participate in another person's emotions while giving them the benefit of the doubt.

- **Developing others**

An empath will take advantage of every opportunity to boost others' confidence, praise their achievements, and congratulate them on their successes. Also, if an empath sees someone struggling, they will selflessly offer friendly or professional advice, mentoring or coaching to help them move past a difficult situation, or at least feel less vulnerable.

- **Leveraging diversity**

This is a process by which emotionally intelligent managers create and develop opportunities for everyone in the team, regardless of their status and expertise. By tapping into their team's individual talents and skills and providing an opportunity for everyone to participate in a project, empathic managers boost team spirit and make everyone feel appreciated.

- **Political awareness**

Being politically aware means being able to pick up on the "emotional undercurrents" of a particular environment or time, and use them to navigate the team's or organization's work. The bigger the group of people, the more likely it is that there will be individuals with hidden agendas. An empath will pick up the vibes of the group—a team, a family, a group of close friends—and deal with them with sensitivity and flexibility.

Emotional Intelligence Across Cultures

Events such as migration, tourism, world trade, and multinational corporations have all helped expand the world into one big, global village. As a result, most societies today are much more culturally diversified than they were fifty years ago. This is particularly evident in the workplace.

However, despite general cultural diversification, most individual cultures have retained their specific social values—which, amongst other things, explains why being emotionally intelligent varies from culture to culture.

Emotional intelligence consists of two key elements—emotions and intelligence. To fully understand how different cultures, understand this phenomenon, you have to understand how different cultures define intelligence. As both physical and social environment varies greatly across the world, so does the relevance of intelligence in different cultures.

In other words, being intelligent in an African, Asian or a western European country will likely not require identical qualities.

In Western culture, intelligence is typically measured by the speed and accuracy of mental skills, as well as by academic achievements. In Africa and Asia, however, social skills play a much more important role in intelligence.

While some cultures are mostly money-driven, for others it's the family and community that are more important. According to the Cross-Cultural Understandings (Lynch, 2004), people in Asia and Africa aim to earn enough to survive, with their main efforts focused on collective family goals and safety of the entire community.

In less developed societies, where poverty and deprivation are common, being helpful and cooperative is a much more desired skill than being highly educated. A helpful person willing to assist others with food or money will help keep his family and neighbors alive. On the other hand, an educated person may be respected because of his academic achievements, but his importance for the wellbeing of a community will be irrelevant until such a time when he starts investing into the society and making their lives easier.

On the other hand, in the US, where money is a symbol of status and power and there are fewer close family links, it's every man for himself.

The West has relatively recently recognized that intelligent behavior does not only relate to academic results. Howard Gardiner proposed a theory that there are several types of intelligence, such as linguistic, logical, musical, naturalistic, existential, intrapersonal, and intersocial.

Overall, we recognize three non-academic types of intelligence. However, most of them are culture-bound; it may not be recognized as intelligence in a different culture.

3 non-academic types of intelligence:

- **Practical intelligence**

This is the ability to solve real-life problems. However, being able to fix a computer doesn't mean you'd be able to fix a yurt in the Siberian tundra.

- **Social intelligence**

A socially intelligent person is able to understand the emotions and behaviors of himself and others—within his own culture. In Asia, where social harmony is the most important aspect of life and where one puts community before self, boasting about your own success would be considered very rude. On the other hand, in most Western countries, people live by the motto, "If you've got it, flaunt it," People will shamelessly promote themselves, often aggressively putting their own interests before anyone else.

- **Emotional intelligence**

Emotionally intelligent people are those who recognize and respond appropriately to their own and others' emotions. In Asian countries, where special importance is paid to balance and harmony, anything that would disrupt the equilibrium is frowned upon. As a result, people often suppress their emotions—they will never let others see when they are blissfully happy or terribly upset. However, in Western cultures, people are encouraged to express their emotions and let go of any bottled-up feelings, but only those from the same culture would tolerate and appreciate such behavior.

Everything is relative, including intelligence. As Dostoyevsky said in one of his books, "It takes something more than intelligence to act intelligently."

Three Emotions at the Root of Success

So, success in life—both on the personal and professional level—is a combination of emotions, intelligence, and attitude. Your perception of what success is may be the key to how you will achieve it, but regardless of your cultural and social background, there are three universal emotions one needs for a long-lasting success and happiness.

3 emotions that are at the root of success:

- **Empathy**

Regardless of your profession or your way of life, you need to connect with people—and empathy allows you to establish a relationship of trust and understanding. What distinguishes empaths from other people is their ability to listen carefully and to read between the lines, if necessary. To become an empath, try to get to a point where you would rather listen to someone else's problems than talk about your own.

- **Motivation**

Motivation helps you stay focused on your goals, keeping you on track despite any challenges. When you lack motivation, self-doubt sets in and you might easily give up or wait for someone else to tell you what to do. To develop or boost your motivation, try to figure out your purpose in life. Keep revisiting your goals, especially if your circumstances change, and work out how best to stop negative self-talk. Remember, the greater the motivation, the greater the success.

- **Patience**

In the modern world, everything is about speed. We eat fast food, drive fast cars, expect quick results, and expect a quick buck. In Western culture, at least, if you're not being fast enough, people wonder what's wrong with you.

However, in business as well as in life, it sometimes pays to be patient. Don't rush to be the first to own something, go somewhere, or do something, and show gratitude for what you have rather than constantly thinking about what you SHOULD have. Success is not about how much you have, but about how much what you have is worth to you.

Food for thought:

1) Do you help others and expect nothing in return? If the answer is no, why not? If yes, how does that make you feel?

2) Think of someone from another culture that you spend a lot of time with—either at work, in a club, or somewhere else. How much do you know about their culture? If very little, why?

3) List three things that help you stay motivated.

Day 3

Intelligence

Is a High IQ a Measure of Success in Life?

While there are many different approaches to the concept of IQ, it is no longer considered the main key to success—although it does help.

No one can deny that a high IQ certainly impacts your ability to earn a good income, achieve academic success, and maintain good health until old age. However, a high IQ score on its own is no guarantee that you'll use the superior intelligence you were born with to achieve outstanding results.

With children and young adults, it is up to their parents and teachers to spot their exceptional intelligence and support them, so they make the most of it. With adults, it's up to their own emotional maturity, determination, and perhaps, vision, to what extent they will use their gift.

So, what exactly is IQ and how is it measured? IQ tests usually evaluate someone's ability to understand, calculate, solve complex spatial problems and reason. They focus on four main elements of intelligence: verbal, numerical, spatial, and logical intelligence.

There are different types of IQ tests—for children, for adults, for people with disabilities—but most have certain limitations. Namely, they test only very specific kinds of knowledge, like vocabulary, problem-solving skills, and so on, but do not measure practical knowledge or knowledge you need for activities such as music, arts, or sports.

Besides, we now know that it takes much more than a high IQ to become a successful professional—many other factors, such as a stimulating environment, a personal talent, and perseverance, play just as big, or even a bigger role in determining your chances of success.

Although scholars disagree on the importance or even relevance of IQ tests, and many claim that its importance has been overrated, everyone agrees that a high IQ definitely helps in some jobs. But, even so, we know that the difference between a mediocre and an outstanding performance often has more to do with one's creativity or motivation than with their intelligence—and these qualities cannot be measured with an IQ test.

There is also the issue of how relevant an IQ score is in different cultures. In societies where intelligence and academic performance is highly appreciated, such as in the West, having a high IQ gives you a much better chance of "making it." While achieving exceptional results will also depend on your personal motivation and self-confidence, a high IQ score in Western culture is appreciated and rewarded.

On the other hand, in societies where strong family and social bonds are key to happiness and success in life, a high IQ may be completely irrelevant to one's societal standing.

A high IQ may or may not help you achieve great things in life, because for true, long-lasting success, your personal efforts will have to be boosted by many other factors, such as family support, available opportunities, cultural values, and more.

Is Intelligence Overrated?

Despite evidence that IQ is not directly linked to one's success in life and that other skills are more, or at least equally important, in Western culture, intelligence still receives a lot of attention. This in spite of numerous studies which show that your communication, negotiation, and leadership skills are much more likely to affect your professional success than your intelligence could.

For example, having good relationships with your customers can bring you more work thanks to the trust you've developed; or knowing how to negotiate the best possible deal for your company, or for yourself, can make you more professionally successful; or skillfully leading your team through a difficult transition period can help you retain your best employees.

Even people with less education and a lower IQ, but who are highly motivated, will have a better chance of succeeding than someone who is exceptionally intelligent and highly educated, but lacks the vision or optimism to keep going through difficult times.

Daniel Goleman, an expert on emotional intelligence, points out that IQ accounts for only about 20% of a person's success. The remaining 80% depends on their emotional intelligence—the various social skills that even those with no access to high education, or those with a lower IQ, can easily master.

Whichever way you look at it, a high IQ is not what you need most to succeed professionally. Things like honesty, flexibility, willingness to work hard, specific skills (like building, driving, IT programming, financial, and so on), good management, and emotional maturity are what, eventually, help you achieve outstanding results.

As it turns out, IQ is not as important for our overall success in life as we were led to believe. Whether we are aware of it or not, we—often subconsciously—choose to be, or work with, people we believe to be honest, efficient, trustworthy, reliable, kind, or helpful, regardless of how intelligent they are. When you choose someone to share your life with, be it personal or professional, their character qualities are much more relevant than their intelligence.

As Robert Sternberg pointed out, the better one's IQ test result is, the worse his practical skills, and vice versa.

IQ vs. EI

The main difference between IQ and EI is the focus. While IQ focuses on academic abilities and pure intelligence, EI is about one's ability to identify, control, and express emotions.

While people with a high IQ make excellent scientists and academics, those with a high EI make good leaders and team players. The answer to which quality is more important lies partly with who you ask, but also with what qualities are sought for a particular profession or situation.

It would be fair to say that both IQ an IE are important for a fulfilled life. However, they relate to different qualities: IQ compares one's mental age with their chronological age, while EQ measures one's ability to receive, process, and manage emotions.

For a long time, IQ was believed to be the much more important of the two types of intelligence—the key to success—we now know its two major limitations:

- **A High IQ score is no guarantee of success**

Superior intelligence on its own—without hard work, optimism, and drive—will not get you very far. Only if combined with other important factors, such as vision and social skills, can it bring long-lasting success.

- **IQ tests are not always relevant**

Even a highly intelligent person cannot know everything, especially if a specific knowledge is completely irrelevant to the culture they come from. This means that IQ tests are applicable only to those from a similar cultural and social background. Besides, most tests consist of written and spoken elements, so non-natives can never do as well as native candidates.

The greatest advantage of a high IQ is that it makes it easier to win a scholarship. Intelligent people enjoy learning and do so easily, so a high IQ makes one a very sought after candidate for a scholarship.

Additionally, in certain professions—particularly those related to science—a high IQ is a definite sign that the individual, able to learn quickly and willing to constantly improve and upgrade their knowledge and skills, will help advance the field in which they specialize.

However, many people with a high IQ are known to suffer from depression and anxiety, possibly because they tend to overanalyze personal experiences and dwell too much on details, often causing themselves unnecessary tension and problems.

Despite the obvious benefits of a high IQ, there is an ongoing debate over how relevant and unbiased intelligence tests are, because it's well known that individuals from more affluent backgrounds, with better learning opportunities, usually do better in IQ tests—though this doesn't mean those with fewer opportunities are any less intelligent.

While this debate will likely continue to rage on indefinitely, perhaps the dilemma of IQ vs. EI is best summed up with the following statement: "IQ gets you hired, but EI gets you promoted."

Food for Thought:

1) Would you prefer to have a high IQ or EI? Why?

2) Which of the two do you think is more important for overall success in life? Why?

Day 4
Relationships

Types of Relationships

A relationship is how we connect to each other and, being social animals, we need relationships to feel "whole."

Although there are many types of relationships, and as many reasons why people enter into them, the bottom line is that we need contact with other people for the sake of our emotional well-being. Relationships provide us with mental stability, physical security, friendship, and help us beat loneliness. And, last but not least, through relationships, we learn and grow.

Humans are complex and sophisticated beings, which is reflected in the many different kinds of relationships we establish and nurture throughout our lives.

5 basic types of relationships:

- **Family relationships**

A family is a group of people living together in a household. related by Roles and relationships within a family are no longer as clear cut as they used to be and vary enormously across cultures, as well as throughout your own lifetime. These relationships usually include your parents, siblings, and extended family.

- **Friendly relationships**

Friendship is a close tie between two people, based on shared interests and emotional bonding. No relationship is static—friendships can also change, but they must always maintain a connection with affection and trust. Bonds established with some friends may last a lifetime, as these are often the people we rely on most during critical times of our lives.

- **Romantic relationships**

In a romantic relationship, you share your dreams, your passions, and your intimacy with your partner. You support and trust each other, and base your relationship on love, equality, and respect. However, a romantic relationship is not a fairy tale—to make it work requires both maturity and patience. These relationships refer to our boyfriends, girlfriends, spouses, and partners.

- **Professional relationships**

Individuals working together share a professional relationship. This kind of relationship exists only so that a particular job can be accomplished. If it were not for the job, these people would probably never develop a connection. Professional relationships are formed among colleagues, team members, managers, employees, clients, customers, and so on. Most people spend long hours at work, so it's worth making an effort to establish good professional relationships with those you spend so much time with.

- **Casual relationships**

According to a number of surveys, many people are addicted to social networks, spending six or more hours every day on Facebook, Twitter, and other forms of social media. These "addicts" constantly check status updates or "stalk" people's online profiles.

Casual relationships can be formed with people we meet regularly or occasionally, which can include neighbors, colleagues, fellow dog-walkers you chat to every day, those you meet through social media or at parties, or clubs you belong to.

Relationships are not cast in stone and often change over time. Many people make the mistake of taking a relationship for granted, forgetting that all relationships require nurturing and "maintenance."

However, we can sometimes outgrow certain relationships or lifestyles. No matter how much you try to keep a relationship alive, if the "glue" that keeps it together starts to dwindle, like your mutual interests or priorities, the relationship will eventually die down, too.

How to Undermine a Romantic Relationship

More than any other type of relationship, romantic relationships make us feel whole, which is why our partner or spouse is often referred to as our "significant other" or "our better half." However, finding someone to share your life with is much easier than actually making that relationship last.

As a relationship is a two-way street, it takes both partners to keep the flame alive.

Making a relationship work takes maturity, commitment, and energy—something many people are naively unaware of, or unwilling to invest in. While there are many reasons relationships fail, the most common ones have to do with honesty.

6 common behaviors that sabotage a romantic relationship:

- **Disloyalty**

You become disloyal if you begin to prioritize other people over your partner, like by continuing to maintain contacts with the previous partner, or being "married" to your work or a club.

Another behavior that many people view as disloyalty is when you prefer doing something with someone else rather than with your partner.

- **Lying**

Dishonesty destroys trust and safety in a relationship. It's particularly bad if a partner pretends everything's fine but, deep down, knows the relationship has no future. People sometimes resort to lying so as not to hurt their partner, but such a relationship is doomed—the longer you keep on lying and pretending, the more you will hurt them in the end.

- **Conditional commitment**

This happens when you know that the relationship you're in is not what you were looking for and, though you remain in it, you keep an eye open for something "better." So, instead of breaking up, you stay in the relationship just to avoid being alone, but all the while actively searching for something that would suit you more.

- **Selfishness/self-centeredness**

Being selfish means it's all about "me" instead of "we"—expecting your partner to comfort you or look after you, while indirectly blaming them when you're not feeling well, as if everything is their fault. This behavior is common in people who refuse to take responsibility for their own lives and feelings. Mature individuals know it's up to them how happy, or how miserable, they feel at the end of the day.

- **Joining forces with someone against your partner**

When you make a coalition with someone else, like your family or friends, to gang up on your partner. The message this is sending is "we are all against you," implying they need to just give in and do as you say.

- **Blackmailing**

People who get what they want from their partner by threatening to leave, filing for divorce, ceasing communication, or even killing themselves.

How High EI Helps You Improve Your Relationships

Believe it or not, most of us could benefit from improving our emotional intelligence skills.

Emotionally intelligent individuals are not only more observant and considerate, but they are also more aligned with their own emotions, and the emotions of others. Western culture promotes individuality and self-centeredness in a way that encourages people to focus on their individual goals. There is very little need to connect with others, which is why many people don't. Your life belongs to you, and you have the right to live it the way you want to. However, in case of problems, you're on your own—this culture is about "every man for himself."

On the other hand, in cultures or communities where people rely more on others for assistance of some kind, they are much more likely to "hear" a cry for help or offer a helping hand before a crisis happens. Only when everyone has at least their basic needs met can the community members relax. The poorer the community, and the more interdependent on each other they are, and the more the community members act as "one."

In the West, we relatively recently recognized the importance of emotional intelligence for our overall well-being, and for the need to at least try and understand the other person's point of view As a lot of interconnectedness has been lost in the developed world, we are now trying to re-learn skills that once came naturally to all humans—to tune in and pick up vibes in our environment.

<u>9 reasons why high emotional intelligence helps you improve your relationships:</u>

- **It improves your self-awareness**

In other words, you get to know yourself better. This could mean anything from realizing how self-centered you might be to learning how to polish your people skills so you stop unintentionally putting people off.

- **You learn to handle criticism**

When you stop feeling that others are out to get you, you realize that, sometimes, negative feedback can do more for your personal development than false and empty words that "you're doing just fine." Unless given maliciously, with the aim to hurt or embarrass you, criticism can help you change direction before it's too late.

- **You stop ignoring your feelings**

Some people, especially the so-called "do-gooders," are so obsessed with the need to do something for someone, it never occurs to them that they, too, have needs that should not be ignored. Many behave like this out of guilt (real or imaginary) and will often ignore their own needs, believing there are those who are needier than themselves.

There is a reason that the mantra all successful people adhere to is "Pay yourself first." Never ignore your own needs or feelings, especially emotions such as sadness, fear, or anxiety, for there is a reason you feel that way. Emotionally intelligent people recognize and stay with their feelings until they figure out what triggered them.

- **You become an active listener**

While it's true that people often take advantage of those who are willing to listen to their problems, being an active listener is basically about temporarily putting yourself second and enabling someone to get something off their chest. Even if there is nothing you can do to help them, just showing that you care is often all the help they need.

- **You learn to challenge your feelings and recognize and understand the triggers behind them**

With practice, this becomes automatic, but at first you may have to stop what you're doing and analyze why you feel the way you do towards someone or about a particular situation. As you become more aware of what makes you feel a certain way, you will learn to apply this to others—you'll be able to pick up on how others react, or are likely to react, to certain news, events, or words.

- **You become more tolerant**

Human population has exploded over the last hundred years, which makes it imperative to learn to be adaptable or more tolerant. We now have to travel in overloaded buses, drive for hours in bumper-to-bumper traffic, and work closely with people from different social, political, and religious backgrounds. Emotional intelligence can not only help us cope in such environments, but even benefit from them.

- **You become more respectful and considerate of others**

By embracing values such as cultural diversity, social complexity, and religious freedom, those with high emotional intelligence can fit in easily to any environment. They are not just tolerant, but are respectful toward and interested in the differentness of others.

- **You understand others' motives and behavior better**

When you stop seeing yourself as the center of the universe, you'll start taking an interest in others and paying more attention to their opinions, feelings, and motives.

- **You learn how to successfully resolve conflicts**

The trick with conflicts is to find a solution before the situation gets out of hand.

- **You start seeing things from other people's point of view**

This is necessary because we are often angry with others because of something they did or said, without taking the time and trouble to try and see that particular situation or incident from their perspective.

Food for Thought:
1) Do you struggle to build relationships with new colleagues when you start a new job? How do you do it?

2) List four ways to make a relationship last. Consider the saying, "It takes two to tango." Do you agree?

3) Consider what you would see if you tried to look at yourself through somebody else's eyes. Think of someone who might dislike you and try to imagine what they feel about you. Why do you think they feel that way?

Day 5
Career

Emotional Intelligence and Career Choice

Being successful in a career has a lot to do with recognizing and making the most of your talents, skills, and character traits. Awareness of these can help you choose a career you are best suited for, which will eventually enable you to live the life you've always dreamed of.

Stop trying to live somebody else's dream or worry you may be letting others down. Choosing a career that you are best suited for also means you are much more likely to feel passionate about what you're doing with your life.

Certain professions require high emotional intelligence—for example, being able to stay calm under pressure, or to deal with difficult situations without exploding or bursting into tears, or to understand and tolerate when someone unloads their negative feelings on you.

Some of the careers that require high emotional intelligence:

- **Sales**

This profession is for relationship-oriented people and those who would enjoy building long-term relationships with their customers.

- **Leadership**

One of the most important skills of a good leader is empathy, for the simple reason that it helps build trust.

- **Psychology**

Emotional intelligence is possibly the most important skill mental health professionals need, as it significantly improves communication between a therapist and a patient.

- **Social work**

Only highly empathic people can successfully work with marginalized or at-risk individuals and families.

- **Politician**

The most popular politicians are usually those who delight in serving the people and are prepared to listen to everybody.

There are many other professions where job success or career happiness depends on a high level of emotional intelligence.

Some professions, like nursing and teaching, are ideal for individuals with high emotional intelligence. If someone with low emotional intelligence becomes involved in a situation or a job which requires emotional intelligence and traits like patience, empathy, and interpersonal skills, he will either not be able to do the job properly or would need much more time and energy to do it well, for the simple reason that those skills are not their greatest professional strengths.

This is why job profiling is so important, particularly for young people who may still not be aware of how emphatic or emotionally detached they are. It takes very different qualities and skills to be a good accountant compared to a good nurse.

Emotional Intelligence in the Workplace

Teamwork is becoming extremely important in the workplace and, as a result, emotional intelligence has become a highly sought-after skill, especially within big corporations that employ thousands of people from very different social backgrounds.

The main reason emotional intelligence is so important in a workplace is that it enables people to work well together and develop good professional relationships, despite likely having little in common.

Therefore, learning to get along with others, dealing with constant change, and being able to successfully work in teams, is what makes people more employable, today. From their side, organizations can help promote the "spirit" of emotional intelligence by creating working environments that encourage tolerance, mutual understanding, and good communication.

<u>4 most common professional relationships in the workplace:</u>

- Relationships between colleagues
- Relationships between management and staff
- Relationships between managers
- Relationships between staff and outside partners, clients, stakeholders, and competitors.

Workplaces with a high level of emotional intelligence in staff and management benefits both the employer and the employee. Staff are much happier when they feel motivated, appreciated, and adequately rewarded, while employers benefit because satisfied employees are more efficient and productive.

More and more organizations are beginning to recognize the importance of emotional intelligence in creating a dynamic working environment, where both staff and clients feel valued and supported. In return, they continue to support the organization—a win-win situation.

Emotional Intelligence and Job Burnout

Although self-awareness and good communication skills usually improve your performance and lower your stress, there are jobs or situations where emotional intelligence—particularly empathy—may actually contribute to job burnout.

Some studies claim that certain professions, like nurses, doctors, and caregivers, especially in countries where hospitals are short-staffed, are much more likely to experience job burnout if they have high emotional intelligence. Their stressful jobs involve direct contact with lots of people, exposure to death and suffering, and long working hours, which makes them highly susceptible to burnout.

On the other hand, there's plenty of evidence that helping staff develop emotional intelligence may actually help them cope with stress and prevent burnout.

While heavy workload and long working hours combined with family life obligations are potentially the major cause of job burnout, a lot depends on the job. If your job enables you to see how your efforts are making a difference, like on maternity wards or in old age homes, you are much more likely to have job satisfaction and be protected from the emotional exhaustion which leads to burnout. This is often not the case for those who work with the general public, or have boring, repetitive office jobs.

Emotional exhaustion is seen as one of the major contributors to burnout. This usually happens when you are expected to exhibit emotions to customers, e.g., smile and be polite, even when customers are rude or aggressive, or when you are perhaps having a bad day. The emotional imbalance between your actual feelings and the feelings you exhibit to the public—if unaddressed and allowed to persist—will easily result in burnout.

Different studies show there is definitely a link between emotional exhaustion and burnout. Prolonged stress makes people feel emotionally depleted, and once that happens, they often have no choice but to start cutting back on their involvement with others.

While this may help them deal with pressure, it often contributes to various negative behaviors, because they may neglect many of their duties and feel they are letting their patients, customers, or clients down.

However, individuals with higher levels of emotional intelligence have the advantage of knowing how to process their emotions before they become negative attitudes or behaviors. So, although empathic people can often spread themselves too thin, they are better equipped to deal with the challenges of stressful professions.

In conclusion, emotional burnout can both protect from and contribute to job burnout. Perhaps the solution is to seek employment you are emotionally and mentally suited for, rather than work a job that clashes with your temperament or personal strengths just because it's well-paid or interesting.

Food for Thought:

1) What is your dream job? How important is emotional intelligence for that job?

2) Think of a conflict you witnessed in a workplace which could have been much more professionally resolved, had the participants' emotional intelligence been higher. How would you have handled it?

3) If still considering which career you're best suited for, ask yourself how much emotional pressure you would be prepared to put up with. Do you easily fake a smile? Do you take criticism personally? How do you deal with other people's pain and suffering? Before investing time and energy in developing emotional intelligence, make sure your time would perhaps not be better spent developing different skills.

Day 6

Leadership

Good Leadership Skills for Success in Life

There are situations when, without strong leadership, it becomes impossible to move forward. Leaders come in many forms, such as pacesetting, authoritative, affiliative, coaching, coercive, or democratic leaders.

However, regardless of their style and agenda, they are there to lead—whether it be a team, organization, family, or clan.

Leadership is about taking charge, giving direction, and deciding how best to achieve the goals set out for a particular group of people.

But, strong leaders also need to have personal charisma and the power to inspire others. As Dwight Eisenhower pointed out, "Leadership is the art of getting someone else to do something you want to be done, because he WANTS to do it."

To be able to guide and inspire others, leaders should arm themselves with a set of strong management skills, as well as high emotional intelligence. They also need a lot of self-confidence and self-esteem, as well as enough stamina not to feel emotionally exhausted after dealing with difficult situations or people.

So, the qualities leaders bring to the table sets out both the style in which they will lead, along with the creativity and confidence with which they will take their team or organization to a new level.

13 qualities that make a good leader:

1) You have vision and can see the big picture
2) You are highly motivated and easily motivate others
3) You have strong emotional intelligence skills
4) You are creative, and your achievements reflect that
5) You are confident
6) You are supportive of your community/team/organization
7) You are a good listener
8) You lead by example

9) You have strong management skills—knowing when to lead and when to step back to let others take over

10) You never stop learning and improving yourself

11) You are not afraid to initiate action and take calculated risks

12) You provide guidance and direction

13) You boost morale in times of crisis

In a business environment, leadership is an important aspect of management. In terms of leadership skills outside of the business world, such as a community leader, team leader, or sports leader, their main role is to make communities or groups stronger, united, and focused, while offering guidance, support, and direction—particularly during challenging times.

Why Emotional Intelligence is Critical for Leaders

As leadership revolves around leading people, strong leaders need to have strong people skills. Of all the mentioned skills that a capable leader should demonstrate, the most important ones are those which make them a 'people person.'

Individuals with high emotional intelligence can gracefully slip into leadership roles—mainly because even if they don't have all the necessary skills, they can easily develop them on the job.

If you believe you are emotionally intelligent, you would likely make a good leader. In which case, developing key leadership skills would not be a problem.

<u>5 leadership skills that high emotional intelligence helps you excel in:</u>

- **Communication**

It goes without saying that a strong leader has to be willing to listen and hear what his team, community, employees, or clients have to say. They also have to be able to clearly convey suggestions, directions, and decisions. While good communication skills are very important in life, they are absolutely crucial in leadership positions.

- **Self-awareness**

Only people who are willing to pay attention to and recognize the emotions of others, as well as be able to read the undercurrents of a team they are leading, can hope to fully understand the dynamics and interactions that may occur.

- **Emotional management**

Being a leader means you know how to manage your emotions, as well as those of others. It's about staying in control without having to control everything all the time.

- **Social awareness**

This skill enables leaders to feel connected with those they lead. Strong leaders are so well tuned into the way their team or community "breathes," they easily understand what triggers their emotions and reactions. This is particularly important in situations that can only be understood and interpreted from the prevailing atmosphere, where a good leader can easily pick up the subtle undercurrents.

- **Conflict resolution skills**

In some environments, or under certain circumstances, this may be one of the most important skills a leader needs. Conflict in a workplace, or situations where angry, unhappy, or rude clients, staff, or customers take their emotions out on you, demand that you stay calm, listen carefully, apologize, and sympathize—without taking it personally.

Food for Thought:

1) Name two people who, for you, are textbook examples of a good leader. Explain why.
2) Do you think you have what it takes to be a leader? Which skills you still need to develop?
3) Leaders often have to make tough decisions, and with some of them, you have to trust your gut. If you know that your decision will make you unpopular—meaning you risk not being re-elected to your post—would you still take it?

Day 7

Shyness

What Makes People Shy?

Understanding why someone is shy is about figuring out what triggers their feeling of awkwardness in the presence of other people. No one is shy when they are on their own—this is something that happens because of other people.

From a scientific point of view, shyness is believed to be a response to fear or a result of difficult personal experiences.

It's generally believed that both introverts and shy individuals are happiest when they're on their own; however, that's not quite true. While introverts enjoy being alone, shy people are often alone simply because they are uncomfortable being with others. As it is human company that makes them feel anxious, they often withdraw from the world. What makes this even more absurd is that, more than anything else, shy individuals crave human company.

What usually prevents shy people from developing normal relationships is that they tend to spend too much time in self-analysis, constantly thinking about how they appear to others and what their shortcomings are.

Surveys show that more than 50% of people consider themselves shy. Some people eventually learn to overcome or cope with it, but many people do not.

<u>3 main challenges that shy people face on a daily basis:</u>
- Low self-esteem
- Fear of rejection
- Self-consciousness

Although shy individuals face more challenges than others, it doesn't mean they cannot take part in social activities, like parties, sports events, or speaking in public. It's only that they'll have to invest twice as much energy—both mental and emotional—to act comfortable in such events than someone who does not have a problem interacting with others.

No one is born shy—whether or not someone becomes shy will depend on both nature and nurture. People are often shy only in certain situations, in front of certain people, or in certain periods of their life.

It's quite common that people who were very shy as children grow up to become confident and outspoken, which is proof that people skills can be learned and improved over time.

Our upbringing also contributes to how we feel about ourselves, as do the culture and religion we grew up in. Many religions encourage feelings of guilt, shame, and self-blame, and when combined with low self-esteem, these beliefs can really damage people. And if one is shy on top of that, they likely wouldn't dare speak about these things to others—only making the situation worse.

Certain events, such as divorce, bankruptcy, losing a job, or spending time in prison can make one change their perception of themselves as well, contributing to shyness and withdrawal.

When Shyness Becomes Crippling

Shyness is most common when people find themselves in contact with new acquaintances. There are many reasons why this makes people nervous, but most often, they may be too self-critical and constantly compare themselves to others. Most shy people almost constantly feel as though they are being appraised by others, which can be what makes them nervous, especially if in the company of people they don't know.

Shy people also seem to focus on the negative—what they're not good at, or how inappropriately dressed they may be. It's like constantly having to listen to a small voice telling you how out-of-place you are.

For some people, shyness stems from poor upbringing. Shy children often come from families where one of the parents (usually of the same sex) was too critical of the child. In that case, the child usually struggles to develop sufficient self-confidence and resilience to deal with the challenges of growing up.

Poor parenting skills may turn an otherwise healthy child into a social cripple, a person whom no one ever taught how to behave in social situations. When someone is shy since childhood, it's often because they never had a chance to learn how to participate in social activities.

Another childhood experience which may leave people feeling shy is too much teasing. Children who grew up feeling unloved, unwanted, or openly blamed for their parents' misfortunes (like, "if it hadn't been for you, I'd be free now," or, "when I think how much I've invested in you…"). If a child is belittled by family members or older siblings, they may grow up with low self-esteem and be used to receiving negative comments. So, in a way, as adults, they almost half-expect others to dislike or tease them. As a result, they may avoid social situations and contact with others as much as they can.

Helping someone who is shy can be tricky because there are so many reasons for shyness, as well as ways people cope with it. However, the worst thing you could do is try to help someone get rid of their shyness by forcing them to make a speech or participate in a social activity if they don't want to. Shyness is best tackled gradually rather than with a "sink or swim" method, when you push someone into a situation they are unprepared for.

Making fun of someone who is shy, hoping they will react by stopping being shy just to prove themselves, is a mean and aggressive way to help someone, and can typically do more harm than good. Shy people can participate in all social activities, but because this is usually stressful for them, they will need time to mentally prepare themselves for the ordeal.

4 ways to tackle shyness:

- **Stop self-obsessing**

One of the things shy people battle with is self-obsession. They constantly think about themselves, analyzing their own behavior, appearance, words, life, family, and so on—always looking for what's wrong and expecting others to criticize them for it. Action: Shift the focus from yourself to others.

- **Launch a counter-attack**

Instead of withdrawing from a situation which makes you feel awkward, stay and confront your fear. It won't be easy or comfortable but, with time, you'll get better at it. Work on it, just like you would work on improving your negotiating skills, foreign language skills, driving skills, IT skills—you learn skills you feel you need. Treat interactions with others simply as a skill you lack, but want to learn. Action: Try to get yourself in situations or with people who make you feel shy and practice counter-attack.

- **Don't be afraid to stand up for what you believe in**

Sometimes, people feel awkward when they stand out from others, like when they look different, speak with a different accent, dress differently, practice a different religion, or eat a special diet. Being just like everybody else is usually easier because you're "one of the herd," and many people adopt the herd mentality just so they are left alone. Action: Look at your differentness this way: if you are different you are special—be proud of it!

- **Enjoy the attention**

If you feel uncomfortable with others watching you, could it not be that they are observing how interesting, stylish, or original you are? When someone is looking at you, they may not be judging you—they may be admiring you. Try to change that negative attitude. Action: When you catch someone watching you, smile and think how interesting, attractive, or elegant you must be for someone to have noticed you in a crowd.

How Emotional Intelligence Helps You Overcome Shyness

The more you read about what causes shyness, the more you realize shyness is a relative term. There are people who are shy in the sense that they are not interested in superficial relationships, and find wasting time and energy on people they don't really want to be with to be a stupid way to spend an evening. These people are very much in touch with their emotions and know what is and isn't important to them, and what sort of people or activities aren't worth wasting time and energy on.

Then, there are people who would give anything to stop being shy, and they try as hard as they can to fit in with others. They work on themselves, and they usually manage to overcome shyness.

There are also those who, for reasons of inadequate upbringing or past traumas, find being with others—particularly in new situations—too traumatizing, and will avoid it as much as they can.

Everyone has their own reason for being shy, and people with low emotional intelligence usually struggle to cope with the complex social roles and norms of the corporate world, or even in personal relationships.

Although most people learn to cope with shyness, sooner or later, if unaddressed, it can start affecting your day-to-day life.

To overcome shyness, you first have to figure out when and why you feel shy. Once you know what your triggers are, it'll be easier to deal with.

Shyness does not have to be a problem, in itself. If you are happy with yourself and your shyness does not interfere too much with your personal and professional life—like if you work from home, or if your lifestyle does not revolve too much around being in new situations and meeting new people—you may be very shy and still very happy.

Emotional intelligence skills help control shyness by keeping you in touch with your own emotions, helping you understand and deal with situations which trigger those anxious feelings.

However, if you are painfully shy because of an abusive childhood or past trauma, or you are in a job which requires constant dealing with the public, then you will likely have to do something about it. How you conquer your shyness depends mainly on your personality.

As the well-known Italian actress Mariacarla Boscono said in one interview, "I cover my shyness by being exactly the opposite. You know, really loud and very Italian. I am an extremely insecure and fragile person, and only the people that really know me know that. But I push myself."

Food for Thought:

1) Some shy children grow up to become confident adults, while some confident children end up feeling increasingly shy with age. How do you think life experiences shape our perception of yourselves? Has your own shyness increased or decreased with age? What do you think has contributed to that?

2) Do you agree that the Internet and the huge amounts of time people spend alone, without face-to-face contact, could be fueling shyness?

3) The famous actor Al Pacino was very shy as a young man. When he became an actor and was thrust into the limelight, he learned to cope with his shyness. In which situations do you feel most awkward, and how do you deal with your shyness?

Day 8
Self-Esteem

Believe in Yourself, Without Being Full of Yourself

Believing in yourself is best if it's nurtured from an early age. However, those who grew up in an unsupportive environment can still learn to develop self-belief later in life.

We often read that something all successful people have in common is a belief in themselves. Believing in yourself has to do with knowing what you want, having an idea of how to get it, and being resilient to pressure and negativity from your environment.

Many people are brainwashed by their families to believe they are not good enough, pretty enough, or smart enough to be successful in life, and they should be grateful with whatever life throws at them, no matter how little that may be. Those who buy into this usually remain stuck wherever they were led to believe they belong and never really find the energy to try and do something for themselves.

Fortunately, even if your self-esteem is low, you can easily improve or develop it once you build a positive self-image and decide you're ready for a change.

6 steps to creating a better self-image:
- **Acknowledge your struggle**

If you know you lack self-esteem, do you know why? Acknowledging that you have low self-esteem allows you to start asking questions like how you can be more confident.

- **Manage your inner voice**

Whatever your inner voice telling you is typically comprised of negative feedback from your parents, your partner, friends, colleagues, or anyone else who has tried to hold you back. There could be many reasons why they're trying to sabotage you, so think of a way to get rid of the negative self-talk and start listening to your own voice for a change.

- **Read motivational material**

This is important mainly because it's an easy way to learn how others with a similar problem improved their own self-image.

- **Practice visualization**

Imagine yourself the way you'd like to be (confident, pretty, popular, fearless, sought-after professionally, outspoken). Then, ask yourself what prevents you from being like that.

Limit negativity

You probably know where the most negative influence is coming from. Limit your exposure to those situations, people, TV programs, or newspapers.

- ### Stop comparing yourself to others

Those with low self-esteem don't do themselves any favors if they constantly compare themselves to people who are more successful. This only helps if it encourages you to do something about your life, not if it makes you even more miserable.

Develop Self-Respect

Self-respect is feeling good about yourself. Those who lack self-respect are usually insecure and often experience feelings of regret, shame, or guilt.

Self-respect can be gained or lost, and can also be improved. Improving your self-respect is not hard, but because it comes from your inner beliefs about yourself, it does take time.

<u>7 things to keep in mind if you want to improve your self-respect:</u>

1) Know where you want to get

Try to identify the traits you would like to develop—what does someone with high self-respect look like? Can you see yourself being like that one day?

2) Accept that you are responsible for your opinion of yourself.

If you don't like yourself, ask yourself why. How do you expect others to like you? What would it take to change your opinion of yourself, and accept who you are in this current moment?

3) Stay away from those who promote feelings of guilt, shame, or fear

We all know people, situations, or topics that make us feel "small" or awkward. Avoid them like the plague, or at least try to minimize the time you spend in that situation or with those people.

4) Walk the talk

Life is tough, so be prepared to defend your views. You will boost your self-esteem by behaving in accordance with what you believe in and by having faith in your values. People respect those who practice what they preach.

5) Learn to handle criticism

This comes with practice, and it's not always easy, even if others say they do it for your own good. Even if what others say about you is not true, by choosing not to take it too personally, you are practicing emotional intelligence skills—"managing your emotions and reactions."

6) Choose your company carefully

Try to surround yourself with people who make you feel appreciated and loved, and in whose company you can be yourself.

7) Stand up for yourself

If you live in an environment where it often feels like it's "you against everybody else," this may be difficult. However, you will look better in your own eyes when you stand up for your beliefs or choices in life. Self-esteem is about how you see yourself—by not being afraid to stand up for what you believe in, you'll be boosting not only your self-esteem but will be forcing others to take you more seriously, as well.

How Emotional Intelligence Reinforces a Positive Mindset

Before you attempt to influence your behavior, or somebody else's, you have to understand how your mind works and how to access it. To be able to control your emotions and reactions, or replace your negative thoughts with positive ones, you need to tune in to your subconscious.

It all starts with acknowledging that negative self-talk influences many decisions you make every day. Certain situations may act as triggers for this kind of attitude, but low self-esteem is known to fuel such negative thoughts.

We often spend our entire lives undermining ourselves with negative self-talk, not realizing that what we repeatedly think about or continually tell ourselves often becomes a self-fulfilling prophecy. We may become aware of what we've done to ourselves with hindsight when, after years of self-abuse and self-sabotage, we look back on our lives only to realize we were our own worst enemy.

However, this is unlikely to happen to emotionally intelligent people, mainly because they are tuned in their emotions and can easily pick up negative vibes from the environment or from their own subconscious. This means that the higher your emotional intelligence, the better control you'll have over your mind.

If you persevere with developing your emotional intelligence skills, you'll eventually learn how to identify stress-induced emotions, and catch your own negative self-talk before it has the chance to affect your mood or behavior.

However, even if you are a master of your own subconscious, you won't always be able to influence what others say or how they behave. Fortunately, even when you are exposed to negativity for extended periods of time, your emotional intelligence skills can help you reduce the effect of such negativity on your own life.

The easiest way to overcome negativity is with a positive attitude. If you are someone who is generally positive about life, this won't be a problem—you probably try to see something good in every situation, anyway. However, if this is not how you normally see the world, you'll have to work on developing a more cheerful and trusting worldview.

The best thing about high emotional intelligence is that it empowers positive attitude, which weakens the impact of negative thinking.

While you are having positive thoughts, your brain is stress-free. The more often you have positive thoughts, the more often your brain is given a chance to relax. It's not difficult being stress-free and having relaxing thoughts when you are happy—it's when things are not going well and your mind is flooded with gloomy, negative thoughts that focusing on the positive becomes challenging. However, with practice, you can learn to switch off and simply spend a few moments getting in touch with your positivity. If you can't focus on anything good, try to think of someone or something that made you laugh. Or think of something nice that happened to you recently. Or look at children or dogs playing in the park, go out and feed the birds, enjoy the colors and scents of your garden. You can shift your focus from negative thoughts if you have something happier to shift them onto.

Your mindset is what guides you through life, determining how you will react in certain situations. People with a positive mindset see challenges rather than problems. They are open to suggestion, accept criticism, and do not give up easily. With a negative mindset, people tend to deal with problems by simply accepting them as fate, are reluctant to change, and often become victims of negative self-talk.

Food for Thought:

1) Do you believe in yourself? If you do, prove it by answering these questions: How much do you like yourself? Do you often say or do things you don't mean to get people to like you? When you think of your future, do you feel hopeful or anxious?

2) In which situations would you not have the nerve to stand up for yourself, but would pretend you agree with the general opinion? Do you think it's always safe to say what you really think?

3) "A positive attitude causes a chain reaction of positive thoughts, events, and outcomes. It is a catalyst and it sparks extraordinary results." –Wade Boggs

    If you agree with this view, think of two people you know (or have heard of) who managed to recover from a major setback in life. What would you do if what happened to them, happened to you?

Day 9
Social Anxiety

When Being Shy Becomes a Mental Disorder

Most shy people eventually learn to cope with shyness and being around unfamiliar people. Social anxiety sufferers, on the other hand, find it impossible to relax in a those settings, no matter how much they try.

People with social anxiety disorder dread being judged, and are usually plagued with feelings of inferiority and inadequacy.

To understand how social anxiety affects people, consider it the opposite of narcissism. While narcissists have an *inflated* sense of self and try to draw attention to themselves all the time, social anxiety sufferers experience a *deflated* sense of self and try to avoid attention. However, at the same time, they believe that everyone is looking at them, talking about them, and commenting on their appearance. Sometimes, they can even start sweating, breathing heavily, and feeling dizzy or nauseous.

Social anxiety, being the third largest mental health problem in many countries, seems to be much more common than was, until recently, believed. This means there are millions of social anxiety sufferers among us, who go on with their lives without us ever noticing the trauma they may be going through every day. Which means, with proper education and self-care, the disorder is manageable.

The intensity of the disorder varies throughout one's life and throughout the day, as do the symptoms. However, most people with this mental disorder experience at least a mild kind of emotional distress in certain situations.

Situations which trigger social anxiety:
- Being introduced to other people
- Being teased or criticized in public
- Being the center of attention
- Being watched while doing something
- Meeting with strangers

What people experience during a social anxiety "attack" will depend on the individual and on the circumstances, but may include fear, blushing, sweating, dry throat, or racing heart.

Self-education helps, but regardless of how much you tell yourself that the fear or discomfort you're experiencing is irrational, you will not be able to stop it.

How Easy Is It to Overcome Social-Anxiety?

If you come to a point where social anxiety starts affecting your performance and relationships, you may have no other option but to seek counseling. Regardless of how good your therapist may be, however, it's up to you—and how much you're prepared to work on yourself—to determine how successfully, if at all, you'll manage to get rid of your discomfort.

Perhaps the worst thing about this mental disorder is that if left unaddressed, it can lead to other problems, such as:

- **Substance abuse**

Some people resort to alcohol or drugs in order to calm down and get through an event that involves public speaking or meeting new people.

- **Relationship problems**

While everybody faces relationship problems from time to time, individuals who lack self-esteem usually lack both the skills and confidence to deal with such challenges. As a result, they sometimes put up with mental or physical abuse for a long time before they summon the courage to do something about it.

- **Career problems**

Unless they learn to manage their disorder, social anxiety sufferers are at a disadvantage when it comes to career advancement, simply because in most professions one needs to have strong communication skills. Trying to spare themselves unnecessary exposure in public, they usually stay quiet in meetings, rarely volunteering new ideas or actions. As such, they are seen as someone who has nothing to contribute to the organization, and might not considered for promotion.

- **Depression**

If their mental health problems and low self-esteem are making them unhappy, lonely, and generally unsuccessful in life, those with social anxiety often end up fighting depression, as well—especially if they are painfully aware of the opportunities they've missed because of their social clumsiness.

- **Loneliness**

Social anxiety sufferers are always not taken seriously and may be teased or taken advantage of, which only contributes to their wanting to withdraw from the world. To them, things may seem harsh and unfair.

The only way to help someone with this disorder is through treatment. However, how successfully someone copes living with social anxiety has also a lot to do with their lifestyle. Depending on what they do for a living, it may be possible to avoid, or at least reduce, exposure to situations which trigger social anxiety attacks.

Emotional Intelligence and Social Anxiety

According to the Institute for Human Health and Potential, emotional intelligence is "the ability to recognize, understand, and *manage* our own emotions, and recognize, understand, and *influence* the emotions of others."

If you look at the situations which trigger social anxiety disorder, and at the competencies and behavior of those with high emotional intelligence, it's easy to see the relationship between the two.

Depending on its intensity, one can learn to overcome social anxiety through *understanding* what triggers it, or with the help of a good therapist. Emotional intelligence is all about *understanding* and managing one's emotions, so by applying emotional intelligence principles of being tuned in to your feelings, you can learn to understand your emotions, figure out the triggers behind them, and use your mind to control your reaction to those triggers.

<u>4 ways emotional intelligence helps you deal with social anxiety:</u>

- **Understand the triggers**

Analyze your potential job requirements and make a list of how much of your time will need to be spent in meetings, interviews, networking, formal events, giving presentations, and meeting with dignitaries. Think how much of this kind of exposure you could cope with and how you would do it. Only then should you decide whether to accept that particular job.

- **Improve your coping techniques**

If you've been in your job for some time, it means you've figured out how to cope with situations that trigger social anxiety. If this is a new job you're about to start, you need to come up with ways to lessen your anxiety while enabling you to function more or less normally. For example, make a list of activities you could delegate to others, those you could avoid or do either over the phone or in writing, and those you absolutely have to deal with personally.

- **Develop your emotional intelligence**

People with high emotional intelligence are usually very tuned in to their feelings, which helps them cope with or predict—and avoid, if necessary—certain potentially challenging situations which may require a lot of negotiations, reviews, and so on.

- **Shift the focus**

The first thing someone with a social anxiety disorder should do to develop or improve their emotional intelligence skills is to stop thinking about themselves and start thinking about the needs and problems of others. By shifting the focus from your fears to somebody else's, you'll be reducing the mental pressure you constantly live with.

The problem is that people with social anxiety disorder generally have lower levels of emotional intelligence. Which doesn't mean they can't learn the necessary people skills, but they will have to invest more effort to become emotionally intelligent than someone to whom interpersonal skills come naturally.

To manage your disorder with emotional intelligence, you will first have to develop it. You can improve your emotional intelligence if you use your energy on analyzing other people's feelings instead of focusing on yourself and dreading the—usually imaginary—rejections and failures.

Food for Thought:

1) Do you know someone with a social anxiety disorder? If you do, are you comfortable around them? If you don't, how do you think you'd be able to work with them?

2) When you are upset, do you always know what the trigger is? If you do know, does that make it easier to deal with the issue?

3) If you had to, how would you describe your ego—as inflated or deflated? Which of these two categories do you think you belong to?

Day 10
Coping with Pressure

The Pressure in the Modern World

Most of us have to work for a living, and typically define ourselves and our status in life by our jobs and the lifestyles they allow us.

Several studies show that despite the fast-paced life, information overload, and constant change many struggles to keep up with, most of our stress in the modern world is work-related.

If you lose your job, you automatically face concern for the future. When your regular source of income is taken away, you are forced to make lifestyle changes, lose touch with many people, and deal with anger, humiliation, or poverty. It's a very stressful situation, especially if you have a family.

Even when you have a job, you probably often worry about the consequences of economic meltdown and potential redundancies—and, to ensure you keep your job, you agree to take on more work, work longer hours, take work home, or work on weekends. Again, a very stressful situation, particularly if it persists.

So, whether you are in a low-paid, dead-end, or highly stressful job, you may be anxious either because of too much work, low pay, or because you don't feel appreciated. All of these situations are demoralizing, especially if they force people to stay in a job they hate or one that doesn't allow any creativity.

In trying to juggle career and family, people—particularly women—often take on more than they can handle. The marketplace has become increasingly competitive, and this encourages more aggressive competition within the workplace.

Negative emotions, such as stress, burnout, fear, rage, sadness, and envy, produce reactions in the body during which certain chemicals are released. These chemicals are directly linked to high blood pressure, cardiovascular disorders, autoimmune diseases, depression, and other health conditions.

We all know about the negative impact that unhealthy lifestyle, chronic stress, and unhappiness have on our physical and mental well-being. Still, we seem to be unable to slow down, as the pace of life will obviously not change anytime soon.

The fast-changing, complex, and high-tech world we live in demands we develop new skills which will make us more employable, more tolerant, and better at managing stress. Emotional intelligence is one of these skills.

How Pressure Affects Your Behavior

Life in the modern world is fast, hectic, and stressful, and most people are just coping as best they can.

In most of the developed world, people live longer than ever before, have a number of phenomenal opportunities, unsurpassed wealth, and enjoy political and religious freedom. Unfortunately, the material wealth accumulated in the developed world does not match the level of personal happiness of its people. While the consumerist mentality, which the modern society is based on, continues to push people to earn more, buy more, and have more, this is taking a toll on their mental, emotional, and particularly spiritual well-being.

There is the additional pressure to be "forever young"—people, particularly women, are expected to look half their age, to be slim and groomed, to have a career, and to always be happy, confident, and politically correct. That's a lot of things to have to worry about constantly.

Combined with the information overload, job insecurity, eating healthy, new autoimmune diseases, the threat of terrorism, illegal immigration, climate change, and the everyday effort of juggling family, career, and social life, it's no wonder anxiety and depression are becoming epidemic.

People react to stress by the fight-flight-or-freeze response, and although this is a time-proven survival technique, it's only effective if the stress does not last for too long or does not happen too often. Which is exactly the opposite of what our lives have become.

To cope with the unforgiving pace of modern life, we find ourselves engaging in lifestyles and habits which temporarily relieve the tension we have to live with—but which, in the long term, can create serious health problems.

<u>5 ways in which stress affects our behavior:</u>
- Overeating or emotional eating
- Outbursts of anger
- Substance abuse
- Social withdrawal
- Chronic exhaustion

To cope with all these opportunities and challenges, we need to learn how to deal with pressure, how to embrace the complexity of modern life, how to diffuse conflict, how to slow down, and how to prioritize.

Our world has changed beyond recognition within the last 50 years. To make the most of what it has to offer, we need to be ready to change with it and, when necessary, adopt new skills and lifestyles which will not only help us deal with stress better, but also make our lives more harmonious and fulfilling.

Why Emotionally Intelligent People Cope Better Under Pressure

Work-related issues are the main cause of stress in the modern world, and being able to manage this stress means that you'll perform better on the job.

The reason emotionally intelligent people cope better under pressure is because they are more in tune with their feelings and with what's going on around them. How does it show?

<u>6 traits of emotionally intelligent people which help them cope under pressure:</u>

- **Self-Awareness**

Emotionally intelligent people are in tune with their feelings, what causes them and why, and are able to recognize or anticipate stressors before they occur. Since they are better prepared, they have the opportunity to come up with ways to deal with them.

- **Awareness of others**

Emotionally intelligent individuals are not only aware of their own feelings, but they can pick up on the emotions of others, too. That means they understand what causes stress to other people and recognize a potentially stressful situation arising, so they can avoid getting caught up in something they're not really involved in. In other words, they know when to offer help and when to stay out.

- **Responding on time**

When they find themselves in a challenging situation or being verbally attacked, emotionally intelligent people, being in control of their feelings, try to understand what had caused such behavior. If possible, they'll even try to diffuse the situation before it gets out of hand.

- **Good listeners**

Conflicts are rare if everyone has the chance to be heard. But, since most people prefer to talk than to listen, that's not always easy. Those with high emotional intelligence often manage to prevent stressful situations because they find time to listen to people who have something to say. That way, they understand what could potentially become a problem and can take steps to prevent it before it happens.

- **Ability to see a broader picture**

Being able to see things from someone else's point of view, emotionally intelligent people are prepared to try and understand why people do things, even if they don't agree with what they've done. Walking in other person's shoes, at least temporarily, is sometimes all it takes to understand them better.

As Jurgen Klopp pointed out, "The challenge is to stay cool enough to handle the pressure at the moment so that you can succeed in the future."

Food for Thought:

1) Have you ever been laid off? How did you feel? Did it impact your relationships with others?

2) How do you deal with stress at home? What about at the workplace?

3) When you see a "storm brewing" in the office, do you try to help or stay out? Why?

Day 11

Why You Need "People Skills"

People Skills You Need to Succeed in Life

People skills are essential for work, life, and social success, and they primarily revolve around communication, tolerance, and trust.

Regardless of your profession or lifestyle, you are probably in constant interaction with others—and the stronger your people skills are, the more successful these interactions will be. However, we are all different, and our ability to interact varies. While to some, this comes easily and they enjoy it, others may find it challenging and stressful. The way a relationship is developed depends on both parties, as well as the circumstances they find themselves in. But, regardless of our individual preferences and personalities, we all need to know how to communicate with others and maintain good relationships with them.

<u>4 interpersonal skills necessary for success in life:</u>

- **Good communication skills**

Good communication skills are about being able to take in information, speak clearly and thoughtfully, and respond timely and coherently. Both verbal and non-verbal communication are equally important, although the latter is usually underrated.

- **Good listening skills**

Not many people enjoy listening to others; they'd much rather talk about themselves. But listening effectively and empathically is often the only way to fully understand what's really going on, and to hear even unspoken parts of the conversation. As the well-known Russian writer Alexander Solzhenitsyn said in one of his books, "The less you speak, the more you will hear."

- **Empathy**

Many people are natural empaths, although this is something you can learn to become. Empathic managers easily understand the needs of their staff, clients, or partners. Being able to understand others' motivations, complaints, fears, or aspirations makes it easier for them to deal with, or prevent, conflict or convince others of necessary change.

- **Conflict resolution**

Conflicts are common in the workplace. Being able and willing to listen, see the problem from the angle of those involved in it, and try to understand what really contributed to the incident is what enables some people to successfully solve—or at least diffuse—a tense situation before it gets out of hand.

Clearly, you need people skills to improve your interactions with others. Some people have a way of dealing with all kinds of people or situations with ease, and have obviously perfected their people skills.

Strong People Skills for Career Happiness

These so-called "people skills" are nothing more than interpersonal skills which enable you to peacefully coexist with others. Good people skills are a sign of high emotional intelligence, which is particularly important for a career that involves a lot of social interaction.

In many professions, it is absolutely necessary that you are willing to listen attentively, communicate clearly, and engage with others on a regular basis in a way that demonstrates your interest in what they are doing or what they are going through.

So, if you think you have strong people skills or if you are willing to develop them, it may be a good idea to choose a career that will make those qualities visible—making it easier for you to become a leader in your organization or field.

Career happiness has a lot to do with doing what you like for a living, so finding a career that helps you showcase your strengths and hide your weaknesses goes a long way towards ensuring you make the most of your skills and life.

While good people skills are important for a successful career in any field, and for successful cooperation with people in general, in some professions, it makes the difference between a good or bad career choice.

Careers requiring strong people skills:
- **Management**

Managers regularly have to deal with others, on many different levels. They are often involved in negotiating, restructuring, coordinating, and resolving conflicts. Different types of managers may need a different level of people skills (like how a financial manager needs much less than an HR manager), but generally speaking, the higher the level of responsibility, the more one needs strong interpersonal skills.

- **Legal profession**

Lawyers and others in this field do a lot of listening, negotiations, persuasions, and conflict resolutions as part of their job, so they need excellent communication and listening skills—as well as a healthy dose of empathy.

- **Helping others**

Someone who works as a nurse, social worker, teacher, doctor, therapist, or school counselor, spends most of their time closely—sometimes intimately—involved with others. To do their job successfully and professionally, only people with excellent people skills and high emotional intelligence should choose these professions for a career.

But what if you lack, or struggle to develop, people skills? Although many things can be learned on the job, you would obviously be choosing a career you have very few "strengths" for. This doesn't mean you can't do it, but it's highly unlikely you would be recommended for a promotion or become a big name in the industry. A lack of these skills can easily kill a career.

8 traits that show you are NOT suitable for a profession requiring strong people skills:
- You can't control your emotions and are short tempered
- You lack self-confidence and you let others see it
- Deep down you don't really believe in yourself, and it shows
- You have poor communication skills and prefer talking to listening
- You're easily discouraged, and if your first attempt at something fails, you choose to quit rather than keep trying
- You don't get along with others
- You are not a genuinely helpful person
- You lack negotiating and networking skills

Perhaps emotional intelligence is best summed up by Russell H Ewing: "A boss creates fear, a leader confidence. A boss fixes blame, a leader corrects mistakes. A boss knows all, a leader asks questions. A boss makes work drudgery, a leader makes it interesting. A boss is interested in himself or herself, a leader is interested in the group."

Food for Thought:
1) List all the people skills needed for the job you're currently in. Which ones are you good at, and which ones do you still have to develop?
2) Are people skills your strength or your weakness? Does your current job match your skill level?
3) Would you be prepared to listen to someone complaining about you and your management skills? How can you learn and improve from it?

PART 2

How to Improve Your Emotional Intelligence

Day 12

Learn to Deal with Your Feelings

Recognizing and Managing Emotions

Not everyone pays attention to their feelings, and this often has a lot to do with one's childhood. Growing up in a loving environment that is both physically and emotionally safe is very different from being raised in a family where children witness violence, deprivation, or substance abuse by one or both parents. All these memories and/or traumas affect one's state of mind, and children usually learn early on that sometimes it's safer not to show how you feel, or to expect kindness.

However, even people with happy childhood memories can struggle to identify or express their emotions.

One of the main traits of emotionally intelligent people is that they are in touch with their feelings. This means they don't ignore them, are able to figure out what triggers them, and learn how best to deal with them.

How do they achieve this?

As feelings are usually a result of your thoughts, attitude, or experience, if you can manage to control those, you can take charge of both your emotions and your reactions to situations that trigger them. For example, if you think about the exam you have to write in a couple of days, you may feel anxious. If you notice that your boyfriend drinks a lot, you may feel nervous or angry if that brings up memories of growing up with an alcoholic father. If you attend a funeral, you may feel sad if that brings back memories of the loved ones you've recently lost.

Feelings range from simple ones—such as joy, fear, or grief—to the more complex, which are a combination of simple feelings and your thoughts and/or images. For example, you may feel sad if a friend tells you his dog was killed in a car accident, but secretly happy it wasn't your dog. Or you may love someone, but at the same time be worried because of their high blood pressure.

Emotionally intelligent people rarely feel lost, mentally exhausted, or confused, because they accept and process their feelings as they occur, instead of bottling them up. Besides, it's not uncommon for people to care more about others than about themselves. For example, you may be sad or angry when your friend experiences a tragic event, but simultaneously ignore your own fears—either because you feel it'll go away (it never does) or because you don't have time to do something about them (although you always find time for others), or because you subconsciously believe you're not worth the attention (because there are people with much more serious problems in need of help).

We all know feelings are contagious, and this is why we, consciously or subconsciously, avoid the company of sad, depressed, or troubled people and instead seek the company of the happy, successful, and positive individuals. Think about how drained you feel when you have to spend time with a friend or a relative who complains or moans all the time—it makes you feel mentally exhausted, but secretly happy you don't have to live with someone like that.

Suppressing feelings is not healthy, especially if this goes on for a long time. Holding on to sadness or disappointment can make you feel depressed or bitter. However, many people are brought up to not show their feelings, and some spend their entire lives never letting go of pain, anger, or resentment.

When you don't deal with your feelings, you can develop many psychosomatic symptoms, such as a headache, ulcer, or high blood pressure. Bottled up emotions can cause muscle tension in the neck, back, or jaw.

According to the mind/body philosophy, when you suffer from tight muscles, you usually hold bottled-up feelings in that part of your body. For example, fear tends to affect stomach muscles, problems can manifest in shoulder and upper back pain, hopelessness in tight neck muscles, and so on. If this is happening to you and you don't want to seek professional help, you can try muscle relaxation techniques or learn how to work through your feelings before they settle in your body.

How to express your feelings:
- **Talk about them**

It's best to find an empathic person willing to listen, but if you have no one to talk to or if the issue is very delicate, you might consider seeing a therapist.

- **Write them down**

If verbal communication is not your thing, write about your feelings. You can keep a journal if you like, or jot down specific emotions whenever you feel like getting something off your chest. If the things you write are very personal and you don't want anyone else to see it, flush them down the toilet after you've read what you've written.

- **Learn how to get rid of negative emotions**

There are many ways to deal with anger, depression, or fear—you can try crying, going for a walk, calling a friend, listening to soothing music, analyzing your emotions to understand why you feel the way you do, withdrawing from people or situations that trigger such negative emotions, deep breathing, or meditation. If none of this helps and the feeling is overwhelming (especially in the case of long-held anger), you may try pounding on or screaming into a pillow, or getting some exercise.

The bottom line is not to ignore your feelings, but take them seriously—especially if they persist. Developing emotional intelligence can help you understand and process your emotions in a mindful way, thus preventing serious health-related problems.

Managing Emotions in the Workplace

The modern workplace has changed a lot over the last fifty years. It usually consists of open-plan offices, high staff turnover, multinational and international employees and employers, high competitiveness, and layoffs. Such an environment requires staff that can cope with constant change, cultural diversity, high stress levels, and job insecurity.

For this reason, employers increasingly look for candidates with high emotional intelligence, as well as the ability to work under pressure. In an increasingly stressful and challenging world, only those who can handle their emotions and manage stress are likely to thrive.

According to Bond University professor of management Cynthia Fisher, the most common negative emotions experienced in the workplace are:

- **Frustration**

This is when you feel trapped but can't do anything about it. Frustration in the workplace is the most common cause of burnout.

- **Worry**

With so many layoffs, it's natural to be worried about losing your job. However, instead of feeling anxious, try to focus on your job and think about ways of improving your performance, to you make yourself more employable. Nervous people usually have low self-confidence.

- **Anger**

This is a very destructive feeling, which many people have a problem dealing with. Very few organizations will tolerate employees who can't control their temper. If you know you have an aggressive nature, watch for early signs of anger before you create a problem for yourself. To control your outbursts, try working out what your most common triggers are and avoid such situations if you can. You can also try attending an anger management course or developing emotional intelligence skills.

- **Dislike**

You don't have to like someone to work well with them. In big teams, there are likely to be many people with clashing temperaments or work styles. No matter what your personal feelings are toward someone, always treat your colleagues with respect and assertiveness.

- **Disappointment**

Repeated disappointments always negatively affect efficiency and productivity, and if unaddressed, can lead to burnout and high staff turnover.

The key thing about nurturing negative emotions in the workplace—be it feelings about your colleagues, management, working environment, salary, or something else—is that these feelings are contagious, and this kind of resentment easily spreads and demoralizes others. This is why a negative person is more likely to be fired, if for no other reason than to prevent their negativity and resentment from spreading to others.

Besides, there are often people who will happily invest huge amounts of time and energy to spite or sabotage their colleagues.

As Reham Khan, a Pakistani film producer, said, "It amazes me to this day to think about women in the workplace who spend more time trying to damage other women's images or opportunities than they do on improving their own abilities."

Day 13
Think Before You Speak

Words Can Heal, Words Can Kill

In some ways, words are the most powerful tool man has at his disposal. They have the power to offer hope and energy, but also to hurt and humiliate. However, when you see how carelessly people use words and how often they unintentionally hurt others or themselves, it seems that not many people are aware of this.

Still, there are those who are quick to apologize for things they've said, but often when it's too late and the damage has already been done, like when you've been embarrassed in public or made to feel small or incompetent in front of your family.

here are also people whose kind, encouraging words can help you overcome the worst traumas.

The people who understand the power of words can easily use them to heal or harm—depending on what they hope to achieve.

3 ways to use words:

- As an emotionally intelligent person, you are not only able to understand and manage your emotions, you can use words in a way that soothes, encourages or makes others feel they belong. Combined with good listening skills, speaking kindly and with humility is probably the best remedy for almost any problem.

- Unfortunately, many people are not good at controlling their emotions, and care even less for those of others. As a result, they speak before they think, and will often say whatever happens to be on their mind without considering the impact their words might have on others. Or, even worse, they may knowingly use their words like arrows to hit and destroy those they speak to.

- There are also people who need to talk non-stop, wasting their energy and the energy of others on trivialities.

The way words are used and the effects they achieve vary from person to person. Emotionally intelligent people typically listen attentively and speak mindfully and with compassion. Self-centered people often talk about themselves all the time. Mean or weak people might use words as a weapon to get back at someone or to hurt them the only way they can.

Words can also be used to teach, empower, soothe, or celebrate, and while different kinds of languages are used for different occasions, we should always speak respectfully and with humility.

Those with higher emotional intelligence understand the power of good communication skills and will know how to align their voice, body language, and words to a topic, person, or situation.

How to Improve Your Public Speaking Skills

Good communication skills are valuable for a successful life, and especially career, because they enable you to express your emotions or thoughts in a confident, professional, and timely manner.

However, if your job requires you to frequently speak in public, give interviews, do sales presentations, and more, it pays to invest in developing your emotional intelligence skills, which will help you connect with others with confidence and empathy.

Good public speaking skills can be learned but will only come with practice. There are many tips on how these skills can be developed and improved, and experienced public speakers eventually create a personal speaking style.

5 tips for successful public speaking:

- **Prepare**

This is how you overcome nervousness. Depending on how much time you have, go through your notes several times, especially if you're new to this. However, over-preparing can be counterproductive, because if you learn your entire presentation by heart, you may sound less genuine. If you're feeling nervous, practice in front of a mirror or ask a friend to be your audience.

- **Match your speaking style to your audience**

If possible, try to find out who your audience is, because both the language and manner of presentation will be different if you are addressing a boardroom of directors, or a group of high school students.

- **Organize your notes**

Even if you've done that particular speech or presentation many times, write down the key topics and main points. Sometimes, the audience may interrupt your presentation with questions, or the atmosphere may be noisy, or there may be a lot of coming and going—it's easy to get distracted.

- **Feedback**

You can learn a lot from others, so either hand out a feedback sheet at the end of the presentation or lecture, or ask someone you trust to tell you how it was. In this case, even negative feedback can be very helpful.

- **Make it special**

Depending on the type of speech, presentation, or lecture you have to do, you may use small things that will make your speaking style unique. Things like jokes, interaction with public, topics, or the way you address them all contribute to making the occasion interesting and fun. To keep the audience captivated, try to grab their attention in the first ten minutes.

- **Body language**

Dress comfortably, but professionally. Practice tone of voice, hand gestures, and eye contact. If looking into people's eyes makes you feel nervous, look over their heads and "address" those sitting in the back row. Or, choose a neutral spot to focus on.

- **Finish in style**

Pick the most interesting part of your presentation to finish with, so you leave your audience craving more.

- **Audiovisual Aids**

Use them as and when suitable, but they are not crucial for a good speech or presentation. People often tend to focus on visuals, so using too much might make them less focused on your words.

Day 14
Take It on the Chin

Learn to Accept Criticism

Accepting criticism without taking it personally is a sign of maturity, self-confidence, and emotional intelligence—yet very few people can do it.

This is not entirely surprising, because those who give feedback are often not adequately trained to do so professionally. Additionally, many people are not well-meaning and will be only too happy to use the opportunity to use their feedback to undermine your confidence.

Be it as it may, we receive feedback in various forms throughout our lives, so learning how to do it professionally and receive it graciously are skills we should all strive for.

There are ways of providing feedback with subtlety, although many people tend to be blunt. This is either because they either can't be bothered to worry other people's feelings, are simply unaware of how destructive criticism can be, or are purposefully being malicious.

So, how to behave if you receive negative feedback? It depends on who it's coming from and why.

<u>7 things to ask yourself when you receive negative feedback or harsh criticism:</u>

- **What's the occasion?**

Was this personal or professional feedback? Was this a job-performance evaluation, or a friend telling you what she thinks about the speech you gave, or your mother commenting on your dress style?

- **How constructive/helpful is the feedback?**

Whatever it is you've been told, ask yourself if it is something you can use to improve your skills, like public speaking, project management, driving, and so on. If there's nothing to be gained from the criticism, why was it given, and why did you agree to listen to it?

- **Who is giving it?**

There is a huge difference if the feedback comes from someone very important to you, like your boss or your partner, or if it's just a friendly (or not so friendly) comment from a colleague or a friend.

- **How bad is it?**

It's impossible to go through life unscathed, particularly in the business world. Those who are very sensitive will probably have a tough time accepting criticism, even if it's well-intentioned. If this is you, try to work on your self-confidence and stop feeling like everything is all about you. Just because someone gave you negative feedback doesn't mean they have anything against you personally. Maybe you DID look awkward in that dress or made a stupid joke at the worst possible time, or failed to meet the third deadline in a row.

- **Do you feel the negative feedback was given maliciously?**

This should worry you only if it comes from someone you depend on, like your boss. Otherwise, accept it as a part of life.

- **Why do you feel bad about it?**

Sometimes negative feedback prompts people to try harder, while others become withdrawn, demoralized, and discouraged from trying again. If you feel really bad about the criticism, try to figure out why. Is it because you're not used to being criticized, or because you had hoped nobody would notice how much you messed up?

Try to analyze the feedback neutrally, as if it were not about you. What message is it sending? What can you learn from it? As Robin Sharma said, "Negative feedback can make us bitter or better." It's up to us.

Admit You Were Wrong

It's not easy to admit you were wrong. Depending on what you've done, it can be so hard that many people choose to live in denial, rather than confess. Or, they may try to find excuses, blame others, write it off to bad luck, or simply lie.

When it comes to making a mistake, you can either admit it or deny it. Those who own up to the error of their ways show they have both self-confidence and integrity. In a way, admitting your mistakes may actually improve your status among your colleagues or peers.

This happens mainly because those who do summon the courage (and decency) to open themselves to criticism demonstrate major traits of leadership and maturity.

If you happen to be in a leadership position, it's extremely important to lead by example. When you admit you were wrong, you are showing everyone else how they should behave, and teaching them that everyone makes a mistake. As a result, others will trust you more, and this may make you more approachable because others will be less nervous about admitting they, too, had done something wrong.

Something we often forget—or choose not to think about—is that when we make a mistake but refuse to acknowledge it, someone else may have to take the blame for it. If you like playing games with your friends and colleagues this way, go ahead, but it will only last until you're found out and, as a result, will probably never be trusted again. When you are caught in a lie, be prepared to accept the consequences. And in some situations, or jobs, there's no coming back from it.

Although we should all try not to make mistakes, the trick is to learn from them, so you don't repeat the same mistake again. And having the courage to admit you were wrong boosts your self-respect—and helps gain respect from others, because you are confident and decent enough to admit you screwed up.

To quote Donald L Hicks, "To make mistakes or be wrong is human. To admit those mistakes shows you have the ability to learn and are growing wiser."

How to Provide Negative Feedback

As a friend, parent, partner, or employer, you often have to provide feedback—sometimes negative. How you do it may not make a big difference to you but will to those on the receiving end.

Hearing the answers to questions like, "How do I look in this dress," "Should I trust him with my savings," or "Did I do well in the meeting," is usually not pleasant to hear, but can be empowering—IF the person giving it has your best interests in mind, and IF you are self-confident enough not to take it personally.

False praise is easy to give, and people sometimes do this if they know that the person who asked their opinion cannot handle criticism. However, in a work situation, this is not possible, and the more sensitive about yourself you are (the less self-confidence you have), the harder will it be to deal with criticism. Negative feedback, especially if the person feels it's underserved or if it happens over and over again, can be very demoralizing and may actually prevent people from trying.

So, if you have to offer criticism, try to make clear why you are giving negative feedback and suggest ways of overcoming the reasons that contributed to it. This is important because, for criticism to be constructive, it should help the person improve themselves, and not undermine their confidence.

7 tips on how to give negative feedback:
- Provide feedback regularly, especially if it's negative, rather than wait to tell someone what you think of their behavior, work ethic, management style, and so on. People may not be able to take in so much criticism at once, but if you touch base with them on a monthly basis, they can gradually improve themselves.

- Never give feedback if you're not feeling well, like when you're angry, tired, hungry, or in a rush. If you are irritated, it will show in your feedback, and the person you are giving it to is more likely to take it personally. Good communication skills and empathy are very important when providing any kind of feedback, and especially when it's negative.

- Prepare for the meeting at least a couple of days in advance. Make sure you have supporting documents, and if you expect confrontation, prepare yourself emotionally, too.

- Do it in a one-on-one meeting, rather than through email. Give the person a chance to hear it face-to-face. Those who dread giving negative feedback to someone they know will overreact may try to get away with written feedback, but this is highly unprofessional.

- Start the meeting on a positive note, listing the things the person does well, then deal with the negative bit by addressing what you think is the root of the problem. It will soften the negativity if you suggest a solution, such as attending a project management course, improving communication skills, brushing up on a foreign language, or whatever the case may be.

- Attentive listening to what the other person has to say about their performance is very important. Listen carefully, especially if it comes from someone you know doesn't have the confidence to tell you openly what they think. You may have to read between the lines.

- If you're a line manager or a senior colleague, help them get where they'd like to be by offering mentoring.

Day 15

Stand Up for What You Believe In

Walk the Talk

Emotionally intelligent people possess self-awareness which, amongst other things, helps them stand up for what they believe in. By being confident enough to know what their values are, and assertive enough to have the courage to stand up and make a difference, they show us how to be true to ourselves and follow our passion.

We know that repeated thoughts or statements eventually become our core beliefs. Some of these beliefs may have been forced upon us when we were young, some we inherited from our family, while some we may have borrowed from others. The reason our core beliefs are so important is because they show what our key values are in life.

Many people are willing to stand up for their convictions. However, we all know it's not always easy—or possible—to be open about what or who you believe in, unless you enjoy confrontation. And it can be very scary, especially if your beliefs go against what most other people want or believe.

Depending on what it's about, having the courage to stand up for what you believe in may make you very popular or create a lot of problems. So, keeping in mind the opposition you are likely to face if you are not afraid to tell the world what you think, make sure you know what you're talking about. Educate yourself on the subject and stay informed. And if you do get a chance to speak your mind, do so in a polite, non-confrontational manner.

4 reasons why it pays to stand up for your beliefs:
- When you are not afraid to stand up and make a difference, you are demonstrating courage and self-respect. As a result, you'll be respected by others, although they may never tell you that.
- You may be an inspiration to others who never dared stand up for their beliefs. Your "coming out" may boost their confidence to speak up for the cause they believe in.
- When you summon enough courage and confidence to speak for what you believe in, you demonstrate that you choose to be yourself, rather than conform to what everyone else is saying or doing.
- If you truly believe in something, follow that dream. Gandhi and Martin Luther King did just that. You're in good company.

Ability to "connect" with others is a special gift that can help you in almost any sphere in life. With high emotional intelligence skills, particularly empathy, you will not only find it easy to understand others, but will also be able to convey messages efficiently and effectively.

When you decide to stand up for what you believe in, find a way to demonstrate how you "walk the talk" and how others could help. There are causes and situations where you simply know that you have to get involved and do something, because if you don't, you'll feel guilty for the rest of your life. Use the opportunity when it presents itself and be true to yourself.

Follow your passion without worrying about what others will say. They may make fun of you for a while, but deep down, many of them are probably mad at themselves for not having the guts to do the same.

This quote says it all: "Stand up for what you believe in, even if it means to stand up by yourself."

Why Self-Awareness Matters

Only those with a greater sense of self-awareness would dare stand up for themselves when they know that "they will stand up by themselves."

Self-awareness is considered one of the key competencies of emotional intelligence. Basically, it's about understanding yourself better—what motivates you, what your main strengths and weaknesses are, what your core values are, how you relate to others, and so on.

When you know all this about yourself, you'll have a pretty good idea how to navigate through life—by developing your self-awareness, you are actually developing your emotional intelligence.

<u>4 basic steps to self-awareness:</u>

- **Understand where you're coming from**

How much do you know about your family history? Your ethnic origin? What's your life story? What effect did your past relationships have on you? How's your health? How do you cope with stress? How would you describe yourself in one line? Who are you? What are you like?

- **Self-reflection**

Try to set aside at least twenty minutes every day to contemplate on the day behind or ahead of you, on your emotions at that particular moment, or on your life in general. If you prefer, you can pray or meditate, instead. In any case, you'll be surprised how much you can "hear" when you sit in silence.

- **Feedback**

Try to get honest feedback from someone you trust but choose carefully who you ask. We rarely see ourselves as others see us. What you hear may not be pleasant, but if it comes from a well-meaning person, it can help much more than false praise. Insecure people or those who find you intimidating will tell you what you want to hear. People who are jealous of you may use the opportunity to hurt your ego with spiteful or manipulative comments.

Those with high self-awareness find it easy to understand others because they understand life. They easily relate to other people's feelings, because they recognize and manage their own feelings well. And the reason they are good at it is because they know who and what they are, and how they got there.

Once you achieve greater self-awareness, you will be able to make the most of your strengths and channel your energy to where it's needed most.

Day 16

Connect

Why You Need People

People are probably the cause of some of the happiest, as well as the most miserable, memories of our lives. They can provide love, care, help, and joy, but can also be a source of energy drain, frustration, disappointment, and anger.

Science proved a long time ago that social interaction is very important for our physical and mental well-being. Although we may not all be very communicative, social support—particularly at certain times of our life, like when dealing with divorce, redundancy, or the death of a loved one—is what often makes the difference between getting over it or sinking into depression.

However, some people can happily live in isolation, and that's okay as long as they enjoy it. But even if cutting yourself off from people spares you a lot of pain and suffering, it also deprives you of joy, company, and friendship. Annoying as they may sometimes be, people are there for a reason.

However, successful interaction with people is a skill not everyone can master. Communicating and connecting with others is an important aspect of life, but many people are clumsy in their relationships, continually hurting others with inappropriate remarks, gossiping, not being there for them in times of trouble, or exploiting them.

There is also the issue of the culture one comes from. In societies where it's common for extended families to live together, and where an average household usually has 15 or more people, living in isolation is, for practical reasons, impossible—but it is also not something people want. When you get used to being around others all the time, you find it difficult to function on your own. As a result, these people function much better in a group.

Modern Western culture, however, is all about independence, autonomy, and self-sufficiency. People are encouraged to follow their dreams regardless of family tradition or cultural norms. The families are much smaller, and once the children turn 18 and leave home, they become even smaller. It's also not uncommon for people to live on their own.

However, regardless of our lifestyle, we all need others to feel whole. Living on your own, either out of necessity or choice, you probably need people even more than those who live surrounded by others all the time.

Regardless of how much you interact with others, you clearly need people skills. Most of us pick these up from family as we grow up. But in cultures where extended families live together, people become good at networking because they pick up key people skills from an early age.

In "self-sufficient" Western society, though, people skills have to be learned through education. Emotional intelligence is the essence of basic people skills that we likely were all good at once, but now have to learn about from books or courses.

But, regardless of whether people skills come to you naturally or you learn about them in a course, and regardless of how introverted you may be, we all need people in our lives.

How important emotional intelligence actually is for human society was perhaps best described by Theodore Roosevelt, long before any books on the subject were written: "The most important single ingredient in the formula of success is knowing how to get along with people."

Be Happy for Others

Being happy for others doesn't come easily to everyone. Those who like people, and who are genuinely happy for others—even for those they don't know personally—are usually people who are emotionally mature and confident enough not to see another person's success as a potential threat to their own.

So, what does being happy for others actually mean? It's about being genuinely glad that someone has made it. But it's also about being grateful for what YOU have, even if you think you deserve much more. Emotionally intelligent people don't compare their success or happiness with that of others. Instead, they continually work on themselves, improving their people skills and their overall understanding of what works and what doesn't.

Being aligned with their emotions and understanding what triggers them, they can easily recognize the first signs of envy, or perhaps anger or resentment for not having tried harder. But, as they are better able to manage their emotions, they don't allow them to interfere with their judgment or behavior.

The key to learning to be happy for others is to stop comparing their success (or happiness, or wealth, or appearance) with yours.

For example, just because your best friend is beautiful doesn't make you any less pretty—perhaps she simply spends more time on self-grooming. Or, just because your cousin lives in a big house doesn't mean you can't, too – perhaps you need to start managing your finances better. Or if a friend landed a great job, perhaps he just invested more time and energy on his education than you did.

Not comparing yourself with others is about separating someone's success from the actual person. Don't forget that success in anything rarely comes without years of hard work, so someone else's success is usually only a sign that they managed their money better, invested more time in education and training, or had better people skills than their competition.

Just like you may have indirectly helped someone get what they want in life, there are people in your life who may help you get what you want—provided you know what it is.

<u>3 tips on how to be genuinely happy for others who seem to have it all:</u>

- **Stop comparing yourself to others**

When you constantly, often unconsciously, focus on what others have, how they look, how happy they are, and so on, you are wasting your energy. Be grateful for what YOU have, although it may be difficult if what you have is very little. If this doesn't work, think of at least two things that you do have—good health, respectful children, a nice apartment, a secure job, a good income. Everyone has something to be grateful for, even if it's less than they think they deserve.

- **Know what you're worth**

This doesn't have to refer to material possessions, because they are not YOU. So, even if you are the only person in your office (or amongst your friends) who doesn't have a car, or who still lives with her parents, or who is working a low-paid job, that doesn't change who you are. We are all special in our own way, and there are probably many things about you that you are appreciated for, like your patience, empathy, or kindness. On the other hand, your financial or marital status does not say what you're truly like, but simply describes how you live.

- **Don't ignore your negative emotions**

When you catch yourself feeling envious, try to figure out what it is about someone else's success that is bothering you. Instead, ask yourself what's stopping you from getting the same thing they have. Then, instead of being envious, be happy for them, and see what you can learn from their success. Perhaps you can "steal" an idea or two.

The key thing to remind yourself of is that others who are successful or happy are not so at your expense. They haven't stolen your happiness from you, nor have they reduced the overall quantity of happiness available to everyone. In fact, they probably worked hard to get where they are today.

Day 17

Reprogram Your Mindset

Why It Pays to Adopt a Positive Attitude

Many people believe that the reason positive people seem to be more successful in life is simply because they are lucky, but the truth is a bit more complicated than that. When you live your life with a positive mindset, you tend to attract positive experiences to your life—love, decent people, professional success, wealth.

Besides, as they always tend to see the bright side of life, these people also cope better with stress, as a result of which they are generally healthier. All this helps them enjoy more opportunities, contributing to a generally successful and fulfilled life.

On the other hand, those who focus on the negative, like problems, past hurts, injustices, the unfairness of life, poor health, and so on, are naive to expect anything positive to happen. What they unfortunately don't realize is that when you focus on the "lack," that's exactly what you end up with.

Life is often unfair, and you need all the energy you can muster to cope with everyday challenges. This is why it's so important to let go of all draining thoughts, emotions, and people because these are the underlying cause of feelings of fear, insecurity, worry, or bitterness.

While some people seem to be naturally positive about life and are optimistic in almost every situation, most of us have to work on developing a more positive attitude and learn how to stop self-sabotage with negative thoughts.

13 steps to develop a more positive frame of mind:
1) Accept change as a normal part of life.
2) Make it a priority to look after yourself and nurture your body, mind, and soul.
3) Learn to identify negative thoughts and stop them before they become part of your mindset.
4) Surround yourself with those in whose company you feel appreciated and accepted.
5) Avoid people who are "angry with life." Their bitterness is contagious.
6) Choose friends who accept you for who you are.
7) Avoid, or limit, negative media.
8) Stay away from energy drains, be it situations, locations, or individuals.

9) If you're suddenly feeling low, try to work out what preceded such thoughts. Finding out what, or who, triggered your negative thinking pattern can help you avoid similar situations in the future.

10) Reduce stress by learning to say NO.

11) Look for solutions rather than focus on problems.

12) Learn to spot opportunities and use them.

13) Try to think of yourself as you would like to be, not as you are. Then ask yourself what's stopping you from becoming such a person.

Another way to remain positive about life is to limit your expectations. This isn't easy in the consumerist and often aggressively competitive world we live in, where we are constantly urged to buy more and earn more, or to be the best, forever young, super slim, and super healthy.

Never forget that life is about choice. When you choose to see opportunities rather than problems, opportunities actually start presenting themselves.

As Wayne Dyer said in one of his books, "With everything that has happened to you, you can either feel sorry for yourself or treat what has happened as a gift. Everything is either an opportunity to grow or an obstacle to keep you from growing. You get to choose."

Redesign Your Life by Reprogramming Your Mind

This may seem like an impossible task to someone who's lived with a negative mindset their entire life. A negative mindset reflects on all aspects of your life—how you relate to your children, partner, work, friends, opportunities, disappointments, or tragedies.

According to the like-attracts-like concept, being focused on the negative means you probably attract people or events that match that thought pattern. When you listen to some people explain why they're so bitter about life and you hear of all the misfortunes they've had to deal with, you immediately understand why they are always so negative—even toxic—towards others.

However, it is probably *because* they approached everything in life with a negative attitude—their job, relationships, children upbringing—without joy and happiness, half-expecting the worst to happen any day, that their life turned out the way it did.

Although your mindset is not cast in stone and can always be changed, it requires a lot to discipline and commitment. In other words, you have to acknowledge that you have a negative mindset, and that it has slowed you down in life and contributed to a lot of missed opportunities, poor decisions, or failed relationships.

So, is it possible to change the direction your life is taking by reprogramming your mind? Absolutely, although a lot will depend on where you are in life. The longer you've lived with resentment and fear, the more effort will it take to change the way you see the world and your place in it.

Emotional intelligence is a tool you can use to help you change direction, but first, you need to be clear about what it is you need to change.

There's a saying that your mind is the key to success and happiness, so if due to faulty programming you repeatedly experienced disappointment and bad luck, all you have to do is reprogram it for success.

8 steps to a positive mindset:

1) Acknowledge

Face it—We've all made some mistakes in our lives. Acknowledge all the opportunities you've missed and all the relationships you ruined because of this, then decide how you'd like to make up for the lost time and energy.

2) Commit

Be prepared for a lot of soul searching, self-doubt, fear, and regret, but remind yourself that unless you work to change something in your life, it will not happen on its own. The worst thing would be that you continue to live your life the way you did until now.

3) Make a choice

Take stock of your life. The path you are choosing will be neither easy nor straight. Make the right choice—choose the attitude which helps your soar, rather than remain stuck.

4) Create a completely new belief system

From now on, you should focus on your strengths and opportunities, not your past mistakes and failures.

5) Don't be afraid of failures

Accept them as a part of life, and an opportunity to learn something new.

6) Boost your self-confidence and self-awareness

Believing a change is possible is what makes it possible.

7) Never stop learning

In the fast-changing world, you need to be constantly learning and improving yourself.

8) **Grow**

Learn from the experience of others who turned their lives around by changing their mindset.

How Emotional Intelligence Boosts a Positive Mindset

Positive thinking is much more important than we realize, because we feel its effects in almost all areas of our lives. Psychologists believe that a negative attitude, such as expecting catastrophes and hostilities and experiencing fear or rage, is actually part of an ancient survival mechanism, because these feelings helped men watch out for potentially dangerous situations or people. And that's what helped them stay alive.

However, as we have moved from a physical to a social environment, we no longer need emotions like that—except perhaps in extreme situations, such as during a war or natural catastrophes. But our brains still work according to this original model, constantly warning us of possible danger.

As our environment has changed a lot since those early days, we no longer need these survival mechanisms as much, and should replace them with new behaviors and thought patterns more suitable for modern-day challenges. There are several tools that can help us achieve this, and emotional intelligence is one of them.

If you are serious about changing your thought pattern, the first thing you should do is get rid of, or limit, negative self-talk. Unfortunately, thoughts that lead to this kind of talk are not always easy to identify, and this is where emotional intelligence can help you.

One of the things emotionally intelligent people are particularly good at is recognizing their thoughts, and the feelings that follow them. This is why they know what to do when they recognize a negative thought or emotion take over.

Emotional intelligence boosts a positive frame of mind, and when you are positive about life, you tend to be more willing to hear others and engage with them on a deeper level.

So, a positive mindset, combined with emotional intelligence, goes a long way to improving your quality of life on all levels, simply because with such an attitude, you form better relationships, cope better with stress, attract opportunities, and not surprisingly, lead a happier and more fulfilling life.

Day 18

Forgive and Get on With Your Life

Emotional Intelligence and Forgiveness

At some point in our lives, we've all been hurt. People cheat, lie, deceive one another, leave, turn back on us when we need them most, give away our secrets, and so on. However, while some hold onto these past hurts, reliving them day after day for the rest of their lives, others decide to let go of them and move on.

There are things which are impossible to get over, such as child abuse or animal torture, there is still something very liberating about forgiveness. However, forgiving someone doesn't mean what they did should ever be forgotten or approved of.

The problem is that the pain and anger caused by the hurt or injustice you experienced will continue to live on in your subconscious, constantly reminding you of that trauma—especially when something triggers the memories of the incident, which is bound to happen from time to time. But when you forgive, you choose to let go of the pain and move on with your life.

Emotional intelligence shows us how to engage successfully with others, and how to manage our reactions to the emotions they stir. It also helps us understand our own emotions and express them as and when they occur, so they don't become bottled up.

A forgiving person is someone with higher emotional intelligence, because they epitomize maturity and ability to move beyond their present emotions.

Sometimes, it can take years to understand and get over an incident, but until you forgive, you remain stuck in the past. And that's the last thing you want to do, especially if your past is not something you want to remember.

To forgive doesn't mean you'll ever forget what happened. Instead, it is about deciding to move beyond the hurt and gain back your power.

However, forgiving is an ongoing process. When you forgive, you may not stop feeling angry about what happened to you immediately, or that you'll ever truly trust that person again, but it's a start. When you decide to move beyond the incident, it's not because you want to make life easier for the person who hurt you, but for yourself.

To forgive takes courage, and not everyone can do it, but the concept of emotional intelligence fosters the spirit of forgiveness—if for no other reason than to bring peace to the victim.

Although vengeance may seem like a tempting option, it takes a big toll on your mental and emotional well-being.

As Mahatma Gandhi pointed out, "The weak can never forgive; forgiveness is the attribute of the strong."

Letting Go of Past Hurts

We've all been hurt, and we usually blame others for it. Sometimes, those who hurt us apologize or try to do something to make amends, but often they pretend as if nothing happened, or stand their ground with a "so what?" attitude.

Being hurt is about justice. We expect someone to make it up to us somehow, or at least to acknowledge what they've done.

However, this process puts all the power in the hands of others. Anger is a powerful feeling and can be self-destructive if targeted toward the self—you may be angry with yourself for having unintentionally contributed to the incident, or for not having reacted differently when it happened.

Emotional intelligence encourages us to acknowledge our feelings, to recognize them and stay with them until they've been processed so we can express them in a suitable manner. This means it can be very damaging if you keep telling yourself you are not angry, or you've forgiven someone, while deep inside, you seethe with rage.

Whatever feeling you experience, be it anger, humiliation, disappointment, or desperation, stay with it. When you ignore your painful feelings, all you are doing is trying to bury the past. Unfortunately, the past has the habit of surfacing, sometimes at the most inopportune moments.

Whatever it is you feel, stay with those feelings. Feel the pain, the hatred, the humiliation, the bitterness. Analyze them so you understand what triggered them, and when you have processed them and are ready to move on, let go. Then, decide to put it all behind you.

<u>3 ways to let go of past hurts:</u>

- **Acknowledge**

Examine your role in whatever situation that caused you pain, and how you could handle a similar situation differently with the knowledge you have now.

- **Decide to let it go**

This is a very powerful process, because it involves a choice—and the choice is yours. You can choose to remain stuck in the hurt or to let it go. This is very empowering and liberating, because the ball is now in your court. YOU decide what happens with the hurt you've experienced.

- **Express the pain**

Whatever discomfort is the hurt causing you—shame, guilt, self-blame, anger, fear—vent it out in whatever way you see fit by crying, screaming into a pillow, writing it out, talking to someone, meditating, praying, or whatever works for you. Otherwise, the negative feeling may stay with you, and become yet another bottled up emotion. Depending on what it is, this may take weeks or years. Feel it, learn from it, and get rid of it.

- **Stop the blame game**

When you blame others, even if you have every reason to do so, you are a passive participant in what happened to you. It makes you adopt a victim mentality, which is very disempowering. Living with this kind of mentality can mean feeling sorry for yourself and doesn't allow you the power to take back control of your life.

- **Don't dwell on the past**

People can spend months and years reliving a painful memory—when their partner eloped with their best friend, when their child died, when they were humiliated in public. But there is no need to analyze such memories for years; nothing will change what happened. Seeking professional help usually speeds up the healing process.

- **Focus on the present or the future, not the past**

When you let go of the past, you are free to focus on the present or the future. This doesn't mean you'll forget what has happened to you, but that's okay. Rather than trying to ignore past events, acknowledge them and let them go. This is important because when you stop crowding your brain with memories from the past, you create space for new experiences and people.

- **Forgive yourself**

Why do we so often find it easier to forgive others than forgive ourselves? Forgiving yourself is about admitting you're not perfect—if there's something you should not have done, or should have said but didn't, at least you'll know better next time.

However, anger and pain because of something you've experienced are sometimes so overwhelming that it's impossible to simply let go. In that case, the anger should be acknowledged and processed in a way that will bring you closure.

Fantasizing about revenge can sometimes help, but revenge itself is not a solution. And as long as you dream of it, you remain stuck in the past.

Before any healing can take place, you should forgive yourself for the part you played in what happened. So, instead of thinking about what SHOULD have been done or how the incident COULD have been avoided, accept the painful reality and try to overcome the whole episode.

While you shouldn't dwell on the past and repeatedly bring back the painful memories by reliving the incident, you should not try to forget it, either. That won't actually make it go away;

it will simply be stored somewhere in your subconscious, waiting for a trigger to come back and haunt you again.

Emotional intelligence can help you deal with what happened by processing the painful memories and expressing them in a way that will bring emotional release.

Day 19
Emotional Manipulation

Are Emotionally Intelligent People Manipulative?

With a higher level of emotional intelligence, people become very good at perceiving, as well as manipulating emotions—both their own and those of others. In a positive sense, this means they can pick up on what's going on and intervene in time to prevent an accident, incident, or a problem becoming bigger than it should.

However, being able to sense and manage other people's emotions and influence their way of thinking and behavior has a darker side.

In the workplace, those with high intelligence levels can easily manage members of their teams. They are good at building and maintaining professional relationships with their colleagues, business partners, or clients. Their key strength is exceptional people skills.

However, as we all know, emotions can be a very powerful tool for those who know how to nurture or manipulate them.

Emotionally intelligent individuals can "read" others easily, especially if they've known them for some time. Being aware of another's weaknesses, preferences, character traits, vulnerabilities, or personal problems, can, in the wrong hands, become a very powerful tool—or a weapon with which to get what you want.

For example, when you know that someone is nervous about a presentation they have to give, by interrupting them while they speak, you can easily make them look unprepared or silly. There are many subtle ways of embarrassing someone or exposing their vulnerabilities in public if you know what will easily upset them. And being aware of problems in someone's private life is potentially very dangerous in a hostile or competitive environment.

So, in theory, emotional intelligence can be used to manipulate others in order to achieve a desired effect—by making someone appear less competent than you, you are indirectly promoting yourself.

These people can be destructive for the team spirit of an organization, and even though they are often eventually exposed for what they are, this is typically not easy because they can simply manipulate their way out of trouble.

On the other side of the coin, when someone achieves extraordinary results thanks to their high emotional intelligence, it is often at the expense of others. So, if you are in a position to influence others and you know you have high emotional intelligence, work to ensure you never use your gift to unintentionally hurt others—try to be empathic, as that will stop you from taking advantage of someone.

Protect Yourself from Emotional Manipulation

Whenever you interact with others, you are at risk of being manipulated. Especially if you are an empath, because some might try to take advantage of your kindness. On the other hand, being an empath, you should also be good at picking up vibes from those you interact with, and this is usually a good way to tell how much you can trust someone.

To stop being emotionally exploited, try to learn about the power of one's energy field, and how best—and why—it should be protected.

<u>7 tips on how to protect your energy field from emotional exploitation:</u>

1) Trust your instinct

Be on your guard if you get a bad feeling around someone, even if you're not sure why you feel that way.

2) Keep a written record of their comments/requests/suggestions

This applies only to a work situation, and is particularly effective if you can get them to send you something in writing, like an email request to go somewhere or do something.

3) Avoid them as much as you can

Sometimes, when you are identified as a suitable "victim" for manipulation, it may not be easy to get away from this person. Especially if they carefully planned their trap and befriended you, first.

4) Avoid getting too friendly with those you don't know well

Although this sounds paranoid, try not to open up too much in front of people you don't know, at least until you get to know them better—especially if they seem too eager to quickly become your best friend.

5) Raise your vibrations

If you realize you've been trapped or cornered by someone with ulterior motives, try to increase your personal power by raising your vibrations. The easiest way to do this is by staying calm and present, which you can do through meditation or by spending more time in nature.

6) If you fell into their trap

If someone you work or live with is known to enjoy toying with other's emotions, be mentally strong and don't allow them to get what they want—to see you blush, cry, make a scene, or shout at them. After several attempts, they'll get bored or realize you're a tough nut to crack and move on to someone else.

7) Use self-love to protect yourself

If you have to deal with a manipulator on a daily basis, boost your morale by giving yourself positive self-talk every day. You can do this with affirmations, or by reading uplifting quotes and spiritual texts that have stood the test of time.

The best way to spot and avoid potential manipulators, and to protect yourself from emotional exploitation, is to understand how they operate. Emotional manipulation revolves around playing on others' vulnerabilities and gaining an advantage over them.

Emotional exploitation can happen anywhere and is not limited to the workplace.

8 tricks manipulators use to take advantage of you:

1) They play on fear

This is probably one of the most common tactics manipulators use, and is most likely to be applied to those who are easy to scare and put off balance. These are usually people who are for some reason more vulnerable than others—the lonely, recently divorced, unemployed, depressed, with serious health or personal problems, or low-self-confidence.

2) They deceive

They do this either by withholding important information, so you find out only when it's too late to do something about it, or by intentionally giving you only bits and pieces instead of the full story, so by the time you manage to put all the pieces together, your opportunity to act may have been lost. This is usually done to gain an advantage over others by making sure they find out about something much later than the manipulator does.

3) They take advantage when you're in a good mood

If you've just heard some good news or are feeling particularly happy, it's much more likely you will say "yes" to things you would normally want to mull over, first. Sometimes, they time the favors they ask of people for when they are most likely to agree. Learn to control your emotions; it's not always safe to let everyone know how you feel.

4) They trap you by favors

Once you owe them, you're trapped—sometimes for life. We all know people who will not only happily do something for you (even if they are the last people who should agree to something like that) but will actually hound you, offering favors you don't even need. You can be sure that, before long, you'll be asked to return the favor.

5) Territorial advantage

Sometimes, a manipulator may try to bully you into agreeing to their terms by arranging a meeting in an environment where they are more likely to feel "at home." It can be their home, their club, their office—somewhere you are probably going to feel out of place.

6) They prepare their trap carefully

Most people prefer talking about themselves than listening to others. Manipulators use this to find out as much as they can about you, so as to know what they could use you for. And while you feel happy you met someone who is so interested in you, the manipulator is collecting information about your family situation, personal problems, relationships, useful contacts, and so on. Be careful what you reveal about yourself to those you don't know well, or who seem overly interested in your life, habits, and routines.

7) They use body language to browbeat you

To intimidate you and browbeat you into agreeing to something, the manipulator may choose to stand too close to you, tower over you if you're sitting or if they are much taller than you, use a deep voice, or stare at you in an effort to distract you. If someone tries to do this to you, it's best not to answer to their demand immediately. Instead, wait for a few moments while you compose yourself before replying.

8) They give you a very short time in which to make a decision

One of the easiest ways to force someone to do what they wouldn't normally is to not give them enough time to think things through. By rushing you, or pretending a decision has to be made urgently, they are hoping you will just agree to whatever they are asking. If at all possible, never agree to be bullied into making a hasty decision.

Day 20

Step-by-Step Guide to Becoming a Better Listener

Verbal Communication

When you know what it takes to be a good listener, you'll see that it's not surprising so few people are. We all have problems, some very serious ones, and having someone to talk to is sometimes all you need to see the light at the end of the tunnel.

However, in the increasingly stressful world we live in, it takes a lot of energy just to cope, so many people simply refuse to invest their energy and time on listening to other people's problems. Or, they simply don't care.

Good listening skills will help you not only with developing high emotional intelligence but will make it easier to read between the lines and hear even things which are not spoken. When you listen attentively, you may sometimes accidentally learn details about people you otherwise may not have known about.

The main reason good listeners are rare is that it requires much more than empathy.

How to develop good listening skills:

- **Be present**

When you are listening to someone, try to focus on what they are talking about, rather than tuning out to think about your own to-do list. The person speaking to you will notice if you are there, or if you are miles away. By listening attentively to someone, you are showing you respect them enough to want to give them some of your time and showing interest in what they have to say. Don't interrupt them while they speak, but ask questions either to clarify what they've just said or to prompt them to tell you more.

- **Pay attention**

You can do this by maintaining eye contact. For this reason, it is best to sit facing the person you are speaking to, rather than next to them. Also, you occasionally show that you understand what they're talking about by nodding your head, or saying, "Yes," "I see," "Mmmm," and so on. This, of course, doesn't have to mean you agree with what they are saying, but it helps them continue because these cues show you're with them.

- **Be patient**

Some people talk a lot while saying very little, others choose their words carefully, while others speak too fast. Listening attentively is not always easy, and can actually be tiring, but once people see that you are focused on what they are saying, they will relax and start talking more coherently and openly. It also depends on what is being discussed. Some topics are not easy to talk about, and you might choose to talk to them about something else first just to get them to relax a bit before you approach a more delicate subject. There is also the issue of culture. In Western culture, people tend to get right to the point. In the Middle East and Africa, however, you never approach a subject directly.

- **Open-minded**

If you already have an opinion of the person you are talking to, being unbiased will be more difficult. If you don't know the person, but they do things you hate or live a lifestyle you disapprove of, you will have to try very hard to stay open-minded about what is being discussed. In other words, try to listen without judging.

- **Body language**

Non-verbal communication skills are sometimes even more important than verbal communication, because they show how we really feel about the person we are talking to. For example, try to avoid crossing your arms across your chest, swinging your legs in boredom, looking through the window, glancing at your watch, or checking messages on your cell phone while the other person is talking. Sit facing them, nodding occasionally while smiling or looking sad, whatever is appropriate.

Don't forget that boredom or irritation easily shows on one's face, so don't think you can pretend you are genuinely interested in them while, in fact, you can't wait for the meeting to finish so you can have a cup of coffee and call home to see if your daughter finished her school assignment. When you are positive about life, you tend to be more willing to hear others and engage with them on a deeper level. Also, if what they say shocks or disgusts you, try not to show it as that might prevent them from continuing. Avoid touching, unless you both come from the same culture where touching each other on the arm or patting on the back is accepted behavior. Watch your facial expression—try not to look bored, shocked, disgusted, or angry.

- **Emphatic**

Real empaths can easily feel the motivation even of people they disagree with, and will readily share in their happiness or pain. Regardless of what your job is, you will on many occasions have to deal with people with whom you just can't see eye to eye. Although many people would choose to stay away with those they don't agree with, emotionally intelligent people don't have a problem interacting with such people. Empathy is universal, and applies even to your enemies.

- ## Solving problems

Don't interrupt people while they talk, except to perhaps ask questions that will prompt them to go on. Neither should you offer solutions to their problems, unless they ask for advice. In many cases, all people need is someone to talk to, not someone to tell them what to do.

Besides, when someone is finally given a chance to talk to someone, they may suddenly see the solution to their problem. Although you may think you are helping someone by offering answers, it's much better if they work out what the best solution would be. If you do it for them, you are taking their power away. You may even be seen as someone who believes they know what's best for others. People should always be encouraged to solve their own problems.

Non-verbal Communication

There are many subtle ways in which to communicate non-verbally, the most common of which are with eyes, voice, and touch.

<u>7 most common types of nonverbal communication:</u>

1) Facial expressions

These are usually universal feelings of happiness, sadness, anger, fear, surprise, and so on are usually the same across cultures.

2) Body posture

The way we sit, walk, or hold our head says a lot about us, although very few people are aware of that.

3) Gestures

These vary across cultures, and special care should be taken if using them with an audience from different cultures—what is normal in one country could be considered very rude in another.

4) Eye contact

This is probably the most important aspect of non-verbal communication. Your eyes clearly show interest, affection, hostility, fear, and so on. Eye contact is very important in one-on-one meetings, but in some cultures, not looking the person in the eye is actually a sign of respect.

5) Touch

This can be a handshake, a hug, a pat on the head, and various other types of touching or holding one another. Touch is a very powerful and revealing manner of communication and varies across cultures.

6) Personal space

The minimum physical space you need to feel comfortable around others is different around the world, but generally speaking, bringing one's face too close to somebody else's is considered either threatening or too intimate, which is why it is often used to signal dominance or affection.

7) Voice

What you say is as important as how you say it. In addition to listening to your words, people often read the tone, volume, and pitch of your voice. A voice easily shows confidence, anger, or nervousness.

Active listening requires a lot of practice and is an essential skill for anyone in contact with people; however, it's a learned skill.

Many non-verbal communication cues are part of a culture or a social milieu, and we usually learn them as we grow up.

Non-verbal communication is important for successful interaction because it enables us to see or feel the emotional state of the person we are talking with—are they tense, angry, relaxed, scared?

Besides, many non-verbal communication cues help us reinforce the message we are sending, or establish a particular relationship with another person. At the same time, the speaker can see how his words are affecting those he is speaking to, to sense if they are shocked, amused, or worried. So, non-verbal communication provides mutual feedback.

Day 21
Putting It All Together

Lessons Learned

What have you learned from this book?

The 21-Day Challenge was meant to highlight the importance of empathy and self-awareness for good relationships, professional success, and mental well-being.

Where to go from here?

If you enjoyed this book and feel this is something you'd like to learn more about, find out what your level of emotional intelligence is. You can download free tests from the Internet, or you can attend a course. Once you know where you are at, make a list of skills you feel you lack or want to improve.

Step 1

To fully benefit from this book, you should find a way to practice these skills. As emotional intelligence is mainly about relationships, you will have to ask your friends or family to let you practice on them. Ideally, you should start applying the principles of emotional intelligence in your daily life, like when you talk to your colleagues, when someone needs a shoulder to cry on, when you try to resolve a conflict within the team, when you are laughed at because of what you believe in.

As emotional intelligence is required in almost every aspect of your life, there will be many opportunities where you'll be able to check if your people skills have improved.

Practice is very important, but so is honest feedback. We can't see ourselves as others see us, so think of someone whose judgment you trust to tell you what they think of you. That's the best way to find out how you're doing and what you still need to work on.

Step 2

Make a list of all the emotional skills you feel you need for your current job, or for the job you'd like to be in one day, and try role-playing. Or, of all the skills mentioned in this book, identify three you know you would most struggle with—like listening attentively, speaking mindfully, or thinking before you speak—and focus on developing them over the next thirty days.

Although we can all benefit from improving our emotional intelligence skills, in some professions they are absolutely necessary and could be a part of your job description.

So, how can you know which skills to work on the most?

If you know you're impatient, you're likely not a great listener. If you talk a lot, you probably often say things without thinking. If you are proud of yourself for not being afraid to say what you think, regardless of who you speak to, you may occasionally say things you shouldn't.

Emotional intelligence is a key tool for better relationships. If you are a people person, you will easily develop new skills or improve the ones you're already good at. Don't forget that you don't learn emotional intelligence in a 5-day course—it's a lifelong process.

Step 3

To move forward, create an Emotional Intelligence Action Plan. Make a list of skills you need to develop and those you need to improve. It can be something like a SWOT analysis. Think of ways or opportunities you'll have at work (or at home) to practice the skills you find crucial for the job you're in.

Emotional intelligence is useful in all spheres of our lives, and you can apply its principles almost anywhere and under any circumstances. So, starting from tomorrow:

- When you next ask your partner or a friend how their day at work was, try to be genuinely interested and actually listen to what they say. If you're too tired to listen about somebody else's day at work, it's better not to ask than to pretend to be listening while your mind is miles away, thinking about your own day at work.

- When you next meet a friend and she starts telling you of the health problems her mother is having, watch your body language, tone of voice, and eye contact, and either show genuine interest or change the subject—your boredom shows.

- When your boss summons you to his office to tell you there's been a number of complaints about you from some important clients, don't take it personally—instead, try to understand what might have caused those complaints.

Step 4

Refine your Action Plan by breaking it down into individual skills you feel you need to improve, and create a weekly or monthly challenge on how to develop those skills:

- How would you improve the way you manage your feelings if you know you have a short temper, or dislike being challenged, or tend to take even the slightest criticism personally? How would you start changing these behavior patterns?
- How would you get yourself to start speaking mindfully if you talk a lot and often say something without thinking?
- How will you improve your listening skills when you know you find listening to other people boring?
- How can you become more open to feedback?
- If you are timid by nature, how would you summon the courage to stand up for what you believe in?
- If you are known as a vengeful and unforgiving person, how would you work on becoming more forgiving?
- If you are an empath who people often take advantage of, how will you make sure you protect yourself from emotional manipulators?

All these skills take repeated practice, which you can do with friends or family.

You will see your progress when you receive your performance evaluation, for emotional intelligence is definitely something people will notice and it should reflect in your evaluation. Outside of work, your friends or family will pick up on the changes in your behavior. Their honest feedback can help you be even better.

Emotional Intelligence in Children

Emotional intelligence can help you improve your relationships, self-awareness, and sensitivity when dealing with others. It requires lifelong learning, and the sooner you start, the better.

When it comes to children, it's best if you nurture these skills from an early age. Today, everyone—including children—is expected to be good at managing different relationships. This means that to be able to successfully adapt to the constantly changing environment we live and work in, children should start practicing basic principles of emotional intelligence philosophy even before they start school.

Those who learn these skills at an impressionable age will find it much easier to fit into the high-tech, high-speed, and culturally-diverse world of the 21st century. By helping children develop empathy and a sense of self, you are preparing them for the workplace of tomorrow.

There are many different ways to do this, but it's easiest if these strategies are gradually incorporated into their daily routines. A lot of this can be done through role-playing and games.

4 ways to encourage emotional intelligence in children:

- **Be the way you would like your children to be**

Be their role model. Behave, speak, and act the way you expect them to.

- **Acknowledge positive and negative emotions in your child**

Learn to recognize different emotions in your children and tell them it's okay to be sad, angry, or hurt. Teach them how to resolve conflicts, and encourage them to openly express love or sadness.

- **Encourage your children to accept and express their emotions**

Children should feel free to talk about how they feel and why. But they will only do so if you create an environment in which it feels safe for them to open up. Never punish them for something bad they've told you they've done, for they may learn it doesn't always pay to be honest.

- **Be realistic**

Don't expect results overnight. This is a lifelong learning process. Emotional intelligence is a sign of emotional maturity, so adjust your expectations to their age.

4 skills to cultivate in children:

- **Empathy**

Can your child see and relate to another person's pain or happiness? Do they sometimes cry for others? Do they feel sorry if a friend lost something? Or when they see a dead bird in the park? To teach your children to empathize with others, you have to be a perfect example of how they should behave. Don't try to fake empathy if you don't really feel it. Children are much smarter than we give them credit for—if you fake, they will, too.

- **Expression**

Children often express their feelings in very socially-unacceptable ways, like by screaming or crying. If you try to stop them, you are effectively preventing them from expressing their feelings—indirectly interfering with their development.

When they scream or cry, all they are doing is venting their emotions. It's believed that if you prevent them from expressing their emotions this way, they will express them in another, perhaps more violent way, like by taking it out on a sibling or the dog, or being destructive.

- **Listening**

Being around children can be very tiring: they ask a million questions, they talk non-stop, and they crave attention all the time. If you are busy, exhausted, or simply not in the mood and ask them to shut up or ignore them, you are sending a very wrong message. To develop into an emotionally intelligent person, a child should be given your full attention whenever he or she needs it.

- **Problem-solving**

Parents often rush to help their children with whatever problem they may be having. However, this makes them dependent on others to solve their problems. To nurture their emotional intelligence, encourage them to find solutions on their own. They may struggle, they may get angry, or even cry if you refuse to help, but when they manage to get it right, it will boost their confidence and will help them grow into independent and responsible adults.

Emotional Intelligence in Teenagers

A high IQ in a child is no longer what parents worry about most. Today, they are encouraged to pay much more attention to their teenagers' emotional well-being. They do this by helping them develop self-awareness and manage their emotions, as well as by boosting their confidence through regular encouragement and praise.

Teenagers are young adults whose brains are still developing, so signs of strong emotional intelligence are not always consistent. However, the main clue is how well a teenager handles their emotions.

8 traits of emotionally intelligent teenagers:

- **They are interested**

Emotionally intelligent teenagers are interested in the world around them. They are curious about life and want to know everything.

- **They don't worry too much about making mistakes**

They accept that making mistakes is a part of life. They don't dwell on past mistakes or hurts, and this is a good sign of resilience and an ability to overcome challenges.

- **They have a positive mindset**

They generally focus on what they are good at, rather than on their weaknesses.

- **They control their emotions**

Emotionally intelligent teenagers understand the power that comes with controlling and managing your emotions. They understand their happiness and success is in their own hands.

- **They differentiate between various energies in their environment**

Emotionally intelligent teenagers recognize those among them who boost or drain their energy levels, as well as those who create negative vibes.

- **They embrace change**

They don't fear change—on the contrary. They can easily adapt to a new situation or circumstance.

- **They don't hold on to grudges**

Emotionally intelligent teenagers are generally quick to let go and move on after an incident.

Closing

There may come a time when you start having a nagging feeling that you're just not coping and that for the challenging times we live in, you need to learn new skills.

You may be lacking skills necessary for the industry you work in, or simply wondering how to improve your relationships—both in and outside of work.

One of such skills that will be very difficult to live without in the confusing and ever-changing world of the 21st century is emotional intelligence.

Perhaps it is that vague nagging feeling that led you to this book. Or maybe you heard about emotional intelligence from a friend. Perhaps you just stumbled across it while searching the Internet.

Whatever the case may be, you are usually attracted to something for a reason. Just like we are drawn to scents which make us feel a certain way, to people we feel comfortable being around, or to books with relatable characters, you may be subconsciously looking for a way to improve your interpersonal skills.

Even if you chose this book with no clue what emotional intelligence is, the fact that you've read it shows that you are interested in learning how to manage your emotions and improve your communication skills.

We hope that after reading the book, you'll understand why those with higher emotional intelligence have a better chance of being successful professionally and feeling more accomplished personally.

A fulfilled life includes a combination of professional and personal achievements, and knowing how to understand, manage, and use your emotions will help you achieve both.

Your path to success depends on many things, but mainly on how well you manage to navigate your way through life. Developing emotional intelligence can help you stay on course.

We hope you enjoyed *The 21-Day Challenge,* and that this is only the beginning of your journey of self-discovery.

Book #2

Anger Management

The 21-Day Mental Makeover to Take Control of Your Emotions and Achieve Freedom from Anger, Stress, and Anxiety

PART 1

Anger – A Cry for Help or a Desire to Control?

Day 1

What is Anger?

Anger as a Powerful Emotion

Anger is a feeling we are all familiar with, although we experience it and express it in different ways. The usual cause of anger is a reaction to an unfair decision or treatment, as well as to criticism, being embarrassed in public, being bullied, feeling impatient, somebody's rude behavior, being ignored, losing, being dumped, and many more unpleasant experiences.

However, while anger is a perfectly natural part of life, it's not something we should encourage. On the contrary—most people try to control their anger, especially in social situations. Perhaps there were times in the distant past when being openly angry was a crucial survival skill, but in the sophisticated and densely-populated world we now live in, different survival techniques will help you succeed.

Like with so many other things in life, there are two sides to anger—it can be both a positive and a negative force in your life. On the upside, anger often serves as a sign that things are not right and that something needs to be done about the situation, like if you are facing unfair treatment, having to deal with rude people, or standing in a queue for too long. However, we often make ourselves angry by having unrealistic expectations.

The downside of anger, especially out-of-control anger, includes a long list of behaviors that lead to ruined relationships, domestic violence, imprisonment, destroyed health, spoiled opportunities, and more.

Often, the so-called primary anger masks the emotions that are the real reason for our aggression. The most common secondary emotions leading to anger are fear—often manifested as anxiety and worry—as well as sadness, because of a real or imaginary loss.

The reason these feelings cause anger is that fear and sadness make people feel vulnerable or threatened, and to stop themselves from becoming overwhelmed with these emotions, people often shift into anger mode. A friend of mine once said that it was only when she was behaving aggressively that she felt truly alive.

By shifting your fear of being dumped by your partner into anger, you subconsciously give yourself a shot of adrenalin, which makes you feel energized and in charge rather than helpless and vulnerable.

If used positively, this boost of energy can actually help you get out of a tricky situation or find a better resolution to a problem. However, if creating this false sense of confidence and control over the situation means you actually become aggressive and start abusing others, the adrenalin rush that created this powerful feeling will probably create more problems rather than offering any solutions.

Self-Anger

Turning your anger and frustration inward, whether you are aware of it or not, is one of the most self-destructive things you can do to yourself.

If you're angry with yourself for not being more attractive, more successful, or happily married, start by asking yourself what's stopping you from getting what you want. If you stay with this question for a while, you'll realize that you either don't really want these things or that the effort of getting them would outweigh any benefits you'd see.

Unfortunately, not having what you'd like or think you deserve is often the result of choices you made in the past which you are now paying for—wrong life partner, wrong investment decision, remaining in a dead-end job, and so on.

Not having what you want is a complicated issue, especially if the reason you can't get something is beyond your control, as things often are. Although having dreams can be a powerful motivating force that can help you overcome setbacks, having unrealistic dreams or not doing enough to make them happen will only make you sad, resentful, and—worst of all—angry at yourself for not having tried harder.

We usually turn anger outward, to other people—like the government, a particular person, or even life in general. However, those who turn their anger inward, toward themselves, usually reach a point where it manifests as self-hatred or rejection of certain aspects of self that they believe are a cause of their failure in life. So, like how in extreme situations, anger can lead to murder, self-anger can similarly lead to suicide.

Anger comes in many disguises—as resentment, ranting and raving, or blame. But it can also be masked by such feelings like impatience, envy, guilt, or low self-esteem.

So, what to do if you are openly or secretly angry at yourself? Besides learning anger management, you can do one of two things.

<u>2 things to do when feeling angry at yourself:</u>
- **Forgive yourself**

    Your failure to be what you think you should be or have what you think you deserve could be due to wrong life choices, or simply unrealistic expectations. However, while acknowledging your mistakes is necessary before you can move forward, beating yourself up over something you did or failed to do will get you nowhere. Instead of wallowing in your guilt or self-hatred, learn from your mistakes, face your demons (guilty thoughts, hurt feelings, disappointment) and stop replaying over and over again in your head that you're a failure. If you can forgive others, why can't you forgive yourself?

- **Work out why you're angry**

    If the reason for your anger is justified, do something about it. If it isn't, don't stress yourself by constantly thinking about how unfair life is, how ungrateful children can be, how selfish, rude, or arrogant people are.

    If you think you deserve better and believe you can use your anger to make others aware of the injustice done to you, doing what you think may improve the situation.

    However, don't forget that anger often breeds more anger, as well as resentment and fear. To prevent self-destructive behaviors and thoughts, stop thinking about the past (and your failures) and shift your focus to the present (and new opportunities).

Learn to Understand Your Anger

Before you try to control your anger, you have to make sure you understand what is causing it—what is REALLY causing it.

Next time you feel angry, try to calm down so you can think clearly about what's making you mad. This is not easy and you'll probably need to try more than once, because we often become masters at fooling ourselves.

<u>4 steps in understanding your anger:</u>

1. **Acknowledge your anger**

    Stop telling yourself (and others) "I'm fine." You can't be fine if deep down you are seething with rage. Unless you acknowledge you have a problem, you won't be able to start looking for a solution.

2. **Identify the key feeling behind your anger**

    This can be tricky, but if you are used to tuning into your emotions, it won't be too difficult. Emotional intelligence is a tool that can help you understand your emotions, and why your anger often masks more intense emotions such as disappointment, loneliness, or abandonment.

3. **Ask yourself why**

    Once you work out what really fuels your anger, be brutally honest with yourself and admit why the fear, sadness, envy, or any other secondary emotion is making you so upset. For example, you may fear the future (if you believe you will be made redundant soon), you may fear loneliness (if you suspect your partner is contemplating leaving you), you may fear death (if you know you have a serious health issue), you may feel sad (because you let someone down), you may feel resentful (because of missed opportunities), you may feel envious (because amongst all your friends, you are the only one still living with your parents).

4. Deal with the secondary emotion

There are issues that can be resolved, and those that are beyond your control. If your anger stems from something that can be changed or improved, work on addressing this so you can close that chapter of your life and move on.

If your anger is caused by a secondary emotion, like fear, guilt, or anxiety, you should find a way to express this feeling in a healthy way.

When you understand what your anger is actually about, it will become much easier to find a way to deal with it. Although figuring out what is making you angry will not make the anger go away, it will at least help you keep it under control.

Anger is a very powerful emotion. The trick is to use its energy as fuel to motivate yourself to improve your life and get where you want to be.

Food for Thought:

1. Think of a time when you were very angry. Try to remember how you felt, how you looked, and how you behaved at the time. Do you think your reaction was justified? How would you react in the same situation today?

2. List three things that make you most angry. Why?

3. How do you react when you witness an angry outburst in public? Do you pretend not to see or hear anything? Do you try to get as far away as fast as you can? Or do you try to find out what's going on?

Day 2
Signs and Symptoms of Anger

When You Can Feel it Coming

Some people get angry very easily. Some might stay angry for days or months, while others can let go of built-up tension through an angry outburst, then simply forget about it and move on—though this doesn't mean those around them can do the same.

Certain people may decide to do nothing about their anger, and instead hold on to it for years, until such a time when they can no longer take it and an angry scene follows. Although many anger-related issues cannot be resolved, the worst thing you can do is let your anger turn into bitterness, be it about life in general or about a particular person or incident.

After an angry outburst, you may feel relieved because you let go of accumulated tension, but it can also make you feel flat, embarrassed, or foolish—not to mention the stress you've created for those who had to witness the scene.

In any case, there are warning signs one is about to "explode." We all learn to recognize these signals from an early age, and continue to perfect the skill as we grow up. Just like we are taught that a dog is getting ready to attack if it flattens its ears, we learn how our parents look or behave when they are mad by watching how they react when they realize we've done something we shouldn't have. Later in life, we learn to interpret the subtle—or not so subtle—signs our partner is about to leave us, or we're about to be laid off.

Being able to pick up vibes from your environment and understand what's going on even when nothing is said is a very useful skill which can sometimes be a real lifesaver.

The tell-tale signs you, or someone else, is about to become angry and possibly dangerous are many, and vary from person to person. However, some of them are common and easy to notice.

16 traits of people prone to anger and/or aggression:
1. They frequently experience road rage.
2. They often blame others for their misfortune.
3. They often feel threatened and believe that others are out to get them.
4. They make scenes when angry.
5. They get angry for even small and insignificant things.
6. They use dominating body language, threats, and screaming to control others.
7. They easily lose their temper.
8. They easily become frustrated.

9. They are unable to control themselves even when they know they'll be sorry later.
10. They have a history of domestic violence.
11. They are in chaotic or problematic relationships.
12. They refuse to accept they have anger issues.
13. They often think or boast about violent confrontations with others.
14. They have been arrested for violence.
15. They drink excessively and are aggressive when drunk.
16. They believe and boast they can easily make others do what they want.

If you know that you or someone close to you is experiencing anger issues, the best thing to do is to explore various anger management techniques which could help not only deal with an explosive temper but understand what it is that makes someone react in such a way.

How Does Being Angry Make You Feel, Look, and Act?

Some people are quick to anger, either because they are short-tempered or because they feel entitled to certain things. Others may need more time to get upset, but their anger may be longer lasting. However, the most problematic type of anger is the kind that leads to physical violence.

Anger is a powerful emotion which affects us on both a physical and emotional level. It not only invokes a strong physiological response, often leading to aggressive and destructive behavior like shouting, thrashing, or violence, it also changes our emotions and encourages certain behaviors we may later not even remember.

Blind rage is particularly common when people are set off for one of these three reasons:

- **Major loss** - For example, a stolen car, a broken-into apartment, or a bag snatched in a restaurant.
- **Grief** - For example, your best friend killed by a drunken driver, your partner cheats on you with someone you trusted.
- **Humiliation** - For example, being belittled in front of others, being insulted because of the way you look, being bypassed for promotion.

While anger can lead to aggression, there's also a positive side to this emotion—it often makes you take steps you might not have otherwise. These steps often lead to change, which does not always have to be external: if you've been bypassed for promotion, you may decide it's time to look for another job, or if your apartment regularly gets broken into, you may decide it's time to improve on security or move to a safer neighborhood.

If you've been angry for years, it may be a sign that something within you needs to change, such as your beliefs, goals, needs, or priorities.

Whether anger will have a negative effect on your life or health, or whether it will prompt you to look deep within and make positive changes in your life, will depend on how honest you are with yourself and how willing you are to embrace change.

Most people who have an anger issue know very well they have a problem, but few decide to do anything about it. If left unaddressed, anger can not only make you a social outcast, but may lead to broken relationships, lost friendships, and even imprisonment.

Anger is like an adrenaline shot which, if not occurring often or allowed to get out of hand, can actually boost your confidence and sense of self-worth. A "dose" of anger, especially if you are fighting for the right cause, can make you feel strong and self-aware.

Just like animals exhibit certain behavior when facing an enemy—dogs raise the fur on their back, cats flatten their ears, horses stamp the ground—people also change their appearance when feeling threatened.

When angry, people may also display some of the behaviors used by many animals. Based on the fight-flight-freeze theory, if they decide they will neither flee nor freeze, but choose to fight, people will often stand tall with slightly spread arms, showing they are ready to fight. They may shout, thrash, or stamp their feet to demonstrate how angry they are, they could become red in the face which makes them look fierce, or they may stare at the opponent or point a finger at him. These body language signals are all part of atavistic behavior, which has helped us survive and which is understood across cultures.

Not only do angry people look threatening, the adrenalin rush makes them feel strong and ready to charge. And when you look and feel threatening, it's easy to go a step further and behave violently.

<u>Physical reaction when feeling angry:</u>
- Increased heart rate
- Increased blood pressure
- Increased breath rate
- Hormonal changes (adrenalin rush)
- Muscles become tense (ready to hit or receive a blow)
- Face becomes red (because of increased blood pressure)

Anger can take different paths and can invoke different emotions, from a desire for physical confrontation to severing communication and withdrawal from the situation or the person you're angry with. However, the physical and emotional manifestations of anger rarely happen at the same time, but are usually spread over a certain period.

How we react to anger depends on our personality, how emotionally intelligent we are, as well as on what caused the anger. Still, certain reactions seem to be common among angry people.

9 stupid and counterproductive things people do when angry:

1. Use bad language
2. Drink excessively
3. Throw or break things
4. Threaten others
5. Refuse to listen
6. Cry
7. Say things they don't mean
8. Behave as if they are entitled to whatever they want
9. Feel proud for demonstrating their strength even over much weaker opponents

So, if you know you're prone to feeling angry, and especially if you often act aggressively, the best thing to do is to start anger management treatment. You can either seek professional help, or you can try to help yourself by reading suitable self-help materials or attending an anger management course.

Anger takes many forms and people deal with it, or struggle with it, in different ways and with different levels of success. However, if you know you've felt angry for a long time, don't assume you're used to it and can continue to deal with it on your own. Bottled-up emotions can change the way you think and behave, even without you realizing it, so it's best to do address it before the accumulated resentment gets you into trouble.

Food for Thought:

How do you usually react when angry? Do you later regret it?

Do you think letting go of bottled up emotions by shouting and screaming at others is okay as long as the person feels less tense afterward?

Some claim that mental or emotional abuse is as bad, or even worse than physical abuse. Do you agree?

Day 3
Why Do I Get Angry?

Many things affect how often you get angry, how long you stay angry, and how you express your anger. Although we all have different anger thresholds, they usually revolve around feelings of personal safety and self-image.

Causes of Anger

Our anger is often based on our interpretation of the situation we find ourselves in. But how we react in a situation also depends on our triggers for anger, which vary from person to person and usually have something to do with our personal boundaries or our view of justice.

<u>4 most common triggers of anger:</u>

1. Feeling threatened
2. Feeling "cornered," helpless, or desperate
3. Feeling you are not being treated fairly
4. Facing injustice (yours or others')

However, we are all different—not everyone may feel threatened, provoked, or mistreated in the same situation. The way we react to challenges has a lot to do with who we are. Our experiences, both those we are currently going through as well as those we went through in the past, affect how we react in a situation, or with people who remind us of something or someone that made us feel unpleasant. The more troubled our life is, the more likely we are to be emotionally unstable, and the greater our need for anger management skills will be.

<u>4 factors that influence your reaction in a challenging situation:</u>

- **Your background**

    If you grew up in a family where it was okay to show your emotions, you will likely continue to be open about your feelings, both positive and negative, as an adult. However, this also means that if you were spoiled as a child and managed to get what you want by throwing tantrums, you will probably continue to exhibit similar behavior throughout life.

If you were brought up believing that it's rude to complain, chances are you worked out how to swallow your pride and hurt early on. The trouble with this attitude is that unless you later learn how to express your anger, there is a danger you may turn it inward, on yourself.

And if you witnessed a lot of family violence, you likely grew up believing that anger is a terrifying feeling, and will try to avoid any kind of confrontation for fear of provoking violence.

- **Your past experiences**

If there are past experiences, like childhood abuse or bullying, that you didn't deal with, you are probably still trying to cope with those feelings of anger even though you may not be aware of it. So, even if you appear happy and confident, deep down, you may still be fighting demons from the past. As a result, you might find certain situations or people difficult to deal with, and if you can't avoid them, being around them is likely to make you feel angry—even though no one would understand why you feel this way.

- **Your current circumstances**

If you are going through a tough time at the moment, facing a divorce, redundancy, serious health issue, or the loss of a loved one, you are probably not quite yourself. As a result, you probably get angry easily, though you may not understand why.

If there are situations that you find personally challenging or threatening and you don't address them, the unresolved issue may find an outlet in angry outbursts—which may happen when you least expect it.

Also, if you are grieving for someone, you may be overwhelmed by conflicting emotions such as sadness, anger, sense of emptiness, guilt, and so on. These contradictory feelings may make it very difficult to cope with otherwise normal challenges, and this may affect how you relate to those you come in contact with. For example, you may snap at others, burst into tears for no reason, or have brief episodes of unexplainable rage.

- **Possible health issues**

Sometimes, certain health issues may be the cause of anger. According to the mind-body doctrine, our emotions and physical health are very closely linked and depend on each other much more than we realize. Anger can have neurological triggers and if you can't stop feeling angry, or you come to a stage where you wake up feeling angry, you should seek professional help as soon as possible.

Anger may also be caused by chronic exhaustion. If you are feeling constantly tired, you will have much less energy to do what you're supposed to, or may find it more difficult to concentrate and persevere with your tasks. For these reasons, you'll most likely be less successful in life which, in turn, may make you feel angry with yourself.

Personal Judgment as a Leading Cause of Anger

How we go through life has a lot to do with our mindset—our values, what we see as right or wrong, what we experience as injustice, how cooperative we are, and so on.

Based on this, it makes sense that our own judgment about a situation will decide if we experience it as a threat or injustice. Basically, it is how WE see the world and what WE think is the right reaction to certain triggers and challenges.

It follows that anger, as an emotional response, is about how we experience reality.

So, if you perceive that a situation justifies an angry response, you will act accordingly. This often means that you may decide to take justice into your own hands, which is how many unnecessary confrontations happen.

If you are struggling with anger issues, try to get to a stage where, before you act or react, you can stop for a moment and look at the situation (an argument, provocation, a stupid joke) from a different angle. Try to see it from someone else's eyes. Give the person who is making you angry the benefit of the doubt. What if your judgment is wrong? What if you are overreacting?

We often react based not on facts, but on what we THINK is happening. And what we think is usually influenced by our experiences, culture, and temperament. This is why insight—our ability to have an accurate understanding of a situation or a person—is so important. And so is good judgment, especially when trying to understand what's going on and make the best decision.

However, many studies show that anger does cloud your judgment, which means it's important to calm down before making any big decisions—especially if you know you have a short temper. A recent study published in the academic psychology journal *Intelligence* suggests people prone to anger are also those most likely to overestimate their intelligence, particularly their ability to make good decisions.

Scientists from the University of Warsaw found a link between quick temper and a slightly skewed perception of intelligence. And this is not because these people are not intelligent, but because anger triggers the release of stress hormones that change the way your brain works. In other words, you need to either learn to control your anger or refrain from making any major decisions until you have calmed down.

Food for Thought:

Do you easily get angry? If you do, what are your main triggers? If you don't, how do you control your temper in challenging situations?

1. If memories of how your ex treated you make you "see red," how can you prevent this past hurt from affecting your future relationships? How often do you get angry because something reminds you of a wrong someone has done to you in the past?

2. Do you hate yourself after arguing with someone, or do you pat yourself on the back because you "showed them"?

Day 4

Anger in Children

Just like anger is a perfectly normal emotion in adults, it is equally normal in children. However, there is a major difference between an occasional tantrum or meltdown and prolonged or intense anger outbursts that can lead to ugly scenes or even harm to self or others.

Why Do Children Get Angry?

When anger in children occurs occasionally and passes quickly, we can assume it's part of growing up. But if it becomes an outburst of very intense emotions that last for a long time, it can easily be a mask for an anger-related health disorder.

Dealing with angry children can be difficult, as most parents will testify. Not only is it exhausting both physically and mentally, it sometimes leaves parents feeling guilty or ashamed if they overreacted to a child's misbehavior.

Most people will agree that when they were children, they were not allowed to get away with many of the things children of today expect as their birthright. Today, children are generally more comfortable expressing their emotions, and they also have different expectations of their parents. This shouldn't surprise us—just like we, as adults, have risen our expectations of our governments, employers, or service providers compared to the generation of our parents, so do children of today expect many things and privileges we were not entitled to while we were growing up.

The worst thing a parent can do when facing an angry child is to try to stop him or her from being angry. When you do that, as many parents do, you are forcing your child to suppress their emotions. If the consequence of throwing a tantrum is punishment, a child will quickly learn that anger is something that should not be displayed openly. But this doesn't mean they will stop feeling angry, only that they will stop expressing their emotions for fear of punishment.

Not surprisingly, such children usually grow up into adults who rarely show their feelings. This, in turn, creates many other problems, because bottled-up emotions will sooner or later have to find an outlet. This explains why otherwise perfectly normal, kind, and tolerant people physically or mentally abuse their families, or even get involved in violent crime.

So, rule number one: never try to suppress or ignore the fact that your child is angry, because there is probably a very good reason why he or she feels that way.

<u>6 common reasons why children get angry:</u>

1. **They can't get what they want**

    Children are more intelligent than we give them credit for, and they quickly learn what works and what doesn't. So, if a child is used to being allowed to eat sweets all the time, he or she will react negatively when that favor is withdrawn. Parents often use such favors as a disciplining tool, and if they use it correctly and the child understands that favors are not automatically granted but have to be earned, everything will be fine. However, if a child assumes it is entitled to something which one day becomes unavailable, it will "fight for its rights."

2. **They are teased by peers or adult**

    Often, gentle teasing is okay and adults sometimes do it to get children to do something, like saying "I know you can't count to 10" so the child will count to 10 to prove them wrong. However, teasing that makes the child feel embarrassed or stupid can easily provoke angry tantrums.

3. **They react to criticism**

    Parents can be extremely demanding, although they believe they do it with the child's best interest in mind. Pushing a child to do something and then criticizing him or her if they fail can make a child angry. However, some children are very spoiled and are not used to criticism—by throwing a tantrum, they are setting boundaries and showing their parents what they can and cannot say.

4. **They are disappointed**

    Parents often make promises they have no intention of keeping, just to get a child to do something or stop crying. For a child that has been expecting to be taken to the zoo or given a new toy, this may be a major blow. On the other hand, spoiled children often bully their parents by throwing tantrums until they get what they want.

5. **Disagreement**

    This happens sometimes when children are playing with other kids. Children pick up basic social skills during interaction with their peers, but if a child is not used to losing or sharing, being put in a situation where this is required can trigger an angry outburst.

6. **Rejection**

    Children, as well as adults with low self-esteem, react intensely to rejection. Being part of a herd is very important to a child, so the reaction to being, or just feeling, rejected by peers or parents may result in hitting, biting, crying, tantrums, or withdrawal.

The easiest way to cope with your child's anger is not to expose them to situations that make them angry. However, this is not always possible, nor would it be a wise thing to do in the long-term. Anger is a part of life, and the best thing you can do for your child is to teach them how to control it.

Some children cope better than others. If your child is prone to anger outbursts, it's best to identify what triggers such behavior and control their exposure to such stimuli, like too much TV, certain games, or the presence of certain children or adults.

If a child takes a long time to stop screaming and tends to become physical when angry, you could be dealing with anger overload. This is not a typical reaction to anger, but is a prolonged outburst where the child is simply inconsolable and unable to stop screaming, crying, or thrashing around.

Anger Management for Kids

To manage anger, you first have to understand what is behind emotional outbursts. Understanding triggers can help you find a solution. In the case of excessive or prolonged anger, you could be dealing with an anger-related disorder. While medication can reduce some of the symptoms of hyperactivity or anxiety, only therapy can provide long-lasting improvement and help keep anger in control.

4 common causes of excessive anger outbursts:

1. Hyperactivity
2. Anxiety
3. Trauma or neglect
4. Health disorders, like learning problems or autism

With young children, "normal" tantrums are common, especially if they feel frustrated or refuse to do something you're asking of them. This is often because very young children can't always explain what they want or how they feel, so they act it out. A tantrum is also the best way to draw attention to oneself, so children often use this as "sign" language to show they are not happy with something.

But sometimes, tantrums happen all the time. If they never seem to stop, or it becomes obvious that a child is unable to control his or her temper, this is usually a sign that you're dealing with a behavior problem.

5 signs that angry outbursts could be a symptom of behavior problem:

1. They don't stop even when the child is older than seven
2. The child's behavior becomes increasingly violent
3. They start getting into trouble at school
4. They can't get along with other kids, so they are often excluded from birthday parties or games.
5. Their behavior starts disrupting family life, like the relationship between parents or with other siblings.

As anger is often the only way a child knows how to react to frustration, parents should take angry outbursts seriously. Instead of telling the child to stop, they should try to figure out what made the child so upset. It is often the feeling of helplessness, quite common in children, that prompts them to express their feelings through anger.

Parents can do a lot to help their children learn how to cope with anger. First of all, they should encourage them to express their emotions, whatever they are, rather than deny them. Secondly, they should find a way of channeling those emotions into something positive. Finding an effective outlet for unexpressed feelings is one of the best ways of preventing them from becoming bottled up.

The reason some children seem to almost enjoy being angry is that an outburst is followed by an adrenaline rush, which boosts their energy. Suddenly, though temporarily, they feel <u>powerful</u> instead of <u>powerless.</u>

But if angry outbursts continue, maybe you as a parent need to reset your own boundaries, adopt a new set of rules, spend more time talking to your child, or take more interest in their life.

Whichever course your child's anger takes, make sure the child understands the difference between anger and aggression. To be angry is okay, being aggressive isn't.

Anger is often a cry for help, especially in very young children who may not be able to clearly explain what bothers them—but even they should be taught how to express their anger in the least harmful way. On the other hand, aggression, especially toward others, should not be tolerated, and this should be made very clear.

Talk to your child as often as you can and try to be aware of what is going on in his or her life, especially outside the home. Prompt them to tell you what is bothering them. To get to a stage where a child will open up, you have to develop a close and trusting relationship.

Don't forget that children copy the behavior of adults, and an excessively angry child may be responding to chaos at home, like alcohol, domestic violence, or abuse.

<u>7 tips on how to deal with an angry child:</u>

1. Praise your child often.
2. Criticize them if you have to.
3. Provide physical outlets.
4. Take an interest in your child's activities—ask about what happened at school, how they like their new teacher, how are their relationships with their peers.
5. Be a role model—if you don't want your child to use bad language or act aggressively, you shouldn't either.
6. Teach children that anger is normal, but that aggression isn't the answer
7. Don't get involved in any conversation as long as the child is screaming. Wait until they have calmed down to find out what has happened.
8. Don't give in to blackmail, but be prepared to listen.

Despite many new approaches to childhood education, discipline is and always will be the key to good behavior. It's about rules and rewards. It's about preventing behavioral problems, and teaching a child what behavior is and isn't acceptable.

As Nicole Ari Parker said, "Raising children is about loving them while trying to figure out how to discipline them."

Food for Thought:

1. Do you think children should get used to receiving criticism, or that they should be spared until they are at least 10 years old? Would too much criticism make them stronger or undermine their ego?
2. Considering their communication skills are limited, do you think children are justified in throwing tantrums? How else could they get adults to do what they want?
3. Think of a relative or a friend who has a child struggling with anger management. What are their parents doing about it? What would you do in their place?

Day 5
Anger in Teens

For a number of physiological, psychological, and social reasons, being a teen is the most difficult period of one's life. When your body is developing from that of a child to that of an adult and your hormones are wreaking havoc in your mind, it's not surprising that you often appear tense and angry.

A teen is but a child in an adult's body—faced with the physical and emotional needs of an adult, but neither fully developed physically and emotionally nor financially independent to be able to fulfill those needs. As a result, they, not surprisingly, often lash out in anger at those they feel are responsible for their unfulfilled needs – their parents.

Why are Teens Angry?

We've all been teenagers before, so we all know how hard growing up can be. In the past, and in some cultures even today, teenagers were more considered to be children than adults. Today, teenagers are—perhaps unfairly—often expected to behave and be responsible for things that normally only adults should deal with.

Handling a child who throws a tantrum can be hard, but it's nothing compared to dealing with an angry and screaming teenager who may be considerably taller and stronger than you.

Teens can be angry with or without reason, and it is up to their parents to curb or fuel that anger. Instead of yelling and fighting back, which may be very tempting but which would only escalate the argument, a parent should try to calm them down.

If you respond to your teen's anger by yelling or threatening, you put yourself on the same level as your child. In some ways, you become equal, which means you lose some of the "weight" at the bargaining table. If this happens, it may be even more difficult to negotiate further. So, whatever you do, don't lose control.

To deal with teen anger, you have to understand what makes them angry. As a parent, you know that although they may try to act like adults, the brains of adolescents are still developing. The way a teen perceives and experiences the world is very different from how an adult sees it, and this should not be used against them.

The problem with angry teens is not that they are often angry for no particular reason, but that they may not be expressing that anger effectively, either because they don't know how to or because they are not allowed to. Unaddressed anger makes people feel powerless and helpless and can sometimes lead to depression or violence—often turned against those who have nothing to do with their feeling of helplessness, but who happen to be an easy target, like pets, siblings, or friends.

The root cause of a teen's anger is usually due to physiological and emotional changes going on in their bodies, as they try to make sense of it. Their social background, as well as the support they get from their families, can either make this process easier or more difficult.

<u>4 things to do when facing an angry teen:</u>
1. Don't use bad language or name-calling, as this will only make things worse.
2. Never make any major decisions, promises, or threats, if you are both in a state. Wait for things to calm down, first. In fact, if both you and your teen are very angry, it's best not to say much. When you have both cooled off, you can address the problem in a more constructive way.
3. Never get physical, because this may easily escalate into violence.
4. Try to listen carefully to what they are saying—their comments or demands may be justified. Even if you don't do anything about it, show you respect them enough to listen to what they have to say. Teenagers often feel ignored or belittled, and this can be a major anger trigger.

Adolescents are often moody and have strong feelings, which means they often can't think straight nor listen to reason. You shouldn't hold this against them—all the physiological and emotional changes they are going through makes them feel confused and angry.

A teenager's anger is usually directed at those they identify as an obstacle to their desires, which is usually their parents. Other times, they may not be angry with you, but because of something that happened at school or because of an argument with a friend.

Teen Anger Management

Although anger is not bad *per se*, to be used positively, it needs to be managed. There are different ways of expressing anger, and the trick is to express it effectively without hurting others, verbally or physically, or creating an atmosphere of discomfort and fear.

Teens may often seem angry, but are not always sure what or who they are angry with. As a result, they may be prone to snapping or sulking.

However, if a teen stays in this angry mode for months on end, without any particular reason, it could be a sign that their anger had turned inward. Those who sulk for extended periods of time may easily sink into depression, or become violent and start bullying others.

Angry teens can often become rude, asking for trouble, and behaving as if they want to turn every situation into an argument. With such individuals, discussing anything calmly is impossible, and almost any conversation easily spins out of control.

If such behavior becomes frequent, it could be a symptom of an anger-based disorder. Unfortunately, these disorders are particularly common with adolescents who were subjected to physical or mental abuse, or who through TV and video games are often exposed to images of violence, or those who were punished for being angry. Teens who received little or no support while growing up are much more likely to develop some kind of anger-based disorder later in life, simply because they never learned nor were allowed to express their emotions properly.

So, how do you deal with an angry teen? Assuming you understand where their anger is coming from, you will help them the most if you create an environment where they feel safe to express their feelings, regardless of what they are.

Another important thing to do is to try and establish a close relationship with your teen and encourage them to talk to you, so you are more aware of the people they socialize with. The older the teen, the more likely their behavior and values will be influenced by their peers, and peer pressure can lead to inappropriate and destructive behaviors.

10 ways to help teenagers handle their anger:
1. Become a role model on how to manage one's emotions.
2. Allow them to express anger.
3. Never punish them by humiliating them.
4. Be aware of who, outside of the home, may be influencing their behavior.
5. Set rules, but don't forget rewards.
6. Be open to negotiations, but say no to threats, blackmails, and tantrums.
7. Encourage intimacy and bonding, so you know what's going on in their life.
8. Never be too busy to listen to them.
9. Allow them to be open about their feelings.
10. Cultivate mutual trust and respect.

Food for Thought:

1. What were you like as a teen? Were you often angry? If yes, how did you deal with it?
2. When confronted by an angry person, what is the one thing you should never do?

3. When reasoning with an angry teenager doesn't work, how far do you think a teacher or a parent should go with enforcing discipline? What do you think happens if parents hold different views on how to address their angry teen?

Day 6
Anger as Part of Grief

Just like you can be quietly or ecstatically happy, you can handle your grief with silent sadness or with a massive show of pain and outrage. Regardless of the way you choose to grieve for something or someone (like a way of life or a loved one), anger will definitely play a part in the process.

Why You Should Neither Ignore, Nor Feed Your Anger

There is a legend that one evening. an elderly Cherokee told his grandson about a battle that happens inside every one of us. The battle is between two wolves. One is Evil. It is anger, jealousy, envy, sorrow, regret, greed, arrogance, guilt, resentment, inferiority, self-pity, lies, false pride, superiority, and ego. The other is Good. It is love, joy, peace, hope, serenity, humility, kindness, benevolence, generosity, empathy, truth, compassion, and faith. His grandson thought about this for a short moment, then asked his grandfather, "Which wolf wins?" To this, his grandfather simply replied, "The one you feed."

Emotions are there to be experienced, not bottled up. However, if you experience negative emotions too often or you stay with them for too long, they can eventually become your reality.

Anger, being a very powerful emotion, should not be ignored—it is actually trying to tell you something. Nor should it be fed and nurtured, until it grows beyond control.

Grief is a very personal thing; there is no one-size-fits-all way to grieve. The way you go about it depends on many things, including your support system, your relationship with the deceased, your religion or culture, and your own coping skills. It takes time to get over the loss of a loved one, and although everyone may encourage you to move on with your life, you shouldn't rush through the process—allow it to unfold naturally.

If the crushing sadness makes you feel like you won't be able to go on, or your burning anger at those who could have prevented the death but didn't makes you scream for justice, grief can be frightening. And this is why many people who go through a grieving process end up alone, at the time when they need support the most.

What happens when you ignore anger during grief:

Ignored or unaddressed emotions often come to haunt us later in life. However, Western culture doesn't encourage people to experience overwhelming emotions. Instead, people are encouraged to block or alter them with drugs, divert their attention from what is happening to them with the hypnotic repetition of positive mantras, or simply engage in various feel-good activities.

It's believed that one of the reasons anxiety and depression are increasingly common is that many of our basic feelings are not expressed, but controlled by keeping them swept under the carpet.

If you're dealing with negative emotions, you should try to understand where they're coming from and try to release them. Negative emotions shouldn't be ignored, but nor should you become stuck in them for the rest of your life.

What happens when you feed your anger while grieving:

If, after a personal loss, you dwell on the injustice of it all and cry for revenge, what you are doing is feeding your anger. According to the Law of Attraction, you get more of what you focus on—so by focusing on anger, you attract even more anger and bitterness into your life.

Instead of feeding it, you should starve it and release it.

No matter how frustrated or let down you may feel because of your loss, the faster you stop wallowing in guilt or sorrow, the faster you can get on with your life.

As Ralph Waldo Emerson so wisely pointed out, "A person is what he or she thinks about all day long."

How Anger Helps You Deal with Grief

Anger is often, but not always, part of grief—it's best to think about it as a state in which most of us temporarily find ourselves. Grief can bring feelings of helplessness, regret, blame, or self-blame, and all these emotions can make you very angry. When you hurt, you often try to find someone to blame, which means grieving people often lash out at others.

However, the energy of anger is sometimes directed inward. Some people can start to blame themselves for what happened, or hate themselves for not having been able to do something to prevent the death of their loved one.

10 common recipients of misdirected anger in case of grief:
1. Yourself, for not having done more to prevent the death
2. The person who died, for having abandoned you
3. Surviving family members, or passengers, for not having died instead
4. Doctors, for not having done more to prevent the death

5. Destiny, for leaving you alone, ridden with debt, powerless, or helpless
6. God, for allowing a good person to die
7. Life, for being so unfair
8. The rest of the world, because life goes on as if nothing happened
9. Others, who have not lost what you've lost
10. Everyone who is happy

In that context, being angry is a way of channeling your grieving energy while you try to make sense of your loss. Anger is also usually followed by an adrenaline rush, which boosts your energy levels, giving you the strength to go on.

So, although anger can be painful and frightening, it also represents personal power—which means that it may prompt you to do something to change the situation you are in. And change means action. If anger is expressed positively, it can be channeled into activism, a process that helps release the pain and the feeling of helplessness.

If, on the other hand, you try to suppress your anger—pretending that "that's how it was meant to be," or "it was God's will," or "there was nothing we could have done," while seething with rage and holding onto your anger—the bottled-up emotions may find an outlet in the form of depression or be misdirected to others, like family or friends.

The best way to cope with anger during a grieving process is by acknowledging your pain, your loss, your fears, your despair, and whatever else you may be feeling.

<u>5 ways to cope with anger during grief:</u>
1. Try to understand how you feel about your loss. Stay with the feeling, even if it hurts.
2. If you feel very angry, try to work out who are you angry with and why.
3. Think of ways to rid yourself of anger in a non-destructive way, like through physical exercise, volunteering, writing, or reaching out.
4. If you can't cope with anger because the person who caused your loss got away with it, confront the person you hold responsible for what happened if that's an option you can take, but don't try to escalate the situation.
5. Seek professional help if you find it hard to go on.

Finally, to be able to grieve and deal with the anger that often accompanies it, you have to understand the six stages of grief that you'll be going through.

6 stages of grief:

- **Shock**

  This is how your mind tries to protect you from overwhelming pain: "What? No, it can't be!"

- **Denial**

  This is how your mind tries to protect you from reality: "No, it can't be true."

- **Anger**

  This is when you start grieving in earnest when the truth finally hits you: "Why? Why me?"

- **Guilt**

  You will sooner or later start lamenting why you hadn't done more to prevent your loss: "If only I'd been there, maybe he'd still be alive."

- **Pain and sorrow**

  This is the hardest and most frightening part of the grieving process, because by then, you are fully aware of what has happened and you are forced to face reality.

- **Release and resolution**

  This is the stage of grief where you start accepting the reality and getting ready to let go of the relationship.

However, having gone through all six stages does not mean you're over your grief. It will continue to come back and haunt you from time to time—to prevent this from happening, it's very important to deal with the pain and close this chapter of your life.

To heal, it's important to go through all the stages of grieving. Then, you can accept the reality, forgive yourself and others, and move on.

Food for Thought:

1. Think of a painful memory you can't get out of your head. Do you realize that by thinking about it continually, you are feeding your anger? What would it take to release it? Why would anyone enjoy wallowing in self-pity?

2. Think of a time when you lost someone. How did you deal with the loss? What was the prevailing emotion—anger or sadness?

3. When a loved one has a life-threatening disease, it gives everyone time to prepare for their departure. On the other hand, when someone dies in a car accident, it comes as a major shock. Which scenario causes more anger?

Day 7
How Anger Affects Relationships

Chronic anger has a devastating effect on relationships—not only because it destroys love and trust, but because it creates a toxic and often unsafe atmosphere at home. Just like gathering clouds can warn us of an approaching storm, chronic anger issues are often a sign of an accident waiting to happen.

Anger as a Medley of Emotions

Anger is a complex emotion and unless it is managed, can be devastating to your health, relationships, and career. If you have an anger problem, it's important to work on it when you are NOT feeling angry, instead of waiting for an angry reaction to try and find the best ways to deal with it.

However, anger doesn't appear out of the blue—it is a response to another emotion or particular triggers.

Just like happiness is contagious, so is anger. When you are angry, it spills over to your environment, even if you aren't making a scene. Those around you can pick up on your quiet anger and, depending on their relationship with you, may feel intimidated or simply uncomfortable in your company. As a result, they may start avoiding you.

Although people in your environment—be it your family, colleagues, or friends—may have nothing to do with the reason you're angry, they often find themselves the target of your anger. You may snap at them, be sarcastic, or openly lash out. And this is what ruins many relationships.

When you start taking your anger out on others, especially if they are in no position to respond or physically remove themselves from you, your anger becomes a sort of bullying. If you know this is happening, the first thing you need to do is acknowledge that you have an anger problem which is getting out of control.

The best way to deal with a chronic anger issue in a relationship is to address the real cause; however, how you approach this will depend on who is having the problem.

If YOU have an anger problem:
- Look for a solution to this problem cool-headed. In other words, calm down first so you can think clearly. Anger releases certain hormones in our brain which can affect the decision-making process.

- Acknowledge your uncontrolled anger is creating problems in the relationship.
- Dig deep and try to understand why you feel so angry. It may have nothing to do with your partner, so why are you taking it out on them?
- Discuss your anger with your partner. Ask them how they feel during your outbursts. Try to see yourself through your partner's eyes and understand how this has been affecting your relationship.
- Together, make a plan for how you can start managing your anger. If nothing else, promise yourself you will refrain communicating with your partner or making any major decisions when overwhelmed with frustration, fear, or rage. Chances are, you will say or do things you'll regret later.

If YOUR PARTNER has an anger problem:
- Help him or her calm down when they are in a state.
- Listen to what they have to say, even if you don't agree with them. Let them speak. Even when people have every reason to feel angry, they will often vent their anger while talking about it, so confrontation is avoided.
- Communication is key for healthy relationships—the more you talk to each other, the less likely you are to have communication problems.

If BOTH PARTNERS have an anger problem:
- Dealing with an angry partner is bad enough, but if both suffer from chronic anger problems, the relationship usually would not work. Especially if neither is used to apologizing, staying calm during an argument, listening, or accepting another's point of view.

Psychologists believe that the main problem with anger is what we do with it—do we manage it, do we ignore it, do we direct it toward others or toward ourselves?

Unfortunately, uncontrolled anger often leads to fighting, blaming, name-calling, or bringing up the past. The more of these things you do to your partner when you're angry, the more difficult it becomes to go back to normal once you've calmed down, for some words or actions cannot be taken back.

We know that anger often goes hand in hand with other emotions, like feeling ashamed, hurt, or frightened. According to psychologists, anger is like an iceberg—only 10% of it shows while the remaining 90%, which is unseen, is what really is making you angry. So, while to others you may appear angry, what you are actually feeling is fear, shame, hurt, and more. Find out what your submerged iceberg is made out of.

During an argument, an angry person will often criticize their partner, which is counterproductive.

Here are 5 signs you're dealing with anger in your relationship the wrong way:
- If you are criticizing the character, rather than the behavior of your partner.
- If the criticism is supposed to make them feel guilty.
- If you are not doing this to improve your relationship, but just trying to let go of your bottled-up tension—criticizing them just to make yourself feel better, regardless of how the criticism is making your partner feel.
- If you refuse to listen to what your partner has to say in their defense, but expect them to do as you say.
- If your criticism is insulting or belittling.

Misplaced Anger

While anger is important, because it often tells us in no uncertain terms that something needs to change, it can also be a destructive emotion.

We live in a stressful and often very unfair world, and not everyone copes well with pressure. When dealing with everything they have on their plate proves too much, some people simply lose it.

Unfortunately, those who find themselves at the receiving end of their angry outbursts are usually not those who caused it, but those they have access to. In most cases, this is a family member.

While one way of managing anger is to make sure you find a positive outlet for your emotions, misplaced anger will easily destroy a relationship, especially if it happens repeatedly.

5 causes of misplaced anger

1. **Suppressed anger**

    As many a wife will testify, women often find themselves on the receiving end of their frustrated husband's emotions. Although talking to your spouse is a great way to relieve tension and frustration, it has to be done in a way that is not harmful. In other words, you shouldn't destress by stressing someone else out.

2. **Desperation**

    Regardless of what it is you feel hopeless about, depending on your nature, you may sink into depression, make scenes, or lash out in indignation.

3. **Not taking time-off**

    The more stress in your life you have to cope with, be it at work or at home, the more you need to take care of your mental health. If you can't afford vacations, at least take weekends off from time to time. The best way to unwind is to get involved in something that makes you happy—that's what hobbies are for.

4. **Negative mindset**

    Some people find it very difficult to see anything positive in any situation. Instead, they dwell on problems (both real and imaginary), wants, lacks, or potential disasters (theirs or global). Not only will this attitude make you feel miserable all the time, it will probably also make you very angry.

5. **Resentment**

    We all feel resentful from time to time, but if this emotion lasts for very long, it can become part of your character. This usually has to do with some injustice done to you, but instead of addressing it, some people choose to wallow in pain and bitterness for the rest of their lives.

The worst thing is that many people are fully aware that their anger is misplaced, but can't or won't do anything about it. For how long your partner will be able to put up with it depends on many things, but even if you are not aggressive when you're angry, misplaced anger is very toxic for a relationship.

5 reasons misplaced anger destroys a relationship:
- It creates a negative atmosphere at home.
- Angry outbursts are unpleasant, disrespectful, and unsettling.
- It's very belittling to be treated like a doormat.
- Chronically angry individuals are difficult to live with because you never know when the next outburst is coming.
- Such people may not be safe to live with, especially if they have a history of aggression.

Food for Thought:

1. What do you do when you feel your partner or friend is angry about something? Do you try to distract them from what's bothering them, or do you get them to talk about it?

2. Some people go for a drink after work so they can relax and diffuse their accumulated tension in order not to pass it on to their family. Others expect their partners to help them unwind, although it usually means they will have to listen to the well-known complaints, objections, or dramas. Which approach do you think is better?

3. If you often have to suppress your anger, how do you make sure it doesn't become bottled up?

Day 8
Anger in the Workplace

Although there are many reasons to get angry, in a private situation—with family or friends—you can say things or even behave in an inappropriate way and still be forgiven. In the workplace, however, the situation is very different. While you and your sibling or spouse may fight regularly and still love each other, if you scream at your colleagues, call them names, or shame them, you are likely to get fired. Most people know this and try to control their temper at work as much as they can, but, this can lead to the most common cause of anger in the workplace—frustration.

Why is the Workplace Anger so Common?

Frustration is the main cause of anger in the workplace. However, what lies behind this frustration is often that these people know that, for one reason or another, they have to remain in the job (or organization) they do not enjoy. This creates resentment, which is a form of long-lasting unresolved anger.

<u>6 reasons people feel frustrated in the workplace:</u>
1. Being passed over for promotion.
2. Having to do what you are told even if you know it won't work.
3. Having to report to a much younger or less intelligent person.
4. Having to report to women (in some cultures, this would be a major blow to many men).
5. Having to work after hours or on weekends with no pay (this is common in organizations planning for layoffs, where many people try to make themselves irreplaceable by showing they are willing to work extra hours for no pay).
6. Having to take the blame for your boss' wrong decisions.

Most employers would rather not employ frustrated employees—they are rarely motivated enough to achieve good results, and can be a potential threat to the organization if they start lobbying against the management.

For you, however, long-held frustration can be a major threat to your health. If unaddressed, the simmering bitterness can lead to burnout, heart disease, high blood pressure, stroke, depression, or other conditions.

And the more you feel you are stuck in your position, the more frustrated you'll feel. If, due to your age or lack of skills, you know you are unlikely to find a better job and know you have to stay with the one you're currently in, or if there are not many jobs available where you live, or if the pay is good, you may feel trapped in a job you hate or with people you have no respect for.

The causes of frustration in the workplace are too numerous to list, but they usually revolve around some kind of a disappointment, like a poor performance evaluation, unfair treatment, being micromanaged, or being criticized too often.

However, disappointment may also be caused by unrealistic expectations. Maybe you assumed you'd be promoted in two years, or that you'd be given a car to go with the job.

The reason you appear angry at work may also have nothing to do with the workplace. If you have a troubled or chaotic personal life, it is likely to affect your professional life, as well—the frustration one brings from home is often directed at one's colleagues. This is a typical example of misplaced anger of browbeaten wives and husbands.

Whatever the cause of your anger in the workplace might be, you have to try and manage it as best you can. Mild irritation is what we all learn to deal with, however, if something happened that made you see red and you feel you're about to make a scene—stop.

<u>8 things to do if you get very angry at work:</u>
1. Take a deep breath or several deep breaths
2. Slowly count to ten
3. Tell yourself to stay calm
4. Try to prevent tension in your muscles, jaw, head, or stomach. Keep breathing and try to loosen your muscles.
5. Walk away from your desk
6. Get out of your office or the building
7. Take a short walk, call a friend, or chat to a colleague you can trust
8. When you have calmed down, think through how to address the problem that made you so mad

How to Deal with Work-Related Anger if You're a Manager

An organization where anger seems to be present all the time is not a nice place to work in. It could be a major HR issue that's making staff unhappy, or just one or two people who, for their own reasons, enjoy stirring things up.

Try to find out who or what is behind this underlying anger. Consider the office safety regulations first, to make sure personal safety is not what's making employees lack focus or drive.

Some problems you may be able to deal with on your own, but in case of major issues, it's best to get professional help, lest things get out of control. Hiring an external consultant to talk to staff often helps, for they may feel less intimidated approaching someone outside of the company.

There may be situations when you have to make unpopular decisions, like redundancies, pay cuts, benefits withdrawal, and so on; however, a negative atmosphere in a company is usually a result of the prevailing culture. Although problematic individuals have to be dealt with, keep in mind that overall dissatisfaction easily turns into anger.

If anger prevails and you can't figure out what may be the cause, perhaps you need to look at this problem from different angles. If it turns out that certain individuals are causing trouble and raising tension (or expectations), it could be that stress from their private lives is spilling over to their work environment. While there is usually not much you can do about their personal problems, you can at least talk to them to see if there is anything you can do to help make things easier at work.

Anger is the workplace can be very difficult to deal with, and many managers turn a blind eye or postpone taking any action for as long as they can. As a manager, though, you must be mentally and emotionally prepared to take action, taking care not to overreact or underreact.

<u>10 things a manager can do to help employees deal with anger in the workplace:</u>

1. Create a professional workplace culture of tolerance and mutual respect.
2. Set rules and expectations and make sure all new employees are aware of them.
3. Encourage communication and, if possible, organize communication training for staff on a regular basis.
4. Be approachable.
5. Provide anger management training, which would show people how to deal with their anger and how to respond to angry colleagues.

6. Deal with inappropriate behavior as soon as possible. The longer you put off an unpleasant confrontation, the more likely it is to get out of hand.

7. Employees with anger issues can create an unhealthy atmosphere in the company they work for, so recommend anger management treatment or fire them.

8. Keep written records of such incidents.

9. Have a zero-tolerance policy in the case of aggressive behavior.

10. In case of major problems, always consult an attorney or an HR professional.

Food for Thought:

1. What do you find most frustrating in your workplace? Is that something beyond your control, or can you do something about it?

2. Were you ever in a situation at work where you took part in an argument you now feel embarrassed about? What happened to make you react like that? How would you deal in the same situation today?

3. If you were a manager and had to fire your best employee for sexual harassment to protect a temp who only started working two months ago, what would you do?

Day 9
Anger-Related Disorders

You may have an anger problem because of a health disorder you are struggling with, or you can develop a health disorder because of a long-standing unaddressed anger problem. In the modern world, anger-related health issues are becoming very common. It seems that as the world gets faster, the people get angrier. Anger can often lead to other negative emotions, like resentment, hatred, self-pity, fear, or aggression, and over time, these self-destructive feelings can turn into disease or illness.

How Anger Affects Your Health

People with chronic anger problems are often those who remain stuck in an injustice (real or imaginary) that has befallen them. There may be a very good reason why someone is angry, but for this emotion to be constructive rather than destructive, it has to be managed.

Unfortunately, many people accept injustice as part of their fate or karma, and live their entire lives feeling angry and bitter. Others, because they can't accept the situation but don't know how to deal with it, become irritable and aggressive. There are also those who are simply short-tempered, and their anger can be triggered by almost anything.

Although many situations are beyond your control, what you do have control over is the way you react. Unless you exert this control, the uncontrolled angry episodes can sap your energy and health very quickly.

We know being angry is not healthy, but it was only relatively recently that the World Health Organization recognized 32 disorders as directly linked to dysfunctional anger, the best-known ones of which are:

- **Intermittent Explosive Disorder**

    Individuals with this disorder display "the degree of aggressiveness which is grossly out of proportion to any provocation or precipitating psychosocial stressor." This disorder is believed to be behind most mass shootings. The strange thing is that most of these individuals don't have a prior history of aggressive behavior. Typically, they are normal, polite, and friendly people. Then, all of a sudden, a rejection or a stressful event pushes them to a breaking point, and they go on a rampage. Their action is supposed to "restore honor or repay the injury."

- **Oppositional Defiant Disorder**

    This disorder manifests as defiance and anger against authority, and is most common in children and adolescents. However, this is not a case of occasional frustration or disobedience. These individuals have frequent tantrums, refuse to comply, argue excessively, blame others for their mistakes, behave rebelliously, and are often vindictive.

What makes the diagnosis of anger-related disorders particularly difficult is that they often appear alongside another emotional problem. This means that if you see a therapist to seek treatment for anger, the real reason for your emotional dysfunction may be another disorder you are probably not even aware of, and it's this that makes diagnosis and treatment difficult.

Anger affects various processes in your body—digestion, assimilation, cell production, circulation, healing, immune system, and more. As a result, if anger persists for months or years, it's very likely to weaken your immune system and to directly or indirectly lead to a number of problems:

- Headaches
- Digestion problems
- Insomnia
- Anxiety
- Depression
- High blood pressure
- Heart attack
- Stroke
- Skin problems

The Most Common Anger Disorders

Anger becomes disordered if the individual exhibits pathological aggressive, violent, or self-destructive behaviors which are driven by chronically repressed anger. Fortunately, most of us figure out how to manage our anger, so anger disorders are likely to happen only to those whose anger was not only not managed, but was repressed for a long time.

Another cause of anger disorder is neurological dysfunction and substance abuse, which both affect the way we control our violent impulses.

<u>6 most common forms anger can take:</u>

1. **Chronic anger**

    This is anger which has lasted for a long time. It usually has a major effect on our immune system and may be the cause of other mental disorders.

2. **Passive anger**

    This type of anger is difficult to identify, because it does not have typical anger symptoms.

3. **Overwhelmed anger**

    This kind of anger happens if there is too much going on in your life, and you can neither do something about it nor can you cope anymore. In other words, this happens when you feel overwhelmed with life.

4. **Self-inflicted anger**

    This type of anger is usually the result of feelings of guilt, shame, or self-blame. It is directed inward and can be very self-destructive.

5. **Judgmental anger**

    This type of anger is common in people who are resentful about a situation or life in general.

6. **Volatile anger**

    With this type of anger, individuals find it hard to control themselves and often display aggressive behavior.

Anger management techniques can help you keep many of the anger-related health disorders under control, and studying anger management materials such as this one can help you understand what you're dealing with.

<u>8 ways anger management helps you deal with your anger:</u>

1. Teaches you about anger and how to use it positively
2. Helps you understand your anger and identify your anger triggers
3. Suggests ways of reacting in such situations
4. Shows you how to relax and defuse anger
5. Helps you identify thoughts and beliefs associated with anger
6. Shows you why dwelling on past problems or hurts is counterproductive
7. Helps you resolve conflicts

8. Helps you identify alternatives to revenge

Food for Thought:

1. Do you know someone with a health disorder? How do you feel in their company? How do you think they feel in yours?

2. Discuss three situations where having anger management skills would help you resolve conflict more professionally.

Day 10

Anger Across Cultures

How you react to anger depends on many things, including your age, gender, and circumstances. However, the definition of anger, and especially of what justifies angry behavior, is largely based on the culture one comes from. In some cultures, expressing your emotions—particularly anger—may be considered very ill-mannered, other cultures encourage people to openly demonstrate how they feel about something. So, while many may consider people from the East as stony-faced and emotionless, to Asians, Westerners probably seem very rude.

Cultural Norms and Emotions

Anger has many definitions, causes, and possible outlets. It is often associated with hurt feelings, frustration, and a desire for justice or revenge. However, as cultures hold different attitudes toward anger, local norms will either encourage or curb angry displays in public.

Comparative studies on the way children are brought up show that in China (as well as throughout the Far East) demonstrating emotions is curbed in children from an early age. Tantrums are usually ignored, and children are left to cry until they have calmed down. Considering their cultural values, this is necessary for a child to develop socially-acceptable behavior.

In many Eastern cultures— Chinese, Japanese, Thai—anger is something that is usually not discussed, especially not in public. Children are discouraged to mention it, e.g., complain about something, or are punished if they do.

In Western culture, however, parents usually fuss and fret over their children, particularly during their fits of anger.

Cultural norms also influence how much anger is considered normal for a man and how much for a woman. In most patriarchal societies, girls are raised not to show their emotions openly— particularly negative ones such as anger. Although things have changed a lot in the last 200 years, in the West, public display of anger is discouraged in girls even today.

On the other hand, boys were, in a way, expected to show a certain degree of assertiveness (often manifested as an angry or aggressive behavior). If they didn't, they were believed not to have the necessary confidence to succeed in life.

Still, in most cultures, boys' anger is tolerated much more than that of girls, even when it leads to aggressive behavior—anger is believed to be what distinguishes them from the feminine characteristics of being kind, quiet, and forgiving.

Display of Emotions in Public

Despite the fact that in the West, anger—especially if it leads to aggression—is discouraged and sanctioned, there is still a disproportionately high level of anger among children. Many believe that it is TV and Internet games behind most of the unhealthy behaviors.

But even very young children seem to show signs of anger and aggressiveness toward others, as we can see with school bullying. For this reason, in the West, everyone is encouraged to talk about their anger problems so they can be addressed and channeled on time—especially children.

Until relatively recently, social status played a major part in how much someone was allowed to express anger. In the West, it was generally believed that the lower classes exhibited more anger—likely because, due to their socio-economic condition, they had more reason to be angry.

In Japan, however, it was those of a higher social status who exhibited more anger, as a symbol of their authority. So, although the display of anger was generally considered very rude and was sanctioned, it was granted only to those who felt entitled to almost anything because of their social status.

While most American citizens don't refrain from expressing anger in public, including making a major scene if they're angry, people in the Far East tend to avoid conflict at all costs. Regardless of how they may really feel—angry, embarrassed, or sad—they will smile. However, this "happy face" is the result of lifelong social conditioning and does not mean they actually feel happy or relaxed.

Cultural norms dictate what is and what isn't allowed, and serve as a guide to socially-acceptable behavior. Western and Eastern cultures approach anger problems in completely different ways. In Western culture, people are encouraged to openly show positive emotions, and manage the display of negative ones, but they are still allowed to express them. In Eastern cultures, people opt for the "middle way" (i.e., Tao), constantly seeking a balance between positive and negative emotions.

They start instilling these values into their children as early as preschool, which means American and Asian children have different reactions to visual stimuli. While in Europe and America, children prefer exciting activities, cartoons, or comics, in the Far East, they prefer calm emotions—smiles instead of laughter, not overly competitive games, or not very excitable stories.

Additionally, while American parents will use every available opportunity to boost their children's confidence, Chinese parents are more likely to downplay their children's good results so as not to inflate their ego.

Finally, bestsellers in America contain much more excited and arousing content when compared to bestsellers in Asia. So, although many believe that we now live in a global village and that our cultures are merging into one, when you dig a little deeper, it becomes obvious that cultural differences are still very present, although often skillfully disguised.

PART 2

Anger Management

Day 11
When Anger Becomes a Problem

While expressing anger is okay, and is actually good for your health, if you do it inappropriately or start feeling it too intensely or too often, it stops being a normal emotion and becomes a problem.

During an angry outburst, your body produces certain hormones. If these are released too frequently or for too long, they negatively affect your health in a number of ways.

So, while releasing anger is an important part of your mental health, this only works if you do so in a way that does not jeopardize your physical health or alienate you from society.

The Primitive Brain

Anger often becomes a problem when your body and mind are not in alignment. Your reaction during a fight-flight-freeze situation is a remnant of atavistic behavior, which was important when we lived close to nature—and still is, for those who continue to live that way.

However, over the past 30,000 years, our bodies and our environment didn't change at the same rate. While our bodies and instincts remained the same as those of a caveman, our physical and social environments changed beyond recognition.

In the 21st century, we are no longer regularly exposed to dangers that would make the fight-flight-freeze instincts necessary for our survival. However, to survive the stress, constant change, and fast pace of the modern world, we now need a very different set of skills—and anger management is one of them.

Numerous studies on the importance of the brain in human development show that the so-called "primitive brain"—the part of the brain that concerns our survival instincts—is much more powerful and important than the part responsible for our cognitive abilities.

The studies show that regardless of how much control we try to exercise over the neocortex part of the brain—no matter how much we try to stick to morals, ethics, and good intentions—when we find ourselves in a life-threatening situation, the primitive part of our brain, the part dealing with instincts, takes over. This, according to neuroscience, explains why we so easily become overcome by rage or fear and are unable to stop it.

This means that although our bodies have remained, from an evolutionary perspective, similar to that of a caveman's, our minds "moved on" and continued to develop and adapt to the changed environment and circumstances.

For this reason, there is often a clash between what we think we should do and what we actually do. As our body's reaction didn't change in face of danger (not only physical danger), the saying "do what you feel is right" makes a lot of sense. However, although your body and your instincts may know what's best for you, you may not be able to act on it. Our world requires that we stick to laws, rules, and cultural norms which often go against our instincts.

Although the world has changed a lot, it doesn't mean we face fewer dangers today than we did all those years ago. The main difference is that the dangers of today don't come from our physical environment, like wild animals, hostile tribes, or starvation, but from our lifestyle.

5 main "dangers" we face today:
1. Chronic stress
2. Overpopulation and lack of personal space
3. Competitiveness
4. Fast living
5. The fast-changing world

As our physical bodies failed to change at the same rate with which our social environment has changed, our reactions to the stress and tension of the modern times is simply the result of our bodies trying to cope with the circumstances for which they were not designed. Therefore, the primitive parts of our brains react to these stressors the same way they would to an imminent attack by a wild animal or any other physical danger.

Unfortunately, not everyone copes well with stress. These stressors, especially if they happen too often or remain unaddressed, often make us angry.

As a species, we are faced with 4 major problems:
- Adapting to an environment that is changing much too fast
- Developing unhealthy lifestyles to match the changing environment
- Coping with stress
- Dealing with anger issues which often result from the stress the world seems to be drowning in

So, does this mean our primitive brain is why so many of us seem to be so angry all the time? Probably not. Our brains are simply trying to help us survive in the face of the threats we face, regardless of what they are. It does not distinguish between a hungry wolf about to attack and an angry boss who threatens to fire you. In both scenarios, you're in serious trouble, and the adrenaline rush is simply there to help you make the best decision under the circumstances and save your life or job.

However, we live in a sophisticated world and even if you are provoked and feel very angry, you should try to control your reactions.

Intense anger can lead to violence, which can result in physical injury, imprisonment, or even loss of life. Even if your anger does not lead to violence, if you express it inappropriately, your position in society may be seriously damaged. Violent and rude people can easily become social outcasts.

If you are known for your temper, others may feel intimidated in your presence and start avoiding you, refusing to have anything to do with your family, or preventing their children from socializing with yours. A poorly-managed temper may cost you your relationship, job, and health.

There are people who act angrily and aggressively not because they can't control their primitive brain, but because they feel good when they are intimidating others. Some may believe people are more likely to listen or respect them that way. Others may act aggressively because they never learned how to manage their anger and simply don't know a better way to express annoyance, resentment, or pain. When someone has been under significant pressure for a long time, they may no longer care how their angry outburst make others feel as long as they release the accumulated tension.

Another problem with anger is that it can become a habit. And as breaking a habit requires determination and perseverance, you may find it easier to stick to your routine rather than try to change it.

If you're struggling with anger, perhaps you should consider anger management counseling, where you can learn how to process it and release it in a way that is neither self-destructive nor harmful to your environment.

Can the Primitive Brain be Controlled?

Being unable to adapt to a changing environment is what's believed to have exterminated the dinosaurs. So, to avoid getting into trouble because of anger—yours or someone else's—you should learn to recognize the first physical signs of the emotion.

<u>7 early signs of anger:</u>
1. Tension in the shoulders
2. Headache

3. Foot tapping
4. Fast heart rate
5. Short breaths
6. Sweating
7. Facial flushing

What these physiological changes mean is that your body is telling you to get ready for action—maybe facing an angry client, being wrongfully accused of something you didn't do, or a possible animal attack.

It's crucial that at this stage you calm yourself down, before you say or do anything. The greater the danger, the more careful you have to be with how you'll react.

- Try to breathe more slowly and concentrate on your breath.
- Try to think what the best way is to resolve the issue.
- If the person facing you is angrier than you are, try to calm them down. Let them say what they have to say and try to get them to talk it over.
- It will help if you haven't used any alcohol or drugs prior to the incident, as both tend to lower inhibition and offer a false sense of power. Most angry and aggressive outbursts happen when alcohol is involved. So, if you're anticipating an unpleasant meeting, don't have a drink to brace yourself for the encounter. All you will achieve is a boost to your ego, which may cost you dearly.
- If you are not in imminent danger, when you've calmed down and hopefully lowered your blood pressure, try to talk yourself into a sensible solution. Alternatively, try to think about something positive.

However, this comes easier to some people than others. If you have a problem controlling your emotions and tend to overreact to provocations, injustices, or stress, it's time to consider anger management treatment.

So, although our instincts often help us get out of a sticky situation, we do need to adapt our behavior to the world we live in. If you know you have an anger problem, learning about anger management can help you understand where your emotions are coming from and how best to express them. However, there are some simple things you can do, starting from today, that will make you less prone to rash behavior or overreaction.

3 simple ways of taming your temper:
1. **Physical exercise**

If you lead a very stressful life, or for some reason often find yourself in situations or with people who provoke an angry reaction in you, you should make physical exercise an essential part of your life, as it will help you release tension.

Well-known psychologist V Schutt believes exercise helps dissolve anger because it helps you channel your emotions. Scientists are still not sure how this happens, but believe it has something to do with the way physical exercise affects the serotonin levels in the brain, which help regulate behavior. Physical exercise is particularly important for those who have aggressive tendencies.

2. Mindfulness

If you are used to tuning in to your emotions, perhaps mindfulness can help you understand why you feel and react the way you do. When you feel angry, how does your body react—what happens in your chest, face, heart, stomach? How do you feel—exploited, helpless, abandoned—and why? What are the thoughts that go through your head?

When you have calmed down, try to discuss the incident that made you angry with the person involved. Try not to start with accusations, but by explaining how the incident made you feel.

Being mindful about your anger is about admitting to yourself that you're not coping well, but also that you don't want to ignore your negative emotions—you want to do something about them. Anger management can be a difficult and long process, so be patient with yourself.

3. Meditation

Meditation is an easy and simple way of preventing anger from getting out of control. Although there are many different ways to meditate, all revolve around self-awareness.

The practice of meditation helps you recognize the signs of anger, so you can learn how to react when you notice anger building up.

In other words, meditation improves your self-control and ability to calm your mind by focusing on something positive. If you practice it daily, you will soon become calmer and less stressed out, which will indirectly change the way you react to anger-provoking situations.

Meditation has been successfully used to deal with problematic adolescents and even in the rehabilitation of violent criminals.

Day 12
Handling Emotions

There is a proverb that "a man without self-control is like a city broken into and left without walls."

Emotions, both positive and negative, are a normal part of our lives—provided they are kept under control. Emotions help us understand how we feel about something or someone, like whether we can relax or should be on our guard, whether we can count on someone or not, how self-confident we should feel under the circumstances, and so on.

Still, we shouldn't allow our feelings to rule our lives, but should aim to take charge of them and rule them, instead. And this only happens if you know how to handle your emotions.

How to Take Charge of Your Emotions

Most of us know, sometimes subconsciously, what sort of situations or individuals push our buttons. And, if we give it some thought, we can better prepare ourselves to face emotionally-charged situations or difficult people ahead of time.

Just like how you prepare for an important meeting or an interview, if you know that finding yourself around certain people or in a certain situation is likely to make you feel angry and act inappropriately, work on bracing yourself for the event.

You can do this by preparing yourself mentally and emotionally for what you think is likely to happen. That way, since you have a better idea of what to expect, you'll be ready to deal with those challenges in a positive and constructive manner.

When you take charge of your emotions, you can prevent the situation from getting out of hand. This is particularly important for situations which are likely to escalate and for those who know they have an anger problem.

So, assuming you find it hard to control your temper or often find yourself in situations which make you behave inappropriately, you should prepare an Action Plan for handling your emotions.

8 things to do when you want to improve the way you handle your emotions:

1. Avoid if you can

Whenever possible, try to avoid the situations and people that are likely to make you angry. Unfortunately, this is often not possible, and all you can do is hope to have enough time to prepare mentally and emotionally before confronting them.

2. Emotions are a matter of choice

With a healthy dose of self-control and emotional intelligence, it's easy to avoid getting angry—even in the company of those who easily push your buttons. Being able to handle your emotions is about taking full control of how you react to anger triggers.

3. Try to make the situation less tense

It's often possible to defuse the tension if you make a conscious effort to do so. For example, if you know that a friend is touchy about certain issues, avoid discussing them. If your boss is particular about punctuality, make an effort to get to work on time. We often do things we know irritate others either because we're too lazy to make an effort, because we enjoy pushing their buttons, or because we are so self-centered we simply don't think about how what we say may make others feel.

4. Ask yourself why certain individuals or situations trigger such an angry response in you

Sometimes, when you are angry with others, you may actually be angry with yourself. It's not uncommon to project what we feel about ourselves onto others. For example, if someone's arrogance makes you angry, are you sure it's not because you reserve arrogance for yourself and are annoyed that someone else is behaving the way you think YOU are entitled to act?

We often say to others what we should be saying to ourselves—"Don't be so impatient," "Why are you so selfish?" So, the saying "It takes one to know one" makes a lot of sense.

5. Try to ignore the triggers

If you know that in certain situations you always get angry, try to shift your focus. For example, if you find the way someone dresses irritating, try to shift the focus from their clothing style to other aspects of their personality, like their work ethics or their empathy. It's easy to get angry if you focus on what you don't like or disapprove of.

6. Change your thoughts

If you can control your thoughts and attitudes, you'll have no problem controlling your emotions—your thoughts create your emotions. When you stop focusing on the negative in your life, such as rude colleagues, unfair working conditions, family struggles, or the consequences of environmental pollution, you will automatically feel less angry. And if you get to a stage where you can feel genuinely happy for others, you will become less judgmental, more compassionate, and will rarely feel angry.

7. Change your reaction

Changing the way you react to a trigger is not easy—it's something you have to work on all your life. However, when you can control your emotions, you have control over your life. By making an effort to choose your response to a trigger, you are taking control of a potentially chaotic situation. It's well-known that anger breeds anger—when you choose to react angrily, be prepared to receive a similar reaction from others.

8. Focus on the solution, not the problem

Instead of constantly thinking about how horrible the people you work with are, try to either change them, change yourself, accept the situation, or find another job. By focusing on the negative in your life, like a disloyal friend, a dead-end relationship, a low-paying job, failing health, you are making yourself bitter and irritable. Wallowing in self-pity and anger can't bring you anything good, so why do it? Why not try to find a solution to your problem, instead of ruminating about the unfairness of life?

How to Control Angry Emotions

We can usually see an angry reaction coming, like when the meeting is not going in the right direction or when we know in advance that a particular situation is likely to turn nasty. This means we usually have time to prepare ourselves for situations which we suspect may provoke an angry reaction, either in us or in others.

If you want to be the master of your life and you know you have an anger problem, try to adopt practices which can help you control both the anger triggers and your reaction to those triggers.

<u>6 habits that can help you control your emotions in any situation:</u>

1. Tune into your inner self

This is a very useful exercise, particularly when you're feeling unhappy, upset, or angry. Start by asking yourself why you are feeling that way. Pay attention to any emotions or thoughts that come up—sadness, anxiety, envy, rage, and so on.

Tuning in is about being in touch with your innermost feelings. It's about reconnecting with your intuition. Most of us have been encouraged not to rely on our gut feelings, but to base our decisions on our logical minds.

Listening to your intuition in the noisy, neurotic, and stressful world can be difficult. Not only have most of our instincts become dormant, but we rarely trust them. Your intuition or gut feeling can be a source of wisdom and, often, your best guide. But to receive this guidance, you have to listen to it and learn to understand what it's trying to tell you. This starts when you tune in to your inner self.

Your inner voice is nothing more than your subconscious telling you what's best for you under the circumstances. However, it may not say what you'd like to hear, and that's often the main reason why you choose to ignore this voice.

2. Develop emotional intelligence

Emotionally intelligent people have great people skills. They are not only in touch with their feelings, but are able to tune in to the feelings of others.

Emotional intelligence enables people to understand themselves and learn where their feelings are coming from. As a result, their reactions are timely and appropriate. They are good at listening, which not only improves their communication skills, but prevents emotionally-charged situations from getting out of hand.

Basically, managing emotions is about working out what triggered a particular emotion and not responding until you've had time to process that emotion. The best thing is that when you can manage your emotions, you can easily manage any situation you find yourself in.

3. Develop a positive mindset

Being positive about life is good for your health, your relations, and your overall happiness.

In line with the saying that "like attracts like," staying positive even when things are not going well is the prerequisite for success. When you are positive about life, it's easy to feel good about yourself, and this makes it easier to deal with anger—both yours and other people's.

4. Mindfulness

Applying mindfulness techniques is very useful when you feel you're beginning to lose it or feel you need more balance in your life. First of all, recognize what's happening (I'm getting angry). Give yourself time to think about how to respond (Count to ten). Respond calmly (Suggest a short break, postpone the meeting for another time, or try to look at the problem from a different angle or in a way that would give both parties a chance to reconsider their position).

5. Identify your anger threshold

You have to know when to draw the line and remove yourself from a situation that is not going anywhere and is likely to get out of hand. Depending on the situation, you may suggest a different approach, consult with someone, or simply walk away. Sometimes, removing yourself from the scene is all it takes to defuse a tense moment. However, it's important you do this BEFORE things get out of hand.

6. Recharge before start running on empty

Negative emotions, such as anger, create negative energy which is not only self-destructive, but quickly depletes your vitality and enthusiasm. To fight back, find out what activities boost your mood and do them whenever you feel subconscious negativity creeping up (this could be taking your dog for a walk, sitting in the garden, meditating, chatting to someone, listening to uplifting music, and so on).

To quote Zen Buddhist monk Thich Nhat Hanh, "When you say something unkind, when you do something in retaliation, your anger increases. You make the other person suffer, and they try hard to say or do something back to make you suffer, and get relief from their suffering. That is how conflict escalates."

Day 13

Emotional Intelligence and Anger Management

When most people think of emotional intelligence, they seem to imagine it as a set of skills that can make them more employable. This is partly true—being a good team player, working easily under pressure, and being able to communicate effectively in a culturally-diverse environment increases your chances of getting hired.

However, these same skills are just as important outside work, and maybe even more so. Your ability to understand and manage your emotions and be able to process them before responding will impact how successfully you deal with challenges on both the personal and professional level.

Emotional intelligence is much more than empathy and good people skills. It's about self-awareness and self-management: the very skills you need if you're struggling with anger.

What's Emotional Intelligence and Why Is It Important

Emotional intelligence skills revolve around the ability to understand and manage your own emotions, as well as those of others. Managing emotions is about understanding what triggers them, but choosing not to respond to the trigger until you've had time to process the emotion. And when you can manage your emotions, you can manage any situation you may find yourself in.

The ability to manage your emotions can be of great help in many different situations, like with decision-making or conflict resolution, but particularly with avoiding situations which could lead to conflict.

For anyone who has contact with others (as most of us do), conflicts are an unavoidable part of life. They are not necessarily bad, because they sometimes help get issues and emotions out in the open. So, if you can control your emotions, you can take control of your life and relationships.

Relationship problems happen both inside and outside of work, and although you would use a different technique when resolving a diplomatic conflict than an argument with a friend, you still need to be emotionally intelligent to successfully address the situation.

Learning about emotional intelligence is not difficult, though it comes easier to some than to others. For people who are empathic by nature, these skills are a way of life, and they—often unknowingly—apply them to whatever they do. On the other hand, those who are not in touch with their own feelings, and who care even less for the feelings of others, have to make an effort to start thinking and behaving in an emotionally intelligent way.

Many people learn emotional intelligence on the job, like when they find themselves in situations that require tolerance, patience, and empathy. However, it's much better to acquire these skills before you find yourself in a delicate situation.

What distinguishes emotionally intelligent people from others is that they know themselves well, so they understand why they think and react the way they do. When you have a high level of self-awareness, you understand what's going on in your mind, even if you don't approve of it. And it's easier to deal with something you understand.

We all get angry from time to time, but an emotionally intelligent person will always try to process the emotion they are experiencing. This is important, since your anger is often just a reaction to something else, even something you may not even be aware of like the memory of an old hurt.

Emotional competency can truly change your life and enhance your chances of success on all levels. There are many techniques at your disposal if you want to master emotional intelligence skills, but to truly benefit from them, you have to apply them to everything you do.

Emotional intelligence is also about developing an awareness of how your behavior affects others—an emotionally intelligent person is fully aware of this, regardless of the situation they find themselves in.

2 main benefits of emotional intelligence:

- **You're in complete control of your emotions**

    When you can control your emotions, you can control your life. And when you can do that, you can take a proactive role in how your life pans out.

- **You easily avoid or resolve conflicts**

    Although emotionally intelligent people are good at resolving conflicts, their main advantage over others is that they know how to prevent a situation from getting to a stage where it becomes an open conflict.

How Emotional Intelligence Helps with Anger Management

Emotional intelligence is mainly about self-awareness and self-management. People who are self-aware rarely allow themselves to get carried away, even when feeling angry, while self-management helps them control their angry thoughts and emotions.

So, if you are often overwhelmed with negative thoughts, which create negative emotions and result in angry outbursts, you need to address your anger problem as soon as possible.

However, if you believe that your behavior does not require therapy, you can try and modify it by improving your emotional intelligence skills. This is only possible if you practice self-awareness, which can be achieved when you start paying attention to and trying to understand your thoughts, emotions, and behavior.

<u>6 ways to develop emotional intelligence:</u>

1. **Self-Analysis**

    If you really know yourself, you will understand why you feel and react the way you do. When you understand the WHY (you react a certain way), it becomes easier to figure out the HOW (you should behave instead).

2. **Self-awareness**

    Learn how to tune in to your emotions, regardless of what they are, and try to understand how they affect your thoughts or decisions. Ask yourself why you feel the way you do.

3. **Understand where your anger is coming from**

    Negative feelings are easier to deal with if you name them. Even if you can't do anything about them at the moment, knowing what you're dealing with is part of the solution.

4. **Don't rush to respond to a trigger**

    Whenever you feel angry, give yourself time to think before responding. Depending on what you're responding to, you may consider putting off your response for later. If that's not possible, simply count to 10, or 50, or as long it takes so you don't say something you may later regret.

5. **Try to tune in to the emotions of others**

    Unfortunately, most people are neither good listeners nor do they have time to spare for others. Try approaching others with an open mind so you can "read" into the situation and get a feeling for how they feel.

6. **Be flexible**

    Accept that regardless of how strong your views on a particular topic might be, there may be situations where you have to be more diplomatic. Be prepared to adjust your words, actions, or reactions to the situation.

7. **Recognize and name**

All emotions—especially negative ones—have to be recognized and named so you can address the REAL cause of your reaction.

8. **Emotional regulation**

   This is about learning how to control your strong emotions, particularly negative ones, and not acting on impulse. Practice by thinking of something that will make you feel hurt, angry, or exploited. Sit with the feeling—feel it, "digest" it—and after about five minutes, "respond" to the person or situation that made you feel that way.

You can't manage a situation (or a team, a relationship, etc.) unless you can manage yourself. We live under a lot of stress, which often makes otherwise peaceful people lash out in anger. Although shouting, slamming doors, or using strong language can help you release that pent-up anger, such behavior is unacceptable in public. The benefits of getting rid of your anger will be weakened by the fact that you'll later have to apologize to those who felt hurt or threatened by your behavior. And it may even cost you your job, or a relationship.

The key advantage of being emotionally intelligent is that you become more aware of how what you say and do affects those around you. It not only makes you a better leader, but also a better human being.

Day 14
Emotional Intelligence

In the overpopulated, dynamic, and fast-changing world, it's becoming difficult to cope—let alone succeed personally and professionally—without emotional intelligence skills. However, the dwindling job market, overcrowded workspaces, and increasing demands on our time all contribute to the stress and frustration we have to deal with almost on a daily basis.

Managing one's emotions is key to emotional intelligence, but this doesn't mean you have to feel positive about life regardless of what's going on around you.

Managing your emotions is about learning to react to fear, frustration, disappointment, or stress in a way that will reduce anxiety and tension in both yourself and others, rather than make an already tense situation worse.

Recognizing and Managing Your Emotions

Our emotions are the result of our thoughts, experiences, and mindset. And although it's not possible to change your past experiences, it is possible to change your thoughts and your attitude.

You may be feeding yourself negative thoughts, or you may be in a situation where you are fed such thoughts by those around you, such as your parents, partner, or friends. Fortunately, thoughts can be changed and the power to change your thoughts and behavior lies with you.

It's unrealistic to expect anyone, no matter how emotionally intelligent they are, to always feel positive about life. Much of how we feel and think has to do with the people we come into contact with or the environments we live in. For example, in a war zone or a poverty-stricken neighborhood, it's difficult to be positive about anything, especially if you feel stuck. Many people feel just bad about themselves or their lives despite having everything they could wish for.

To manage emotions, you must never suppress them. This is why many therapists disapprove of mantras and positive affirmations. Instead of acknowledging you are sick, without an income, or in a messy relationship, by repeating a positive mantra—"I'll be fine", or "I am healthy and full of energy" or "I am confident the Universe will provide"—you are wasting time waiting for someone else to provide a solution to your problem.

Positive affirmations can be very helpful when you're feeling down, because it's definitely better to believe your circumstances will improve than it is to tell yourself you're in a hopeless situation. However, this only works as a temporary measure, until you find a creative solution to your problem. In other words, positive affirmations are simply a tool for boosting your self-confidence until you actually do something about the problem. The focus is on action.

There may be occasions when pushing your emotions out of your mind may help you deal with them. When powerful feelings stay bottled up for too long, especially if they concern a traumatic experience, they can affect your behavior, health, and mindset.

Managing emotions is not about repressing them, but addressing them in a positive and constructive way.

3 tips on how to prevent negative emotions from becoming bottled up:

1. **Talk about them**

    Emotions become bottled up because some experiences are not easy to talk about, you may not know how to express your feelings, or you may have no one to talk to. Some people may also think expressing emotions is a sign of weakness.

    An emotionally intelligent person knows that releasing emotions is an important part of mental health, necessary for your emotional and mental well-being.

    Unaddressed emotions eventually become emotional baggage, which some people carry around their whole life. Your emotional health depends on your memories and experiences, and the more traumas in your life, the greater the need to unpack that emotional baggage and let it go. On their own, old wounds may heal on the surface, but memories of shame, grief, guilt, or regret can create scars which, if unreleased, may stay with you forever.

2. **Write them down**

    If you can't talk about your emotions, try writing them down. That way, you can still get them out of your system without anyone learning about your secret. To make sure no one sees, destroy the written evidence once you've finished.

3. **Learn how to get rid of negative emotions**

    There are many ways to let go of anger, fear, sadness, jealousy, and other negative emotions. If these emotions are so overwhelming they are preventing you from leading a normal life, you should consider therapy. If they are less problematic, you can try self-help techniques, like physical exercise, journaling, self-therapy, meditation. Getting rid of negative emotions is particularly important if you have low self-esteem and a tendency to turn your anger inward.

However, try as you may, some types of anger may not be possible to get rid of. Either because the injustice done is unforgivable, like child abuse, or because you simply can't get over something, such as someone much less competent than you being promoted and becoming your boss.

However, although anger may be justified, holding on to it is not. If the damage cannot be undone, for your own peace of mind, you should try to resolve the negative effect of anger. This is crucial because as long as you're holding on to it, it will continue to harm you—without you even realizing it.

The Burden of Unresolved Anger

We often, unknowingly, hold on to anger by revisiting painful memories from the past which we can't or won't let go.

To let go of the anger, you first have to understand how self-destructive it can be and how it can cause many problems without you even realizing what's going on.

All emotions need an outlet. When anger is not released, it affects your body, which affects how your mind works, which in turn affects what sort of emotions you end up living with. Instead of letting repressed anger rule your life, take charge by letting go of everything that is no longer serving you, or that is undermining your health and well-being.

<u>4 steps to letting go of anger:</u>

Step 1: Are you aware of how anger is affecting your life?

To see the full impact of how anger is making you feel and behave, write down the answers to these questions.

1. How does anger make you feel?
2. How much time each day do you spend feeling angry?
3. Do you often wake up feeling angry?
4. Is anger often preventing you from falling asleep?
5. Do you indulge in comfort foods or alcohol when feeling angry? Does it help?
6. How does anger affect your performance at work?
7. How does anger affect your personal relationships?
8. What would it take for you to let go of this anger?

Step 2: Imagine your life without this bottled-up anger

Write down your answers.

1. If you didn't feel angry, how would you feel in the morning upon waking up?
2. If you didn't feel angry, would you drink less?
3. How would not feeling angry affect your relationships?
4. How would not feeling angry affect your performance at work?
5. How would you feel about your future if you didn't have this anger?

Step 3: Accept the things you cannot change

Have you identified the real cause of your anger? If you could turn back time, what would you do differently that would make it possible to live free of anger?

1. List three things you would change in your behavior.
2. What's stopping you from changing those behaviors now?
3. Can you accept your regrets as mistakes you can learn from?

Step 4: Acceptance

Think about your anger. Write down your answers.

1. Are you in any way responsible for the hurt that's making you angry?
2. Have you considered the possibility that the person who made you angry had no other option?
3. Have YOU ever done something similar to someone else?

Step four can be painful but is very powerful. Depending on the source of your anger, it may take you a long time to get to a stage where you can look at the problem from the other person's point of view.

It's believed that only once you take full responsibility for your anger, and understand your own role in it, can you truly get over it.

Day 15

Mindfulness

Mindfulness is about being fully focused on what's going on around you, what you're doing, what you're saying, and how you're feeling. Although this probably sounds simple enough, it's easier said than done—our minds are not easy to keep still.

Due to stress, information overload, or busy lifestyle, keeping your mind from wandering can be quite a challenge. The racing thoughts, the inner chatter, or things you unconsciously worry about all the time, can make your mind cluttered and restless.

The key to mindful living is the focus. A mindful person is totally in the moment, whether he's playing with his child, working, eating, making love, rock climbing, or writing a letter to a friend. He's aware of the effect his words or actions may have on others, so he thinks before he speaks or acts.

Mindfulness can be learned and it can also become a way of life; however, it does require an effort on your part to keep your mind focused on one thing amidst all the distractions that surround us. Many activities can help you cultivate this personal development technique, such as yoga, meditation, visualization, and sports.

How Mindful Are You?

Practicing mindfulness has many benefits for your health, happiness, work, and relationships. Both science and experience show all areas of your life improve once you start living mindfully.

However, being mindful in this day and age is not easy. Studies indicate most people spend nearly 50% of their waking hours thinking about something that has nothing to do with what they are doing, and this indirectly affects their performance, creativity, concentration, and well-being.

13 things a MINDFUL person does:

    1. They find it easy to focus on tasks.

    2. They make good use of their time.

    3. They get things done promptly.

    4. They are not easily distracted.

    5. They prioritize and stay focused on the most important things.

6. They always find time to respond to emails, meet friends, and visit family.

7. They are fully present during meetings.

8. They find it easy to concentrate on what they're doing.

9. They think before saying something.

10. They choose to "sleep on it" rather than make a hasty decision.

11. They stay calm under pressure.

12. They are fully aware of how they feel about someone or something.

13. They find it easy to understand how others feel.

8 things THOSE WHO LACK mindfulness do:

1. They are often surprised by what they say or do.

2. They often multitask.

3. They worry about work even after leaving office.

4. They often forget things other people say, things they read about, or promises they make.

5. They are uncomfortable sitting still or being quiet for long, and would rather be doing something.

6. Their mind wanders.

7. When they are upset, they can't stop thinking about it.

8. They often have trouble sleeping because their thoughts keep them awake.

Our scattered minds do the best they can to keep track of all the things we need to remember. However, in this stressful world, we wear so many hats in a single day that it's small wonder we are often highly-strung and anxious.

3 simple mindfulness exercises that will force you to slow down and focus on something:

1. Mindful observation

This exercise will help you notice, perhaps for the first time, how beautiful, unusual, or interesting some things you never thought about before are.

Choose an object from your immediate environment, like your garden, the park you walk your dog in, or something you keep on your balcony. It should be something that's been there for years, which you never bothered to notice before—a flower, a bird that visits your bird feeder, a piece of rock, a fallen tree trunk, a tree in full blossom.

Look at the object for as long as you can stay focused. Relax as you do so.

Examine its shape, color, and size, picking up even the tiniest details. As you do so, try to tune in to this object and imagine what its purpose in the web of life must be.

If you can get yourself to stay focused for 15 minutes without answering your phone or talking to someone, you'll be amazed at how refreshed you'll feel afterward.

2. Mindful immersion

This exercise is about finding contentment in what you do instead of moving continually from one activity to another. The purpose is to enjoy whatever it is you are doing at the moment.

For example, if you are involved in otherwise boring and repetitive work, such as doing housework, working in the garden, or sorting out files at work, try to approach these tasks from a different angle. Make your work more creative.

Pay attention to every single detail of your activity, as if you had to describe to someone how such a job should be done. Focus on what you are doing, and focus on how your body feels, how your muscles move as you lift or move things around.

By becoming aware of every step and immersing yourself in it, the job will be finished quickly. You'll stop thinking how boring it is and you'll stop pushing yourself to get it over with as soon as possible so you can move on to something else. You may even start enjoying it.

3. Mindful loving

When you are mindful in love, you don't wait for someone's birthday, anniversary, or Valentine's day to reflect on the importance of that relationship in your life. From time to time, stop and look back on the connection you have with a friend, spouse, or a parent. Reflect on all you've been through, appreciate that they are in your life, and show them you care. Don't just *think* about how much they mean to you—tell them how you feel.

Mindfulness and Anger Management

Cultivating mindfulness helps you reduce both the frequency and the level of the anger you experience.

Mindfulness is about being fully present in whatever you do. To some, this comes naturally, but most of us have to learn how to cultivate mindfulness. And one of the easiest ways to learn this is through meditation.

The practice of mindfulness meditation does not have to be complicated. You can do it while walking your dog, sitting quietly in the garden, listening to uplifting music, or as a part of other activities such as yoga, sports, or knitting. Simply put, mindfulness is about being "centered," without being aware of it. With practice, it becomes a way of life.

Mindfulness can make it easier to cope with life while improving your physical health by relieving stress, lowering blood pressure, and reducing chronic pain.

If your life decisions are made mindfully, it means you will have thought them through. For example, if you decide to go vegan, a mindful approach to this decision should be well thought-through and creative.

5 characteristics of mindful vegans:
- They understand and accept the challenges that a new way of life brings.
- They are prepared to leave their comfort zone and give up the things they are used to, in order to allow new tastes, experiences, and people into their lives.
- They have a strategy on how to deal with crisis, cravings, or self-doubts.
- They are not afraid to stand up for what they believe in and are prepared to explain, but also defend, their way of life without confrontation.
- They prepare and eat their food mindfully.

So, how do you apply mindfulness to anger management?

While some therapists recommend controlling anger—by counting to 10, or by hitting a pillow—others disagree with this approach as they believe this only heals the wound on the surface, while deep inside, it continues to fester. Instead, they recommend addressing the real problem behind the angry outburst, not the anger itself.

Regardless of their approach to anger management, more and more therapists recommend replacing traditional anger management techniques with mindfulness techniques.

Mindfulness is a very personal experience and there are many different ways of doing it, but, you can apply these steps to almost any activity or any situation.

7 basic steps to mindfulness:

1. Find a quiet spot to sit down and relax.
2. Set a time limit, like five to 10 minutes.
3. Still your mind and if it wanders, bring it back.
4. Become aware of your body: notice how your knees feel, how warm or cold your feet are, how tense or relaxed your abdomen is, or if you have any pains or aches.
5. Become aware of the noises around you: try to guess which bird is making that particular noise, what's going on in the street, whose dog is barking.
6. Become aware of any unusual smells: a neighbor having a barbecue, your roommate making a cup of coffee, the scent of lilac in the garden.
7. Slowly come back.

Day 16
Meditation

Numerous studies confirm that meditating for just 20 minutes a day, every day, can have numerous positive effects on both physical and mental health. This is largely because meditation relaxes the mind, which in turn reduces anger and anxiety, lowers blood pressure, and helps you feel grounded.

For those who practice it regularly, meditation can become a way of life. It can also help you come face to face with the feelings you keep hidden from others—or yourself. In the case of those who've suffered trauma or some kind of emotional or physical abuse, meditation can bring healing from the pain, shame, or guilt that is often present. This type of healing is particularly effective if you carry a lot of old, repressed anger.

Meditation is a skill, which means it can be taught and perfected with practice. There are many different ways to do it, and you can choose the style that suits you most based on what you want to achieve with it (e.g., calming vs. insight meditation), or which tradition, culture, or spiritual discipline you want to follow.

Of the dozens of types of meditation practiced today, the most popular ones are guided or unguided meditation, walking meditation, Buddhist meditation, Transcendental meditation, and meditation for sleep, for stress, for anger, for compassion.

The point is, there is no right or wrong way to meditate. Meditation is a very personal experience, and you should choose the one that works for you.

Where to Meditate

Meditation does not have to be a complicated affair, with a special practice space, dimmed lights, and uplifting music. Ideally, it should be practiced in a space dedicated to that purpose, however, that is optional.

Some people go to great lengths to create special effects in the meditation room, but these help only in the sense that they create an atmosphere in which it becomes easier to switch off and relax, and are in no way essential for successful meditation. With practice, you can learn to slip into a meditative state anywhere, regardless of the external and internal "noise."

3 things to bear in mind when creating a meditation space at home:
- **Find a space**

Very few of us can set aside an entire room for meditation, so meditation space is usually a corner of a room which has another purpose, like a bedroom or a study. The meditation space can also be a table decorated for that purpose, a bookshelf, or even a tree trunk or a bench in the garden.

- **Decorate the space**

    This is what will make it conducive to meditation. As meditation is a very personal experience, anything that helps you enter a meditative state is fine—a statue of Buddha, unusual pieces of rock or wood, crystals, candles, photographs, flowers, dry leaves, fruits.

- **Make your space sacred, i.e. special**

    You make your meditation space sacred by making it look and "feel" special compared to other parts of your living space. This is why you should never keep "mundane" things in it, like books, magazines, food, or clothes.

Health Benefits of Meditation

While, for most people, meditation is a relaxation process, in Ayurveda, it's a detoxifying one—it helps clear "waste" products from the mind. It revolves around training your mind to focus and release negative mental energy that affects your thoughts, emotions, and behavior.

Meditation affects all aspects of our being:

- On an emotional level, it's an effective tool for beating stress, depression, and anxiety.
- On a mental level, it helps still your inner chatter so you can concentrate and relax more easily while ignoring distracting thoughts.
- On a physical level, it calms you down. When your heartbeat slows and blood pressure drops, your brain produces alpha, instead of beta waves. After spending some time in this relaxed but alert alpha state, you'll feel as refreshed as if you've had a nap.

Numerous studies show that regular meditators are generally healthier than non-meditators, and that meditation helps not only with stress-related disorders but with many other modern-day diseases like migraines, irritable bowel syndrome, asthma, anxiety, mild depression, high blood pressure, and heart disease.

Meditation techniques

Meditation is about stilling your mind and emptying it of distracting thoughts. It's best if you can meditate at the same time and place every day. How long you do it for is unimportant, as long as you do it properly. If you are new to meditation, start with 10 minutes a day, and by the end of the week, you should start to notice improvements.

Basic meditation technique:

1. Sit comfortably—either in the lotus position or, if your back is weak, in a straight-backed chair with your feet on the floor.
2. Close your eyes. Calm down.
3. Breathe slowly and steadily.
4. To keep yourself focused, you can repeat a mantra and gaze at a *mandala* or a candle flame. This is optional.
5. When you have finished, slowly open your eyes, move your arms and legs to encourage circulation, then stand up. Have a glass of water to ground yourself, as some people feel dizzy after sitting still for a long time.

Types of Meditation

The type of meditation you choose to do should be the one that works for you and should address the reason you are doing it—to calm down, to gain spiritual insight, to sleep better, and so on.

Meditation for stress and anxiety

Life is stressful as is, but if your day starts with traffic-induced stress and ends the same way—especially if you spend long hours getting to and from work—this can quickly become too much.

The reason consistent, daily meditation is so effective for stress-management is that it helps you reprogram your brain so it becomes less reactive and more responsive.

Stress usually makes people worry too much, and the racing thoughts make it difficult to focus on anything. Meditation is a very useful tool to quiet an overactive mind. With regular practice, you can learn how to detach yourself from the endless thoughts—not by forgetting about them, but by controlling how much you stay with them.

Meditation for anger

While there are different forms of meditation to choose from, the so-called "anger meditation" is aimed at addressing your anger problem not by controlling your anger, but by letting it run its course.

To this effect, meditation helps shift your focus from thinking about who or what made you angry to the actual feeling of anger. Feel the rage, embarrassment, frustration, or whatever other emotions your anger provokes. If there is a part of your body that is hot or burning with anger, like your face, stomach, or head, become aware of it.

Focus on that spot, and start breathing slowly and deeply. Try to bring your breath to that area. Keep going until you can feel the negative energy dissolve.

Meditation for sleep

This type of meditation teaches you not to get caught up in negative thoughts before going to bed. For many people, it isn't until they go to bed, or just before they do so, that they can finally slow down and relax. It is then that they start mulling over the day behind them or ahead of them. So, instead of getting themselves ready sleep by slowing down, they activate their mind by thinking about the various problems they have to deal with or the tasks awaiting them in the morning.

Meditation for sleep is usually a guided meditation that will help you let go of whatever you are thinking about until you become relaxed enough to fall asleep. This process revolves around the fact that meditation helps lower the heart rate and encourages slower breathing.

To help fight insomnia, don't think, read, or watch anything exciting that could start you thinking or worrying. Instead, focus on something calming and peaceful, like a photo, music, or thought, and watch your body wind down as it prepares for sleep.

Guided vs. unguided meditation

In guided meditation, you are led through meditation "moves" by a teacher who takes you through all the steps of a particular meditation technique and who suggests how you can apply what you've learned into your everyday life. This type of meditation is particularly good for beginners.

During unguided or silent meditation, you meditate on your own, either completely alone or as part of a group, and no one explains the process. This can be as simple as sitting quietly and concentrating on your breath while emptying your mind of distracting thoughts, or you can apply a particular meditation technique (like meditation for anger, sleep, and so on).

Zen meditation

Zen meditation focuses on breath and how it moves through your body. You think of nothing and let the mind "just be." With this type of meditation, you cultivate both mindfulness and alertness.

Mantra meditation

With this type of meditation, instead of focusing on the breath to quiet the mind, you focus on a mantra. Your mantra could consist of a syllable, word, or a phrase which sums up what you believe in or what you aspire to.

The philosophy behind the mantra meditation is that the subtle vibrations associated with the repeated mantra can encourage positive change, boost self-confidence, reduce fear, and encourage empathy. Basically, a mantra should guide you in the way you want to live your life, so you choose a mantra that strikes a chord with you.

You can choose a quote:

- "Our greatest glory is not in never falling, but in rising every time we fall." (Confucius)
- "A person is what he or she thinks about all day long." (Ralph Waldo Emerson)
- "Opportunities don't happen, you create them." (Chris Groser)
- "They cannot take away your self-respect if you don't give it to them." (Mahatma Gandhi)

You can also create a personal mantra which sums up your goals and aspirations:
- I can and I will
- Live simply
- I write my destiny
- Seize the day

Transcendental meditation (TM)

TM is a silent mantra meditation, usually practiced for 20 minutes twice a day, although there are many variations. You meditate with your eyes closed and repeat a mantra assigned to you by your teacher. While you meditate this way, your thinking process "transcends" and is replaced by a state of pure consciousness.

Unlike other types of meditation, TM requires formal training by a certified teacher. It does not require concentration or contemplation, just breathing normally and focusing your attention on the mantra.

Some studies suggest that this type of meditation is not a good choice for those suffering from a certain psychiatric condition.

Walking meditation

During walking meditation, you are physically active and focused on the experience of walking. You walk very slowly and concentrate on your breath. Ideally, you should do this in a place where you will not be distracted by either people, traffic, or scenery.

You can practice barefoot or wear light shoes, and you can walk in a circle if you are doing this in a small garden. Try to be aware of the sounds around you and of yourself moving in that particular location. Walking meditation is a great technique for improving concentration.

The internationally-renowned self-help author and motivational speaker Wayne Dyer had great advice how life should be lived: "Become slower in your journey through life. Practice yoga and meditation if you suffer from 'hurry sickness.' Become more introspective by visiting quiet places such as churches, museums, mountains, and lakes. Give yourself permission to read at least one novel a month for pleasure."

Day 17

Zen Buddhism and the Importance of Living in the Present

What is perhaps the most striking difference between Zen Buddhism and Western culture is the understanding of happiness. While most people would define happiness as getting what they want—having a certain way of life or certain material possessions—Zen philosophy is based on the idea that we should stop expecting our lives to develop the way we think they should.

Unfortunately, the more we look for something to make us happy, the more likely we are to be disappointed. But for Buddhists, true happiness is a state of mind, and they look deep within when searching for it.

Zen tools that can help you reach a stage when you start looking for fulfillment within, rather than without, are meditation, mindfulness, and the practice of loving kindness.

Living according to these principles not only makes it easier to find your bliss, but makes it very difficult to develop any negative emotions—particularly anger.

What is Zen About?

While interest in Zen Buddhism is growing, many believe that following this philosophy is not possible in the 21st century. It's true that the modern world is very different from the time when Buddhism first appeared; however, the main obstacle to a Zen way of life is that obsession with material possessions, consumerism, and personal ambition—not spiritual development—have become the core values of Western culture.

Zen is about peaceful simplicity, but the stress of everyday life makes it difficult to aim for harmony within. Still, it's possible to embrace Zen values if you manage to slow down and live mindfully.

5 steps to adopting Zen philosophy amidst the chaos of modern life:

1. Find your meditation technique

Meditation is key for the Zen way of life, so choose how you want to do it. There are many styles to choose from, but the most important element of successful meditation is being focused. If you have a busy lifestyle and multitasking helps you cope, be prepared to give up that way of life. Your overall performance and results in anything you do will improve greatly if you start concentrating on one thing at a time.

2. Enjoy the moment

Learn to be content with who you are and what you have. When you learn to accept the life you are living, you stop worrying, and when you are free of worry you enjoy life more. Savoring every moment amidst the stress and chaos we're drowning in is not easy, but it's the only way to keep life from passing you by.

The well-known Vietnamese Zen Monk Thich Nhat Hanh said it all: "Drink your tea slowly and reverently, as if it is the axis on which the world earth revolves slowly, evenly, without rushing toward the future."

3. Look for happiness within

Some people are happy wherever they are, while others are unhappy, regardless. It's pointless to look for happiness in far-off places, better-paid jobs, or faster cars. Happiness is wherever you are right now, because it is within you. Instead of searching for it far and wide, look deep within.

4. Do one thing at a time

Most people have to juggle family, career, and social life, so multitasking has become a way of life. However, when you live like this, all you are doing is shifting your focus from one thing to another throughout the day. When you are not fully focused, and instead trying to do several things at the same time, a lot of your energy and time is wasted. You achieve much more if you give your full attention to whatever you're doing, rather than hoping to get more things done by taking on multiple tasks.

5. Be kind to yourself and others

In some ways, Buddhism and emotional intelligence are based on the same values: understanding, empathy, and forgiveness. When you learn to forgive (both yourself and others), you stop judging and blaming. When you try to understand why someone has done something that upset you, you stop feeling angry. When you practice gratitude, you realize how good life actually is. Whatever you decide to do, don't underestimate the power of kindness.

Zen Approach to Anger

We all get angry from time to time, but we deal with this powerful emotion in different ways. Some cultures repress it, while others express it freely—some even enjoy the feeling.

From the Zen point of view, feeling angry is simply wasting your energy on a mental state which serves no purpose. Buddhists approach anger in a pragmatic way—while they don't deny it, they will do nothing to help it grow.

While psychologists tell us anger is normal and we should express it in a constructive way, in Buddhism, anger is seen as the most negative and destructive force—one which can easily destroy all the good in the world. So, they approach anger in a typically Buddhist way: by neutralizing it with non-anger.

5 Zen things to do when you start getting angry:

1. It's OK to be angry, don't deny it

To Buddhists, fear and anger are energy-draining emotions which can control your life if you let them. With patience and practice, you can learn to avoid these mental states.

2. Learn how not to get angry

In Buddhism, anger gets a bad reputation—mainly because it revolves around ego. Still, Buddhists believe in practicing loving kindness even with those who make them angry. Buddhists don't behave aggressively when angry, nor do they try to suppress anger. They deal with it by observing it, but not participating in it. In other words, they neutralize it with understanding and compassion.

3. Cultivate patience

If you can't help feeling angry, give yourself time to calm down so you can communicate without making a scene or causing harm. Acknowledge the anger and embrace it. Wait. Given enough time, and your anger will vanish on its own. Patience gives you the chance to analyze your angry feelings and understand why you feel a certain way.

4. Don't feed anger

While some therapists recommend venting your anger in a way that will not cause harm, like pounding on a pillow, Buddhists believe that when you express your anger, either verbally or physically, you help it grow. When you ignore it, though, you starve it.

5. Compassion takes courage

Many people feel strong when they are angry, probably because of the adrenaline rush that floods the brain, and regard those who never show anger as weak cowards. In Buddhism, it's the other way around.

Buddhists believe showing anger is a sign of weakness, while having the strength to acknowledge anger, or the fear you feel when facing an angry person or when in a dangerous situation, is a sign of real strength.

Like most Eastern philosophies, Zen Buddhism teachings focus on acceptance and patience. Zen teaches us to be observant of what's going on around us and to embrace both the good and the bad, for there is a reason for everything.

As Robert Green pointed out, "Everything that happens to you is a form of instruction if you pay attention."

Day 18
Inner Peace Techniques for Anger Management

None of us go through life unscathed and, over time, we all devise various coping strategies to help us deal with stress, problems, anger, and disappointments. However, not all coping strategies are healthy.

The unhealthy coping strategies are what most people typically fall back on, mainly because these require the least effort and offer instant gratification. Unfortunately, they often have long-term negative effects on our health. These strategies include alcohol, drugs, antidepressants, smoking, and comfort eating.

On the other hand, healthy coping strategies, which offer a better long-term solution, are not always easy to implement and it may take quite some time for the first improvements to show.

Healthy anger management strategies are based on techniques which help you take control of your emotions and minimize the effects of angry outbursts. Eastern philosophies, such as Buddhism, Taoism, and Yoga, recommend gentle, yet powerful and effective, ways of managing anger that focus on inner peace and self-discipline.

The Tao of Inner Peace

Taoism is a belief system that promotes self-acceptance, inner peace, and flexibility. The reason Taoism and other Eastern philosophies have become so popular in the West is that as life becomes more complex and people find themselves facing overwhelming challenges on all levels, they try to find an alternative way of dealing with stress and restoring inner balance.

Taoism teaches many things, the most important of which is that the past is behind you and the future is not here yet—you should focus on the present moment. And this is why these ideas are so difficult for many to grasp. In the West, people spend their entire lives ruminating about their past mistakes and worrying about how they'll cope with the future. Being overwhelmed by uncertainty (because they constantly worry about the future) and mentally exhausted (from constantly thinking about what happened in the past) are the main reasons why anxiety, depression, and mental disorders are rising to epidemic proportions in the developed world.

Tao is big on forgiveness, so its approach to anger management is to forgive. Whether or not you forgive doesn't really matter, however, as it won't change what happened in the past. Which leads us to Taoism's key take on life—acceptance. Accept the past for what it is, because it's been and gone. Focus on the here and now.

Taoism is not a religion, but a belief system whose main doctrine is that only harmony within people can create harmony in the environment. It deals with anger by cultivating empathy, even for those who make practitioners angry. Through the constant search for inner peace, Taoists develop the ability to understand the suffering of others—even their enemies—without judgment.

<u>4 Taoist tips on achieving inner peace:</u>

Find your own happiness

People need different things to feel fulfilled. There is no recipe to finding happiness, because happiness means different things to different people. It's only when you find your own meaning in life that you will have found true happiness.

Peace is not around you—it's inside you

To reach a stage where you can find peace amidst crowds, noise, and chaos, you have to be able to switch off—regardless of what's going on around or inside you. This is achieved through meditation, which is a great tool for developing self-discipline.

Drop expectations

Expectations are a major cause of anger, because they make you over-ambitious, competitive, and frustrated. People are rarely satisfied with what they have and always want more. According to Taoism, the more you expect, the less you become: the key to happiness is to live in the present and practice gratitude.

Simplify your life

When you declutter your life and your mind from all the unnecessary things, thoughts, and information, you create space for the people and experiences that really matter.

Yoga

Despite the way many people approach yoga, it is much more than a workout. It's a spiritual tradition that brings together the body, mind, and spirit, and *asanas* are only a small part of it. According to yoga philosophy, the main purpose of physical exercises is to prepare the body for long periods of meditation, because you need to be mentally strong and physically flexible to be able to sit still for extended periods of time.

 inner balance. Its three main elements are *pranayama* (breathing exercises), meditation, and *asanas* (physical exercises). And this is where many people who do yoga get it wrong.

To most people (in the West, at least), yoga is merely a way of exercising their bodies. However, although these exercises have proven health benefits, that's not what yoga is really about. Without *pranayama*, ethical practices, and meditation, you are not really practicing yoga.

This means that if you can do only simple poses but understand and follow the philosophy of yoga, you are at a much higher level of yoga practice than someone who can do even the most demanding exercises without understanding why they are doing it.

There are many different schools of yoga, but they all revolve around balance in the mind and body. And, just like other spiritual traditions, yoga can teach us how to react to anger without repressing it or acting aggressively.

According to yoga philosophy, anger should be avoided at all costs because it undermines the very essence of yoga—achieving happiness and freedom.

The ancient yogis firmly believed in and practiced the mind-body approach to life. To them, anger was a kind of blockage at the mental, physical, or spiritual level. To free up the blocked energy, they used a combination of asanas, *pranayama*, and meditation techniques as main anger management tools with which they distracted the angry mind from the negative thoughts. The basic yoga model for controlling anger is to stop the inner chatter (with meditation) and shift the focus from the anger trigger to exercise and breathing (with *asanas* and *pranayama*).

These practices help with anger management by putting you in a mental state which promotes tranquility and boosts self-esteem while improving your physical health through balancing the production of hormones.

<u>3 ways yoga helps control your anger:</u>

1. **Yoga calms you down**

Meditation and breathing techniques are the essence of yoga. They help you stop the inner chatter—and once that happens, it's easier to feel relaxed and stress-free. Anyone who has attended a yoga class knows how light and calm they feel afterward. This is because yoga practice reduces stress hormones (cortisol and adrenaline) and induces the relaxation response (by raising levels of oxytocin, a hormone that reduces blood pressure and improves the levels of certain neurotransmitters that are usually low in those who are overwhelmed with negativity). And it is only in this relaxed state of mind that we can clearly "see" the real reason for our anger or anxiety and come to terms with it. So, there is science-based evidence that yoga practice starts a number of positive chemical changes within your body.

2. **Yoga boosts your confidence**

Doing yoga helps build your physical and mental strength, which in turn boosts how you feel about yourself and your body. As your body becomes more supple, your skin more radiant, and you begin to walk more gracefully, you can't but feel proud of yourself. Another reason your confidence soars is that yoga improves your health on both the physical and mental levels, which indirectly affects how you feel about yourself and your life.

3. Yoga unblocks your energy

Yoga is all about the balance of the body, mind, and soul. For this to happen, the energy within your body has to flow freely. Unfortunately, it is often blocked due to prolonged stress, chronic fatigue, repressed emotions, fear, or depression. As a result, emotions can become unbalanced, and you may easily become overwhelmed with negativity. When energy "flows" freely, so do your emotions, and healthy emotions produce healthy thoughts.

There are several asanas that are particularly powerful when used for the release of pent up anger and frustration, and *garbhasana* and *koormasana*are believed to be the most eficient ones.

According to the well-known yoga teacher and author, TKV Desikachar, "The success of yoga does not lie in the ability to perform postures but in how it positively changes the way we live our lives and our relationships."

Day 19

Cognitive Behavioral Therapy

Anger can have many triggers and, depending on one's temperament, culture, and level of emotional intelligence, can be a positive or a destructive force. We start learning about anger management from the moment we are born: babies cry with anger if they are left hungry or wet; some children throw tantrums if they can't get what they want, while others try to get the same thing by being nice and sweet; and as adults, we learn to deal with frustrations almost on a daily basis.

However, when we find ourselves in situations that are far too complex to be resolved on our own, or when faced with mental health disorders which require a professional approach, it's best to seek a good therapist.

Anger Management Counseling

Counseling works for many mental disorders, including anger management. While there are many different approaches to this problem, perhaps best-known is cognitive-behavioral therapy (CBT). The best thing about it is that you can achieve considerable improvements relatively quickly, in about two months.

CBT's approach to anger management is to address a combination of situations and beliefs which may have contributed to how you feel about yourself, as well as to the reasons when and why you experience anger. It focuses mainly on your childhood experiences and treatment, including the beliefs you were fed with and whether you were mistreated or belittled.

However, there are many other types of therapy, and the anger symptoms you are experiencing may help you decide which one would be the best for you.

<u>3 types of anger symptoms:</u>
1. **Physiological** (rapid heart rate, shaking, aggression towards others, etc.)
2. **Cognitive** (difficulties concentrating or remembering, dreaming of revenge, etc.)
3. **Behavioral** (arguments which result in violence, reckless driving, alcohol abuse, etc.)

People struggling with mental disorders often struggle to determine which therapy would work best for them. With so many options to choose from, it's perhaps best to consult your doctor for advice on this. Still, you should also familiarize yourself with what each therapy consists of, for there may be some that would suit you more.

Different anger management therapies:

- **In-person therapy**

    This is when you see a therapist on a regular basis over an extended period of time. It can be over the phone or online, in a group or on a one-to-one basis.

- **Online counseling**

    This is a relatively new type of counseling and requires you to have a computer or a smartphone. For many, it offers an original and innovative method of treatment. Although this type of therapy would save you a lot of time, it may not suit those who prefer face-to-face interaction or lack IT skills.

- **Group therapy**

    The best thing about this kind of therapy is that it provides both a therapist and a support group. This type of counseling is often preferred by those who enjoy being part of a group and don't mind discussing their problems in front of other people. They also stand to benefit from listening to what sort of problems others may be facing and how they cope with them.

- **Residential anger management**

    This type of therapy is more intense and is used for people whose lives have been severely affected by their inability to deal with anger. On the upside, clients are away from their everyday life and can focus completely on the therapy, but this kind of treatment takes a lot of commitment, and not everyone is able to be away from their job or families for an extended period of time.

Another option is to treat anger management with medication, which usually involves antidepressants, mood stabilizers, or antipsychotic drugs.

Medication is prescribed to patients with severe anger problems, but usually only as a short-term solution until they have calmed down and can start therapy. Drugs are generally avoided, as they often come with side effects and there is the possibility of addiction. For this reason, medication is usually recommended only as a temporary solution.

Cognitive Behavioral Therapy (CBT)

Cognitive behavioral therapy (CBT), which is successfully used for many different disorders, is based on the idea that the best way to stop the vicious cycle of negative thoughts, emotions, and behavior is to replace the destructive thought patterns with positive ones.

CBT is very effective in anger management and focuses on teaching patients both how to control their thoughts and emotions and how to interpret them in a positive way.

7 steps of anger management with CBT:

1. **Avoid negative thoughts**

   Those who are always negative about life will never be able to see anything positive around them. If your mind is overwhelmed with negativity, you need to learn to look at life from a different angle and realize that things are not as bad as you may have thought.

   CBT is about looking at the world, and your life, with more objectivity, and realizing how much your negative thoughts "color" your experiences. When you learn to change the way you react to situations which provoke negative emotions, you will know that your anger management therapy has succeeded. For example, stop feeling that jokes about overweight people are always aimed at you, stop beating yourself up for not having done more for your grandparents while they were alive, or focus on improving your performance instead of worrying you might lose your job.

   Your thoughts affect your feelings, and vice versa—a negative thought pattern eventually turns to anger or self-anger. You don't have to have happy thoughts all the time, but neither should you focus only on thoughts which make you fearful, anxious, or angry. It's not a cliché that a positive state of mind creates opportunities and attracts positive experiences.

2. **Identify where your anger is coming from**

   The main aim of CBT therapy is to get patients to understand what initiates the cycle of negative thoughts, and to learn to avoid them or stop them before they get out of hand. Almost anything can be a trigger to a negative emotion, but it's the way you react to a trigger that decides whether it turns into a negative thought or behavior, or whether you simply register it and let it go.

   Get into the habit of analyzing your anger. Is there a pattern? Is it getting worse? How often does it happen? Are triggers always the same? If you know where your anger is coming from, you can either avoid the triggers or be mentally prepared to face them.

   It's the way you interpret a thought, a memory, a comment someone makes, or an event that either improves or clouds your judgment. This is why negative self-talk can be so destructive.

3. **Cultivate a nurturing environment**

   People in your environment can be a pillar of comfort and support or a cause of constant sabotage. They can help pick you up when you're down, or make you feel even worse about yourself than you already do. This is why choosing your company is so important, especially if you are oversensitive and tend to take things personally, or have a problem controlling your temper. If your reaction is easily triggered, and especially if you have a history of violence, you should try to surround yourself with people who are least likely to push your buttons.

This is not always possible, but what is possible is for you to make some changes in your behavior or daily routine to better avoid situations which make you angry. For example, if you have a problem with road rage, consider taking public transport or finding an alternative route to work. If you have a problem with certain individuals, try to get them to meet you on neutral ground, like in a coffee shop or a park, rather than at their office or home, where being on their "territory" may make you feel more vulnerable and less in control of your emotions.

4. **Respond quickly to negative emotions**

How quickly you react to a negative thought will decide how successful you are in preventing that thought from becoming a thought pattern. Negativity breeds negativity, so the trick is to prevent a negative thought from becoming a negative emotion, which can become a negative reaction.

5. **Learn to identify your threshold**

Sometimes, a change of scene is all it takes for anger to subside. This could mean walking away from your office for a few moments, from your flat for a couple of hours, or moving away from your parents' home. Many conflicts happen as a result of a lack of "breathing space," so when you feel you're beginning to get angry, if possible, remove yourself from that environment for a while.

Some people can quickly come up with ideas about how to respond to an anger trigger, others need more time to think about how to react. Although it's not possible to walk away in the middle of an important meeting or a job interview, when you feel anger rising, at least take a couple of moments to compose yourself. Simply, count to ten or take a few deep breaths before responding.

6. **Weaken your triggers if you can't prevent them**

Learn how to think rationally so you can calm yourself down when under stress and don't take it out on others. A negative thought allowed to get out of hand can lead to rage which is often targeted at those who happen to be around, even if they have nothing to do with your problem.

If avoiding a trigger fails to work, at least try to weaken it by developing a positive thought or repeating a positive affirmation which will counter the negative thought that makes you angry—if you think you are not popular, think of those who actually enjoy spending time with you; if you're angry with yourself for being overweight, think of all those people who were once overweight, and managed to get fit through their own efforts.

If you feel very negative and nothing seems to make it better, try doing something drastic. First of all, leave the place where the negative thought happened, and avoid reading or watching any negative material (like news dealing with war, terrorism, or the destructive effects of climate change). Don't talk to those who are always complaining, sad, or depressed. Although watching news can serve as a distraction from your negative thoughts, it can also make them worse. Fear-provoking news, movies, or sermons will only feed your negativity, while what you need to do is starve it of energy.

7. **Improve communication skills**

    Lack of communication is very often the main cause of misunderstandings, arguments, or angry scenes. When you learn to communicate effectively and know how to express your feelings, you will see that many of the situations which make you angry will disappear. Most people prefer talking to listening and, very often, this is where the problem lies. For example, if you had listened carefully, you would have understood what the client really wanted, or if you let your friends know how much it upsets you when they mention your acne problem, you wouldn't end up angry and hurt every time someone brings this up.

8. **Challenge your thinking**

    It's not easy to admit you were wrong. After you have identified your anger triggers, ask yourself if perhaps there may be other reasons for your anger which the triggers have masked? What if what you think someone meant is not true? Is there another way to think about the incident that provoked such a violent reaction in you? Challenging yourself takes courage and maturity, but you'll be surprised what you can find if you dig deep enough.

A negative mindset is never the result of a single negative thought. It is the consequence of a series of negative thoughts which you have lived with for some time—maybe all your life. Be mindful of your environment, the people you socialize with, and the things you read and watch, as all that contributes to your state of mind.

Day 20

Nutrition for Stress Relief

Your diet is not only the fuel that keeps you going, it also affects how often you'll get sick, how quickly you'll recover, how much weight you'll gain, how long you'll live, and more.

There is a reason Hippocrates said, "Let thy food be thy medicine and thy medicine be thy food."

Diet does not only help maintain good health, it can also be used as a natural medicine to correct certain imbalances—more fiber will improve digestion, less unhealthy fats will reduce your chances of heart disease, less salt will lower your blood pressure, antioxidant-rich foods will lower your risk of cancer.

Mood-enhancing plants can be used to soothe a troubled mind and ease many psychological problems, and you don't have to be ill to reap these benefits. You can use them to lift your spirits, bring tranquility, calm down, achieve mental clarity, or aid meditation.

According to Ayurveda, combining foods of different colors is the best way to eat, but a new study reveals that this kind of diet is not only nutritious and physically healthy, but is also good for your mood—different colors carry different energies and these have a direct influence on your mood. Whether you are aware of it or not, color stimulates your emotions and motivates your decisions.

Fight Mental Disorders with Nutrition

Although we are all affected by stress, not everyone knows that it can be controlled with a diet. Certain foods provide natural protection from stress simply because they increase the levels of hormones in the body that naturally fight stress. As well, there are foods and beverages that reduce stress by lowering the levels of hormones that trigger them.

<u>7 foods that help you beat stress:</u>

1. **A warm drink**

    We all know that a cup of tea will calm you down, a cup of warm milk or cocoa before going to bed will help you sleep peacefully, and that a cup of soup helps if you're not feeling well. It's not so much the nutrients from these drinks that provide a sense of calm and healing, but the warmth of the beverage itself. For a number of reasons, there's something very comforting about a warm drink.

2. **Dark chocolate**

   As all chocolate lovers know, the taste and smell of chocolate alone are enough to reduce stress. Besides, dark chocolate is rich in antioxidants, which are known to fight stress as well as protect the body from free radicals. If taken daily, it can help you improve your heart health, lower the blood pressure, prevent some types of cancer, as well as produce endorphins which will improve your mood. If taking it daily, you shouldn't take more than 30 grams.

3. **Healthy Carbs**

   Carbohydrates increase levels of serotonin, a chemical that boosts mood and reduces stress, which indirectly improves cognitive function. However, there are healthy and unhealthy carbs. To improve your mood and reduce stress-induced anger, include the following foods in your daily diet: sweet potato, brown rice, oats, quinoa, buckwheat, beetroots, beans, chickpeas, carrots, mangos, bananas, blueberries, and apples.

4. **Avocados**

   Rich in omega-3 fatty acids, this is one of the healthiest fruits you can eat. These essential acids are known to reduce stress and anxiety, boost concentration, and improve mood.

5. **Fatty fish**

   Another great source of omega-3 fatty acids, which not only beat stress but ease depression. The best source of omega-3 fatty acids are tuna, halibut, salmon, herring, mackerel, sardines, and lake trout.

6. **Nuts**

   Nuts are full of vitamins and healthy fatty acids. They are particularly rich in vitamin B which neutralizes the effects of stress. Add almonds, pistachios, or walnuts to fruit or vegetable salads, muesli, yogurt, or soups.

7. **Vitamin C**

   High levels of vitamin C help reduce stress, so eat fresh fruit and vegetables or take supplements.

Our bodies respond to threatening situations by sending signals to the brain that it's in trouble. The brain reacts by requiring food that will help it think more clearly and be ready for a physical response—fight or flight.

The main threat we face today is that of prolonged stress, which our bodies react to in the same way as when confronted with physical danger. However, after the threat has passed or after you've escaped, your body goes into a recovery mode characterized by an increased appetite to recover from the shock and exhaustion. It is at this stage that many people reach for comfort foods to calm down and recover the energy lost during a stressful situation.

This is how most of us fight stress. However, there is a healthier approach to stress-relief.

3 tips on how to manage stress with diet:
- On a stressful day, eat less and more often.
- Eat plenty of fruits and vegetables to get the nutrients needed for fighting stress.
- Avoid or limit caffeine-rich foods, such as coffee, tea, soft drinks, and chocolate.

Nutrition and Anger Management

Anger behavior ranges from screaming into a pillow or going for a run all, all the way up to murder, and as many people with anger problems end up in jail, even mild anger outbursts should not be ignored—especially if they happen repeatedly. There are different ways of treating anger disorders, one of the easiest being with a healthy diet.

Studies suggest that uncontrollable outbursts of anger are only one of the many symptoms of various mood disorders, like depression, anxiety, insomnia, addiction, and so on. Interestingly, most such individuals have hypoglycemia—a sugar handling problem.

The reason hypoglycemia is common in chronically angry individuals is because such people are often exposed to unnaturally high levels of adrenaline. In stressful situations, when the brain anticipates energy starvation, it triggers the secretion of adrenaline.

When that happens, there is a rush of adrenaline to feed the brain, as well as activation of the fight/flight hormone. In such a state, people become either defensive or aggressive.

Fortunately, this problem can be solved without drugs through a hypoglycemic diet based on four simple rules:

1. Avoid sugar and sugar-rich foods
2. Eat high-protein foods (fish, eggs, chicken, beef)
3. Snack every three hours on complex carbohydrate foods, including whole grains, fruits, legumes, green vegetables, and starchy vegetables, to help with the slow release of glucose
4. Eat plenty of green vegetables and fresh fruits
5. Take supplements such as vitamin B-complex, vitamin C, vitamin D, and probiotics.

Those who follow a hypoglycemic diet quickly normalize their blood sugar levels and stress hormones adrenaline and cortisol, which are responsible for mood swings, depression, anxiety, alcoholism, and other mental disorders that often lead to angry outbursts.

More and more scientists believe that what we eat contributes to how angry we feel, and numerous studies show that a diet high in trans fatty acids is directly linked to increased aggression.

Trans fats are unhealthy fats found in the foods we enjoy the most—French fries, fried and battered foods, pies, margarine sticks, shortening, frostings, pancakes and waffles, ice cream, ground beef, processed meats, cookies and cakes, biscuits, crackers, frozen dinners, and canned chili.

Giving up your favorite foods is not easy and is best done gradually over a couple of months, otherwise you may not be able to cope with the cravings. However, if you're struggling with an anger problem and know that nutrient deficiency is a major cause of your behavioral abnormalities, switching to a healthy eating plan will make a significant improvement.

The reason processed foods are so bad for your health is that they are nothing more than empty calories, which not only lack nutrition but also contain a lot of unhealthy color and taste additives. Only with a healthy diet will your body be able to produce the chemicals and hormones it needs for clear thinking, healthy mood, and balanced emotions.

In conclusion, you can keep your anger problem under control without therapy if you change your diet and stick to it.

Try a mood-stabilizing diet for a month, and see how your behavior changes and your mood improves. As Bethenny Frankel pointed out, "Your diet is a bank account. Good food choices are a good investment."

<u>Mood-stabilizing diet:</u>
1. Mood-boosting foods: fruits and vegetables—the less processed, the better
2. Plenty of dopamine-building foods: fish, poultry, eggs, and leafy greens
3. Omega-3 rich foods to fight depression: fish, flaxseed, chia seeds, walnuts
4. Magnesium-rich foods to support sleep and relaxation: almonds, spinach, pumpkin seeds, sunflower seeds
5. Vitamin D-rich foods to prevent mood disorders: fatty fish, egg yolks, liver
6. Limit sugar

Day 21

Putting It All Together

The idea behind writing this book was to showcase how you can transform your life by taking control of your thoughts. And when you control your thoughts, you can better control your emotions and your behavior.

In the stressful time we live in, our patience and tolerance are often challenged. Stress typically leads to more stress, and mental health problems are often the result of this vicious circle.

Negativity is a common side effect of chronic stress, as is poor anger management. And the reason people develop a negative mindset is often not because they have a negative attitude to life, but because they are overwhelmed by stress and anxiety.

So, how do you break this circle of stress-negativity-more stress-anger-more stress-more-negativity? By understanding where all this negativity is coming from, and by acknowledging that many times it is not stress, but your own self-limiting thoughts that make you see everything in a negative light.

Unfortunately, becoming positive doesn't happen overnight, nor can it happen on its own. That's something that has to be worked on, and that usually includes making some big, life-changing decisions.

Remap Your Mind

In a culture obsessed with youth, beauty, and fitness, one is constantly reminded of what they should look like. As a result, we have a trillion-dollar health and wellness industry which cashes in on the idea that there is no reason we should not all have perfect bodies, beautiful white teeth, and flawless skin.

However, while taking care of your body is important for your well-being, it doesn't mean you should neglect the part that often stays well-hidden, sometimes even from you—your mind. And just because your emotions and thoughts cannot be seen, while your teeth, body, and hair can, doesn't mean they are any less important.

In the overpopulated, fast, and competitive world of ours, it's easy to reach a stage where you become so overwhelmed with life that you can no longer keep track of all the changes taking place around you. Your brain can only take so much—when it can no longer manage the overload, it may respond by developing a mental health disorder.

If you can't manage your thoughts and feelings, you start living on auto-pilot: barely keeping your head above water, struggling to deal with the stress, fear, and anger that your life seems to be full of. Is it surprising that mental disorders are spreading like wildfire? Some studies even suggest that poverty is not the main reason for the rise in recorded crime, but the real reason is the increasing number of stressors that people are just not coping with.

So, when you hit a low point in life—or even better, before you do—why not do something to prevent the emotions of anger, frustration, and sadness from taking over your life? Take responsibility for what you are going through, but don't give in to defeat.

If you can afford it, go on a mental makeover retreat. If you can't, you can turn over a new leaf by giving yourself a mental makeover without leaving the comfort of your home. Just like you can revamp your body, you can remap your mind with a new approach to life.

Mental Makeover

Mental makeover techniques are about successfully overcoming challenges, taking control of your emotions, and staying healthy and happy. They revolve around high self-esteem and a positive attitude.

<u>10 tips on mental makeover:</u>

1. **Know yourself**
   When you know yourself, you understand what situations make you feel uncomfortable and you avoid them when you can, or you come up with ways to deal with them in an emotionally-intelligent way. There is no recipe for happiness and contentment—it's good to understand what makes you happy so you can do more of it.

2. **Take control of your emotions**

   For good mental health, it's very important not to hold grudges or keep emotions bottled up. While the best way to let go of unexpressed emotions is to talk about them, if there are issues you don't feel like discussing or if you have no one to talk to, you can choose a non-verbal way of communication—writing, journaling, painting, singing, or dancing. The trick is to learn to express your emotions in a way that's not offensive to others or harmful to you.

3. **Keep your brain in shape**

   The reason the mind deteriorates so quickly once people go into retirement is that it's no longer stimulated. While you work, you are constantly under some kind of stress and pressure, and although this can be bad for your health, it keeps your mind alert.

To prevent, or at least slow, mental deterioration, think of games or activities that would keep your brain occupied. If you lack company, get a pet. If you like reading, join a library. Go for lectures, do crosswords, play sports, join a club, learn a new language or skill. When you cultivate new interests, you open the door to new people and new experiences in your life.

4. **Learn to enjoy life**

   Why is this so hard? Some people feel uncomfortable, even guilty when they're enjoying themselves. Others don't know how to do it. Some feel it's a luxury they can't afford. Enjoying life is about finding pleasure in what you do, and it's not a luxury for it does not have to cost you anything.

   Depending on your financial situation, it could be something as extravagant as an exotic vacation or as simple as meeting a friend for coffee, planting some flowers in your garden, or taking part in a dog show. Learning to enjoy life is about finding a way to feel happy, regardless of what you do or where you are. Enjoying life is about being happy to be alive.

5. **Meditate**

   Meditation is a great way to still your mind and stop the inner chatter so you can "hear" the important stuff. Long-term daily meditation improves your health, and actually rewires your brain so you become calmer and better able to handle difficult situations. You also become more open-hearted and able to see things from others' points of view. In other words, you become more emotionally intelligent. It may sound like a cliché, but meditation does change people.

6. **Cultivate mindfulness**

   If you embrace mindfulness as a way of life, you choose to be fully aware of your thoughts and emotions. The reason mindfulness is so important for your mental health is that it makes you feel "centered" and helps you cope with whatever life throws at you. It also improves your physical health by relieving stress, and can even reduce chronic pain. When you live mindfully, you are fully present in whatever situation you may find yourself.

7. **Focus on what you want, not on what you don't want**

   One of the best ways to develop a positive mindset is to shift your mind from what you DON'T WANT and DON'T HAVE, and from what you CAN'T DO, to what you do want, have, and know. However, you have to approach this mindfully, because focus without intention gets you what you don't want.

8. Healthy diet

Food has a very real effect on our physical performance (by providing energy), mental activity (by providing mental clarity through vitamin- and antioxidant-rich foods), and emotions (by calming or alerting us, like chocolate, sugar, caffeine, tea). For long-term wellness, choose a diet that supports you on all levels of your being.

9. Boost your self-image

A true mental makeover is impossible if you struggle with low self-esteem. This is about how you think about yourself, what your appearance says about you, and how approachable you are. Without a positive self-image, you'll find it hard to get far in life. Perhaps the easiest way to improve your self-image is to think about yourself as you would like to be. As Napoleon Hill pointed out, "What the mind can conceive and believe, it can achieve."

10. Develop emotional intelligence

If your life is not too unbalanced, most of your mental blocks can be overcome by developing emotional intelligence skills, which you can learn from self-help books such as this one or from attending an emotional intelligence course. As an emotionally intelligent person, you will always be in touch with your inner world and rely on your self-awareness to guide you when making a decision.

Perhaps, the success of mental makeover depends on how much you believe in yourself. As Roy Bennett put it, "You are braver than you think, more talented than you know, and capable of more than you imagine."

Book #3
COGNITIVE BEHAVIORAL THERAPY MADE SIMPLE

The 21 Day Step by Step Guide to Overcoming Depression, Anxiety, Anger, and Negative Thoughts

Introduction

Do you ever feel like life seems to take extreme delight in brutally dealing with you as far as unfair outcomes? Do you struggle to sustain any sort of relationship in your life? Have you recently experienced an embarrassing emotional outburst that just seemingly happened for no particular reason? If you can relate to these scenarios, then you are not alone. Millions of people struggle with life daily and are unable to find healthy coping mechanisms. However, this book empowers and facilitates your journey to a brand new you that takes just 21 days!

Cognitive Behavioral Therapy made Simple: *The 21 Days Step by Step Guide to Overcoming Depression, Anxiety, Anger and Negative Thoughts* provides practical solutions for dealing with your emotions. As a result of each page, you will gain a deeper insight into who you are as an individual and why you probably act the way you do. This book will achieve the following goals:

- An in-depth analysis of anger, anxiety, depression, and negative thoughts
- The most effective methods used in cognitive behavioral therapy
- Simple steps you can implement daily to transform your life in just 21 days
- How to control your emotions and subsequently take control of your life
- How to be assertive without being aggressive in your relationships with others
- A practical guide for living your best life now

Many books that talk about cognitive behavioral therapy tend to be overly clinical in their approach and esoteric in their methods. In turn, these types of "medical jumbo jumbo" makes it extra difficult for the average person to clearly understand the concept, much less internalize the message enough to apply it to practical use in his or her everyday life. This book brings your common emotional problems to the forefront. It then breaks down the solution that is cognitive behavioral therapy, which essentially is all about putting you in better control of your emotions.

To ensure that you get the most from this book, there is a step by step guide included in the book for daily application. Those steps will get you from where you are now to exactly where you want to be in the future. There is no magic to it. All that is required is a little effort from you, and it starts by you simply flipping to the next page.

Ready to begin this exciting journey to a brand new you?

Dealing with Overwhelming Emotions

There are days when you wake up and you are super excited to take on the day. And then you have those occasions when you awaken, and you immediately regret it. It suddenly feels like the sun is too bright, the bed is too soft, the birds are chirping too loudly, and other people are just too happy. During those kinds of scenarios, the world feels unjust and cruel, and you would rather retreat to the confines of your duvet than face the world's injustices.

It may sound a tad too dramatic, but this experience is the reality for many people. If you are reading this book, perhaps you fall into this category. What you are experiencing is likely a myriad of emotions hitting you at the same time with such high intensity. It is like being struck by an airplane, except instead of having physical injuries, you get emotionally battered and overwhelmed. The world we live in today makes things even worse. The pressure to achieve so much in such a little time creates stress that is both toxic and damaging for your physical and mental health.

Nobody makes a deliberate decision to live his or her life in this manner. So, it is safe to say the people we surround ourselves with and the experiences we have had in life play a strong role in molding and shaping us into who we are and what we feel presently. Think of emotions as our psychological and mental defense mechanisms. When our bodies are infected with a virus, our biological defense mechanisms activate by creating antibodies to combat those viruses. In the same vein, when you have a negative experience, emotions stimulate to help you cope with the situation. If you are being attacked, you become afraid, thus fear triggers your survival instincts.

When you have been violated or unjustly hurt, for anger is stirred to help you stand up for yourself. But outside the regular natural response to life situations, if these emotions are activated frequently, they become a default setting: and when your default emotional setting comprises of negative emotions, your mind becomes a breeding ground for more negative emotions, which are even more dangerous than the initial emotion that generated the entire process in the first place. It is like a chain link. Fear begets paranoia which begets distrust that in turn begets anger, and it just keeps going. This chain of events takes you on a downward spiral that warrants external intervention to rectify.

When you get to that point where it seems like you are feeling everything, you are totally overwhelmed by emotions. Left on its own, you can quickly become extremely toxic. But don't despair, there is a solution. But before we get to that advice, let us look at some of these negative emotions and how much impact they have on our lives.

Anger

Anger is an emotion that has received a ton of negative press. In its regular state, it is an emotion that responds to situations where there is a perceived wrong. Sometimes, anger is in response to something done to you and in some cases, it is in response to something done to other people. The wrong in question doesn't have to be an actual physical thing. Words have a way of provoking anger. Perhaps your beliefs are being slighted and they can instigate anger in you.

People respond to anger in different ways. Because of the volatile nature of anger, some people opt to internalize their anger. This approach is a temporary measure, but the long-term effect could be just as devastating as a spontaneous outburst of anger. Anger, if left unattended and unaddressed, can simmer beneath the surface, thus masking its true intensity until a small and insignificant incident triggers a violent eruption of emotion. When you succumb to these violent compulsions, you end up hurting yourself and those around you.

When people are in the middle of these violent outbursts, they are caught in this haze that seems to rob them of control. It is like the flood gates of their emotions are broken, and everything just rushes in huge massive waves that sweep anything and anyone in their wake. In that chaos, the person who is angry is unable to distinguish between friend or foe, adult or child, and in extreme cases, the violent expression of anger could be physical. But just as quickly as this haze takes over a person, it dissipates within moments. In essence, it can leave a trail of hurt and guilt.

People who are at the receiving end of an anger haze are not the only ones who are hurt by it. Those who express anger bouts are also injured by their actions and they are ashamed of it. This shame triggers guilt. And guilt, in turn, triggers anger, which leaves you trapped in an anger cycle. Each time you experience an anger outburst, you hurt others and feel hurt by the fact that you did. As a result, you feel ashamed, which brings you right back to anger again in a vicious cycle.

That said volatile anger is not the only form of expression. Some people are passive aggressive, and some people prefer to completely shut everyone from their lives when they are angry; and then you have people who tend to do a combination of different forms of anger expression. Whatever category you fall into, there is a way to get better control of your anger.

The goal is not to stop being angry entirely. Not only is that impossible, but it is also unhealthy. Remember, anger is like any other emotion you experience, which means it has many benefits, too. What we are hoping to achieve at the end of the book is to get you to a point where you can express your anger in a healthy and positive way. Because yes, it is possible to be angry, get the message you want to pass across and still ensure that everyone, including you, has a positive experience from it.

Anxiety

Like anger, anxiety is one of those negative emotions that actually acts as a defense mechanism to protect us. It is a biological response to stress. The concept of stress was probably reintroduced into the society about a decade ago, but it is something that has always been present for as long as humans have existed. If you are making comparisons, the main difference between earlier eras and now is the source of stress. There are numerous stress triggers in the world we live in today, and because of the way the modern society is structured as well as the advancements we have made in the areas of technology, these stressors are right in our homes. This would probably explain why stress is one of the most common mental ailments in today's world.

Stressors could be anything from your job, your relationship, your money issues to the actual real threat of danger. Anxiety basically helps you cope in stressful situations, and it is not to be confused with fear, which activates your survival instincts in situations where you feel your person is threatened. It is okay to feel anxious about certain things. It keeps you alert and helps you prepare for whatever it is that is making you apprehensive. However, when these feelings of anxiousness seem to paralyze you and prevent you from engaging in your normal routine activities, you have veered into an anxiety disorder.

Anxiety is often rooted in fear, and it can start making its manifestation from early childhood. Another cause of anxiety is an experience. An ugly incident that traumatized you could cause your anxiety levels to go into overdrive. According to researchers, people who come from families where there is a prevalence of anxiety disorders have a high chance of developing an anxiety disorder themselves because of the genetic component. Whatever the source of your anxiety disorder, it can have a strong negative impact on your daily life experience.

Like anger discussed in the previous chapter, anxiety is not an emotion that you want to eradicate entirely. Lack of any anxious feelings could lead to an even more dangerous mental situation for you with strong physical implications. Without any form of anxiety, it is easy to become reckless and show complete disregard for life. Without anxiety, you would sign up to jump out of a plane in midair, without paying any attention to safety precautions.

The goal of this book is not to stop you from feeling anxious. The objective is to get you to that point where you openly confront those hidden fears, and in so doing, you are able to take back control instead of letting those fears control you. With each step that you take in this program, you actively change the narrative that is your life, from someone whose life and important life decisions has been shaped by their fears to someone who is deliberately taking off the limitations placed on their lives. This is where we [by we, I mean you and I] get to witness a brilliant transformation and the only thing scary about it is the potential you have to lead a great and adventurous life that is only dictated by you.

Depression

Everyone experiences depression at least once in his or her life. The expression of it varies from person to person, although there are classic symptoms and the circumstances surrounding the depression go a long way to determine the intensity and duration of it. Depression happens as a result of immense sadness. That is not to say that every time you feel sad, you are going to get depressed. Sadness is the base level and at this stage, what you experience is a natural reaction to an event that caused hurt or loss. It plays an active role in the healing process after a traumatic experience.

But when sadness lingers on for too long, the outcome is depression: and when one is in this state, life becomes one of existence rather than of living. Depression manifests in people differently. Some people are unable to perform even the basest task. They remain their beds, unable to eat, drink or even function. It cripples their lives so much so that there is a complete lack of interest in living. Their mental health is unstable at this point as they lose the will to live. If left unchecked and unattended, they might give into to the lure of suicide, believing that only death holds the answers.

For some others, their own experience is quite the opposite: they are able to carry on life with every sense of normalcy. In fact, you might even find them laughing, joking and entertaining the crowd as the life of the party. But underneath that happy façade lies extreme sadness and pain. They use their joviality to mask their true state of mind. It is only if you are very observant that you would catch glimpses of their depression. And even then, they "snap out" out of their emotional vulnerability and resume their theatrics until they just can't bear the weight of their depression anymore. Again, if left unchecked, the end could be just as disastrous as people in the first group. The only difference is that no one ever really sees their actions coming.

And then you have people who exhibit a bit of both. One moment they are extremely happy, and the next moment they are down with overwhelming sadness. Many sufferers of depression also experience heightened anxiety and mood swings interspersed with moments of angry outbursts. Besides the emotional effect, depression also leaves its mark physically. Sufferers are likely to experience headaches and back pain in addition to tiredness. They feel exhausted all the time, have trouble sleeping, thinking and even speaking.

Depression peaks when the sufferer starts contemplating suicide. At that point, it is important to seek help immediately. The transition from sadness to the point of suicide does not happen overnight. It is a process that accumulates slowly without even the sufferer's awareness. Like anxiety, it can be inherited, so look up your family's history of mental health. With better knowledge, you are better able to fight. In the upcoming chapters, you will learn what your stressors and how to control them in such a way that they do not end up negatively affecting your mental health and happiness.

Negative Thoughts

We all have inner dialogues with ourselves. Our thoughts and opinions about events, people and even ourselves are prominent topics for these internal discussions. When you observe yourself in the mirror, it doesn't just end there with the glimpses of yourself. Your mind stores that information and then processes it. After processing the information, your mind links events and things in general to this information. For instance, if your favorite jean takes a tad more forceful energy to wear, your mind relates it to the slight bulge you saw earlier in the mirror and tells you perhaps, you need to cut back on the sweet foods as you might have gained weight. At this level, your reasoning is perfectly rational and within the normal limits.

However, things start to take a different turn when your mind starts pointing out absurd events that have nothing to do with the image it saw, and the links are usually very negative. For instance, if you walk into a room that was buzzing with conversation prior to your entrance and your mind feeds you with thoughts linking the sudden hush to your weight gain, that is negative. Perhaps you experienced a loss or were passed over for a promotion, and you start thinking it is because you are too fat, your inner dialogue has taken a very negative turn. These examples are just trivial samples, but they articulate how negative thoughts work. The situations around you are processed internally and fed back to you in a way that completely demoralizes you.

Many people have been prompted to take actions that they normally wouldn't have taken by their consistent negative thoughts. Initially, you would reject the information you are being fed, but when you continuously meditate on those thoughts over time, you would start to believe them until they would almost become a reality for you. Harboring negative thoughts not only affects your mental psyche, but it can also destroy your relationships. This is because those negative thoughts affect your ability to objectively assess your relationships. Your reaction to those thoughts could vary. It could put you in a perpetual state of anger, which can spiral out of control. We already what uncontrollable anger can cause. It can also leave you depressed and unable to function at optimal levels.

In relationships where there is a complete absence of trust, the root cause is usually negative thoughts fed by events that have either been misconstrued or unresolved. It is mentally exhausting to stay focused on negative thoughts. It is like a dark cloud that blots out the sun leaving you unhappy and unable to take notice of the things that actually really matter. Such is the nature of negative thoughts. But as gloomy as this outlook is, it is very possible to retrain yourself to think in more positive terms. With consistent practice and deliberate effort, you can control how you process information and give yourself positive feedback. Cognitive behavioral therapy is key in this process and the next chapter explores how.

Cognitive Behavioral Therapy

Think of yourself as a slate that has so many words, images and texts scribbled over it in a way that makes it impossible to make sense of anything. You cannot tell where one text starts and where the other ends, but you are certain that they are all linked together in a way, but you just can't figure out how. If you were confronted with such a board, you would be saddened by its current state. It is not like a puzzle that you already have a clear picture of what the end product is meant to be. To make sense of this slate, you would have to get to the root word or foundational phrase. When you find that foundation, you may have to erase certain words and replace them with suitable alternatives; in sum, it is only as you piece each new word that you begin to see a semblance of normalcy. This process is what cognitive behavioral therapy encompasses.

When you find yourself acting, thinking and speaking in ways that you ought not to due to excessive anger, crippling anxiety, overwhelming depression and an upsurge of negative words, it would be impossible for life to make sense. This is because everything you do would be filtered through these emotions. It would seem as though everyone in the entire world is out to get you. Every step you take would seem to be steeped heavily in led. Little events spark up rage in you so volatile that it would seem you are carrying a little hurricane on the inside of you that is spinning everything out of control and destroying everything in its path. And it doesn't matter if it is raining outside or the sun is shining so bright, since you have your own personal thunderstorm complete with thick dark clouds and heavy showers that are programmed to flush out any happy thought or feeling. No wonder you feel the way you do. Your slate is completely messed up.

With Cognitive Behavioral Therapy (CBT), you start to understand why you feel the way you do. It is only in answering the question of why that you can determine how you can tip the scales in your favor. You did not wake up overnight and began to feel the way you do. Even if your condition is inherited, there are several behavioral patterns you have established over time that cause these conditions to set in. With Cognitive Behavioral Therapy, you can identify those behavioral patterns and offset their influence by deliberately replacing them with better behavioral practices that are more suitable. CBT is most effective in the mental conditions mentioned in the previous chapter. Although it has also been known to be used in the treatment of long terms ailments like irritable bowel syndrome which can be controlled by better eating behavior.

However, it is important to note that Cognitive Behavioral Therapy is not designed as a curative measure. Far from it. Instead, it helps you cope better with those conditions by effectively helping you take control over your emotions. For CBT to work, you will require the following in equal measure:

- Consistency
- Diligence
- Willingness
- Honesty

Within the context of this book, we are taking a slightly different route. Rather than sitting on a couch with a therapist, you would be going straight into the issues and taking proactive steps to resolve them. The goal is to help you establish new behaviors that you manage anger, anxiety, depression and negative thoughts. They say that it takes 21 days to develop a new habit. But that is not the reason we (you and I) are working with 21 days. I looked at these emotions discussed in this book and discovered that while our experiences differ, there are certain fundamental factors that can contribute to aggravating the situation. At the same time, there are specific behavioral elements that can be introduced to reverse the experience and bring you to a place where you are better able to cope with whatever is happening.

These daily exercises are very simple, but the effect is powerful. Some must be conducted repeatedly to have an effect. However, if done right, you can notice a significant difference from the first try. Others must be combined in specific scenarios for maximum impact, and I have carefully pointed those out as well. To get the desired results, it is important that you are deliberate in taking each action. It also helps to curate your experience post the action. This would help you put things in perspective and give you some insight into problematic areas. Remember the slate we used as an illustration at the beginning of this chapter. There is so much going on in your life right now, and none of it is probably making sense.

We (you and I) are using Cognitive Behavioral Therapy to retrace your steps, realign your behavior with the emotional results you are hoping to achieve and generally bring you to a place where you are emotionally balanced and content in who you are and the experiences you have in life. Because let's face it, life will always have those terrible and unfair incidents happen to us even though we are not quite deserving of those situations. But we don't have to let those incidences define us. When we root ourselves in our true identity, we will not be easily phased by what happens on the outside. There will be moments when you will slip. And that fall will discourage you from going forward. A momentary slip is not the end of the world. This is what makes you human. The part that makes you extraordinary is making the choice to get up from that fall, put the pieces that were broken apart and resolve to be stronger for it. You are made of more, and over the next 21 days, you will discover just how amazing you are!

Day 1

Get real with your emotions

One mistake that is a common practice among people who are battling with emotional issues, like the ones formerly discussed is the need to hide or bury their feelings. We are programmed to think that suppressing those feelings or denying them can somehow make those feelings fade away or disappear in time. Ironically, the opposite is what happens. When you choose to hide away what you feel, it simply stores away in the recesses of your mind. In that hidden corner, it continues to grow. And to facilitate its growth, it feeds off the other positive thoughts that occupy this section of your mind. There it will blossom and birth a not so docile version of the original emotion that started it in the first place. And at the next prompting, it will flare up and overcome your impulses causing you to react negatively.

This is why in some cases associated with anger, it would appear it is just a small incident that triggered the outburst. The fact is, that anger has been there for a while. It was slowly simmering beneath the surface giving you the illusion that by not responding to it the first time, you were able to squelch the feeling when the opposite was the case. And this applies to anxiety, depression and negative thoughts as well. The need to bury our emotions can be attributed to various factors such as our personalities or social upbringing. For instance, people who hate confrontation and act like people pleasers are more likely to not want to react in anger. If you have been angry in the past, whether it was your childhood or in your adult years and you were shamed for that display of emotion, the chances of you reacting in anger now or in the future are very slim.

This would also explain why many men secretly suffer from depression. You were told right from the time you were small that boys don't cry. So, even when you are hurt rather than respond to that hurt, you tend to bottle it up and stow it away. When I talked about depression, I specified that sadness is a very important part of the healing process. So, if you don't allow yourself to feel sad, you will most likely never fully recover from the pain. This goes on to sow a seed in your heart bears depression in full season. I could go on and give many illustrations on how we bottle our feelings and how the resultant effect could be the emotional instability that is being experienced now.

Hiding your feeling is a habit that needs to be broken immediately, and I can understand how this may not be something that you can deal with right away, but I didn't come here for halfway results. We (you and I) are going to do this now, and I will start by giving you a few facts to help you come to terms with the importance of this step.

1. Emotions are not gender sensitive.

Contrary to what you have been told, there are no emotions that are unique to gender. Being sad is not a feminine trait and neither is crying. If you have been hurt or are currently hurting, embrace the pain. Nobody likes to be sad. Not even the women whom you have been told are prone to sadness. But this is a part of human experience. The same goes for anger. Anger does not happen to you simply because you are of a particular gender. If your rights have been trampled on, anger alerts you to this. Sometimes, you may be right in that anger or maybe not. But this is not the stage to rationalize rights or wrongs. You are feeling it because you are human.

2. Emotions are not a display of weakness

I find it highly ironical that we are only able to discover our true strengths when we embrace our emotions. But this is the fact. Emotions don't just happen. They are activated, and those triggers alert you to things that are important to you. Surrendering to those emotions does not in any way diminish your capacity or potential for strength. Instead, it keeps you grounded in what you value, and it is when you are grounded that you can control your emotions. So, to learn to control your emotions, you have to learn to embrace them.

3. Emotions are unhealthy for you

There is no emotion that is unhealthy, and this feeling includes anger, anxiety, sadness, and even negative thoughts. It is your reaction to them that is classified as unhealthy. Anger helps you stand up for your wants and needs, sadness helps you cope with loss, anxiety alerts you to danger in your environment, and negative thoughts keep you from building castles in the sky. Denying these emotions would mean refuting these benefits and this what results in the problems you experience.

Now that you have a better understanding of the importance of emotions, you are now in a better position to embrace your real emotions. However, this is not license for you to go berserk. This chapter is not a do-all-you-want-to-do ticket. It is meant to help stay in touch with your emotions and controlling how you respond to them at the same time. Here is what you should do:

1. Find a physical release.

Mental rationalization is not always the best way to get real with your emotions. Sometimes, you need to do something physical to release it. Things like doing a workout, yelling into a pillow or even smashing something (be careful with this last bit) can help relieve you, especially when what you are feeling is very intense. This is why crying is very recommended. People say cliché things like crying doesn't help, but that is because they don't know better. It really helps.

2. Correctly identify your feeling at the moment

When you are in the heat of the moment, think about what it is you are really feeling. You may be looking at the person who possibly triggered your anger and thinking you hate the person, but in reality, what you are feeling isn't hate. You feel angry.

3. Direct your feelings appropriately

Perhaps you just broke up with someone, and you are in that phase where you think all men are scum or all women are horrible? Going with this attitude can breed anger, anxiety and subsequently depression. The right thing to do is focus on your partner who hurt you and feel what you feel towards him or her. Use this same strategy in all your dealings.

Getting real with your emotions can be a scary prospect, but when you get right down to it, you will save yourself a ton of pain and emotional turmoil in the long run.

Day 2

Put your feelings to words

When I was younger, I remember getting into squabbles with my siblings over the stupidest things and my mother would always intervene. I recall remaining angry and stone-faced right up to the point where she would ask us what happened. Then as if on cue, my voice would crack with emotion, and the tear gate would open. I would be babbling incoherently as I try to recount the event the way I recollect it happening. This happened whether I was the victim or not. Even as an adult, I have experienced this as well. Although I rarely ever get into altercations as much as I used to when I was younger, I have always noticed that whenever I was in a heightened emotional state and reacting to it, if I was asked to narrate the events that led up to that outburst, I always wind up extremely emotional. I am extremely certain that if you look at your history, this might be the case for you as well.

As a matter of fact, I never honestly realize the true extent of my emotions right up to that point where I have to explain it. This is the power of articulating your emotions. Now that you have taken the brave step to be real with how you feel, this next step is to help you explore the depth of those feelings. You don't have to do this in the presence of people if you don't want anyone to witness your emotional moment. This is not about anyone anyway. The objective is to try and discover how deep those feelings go. Sometimes, by articulating your feelings, you are given a perspective of the situation that allows you to see things objectively. You may be surprised by the conclusions this new objective offers.

For starters, in articulating your feelings, you might get to filter through your emotions and find out what is really putting the bee in your bonnet so to speak. In the heat of your emotions, it is difficult to see beyond what you feel but expressing them forces you to do so. Another surprising conclusion that you may come to is the fact that you may be making a mountain out of a molehill. That is not to say your feelings are trivial an don't deserve to be taken seriously. But in situations where emotions and tensions are running high, the slightest thing can trigger an unpleasant reaction. So, if you keep focusing on your reaction to this small incident, you will probably keep dancing around the issue without getting real solutions to the main problem.

This may feel contrary to the importance of staying with the moment, but I promise you that it isn't. If anything else, it is actually aligned with this sound advice. By articulating your feelings, you are able to stay in the moment because you are talking about what you are feeling right now. But it doesn't end there. This process helps you explore where those feelings are coming from, and I cannot emphasize how crucial this is for emotional growth and mental stability. So, now that we have established what this is about as well as its importance, how does one go about expressing one's feelings?

I can understand that this is not something that comes easily to most people. Already, you are at a place where it feels like you are experiencing a kaleidoscope of emotions and being asked to express them might require you to go deeper into those emotions which can be painful. However, you are going to have to apply the same courage, too, to embrace your real feelings to tick this off your 21-day list as well and when it comes down to it, you will find that it is much easier than you think, especially since you have faced down your true feelings.

So, to carry out this task successfully, you will need a journal. You could try using your phone or any other technology that is available. However, when using technology, resist the temptation to use emojis and emoticons to describe your feelings. Having those characters may look cute on your journal and perhaps cut back the time it would take you to articulately write out your thoughts in half, yet it also reduces the benefits you would have enjoyed by going through the process the prescribed way. A trick that worked for me was having two journals: one for chronicling my emotions in the heat of the moment and the other for when I wanted to reflect on how I felt about my emotional onslaught earlier.

Next, you would need to find a quiet time to do your emotional journaling. It could be at any time of the day. Just choose a moment when you can gather your thoughts. The location may not really matter much as long as you are able to sit quietly without anyone or anything disrupting your process for at least 15 minutes. If like me you decide to go the double journal route, you would save the quiet time for reflecting on your thoughts. When trying to journal in the heat of things, you would still need to take yourself outside of the situation and find a space for yourself. Don't hold back when you are writing. Your emotions at the moment may seem ugly, and you instinctively want to deny them, but we talked about the dangers of doing so in the last chapter. Embrace what you feel and write out your feelings in plain but honest terms.

Now, you don't have to be a poet to release your feelings. Although, if you happen to find yourself waxing lyrical as you jot down your feelings, that's fine too. We are not looking for perfection or the next book that would win the Pulitzer Prize. All you have to do is be honest with how you are feeling. If at the end of the day the words barely covered a quarter of a page or maybe you wound up doing three pages, it is fine. What matters is that the words there reflect the true state of your mind. Plus, I suspect that if you keep at this consistently (that is, writing out your feelings), the words would come to you much easier. Each entry would become more voluminous than the last.

The final stage in this process is reading what you have written. To do this, you have to step down from the throne of judgement as we have a tendency to judge ourselves too harshly. At the same time, you would have to take off any rose-tinted glasses you might be wearing. Honesty is a necessity if these steps are going to work for you. Objectivity is another requirement. You may be confronted with feelings of shame, guilt, and disgust as you read what you are feeling especially when reading the journal written in the heat of the moment. Let those feelings wash over you, but don't let them guide your actions going forward. And if you find yourself being overwhelmed by those feelings, it is time to take the next step.

Day 3

Talk to Someone

Our human need to interact with other humans often compels us to skip the first two steps and going straight for this stage. If you are lucky enough to have understanding friends who try their best to get where you are coming from and provide actionable solutions. In the very least, they would give you words that comfort and console you. The problem with this is that this only provides a very temporary reprieve from the emotional turmoil you are going through. And most importantly, there is a very high possibility that the conversation you had with them is one-sided and not honest. This is through no fault of yours.

Without taking the first two steps we recommended, you may not even be fully aware of what you truly feel. Your conversations about your feelings would skim the surface of your emotions without exploring it in its entire depth. And without getting to the root of the problem, your friend or whoever you confide in about these things may not be capable of proffering a solution that has lasting results. That is, unless you are speaking to a professional therapist who would help you sieve through the tangle of emotions to get to the root of what you are going through and even then, you will have to do the two things we mentioned earlier. The only difference is that your therapist would be guiding you through it.

You can only get the full benefits of having this talk with someone when you have come to terms with what you feel. Now, the purpose of this step is to get an external opinion on your emotional state. Again, this is not about judgement or seeking validation for what you feel. This is about helping you get past those dangerous emotions to a place where you can experience the true pleasures and joys of life. So, bearing this in mind, it is equally important that you are very selective about who you approach for this phase. The fact that they have been your closest friends for years or share blood with you does not automatically qualify them to take this important seat.

There are prerequisite qualities they must possess; and while I appreciate your desperation in seeking out someone to talk to, I have to emphasize that talking to just about anyone might prove to be more detrimental to your already fragile emotional state. Remember, we started out this journey to put a stopper on these emotions that appear to be taking over your life. Seeking out someone who is only capable of putting a Band-Aid on a bullet wound would lull you into a state of false security, thus leaving you to fall deeper into that emotional wormhole. So, to avoid this pitfall, be diligent in appraising the person you seek.

For starters, this person has to be someone you respect and who respects you in return. It is important to establish this from the onset because you are going to a place where you are going to be completely vulnerable to them. In your bare state, a person who has no respect for you would only be capable of seeing the flaws and not the potential for what you could become. And a person who can only see the flaws in you cannot in anyway proffer the answers you seek or even the companionship you need because he or she would only amplify the problem.

The person you go to has to be able to show emotional empathy. It is even better if you are aware that he or she been through a similar situation and have been able to come out of it. Emotional empathy helps them connect with where you are coming from without judgement. The absence of this would result in a talk down filled with criticisms and this is one of the last things you need. That is not to say the person dishing out those criticisms does so out of malice or hate. He or she just doesn't get your perspective.

Another quality the person you are turning must possess is honesty. We often trust people who we know to love us with issues like these, but it is very possible that the love that they feel for you hinders them or blinds them from being honest with you. In fact, their reaction when hearing what you are going through might be to bundle you up, wrap you in the fluffiest cotton clouds and then put you in a pain-free bubble where you no longer have to go through the things that you are going through again. These are good intentions but they do nothing to help promote your mental well-being.

Instead, you want someone who would face down those demons and be candid in his or her assessment. Be careful with people who are too honest though. And by being too honest, I mean people who blurt out the first thing that comes to one's head without thinking of the effect it may have on you. Honesty from a place of emotional empathy is what you need.

Finally, this person has to be someone who on some instinctual level you can sense that he or she has your best interest at heart. You have to have had some sort of relationship with him or her in order to establish this fact. And this relationship has to be based on trust. It may seem like you are asking for a lot when looking for all of these qualities in one person but bear in mind that your emotional well-being is at stake. Plus, if you pay close attention, that person may be closer than you think.

Perhaps a counsellor in your local church group, a close friend you may have known for years or even an older relative whom you are tightly bonded? In some cases, this person may be someone who you have a passing acquaintance-ship with. Just keep an open mind and if you feel there is no one who matches any of the criteria, go ahead and schedule a session with a therapist. He or she also in a good position to help you make sense of what you are feeling, and you can always expect a practical solution.

Day 4
Feel the music

I mean this bit quite literally. Music has an immense therapeutic effect on your mental health and not a lot of people understand this power. Before we go into how music helps you feel better, let us take a trip down history lane because contrary to what you think, music therapy is not a nouveau hippy concept that just sprang up. Its use and prevalence can be found in Greek mythology and even in elements of ancient Egyptology. The Greek god of the sun allegedly used music as a conduit for healing. Thus, it was widely believed that for one to possess health and healing, there must be a corresponding harmony in the music and what happens when the strings of Apollo's symbol, the lyre is in tune. Similarly, in ancient Egyptian culture, Asclepius, believed to be the son of Apollo, apparently cures mental ailments with music.

Leaving the realm of mythical gods and their powers, let us see the presence of music therapy in our culture. Native Americans believe that for all-round health, there has to be a balance of harmony between mind and body. When a member of the tribe falls ill, it is believed that this balance is out of order. To facilitate healing, the native shaman or healer would use a combination of herbs, potions and music. The music used is usually a blend of a song, dance and chance routine involving musical instruments and this music is often said to be inspired by visions and dreams. This takes us to one of the most depressing times in the history of humanity; the first and second world wars. Beyond the physical ravages of war, these battles took a strong emotional toll on the soldiers and understandably so. It was recorded that apart from the medical personnel assigned to treat ailing soldiers, musicians volunteered their services in hospitals. They went to perform their craft for the wounded, and it was observed that patients showed a positive response to these performances.

You are not deep in the trenches fighting with guns against an enemy seeking to destroy you as well, but the battles that you fight within can take the same emotional toll on you. And the casualty of this internal battle may not be on the same scale as a worldwide war, but you have just as much to lose. In essence, there is too much at stake to not take cognizance of any solution that is being proffered. Modern day music therapy has advanced beyond a song and dance routine. With the studies that have been conducted on the subject, the practice is much more deliberate and accurate in its delivery. But before talking about how music therapy works and how you can bring this into play in your situation, let us look at what the benefits of music therapy really entail.

For starters, it helps you redirect your focus from the emotional turmoil you are experiencing. When you listen to music, you become enthralled by the harmony of the sounds and this sensory experience transports you to another world where your current feelings or mood are shifted out of focus. This can immediately or gradually prompt you to change your mood. With the right kind of music, you are able to gain mastery over those negative emotions because right after distracting you from your pain, you are lulled into a relaxed state of mind. It is from this place that you can then start letting in the positive emotions enter. You can motivate yourself in areas where you previously felt you were unable to cope. And it is from this place that you can start feeding yourself with positive images that will counteract the negative images that you previously had.

Apart from psychological benefits, music therapy also has a good impact on your physical health. When you are stressed and experiencing anxiety at peak levels or perhaps you are in that anger haze we talked about, your blood pressure rises up as well. And when your blood pressure rises, your breathing is impacted as well. Listening to music can lower your blood pressure and help you regulate your breathing. And these are just on the surface. Including music therapy as part of your routine will go a long way in improving your mental health.

Music therapy is an aspect of cognitive behavioral therapy in that it helps you replace those negative behavioral patterns that have led you down the path to where you are now. By replacing those negative behaviors or thought processes, you can pull yourself out of the proverbial rabbit hole. Now, this measure is a step you are taking today, but like everything else I have included on this list, it requires repeated practice to obtain maximum results.

However, do not be quick to rush to your playlist just to listen to your favorite brand of music. We all respond to music differently and while certain genres of music may resonate deeply with you, the psychological effect may the opposite of what you are hoping to achieve. For instance, if you want to relax when you feel angry or anxious, listening to rock music is certainly not going to help you achieve that as it amplifies your feelings of anger and raises your discomfort levels. The same thing happens when you are in pain. Classical music on the other hand is known to have a soothing effect on the mind. If you listen to songs typically used in meditations, you hear a combination of soft musical elements like wind chimes, flutes and the likes.

But that is not to say that your options are limited to classical music and meditation chants. Certain audio books could also be helpful as could your favorite artists if their lyrics do not invite you. When you listen to music, observe how you react. This may clue you in regarding what kinds of music would work best for you. If your pain levels, anxiety and anger decrease, you are listening to the right stuff.

Day 5
Take things outside

One of the classic behavioral patterns that help nurture and groom an environment that dysfunctional thinking thrives in is the act of seclusion. Hiding yourself away from people and the world in general makes you more prone to thinking negative thoughts and basically living inside your head. You may tell yourself that, hey, you go out. You go to work, you drop the kids off at school, and you even do the grocery shopping in person. But, if you are honest with yourself, those actions do not necessarily count as "going out."

Many people like to use the excuse that they are introverts and feel more comfortable in their own space and so on. This is just that...an excuse. It is very possible to be an extrovert who attends every neighborhood party and has tons of friends who still engages in behaviors that are not healthy and part of the recommendation for changing those unhealthy behaviors would be to go out. "Going out" in this context is more than just routine practices or your interactions with people. What I mean here is taking yourself outside your comfort zone.

I can almost hear the crickets doing their thing in your mind after I made that last statement and I was totally expecting your reaction because it is perfectly natural. When we are confronted with highly emotional situations like these, it is instinctive to want to stick to the familiar for comfort. But there is a need to balance this experience of comfort with new experiences that would feed you thought process. Anger, anxiety, depression and negative thoughts are emotions that feed off your experiences, especially past experiences. They hold you back from enjoying your life in its full form. And when you are in this state, you are deprived of life's wonderful adventures leaving you to recoil back to those old experiences that feed the negativity...Do you see the pattern established here?

It is a repeating cycle that does nothing for your well-being. And since we are all about replacing old habits with new ones, you can see the need for going outside of your comfort zone. The prospect of going out into the world on your own can be scary and daunting. But if you continue to think of the world as this big place of unknowns, it will remain scary and I don't see you going outside with your mind in that state. Also, this is not saying that you should suddenly go from 0 to 100 just to get a new experience as that could backfire in terrible ways. Let us say you have a fear of spiders. Yet skipping all the steps to facing your fears and just heading straight to a museum of arachnids is insane and unadvisable.

Going outside here refers to doing things that are more in line with your interests. Say you have an interest in arts, attend an art exhibition. You can take things a step further by attending an art event that promotes a social change. Seeing people take this thing that you are interested in and use it to provoke positive change might just be the encouragement and inspiration you need to get out of your head. If your life revolves around work, take yourself outside the work environment. As a matter of fact, activities that are related to work should be avoided in this time frame that you have allotted to enjoying these new experiences.

It does not have to be anything grand. Skydiving is aspirational but let us keep our feet grounded for this one. Go out for a quiet stroll through the neighborhood. Stop and smell the flowers (literally and figuratively), observe the changing colors in your neighborhood. Catch a sunrise and watch a sunset, take a hike along the beach, go to your favorite restaurant and order something you have never eaten before. Stop and watch street performers do their thing, volunteer with an NGO, etc. This is what "going out" means. If you have the mind to make new friends, go ahead but that is not a prerequisite to this process.

This process is simply about doing new things. And if you find certain new activities more appealing, go ahead and repeat them. Look for things that bring joy to you, no matter how small. Things that make you feel relaxed without experiencing any of the feelings that brought you to this point in the first place should be encouraged. Apply caution with certain activities though. For instance, if the source of the negative emotions you experience is linked to your body weight, going all out on food splurge might have you feeling guilty in the end. And we all know how the guilt cycle manifests. Embrace your love for food but be conscious of the effect unhealthy eating behaviors would have on your weight and health in general. And then in keeping with the theme of taking things outside, look for a nutritional program that allows you to eat the things you want but in a healthier way.

Have a reward day where you treat yourself to a dainty dish that is tasty but still within the limits of what is considered healthy. It is a delicate balance but when you get right down to it, it is all about ceasing each moment and enjoying it. This gives you more positive things to think about. Bear in mind that some of these experiences may not turn out to be completely positive and this is okay. When that happens and you find yourself sinking back to that dark place, begin at step one and get right back to this point where you are ready to try out something new. Remember, new experiences create new thoughts!

Day 6
Get Physical

Exercises have tremendous health benefits and one of those benefits is a significant boost to your mental well-being. You may have heard incessantly because it is true. These benefits are experienced regardless of your age. The impact of exercises is particularly helpful for people who are suffering from anxiety, anger, depression and negative thoughts. And the best thing about this advice is that you don't have to suddenly become a fitness buff to reap the benefits. You don't have to sign up for a gym or get kitted up head to toe in sports gear for that matter. In essence, simple adjustments to the way you do certain physical activities are adequate to make an impact.

Exercises are not about running a 5k, doing a hundred bench presses in one sitting or doing some kind of impressive physical feat. Although, if you can do these things, that is good for you. It goes deeper than that. A short five-minute workout session can provide you with instant benefits. In fact, it has been proven that mild to moderate forms of depression can be treated with exercises. The effectiveness of these exercises on this form of depression is akin to taking anti-depressant medication and the best part about it is that you do not get the side effects associated with the medications. When it comes to anger and anxiety, I feel like this is a no brainer as exercise provides an outlet for those emotions. You hear people say things like they are going to let off some steam. This is exactly what exercises do for emotions like these.

With each movement of your body, you are releasing the internal tension you feel: and by the time you are done, the worst of the storm has passed. This correlation is because when you exercise, the body releases endorphins in your brain. Endorphins are also known as the happy hormones. They help cause you to relax and improve your mood. Also, let us not forget the mind-body connection that was discussed when we talked about music therapy. Exercise puts your body in alignment with your mind, hence causing you to focus. The combination of all these benefits results in an overall healthy state of mind.

After hearing all the great things that exercise ca do I can see how you want to rush to the nearest gym. However, if you have not engaged in physical exercise for a while, you might want to start off really slow. This would give your body some time to adjust to the process. You might experience muscle aches and body pain after the first try. Take baby steps and let your body guide you.

Day 7

Give Yourself Permission to Heal

In my experience, no matter how selfish we are in our actions or even in our dealings with others, we are most critical when it comes to dealing with ourselves. Even people who have a tendency to pass the blame to anyone but themselves still find that they are trapped in a cycle of self-loathing. And if left unchecked, that self-loathing quickly grows into dark emotions that paralyzes them and binds them to living a life that can only be described as hellish. This is even worse for people who tend to be people pleasers. Because their confidence is attached to their ability to ensure that everyone around them is happy, every failure becomes a red marker in their psychological ledger and continues until their emotional scars are torn, which causes tremendous psychological pain. And this pain leads us to where we are today.

One of the many truth nuggets throughout this book is that it is impossible to please everyone. Even *you cannot please you* 100% of the time. Accepting this truth is vital to helping you with the subject matter of this chapter. You should also note that failure to please someone does not diminish your value or sense of worth. Now that we have laid the foundation for this chapter, let us go in depth into what you need to do today.

I have no idea what pain you have lived through today. I don't know of the emotional battles and the psychological war that rages within you. I have had my fair share of pain: and while you may be able to empathize with my pain and vice versa, it is safe to say that our scars are different. Pain is a part of human existence. At some point, you will be hurt, you will lose someone you care deeply about and you will feel acute pain that has nothing to do with your physical person. But along with that pain accompanies the prospect of healing. It is life's way of keeping the balance.

When you scar physically, almost immediately, the healing process is activated. You may still feel the pain over a few hours, days or weeks depending on the extent of the injury. But it does not negate the fact that healing is happening somewhere underneath it all. However, there are certain things that could slow down or completely halt the healing process. If the wound is not cleaned and treated properly, it could become infected and worsen the state of the wound. In some instances, you would need to cover the wound to protect it from outside elements that might contaminate the wound and trigger an infection. For injuries that are very complicated, you may have to seek out professional medical options to facilitate healing. All of these processes apply with psychological injuries, too.

When you suffer psychological trauma, the shockwave of pain and other elemental emotions such as fear, anger and sadness alert you to this. These primary emotions could be experienced for hours, days or weeks and like the physical injuries we discussed, the timespan would depend on the extent of the trauma. Plenty of us have a tendency to get frustrated at this point and who can blame you? Emotions like these force you to relive the moments leading up to and during the trauma and each replay is worse than the actual event that occurred. If you are in this phase, it is time to cut back on any activity or thought process that you engage in that feeds the habit of blocking out your feeling. Think of it as cleaning the wound so to speak. When you want to clean and disinfect a physical injury, the chances are it will hurt. But if you skip that process because you want to avoid the hurt, you leave an open door for infections and we all know how that would end.

Accept that pain is necessary for healing. Accept that you are not going to get back to feeling "normal" overnight. Accept that what has happened while utterly tragic and unfair has happened and you cannot change that. Now when you have opened yourself to this, there are things you shouldn't do to ensure that these acceptances keep the door open for healing. It is tempting to want to skip to the future where your pain becomes completely numb or a dull throb at the very least. Don't. At least not today. Focus on the right now. Look at the progress you have made in the last few days. Acknowledge the successes you have achieved.

This helps to affirm the fact that you are in control of these emotions and not the other way around. Things may have happened to you, but now you have chosen to happen to things. If you are confronted with images, words or events that remind you of the trauma you have just lived through and your emotional experience takes you to ground zero where it feels like you are reliving everything all over again, resist the urge to question your progress. It is like poking the area around the wound every 5 minutes and wondering why you still feel the pain. You need time to heal and you need to give yourself permission to do just that.

Everyone has his or her own healing pace, regardless of the extent of the trauma. What is important for you to do is to put aside your expectations of your healing timeline and focus on the progress you are making. It can get pretty frustrating because sometimes it is hard to see how far we have come; but in truth, each step you take on this journey takes you farther away from the darkness that threatens within. You just have to remind yourself that the person you are today is better than the person you were yesterday.

For deep and painful wounds, healing begins on the inside in places we cannot see but as time progresses, you begin to notice the difference on the surface. The same philosophy applies here. Be patient and stay true to the process.

Day 8
Start Daydreaming Again

Remember those days long before the darkness took over your mind and your life…time when you would sit back and dream of an alternate life featuring a better you and all of those elements in life that you cannot exactly pinpoint? But somehow, they just complete you. Recall how you would dwell on those dreams and have a silly grin on your face? Those were the good old days yeah? Those dreams have become something relegated to the back of your mind or the bottom of your to-do list by adulthood and life's treacherous experiences. They may seem like relics from a past that you no longer wish to acknowledge. Perhaps, they symbolize your failures or remind you of how silly you once were?

But believe it or not, that silliness is exactly what you need now. Part of the root cause of the emotional trauma you are experiencing is the fact that you have chosen to put your focus on the unpleasant experiences you have had. Some of us give the excuse of "being real." Under the guise of being realistic, we deprive ourselves of the simple pleasures of daydreams and choose instead to align our thoughts with constant reminders of the darkness from our traumas. This behavior traps us in an endless cycle of gloom and depression.

When you talk about daydreams, people think of escapism. A dodgy way to disconnect yourself from the responsibilities of the present and immerse yourself in a world that does not exist. And we cannot dismiss these worries. Many people have been led down the wrong path with their daydreams and fantasy so you would be right to apply caution. However, most creatives, inventors and innovators harness the power of daydreams to renew their sense of purpose, motivate themselves and develop new solutions. You may not be in any of these three categories, but we are going to use the techniques these pioneers used to get to the next stage in this process.

For creators and innovators, using visualizations and daydreams provides a roadmap to where they want to go or what they hope to achieve by setting an aspirational tone. For instance, a novelist would visualize her book's characters in detail. These particulars are usually so vivid that at the end of it, this completely fictional character has a birthday, personality quirks and whole other attributes that when she talks about them in her book, so it becomes almost difficult to determine if those characters never existed in the first place. Today, you are going to do the same thing. Of course, there will a few differences when you look at how the novelist goes about writing her stories, but the objective will be the same.

Instead of thinking of it as indulging in fantasies, approach it instead as you are re-writing your story. Go to that moment hurt or traumatizes you the most. It is a painful journey to take, but it is a necessary one. Now when you get to that moment, in place of replaying the victim role, be more assertive. This is your imagination at work, you are in complete control. So, take back the power that was taken away from you. This does not alter the physical reality of what has happened but the impact of this process on your psyche is tremendously beneficial. And these benefits can extend into the physical aspects of your life. If you are looking for more reasons to start daydreaming today, here are a few:

1. Psychologists believe that these do-over daydreams as they are often called have the power to provide both relief and release when you are actively trying to resolve issues of anger, guilt and frustration over a traumatic emotional experience. Essentially, they help you let off steam.

2. Daydreaming is a form of self-hypnosis albeit in a very minute capacity. If channeled correctly, you can use it to change your perception about certain scenarios. In fact, it is so powerful that you can integrate it to alter behavioral patterns that you feel or are very certain has an adverse effect on your mental health. For a program that seeks to help you transform your life in just 21 days, this is very important.

3. Indulging in daydreams can make you happier as a person. This approach is because, through the alternate reality you have created, you are able to envision what you want and if those dreams are rooted in positive seeds, you inspire yourself with renewed hope. Over time, this hope would nurture an enthusiasm for life that will eventually pull you from any depression.

These benefits are culled specifically for you but there is so much more to daydreaming than what I have listed here. If revisiting the event that traumatized you feels overwhelming, you could try focusing on the kind of future you would want for yourself. For instance, you might try picturing scenarios that got you upset and angry. Say an altercation with a colleague at work. Now, try as much as possible not to play out a revenge scenario where you empower yourself with this superhuman strength that enables you physically defend yourself, halt the offending colleague in his or her tracks and at the same time impress the rest of your co-workers.

This kind of fantasy might leave you feeling temporarily good, but it does nothing to correct the kind of behaviors that get you into trouble in the first place. The focus of the daydream should be on a specific behavior. Let's say you have a tendency to lay back when you are being attacked. Perhaps you have talked yourself into believing that this behavior helps keep the peace? On the surface, what this does is ensure that that you avoid getting into altercations or situations that make you displease people further. This would leave you with unresolved feelings of anger, shame and if unchecked, depression.

The ideal daydream for this would be a scenario where you speak up for yourself. At first, you would get a rush of relief from this and then with consistent practice, you will get to the point where you are emboldened enough to speak out in real life scenarios. And that dear reader, is the point of the process to get you to take a more active role in the transformation of your life. Your imagination and thoughts have played a major in contributing to your emotional turmoil. Today, you are taking over the reins, redirecting your thoughts to a more positive path and wielding the power of thoughts in the transformation of your life. I am getting excited just thinking about the great things you can achieve from here.

Day 9
Create a Gratitude List

This bit is pretty straight-forward, but the impact on our lives is tremendous. You see, the foundation of the negative thoughts that stir us in the wrong direction emotionally is our focus on things that we feel we should have, but we do not. These things are not always material. It could be the love and full attention of a partner, the ideal job that doesn't take too much from you pays you oodles of money and plenty of vacation time and the list goes on. Sometimes, it could be something as simple as hearing the person who hurt you so bad offering a genuine heartfelt apology.

We focus so much on these things we want to have that despite the things we do have, we are rendered impotent and incapable of moving on because we have associated our sense of worth with what we do not have. Without that job, you cannot be a competent provider for your family, without that apology you cannot move on with your life, without the attention of your spouse, you feel unloved and unwanted. So, we justify our negative emotional state with the absence of these things that we crave. I know that you cannot see this now but as long as you are alive, you are standing on the precipice of great and wonderful possibilities every day that you are awake.

Happiness is at your door. All you have to do is open that door. However, when you continue to dwell on the have-nots and value yourself accordingly, you close yourself off to whatever chances you may have at happiness. If you are the spiritual sort, your prayers become an endless loop of requests for those things that you desire and when you do not have them, you become disappointed. And when this happens on a daily basis, you have just bought yourself a one-way ticket to Depression-Ville.

If you have taken every step of this journey so far, you will discover a common pattern. A truth that is obvious but not many see. The fact that the power to change all of this is in you. You hold the key. It is not the job that you seek that is going to change your life. The money that it pays would provide some amazing experiences and perhaps make life a little easier to handle, but I can guarantee that even if you are offered this job in the next three seconds, your happiness will not last beyond the first paycheck. And this is because the job is just a quick fix, like a Band-Aid for a surgical wound. The genuine source of happiness that can take you through life is in you and thankfully, this is something that you already have.

I can almost hear the gears shifting in your head. "Me?", you probably wonder. Well the answer is an emphatic yes. Your happiness is in you. Again, let us not distract ourselves with the have-nots. But I have a pot belly, I am overweight, if only I were thinner etcetera. Those are irrelevant. I have been privileged to know amazing people who were rendered completely incapacitated by debilitating physical ailments and yet, even in their paralytic state, they were able to find joy and happiness. Their joy was so contagious that the moment you came into their presence; you cannot help but be infected by it. So, whatever it is you are going to say is just an excuse. And you have got to stop making excuses. You are more than that!

Instead of focusing on the have-nots, try to be more conscious of what you do have. I can understand and even empathize with the tragedies you have had to survive in your life, but we are past those hardships now. They have happened or may be happening, but so is the good stuff. There are many good things going on in your life every day if you know where to look. One thing that helps points us in the right direction is the gratitude list. As I mentioned earlier, this is pretty straight-forward. It is simply a list of things that you are grateful for each day.

Items on your gratitude list do not have to be grand. And it doesn't have to be mundane, either. It should be things that you are genuinely grateful for. You don't have to look too far for these things. I have this yellow flower pot in my garden. I have a mix of flowers in them and when they are in bloom, it just lights up the entire space. Even when the flowers are not in bloom, this quirky pot makes a striking feature that just lifts my spirits when I see it. This pot always makes it on my gratitude list. My garden and the moments I spend there would definitely be duller without it. Another thing that makes my list if I see it is a sunrise. It doesn't matter if it is a spectacular Instagram worthy type of sunrise or just this bright light gradually peeking from the skies, I am always moved when I witness one. It is like seeing the birth of the day.

These are just a few samples of what makes it to my list. Of course, it is much more extensive than that. But whether it is a smile from a stranger, a pat on the back or the fact that you were able to complete a task, as long as you derived some sort of joy from it no matter how small, it should make its way to your gratitude list. No matter how grim your situation is, look for those little rays of lights and record them. Before you begin your list, you need to get the right type of journal. It doesn't have to be grand and fancy, but it should be visually stimulating enough to get you excited about filling its pages with the things you are feeling grateful for. You can take a bland journal and personalize it. The more personal the journal feels to you, the higher the chances are that you will use it frequently.

When you have purchased the journal, set aside a specific time of the day to make your journal entry, make a ritual of it if you will. I like to do it towards the end of the day by the pool while I enjoy my cigar [it is an expensive habit, but it is one of my very few indulgences). Pick a time when you feel more relaxed and less distracted. Turn off your phone, have a favorite dessert nearby, put on some music. Basically, anything that puts you in a good place. Then you make your entry. Don't panic if you can't fill a page on your first entry. It might take a while to get into the habit, but keep at it. Consistency is key. And before you talk yourself out of doing anything, hang in there and really look deeply. There are tons of things that you can appreciated. You only need to look closely.

Day 10

Meditate

For someone who has lived in one's head for quite a while, the thought of spending more time inside there might not seem like the ideal solution especially given the negative situation of things up there. But, to make the advancement to the next stage, meditation is a necessary part of the process. I believe that the misconceptions people have about meditation are based on what the media feeds us. We hear meditation, and we think images of a person wearing white and sitting on a spot with a good view of the sun oom-ing and ah-ing to the chants of crystals clanging somewhere in the background — not a very relatable image, I must say.

Meditation is more than just the rituals the new age enthusiasts have pedaled in order to sell the idea to the rest of the world. It is a combination of breath control techniques that help us to consciously channel our inner thoughts and regulate the tide of our emotions bringing us to a place where we are completely relaxed, focused and in control. The objective of this exercise is not control although it is a desirable outcome. The ultimate goal is focus.

When you are in a highly emotional state, you are drawn in a million different directions. You become lost in the sea of emotions you are experiencing and are unable to focus on what is important. Being in this state can cause you to take actions that have no valuable benefit to you whatsoever. Meditation pulls you from this brink of confusion by creating what I like to think of as an imaginary pipeline that allows those emotions to seep out and then bring you to an emotional ground zero where you can begin to isolate the cause of the problem before reacting to it objectively. You are able to do all of these with guided breathing among other techniques which will be included as you advance.

The mental benefits of meditation are infinite, but I will stick with the ones that really stand out in context of your current situation:

It improves mental clarity.

1. It is effective in drawing out the negative emotions that affect your day to day living.
2. It enables you to identify the real truths in your situation.
3. It helps you stay more organized.
4. It prevents you from making irrational decisions in the height of your emotional turmoil.
5. It offers you more control over emotions like anger and depression

6. It allows you to cope with the emotional aftermath of extremely traumatic events.

Meditation is not just the fad of the moment. Elements of it can be found in just about any religion so, you do not have to be concerned about imbibing foreign cultures that may violate your own personal beliefs. Meditation may be an active ritual for the Buddhists, Hinduists and others, but we can all benefit from using it. The difference is how we segue into it. Some people require chants, incense, lit candles and a specific outfit to do it, but you can reap the full benefits of meditation without having to go through those rituals. All you need is a quiet place that enables you to calm your thoughts and focus on your breathing.

Meditation is not determined by the time of the day, either. You do not need sunrise or sunset or even the time of the day when the sun is at its peak. What you need is the time of the day when you can hear your own voice the loudest. If you are single, live alone and you work from home, you have all the time in the world to yourself. For married folks with kids, determining the precise time may be a bit trickier. Right before the household awakes and you begin your day might be a perfect time. The house is quiet and the activities needed to get things along can wait a few more minutes. Use this time to meditate. Some people may prefer the end of the day when all is said and done and everyone has crawled into bed to rest for the night. The only problem that I see with this is that you might be too exhausted to really get into meditation mode.

I have a friend who is a stay at home father. He swears that his perfect meditation time is somewhere between 10 and 11. Everyone has left the house, the basic chores are done and he has even done a quick check for those important emails. So, instead of using that time to follow up on the rest of his chores or work, he meditates. This just goes on to illustrate that the best time of the day is not dependent on the hour or the direction of the sun.

Now that you have sorted out your meditation time, the next thing is to set the tone for it. Some people like the bright light, hence the importance of the sun for them. I like lights too, but when they are too bright, they distract me. Instead, what I do is draw the curtains closed, turn off all the lights and take out a candle. I like scented ones because they relax, me and the light of the candle helps me to focus my thoughts. If you are at work, you may want to do your meditation around lunch time when things generally slow down and people generally go out for lunch.

The next thing to consider is the duration of the meditation. One hour, 30 minutes, ten minutes... No amount of time is too long or too short. As long as it does not interfere with your regular routine and it is done right. For a beginner or a really busy person, you can start with 5 minutes a day. As you begin to reap the benefits, you can increase that time limit to what suits you. Just ensure that you are getting the most of your time. After picking the ideal time of the day that works for you, the next step is to pick a spot. Again, nothing grand is required.

You can do it on your bed. Just make sure that it is an uncluttered space that offers a little privacy.

Next, choose a meditation position. You can choose to lie down, sit down or go for the more traditional meditative pose if you are more comfortable with it. Most people have a tough time getting through the next part which essentially involves you sitting down for a period without thinking. There are meditation tapes and apps to help you with that. Or you can just light a candle and fix your gaze on it. Let all your thoughts and feelings be directed towards the candle. Do this consistently for a few days and you would begin to experience a clutter-free mind, even if it is just for a few minutes a day.

Day 11

Pay Attention to Your Diet

There is a popular saying, you are what you eat. Many fitness enthusiasts and experts have translated this to imply that your physical health is determined by what you eat. While this is true, things are a lot deeper than that. Your diet is instrumental in your emotional and mental well-being. There are studies that have indicated that people on a diet that is rich in vegetables, fruits, beans, fish as well as unsaturated fats like olive oil are less inclined to suffer from depression. This research barely covers the surface of what could potentially be a revolutionary approach to resolving mental issues.

Granted, it would be inaccurate to suggest that whatever mental and emotional health issues we have are a direct result of the type of food we eat, we cannot be dismissive of the important role that our food plays in contributing to our state of mind. There situations where people develop an unhealthy relationship with their food. There is a reason why certain foods are labelled comfort foods. They feed our emotional needs at the time. When we are experiencing certain emotions, we lean on these comfort foods to help us feel better. Many, these so-called comfort foods are not 100% healthy in the first place. Gorging on them in a bid to alter our negative emotional state would only amplify the negative effect these foods would have. And it is this unhealthy emotional dependency on food that has caused severe health complications for some people.

Food addiction can result in obesity, high blood pressure, diabetes and even heart diseases. People who struggle with food addiction also find themselves struggling with poor confidence, depression and low self-esteem and this battle tosses them into the continuous cycle that starts with poor emotional health and then leads l to poor eating habits that cause health complications and then brings them back to negative emotional health. Food addiction happens in two ways: those who overfeed on these comfort foods and then those who get their pleasure from not eating at all.

If you have read physical health journals and articles in relation to food, you likely encountered a the word "anorexic, : which refers to an eating disorder that makes people super conscious about their weight and what they eat. This is the very extreme end of what I am asking you to do today. And the reason I am really going in depth with this is because people have a tendency to replace one unhealthy habit with another unhealthy habit. So, if I say pay attention to what you eat, it is quite possible that to escape your emotional turmoil, you might fixate on the role that food plays in your mental well-being and possibly take things to the extreme.

To avoid that, I have decided to educate you on what could possibly go wrong if you find yourself taking things to the extreme. In cases involving anorexia, sufferers either sustain themselves with very little food in their bid to maintain their weight or they do what is generally referred to as a binge-purge where they consume a lot of food and then force themselves to immediately rid the food from their system by either sticking their hands down their throats to make them vomit or taking laxatives. This form of unhealthy food relationship also leads to health complications which can be fatal. Sufferers also get trapped in a cycle that is similar to the one we talked about earlier.

Now even if you do not belong to either group, it is important that you start giving more thought to the food you eat. Instead of just eating to survive, make it your mission to eat to thrive. Paying attention to what you eat requires you to be more conscious about what you eat and when you eat it. It also means eating the type of food that is best for you. For instance, if you have a medical condition like diabetes, there are certain foods that are simply off limits for you. In other words, what constitutes as healthy for some other person may not be right for you.

So, to kick start this process, go over your recent health records and if you don't have those, now would be a good time to talk to your health care provider. Know your current health status and discuss your options with your doctor. Don't make the mistake of jumping on the trendiest diet fad without proper consultations with your doctor. While your intentions may be good, the outcome could prove to have little benefit for your body. If you are given a clean bill of health, the best diet you can go on is a balanced diet.

A balanced diet ensures that you get the right amount of all the nutrients you need and you get those nutrients in the right daily proportions. If you are already on a restrictive diet like being a vegetarian, you will have to work hard at making sure that you make up for those aspects of your diet that are missing. Top up the protein that is missing in your diet. Red meat has its benefits, but it does not mean that if you are not eating red meat, you won't be able to enjoy those merits.

If you choose to go the diet route, like the Whole 30, which focuses on eliminating certain foods from your diet for a whole month and then reintroducing them later on, or maybe your nutritionist recommends the DASH [an acronym for dietary approaches to stop hypertension] diet, which is a salt-free diet, it is important your diet includes fruits and vegetables. They are vital for your physical and emotional well-being. Taking an active role in controlling what goes into your body can give you a good confidence boost. However, be cautious when setting the bar for your expectations for results. Don't expect to morph into the perfect body size after each meal or presume that your health status will dramatically change overnight.

The goal is not to transform your body; rather, the aim is to cultivate healthy eating habits that would serve you in the long term. However, this should not stop you from enjoying the benefits when they eventually come. Also, do not be afraid to stop a diet if you notice that the effect it has on you is affecting your health negatively. While some diets may boast of many great health benefits, it does not exactly guarantee that it is going to be the right fit for you. Be open to exploring diets, start with the ones recommended to you by your doctor or nutritionist. Chances are, you will find the best diet for you from their lists. Most importantly, have fun with your meals. Being on a diet is not necessarily boring.

DAY 12

Develop Your Own Mantra

If you are an avid follower of Hinduism or Buddhism, you are probably familiar with the word "mantra." Essentially, a mantra is comprised of words or sounds that repeated during meditation to help you focus. The long and protracted "ohm" sound is one of the most popular meditation mantras. They are a very important part of the meditation routine. However, for this task today, mantra takes on a different meaning, as I am not really talking about meditation. The mantra I am referring to has more to do with shaping your life and mindset in this phase. And today, you and I are going to work on allowing you to discover your power mantra.

When you start up a company, one of the things you need to work on is branding. This helps your customers identify you from the sea of choices available to them. A lot of the work that goes into the branding of a company is more focused on the aesthetic aspect. These companies strive to influence the market's opinion of them with the help of logos, brand colors as well as the fonts used in all of their marketing materials. However, the element that really defines how the company operates is tan organization's motto. In the same vein, the clothes you wear, the way you wear your hairstyle and all the physical stuff are just aspects of personal branding.

You can use your style to influence people's perception of you. But the thing that really defines how you interact with people, reacts to situations and generally carry yourself is strongly influenced by your personal beliefs. When we hear beliefs, we start thinking religion and culture. And to be honest, our religion and customs heavily influence our behaviors, but think about this for a second. If our beliefs were really rooted in our religion and culture, there is a very strong possibility that people who share the same customs would be more like replicas from a factory than the unique individuals that we are.

The differentiating factor for us is what we believe in personally. And even though you may not have given it a definition yet, the fact is you have a mantra. When you do not make the conscious effort to choose the mantra that defines you, life and everything else that happens to you will make that decision for you. And this is one of the reasons why many people are trapped in a destructive emotional cycle. There is a popular saying that if you don't stand for something, you will fall for everything. Today, you have to take the bold step of defining you. The mistakes you made in the past, the failures that you are living through in the present as well as your fears and concerns for the future are aspects of choices you make that have affected or will affect you. But they do not define you.

In the previous chapter, we talked about the "you are what you eat" phrase. Like aesthetics, this premise influences one aspect of you. Mantras are like your mental food. And because we know how strongly the mind influences our behavior, this makes a great case for choosing to define yourself. And now that we have established that, we have to go to the next step which is selecting the mantra.

Mantras in this context could be anything from a favorite celebrity quote to something culled from your favorite ancient Greek philosopher. Whatever you choose, do not fall for that socially trendy type of quote just because you feel people would think it is cool. Like with everything that has to do with your emotional wellbeing, the final decision is up to you. From the moment you were born, there are several voices competing for a space in your head. These voices are telling you how to do things, how to live your life and basically how to exist.

Now is your opportunity to create and horn in on your own voice. Let this voice take root deep within you and drown out every other belief system or voices that have held you down. The mantra should resonate with your innermost thoughts and desires. That is how you can tell that you are on the right track. It does not have to be "deep". But it should be something that every time you hear the words or speak the words, it changes your countenance for the better. Something as simple as "you are powerful" may be all you need to put your confidence together.

You can also have a mantra for different situations. Like if you are going to be making a presentation at work or maybe you have to speak in front of a crowd, you could choose a mantra that gives you the courage to step up and own the stage you are given. For times when you are experiencing some emotional lows which are very common if you are combating any of the negative emotions we talked about in the beginning, you can find mantras that will empower you to keep the darkness at bay.

When you find the right mantra, the next thing you might be thinking is how often you would need to say those words for them to have any effect. The only correct answer to that question is "as often as you need it." An old friend of mine used to reiterate, "motivation is like a bath: you need it every time you get dirty". And I agree with him 100%. Your mantra is not going to be a one-time-fix-it type of word that you just say, snap your fingers and everything falls into place. I wish there was a word or phrase like that but until that word has been discovered or invented, you are going to have to do your own behavioral conditioning every time you think you need it.

Say the words with conviction. Repeat them in sequence if you have to, but ensure that you are rooted in these words every day. As you evolve, you may have to take on new mantras. But you should always have that mantra that defines you no matter what. Find those words, speak those words, own those words and become those words. It would take a while for you to get there, but for today, let us settle for activating the inner victor within you with your own words!

Day 13

Practice Relaxed Breathing

Breathing is one of those reflexive activities that we take for granted every day. When a healthy baby is born, his or her first instinctive reaction is to fill up their lungs with air by simply inhaling and the same breath that they exhale, they release their first cry. Breathing is one of aspect that characterizes our nature, but we never truly realize the importance of this until a time comes when our breathing is compromised. Now don't panic because I know that the opening of this introduction sounds like a prelude to a doomsday warning. On the contrary, what I am trying to say is that there is more to breathing than merely inhaling oxygen and expelling carbon dioxide.

Earlier on we talked about the benefits of meditation and how we can use this to influence our emotional health positively and one of the things that people use to channel their focus during meditation is their breathing. This here is taking things to the next level. While the concept of relaxed breathing may sound like one of those new age mumbo jumbos, the truth is this is something that has been around for a while now. The use of relaxed breathing in modern medicine dates back to the 70s. However, my research reveals that this has been in existence for much longer.

Before you write off relaxed breathing as a wonky hack, here are some of the wonderful benefits of relaxed breathing:

1. It helps you to de-stress by filling your body up with oxygen and then getting your heart rate back to normal when your anxiety levels are sky high.
2. It plays a role in detoxifying your body by using those deep breaths to make your organs and systems more efficient at ridding the body of toxins.
3. On those days when your energy levels drop low on the scale, you can use relaxed breathing to give yourself an energy boost.
4. You can give your heart a good workout when you do those deep breathing exercises.
5. You can regulate your weight and burn fat with deep relaxed breathing.

With the kind of benefits, you would wonder why people aren't talking about this as much as they should. Chances are, they have been talking about this. You just haven't been paying any attention. Since our focus is on getting you to change your habits to improve your emotional well-being, we are going to capitalize on the emotional benefits of relaxed breathing.

Stress is one of life's experiences that we cannot escape. The source of stress for everyone is different as is our tolerance level for stress. However, when stress is triggered in our bodies, our biological and emotional reactions are similar. The physical reaction to stress can range from headaches to a drastic drop in sex drive. Emotionally, you could experience anxiety and anger outbursts. Some people become withdrawn when they are under stress and this can lead to depression.

We can't stop stress. It comes with the territory of life. But, you can stop the adverse emotions that are usually a byproduct of stress in their tracks. The normal breathing for most adults is usually shallow breaths that do not go past their chests. Deep breathing goes all the way down to your abdomen. It does not have an aesthetically pleasing effect as it gives you a puffer fish appearance with the blown out tummy and all. But this is the only way you can get the most out of your breathing. When in a heightened emotional state due to stress, instead of reacting to those emotions, you can reduce them down to reasonable limits.

So, the next time you feel a rage bubble coming on and you want to let it out by lashing out at the nearest person or thing, take a deep gulp of air and then let it out slowly. Focus on your breathing when you do this. When we are upset, we take shorter breaths and this limits the diaphragm's range of motion causing a restriction of oxygenated air to the lower parts of the lungs. The physical manifestation of this is anxiety. Deep breathing helps you cultivate a healthy response to stress. One of the healthier responses to stress is called the "relaxation response."

According to the Harvard journal that was referenced for the research on this subject, relaxation response is a state of profound rest. Meditations, yoga as well as repetitive incantations or prayers have been known to induce this relaxation response. Another simple yet effective way to kick start this response is deep breathing. By focusing on your breath, you can guide yourself into extricating your emotions from your thoughts and entering into this state of profound rest.

Deep breathing sounds pretty straight-forward but there is more to it than just taking puffs of air. To get it right, what you first need to do is to take yourself immediately away from the source of the stress. Even if you are in a workplace, distance yourself from the stressful work or the stressful coworker. You may be tempted to react immediately but that is only going to worsen the situation. Instead, find a quiet and isolated space, just like you would if you were going to meditate. Get a good spot to either sit or lie down. Being on your back is preferable, but you can still get good results from a sitting position.

When you are in position, take a normal breath. Then, inhale slowly through your nose and let your chest as well as your lower belly rise as you do so. This fills up your lungs with air. Next, breathe out slowly through your mouth. Keep your focus on your breathing and repeat this until you start to feel the tension slowly slip out of your body. Once you have practiced and nailed this breathing technique, initiate it any time you feel stressed in any way. Getting yourself to calm down on the brink of a blowout is a habit that will pay off eventually in the long run.

While there are plenty of benefits to this, there is one downside. If you have a history of respiratory problems, you should talk to your doctor about this as this may cause complications in unsupervised situations.

Day 14

Gain Mastery Over Your Emotions

In the days leading up to your second week on this journey to reclaiming your life, I am very certain that you have been equipped with knowledge that ensures you can now accurately distinguish your emotions. And if you have religiously followed the daily steps that have been listed out so far, you have a fair handle on your emotions. The exercise you did yesterday is about learning to get your emotions under control. Today, I would like to push you to take things further. Instead of just putting a lid on your emotions, you can master them.

The emotions that we talked about in the beginning, the anger, the depression, fear and anxiety…these are intense emotions that can threaten to overpower you when they are being experienced at their peak. What you have been practicing so far acts as a barrier reef that stops the wave of emotions from crashing over and completely destroying you. Another thing we addressed with these emotions is that they have a positive side to them. Anger serves to embolden you to stand up for your right and what you believe. Anxiety and fear are your instinctive defensive mechanisms to protect you when you are threatened while depression and sadness help you cope with loss.

Shutting these emotions out would compromise your total wellbeing because without them, you make yourself extremely vulnerable. Conflicts, crisis, calamities and chaos are things that we will all experience more than once in our lives. These emotions are all part of living. And these negative emotions are there to help you navigate through those kinds of situations. Therefore, pushing back those emotions only serves you temporarily. In the early stages of this journey, it was more important to build your mental and emotional foundations before letting the dark emotions in. Now, you are ready to confront your demon so to speak.

In this chapter, we will address each emotion discussed in the first 5 chapters of this book and then look at how you can channel your reaction to them to serve you better. Unlike the green Hulk from the famous Marvel comics, we are not trying to lock the "monster" away. Oh no. we want the monster to step into your world. Only, you will be the one at the driver's seat. Don't fret and worry about losing control. This is something that may start off a little difficult for you, but with practice and consistency, it is certainly something that you can do.

Anger

Anyone who has ever reacted to their anger in a fit of rage will know that anger can be quite venomous. Its effect on both the person who is angry as well as the person who is on the receiving end of that anger can be likened to that of a hurricane. It has been known to sever relationships, tear down empires, and lead to wars between nations. But, did you also know that it can inspire creativity? Some of the greatest movements that altered the course of humanity were inspired by anger.

In other words, anger can be used to your advantage. Next time when you feel a rage ensuing, use the techniques you have learnt so far bring the violent bubbles down to a gentle simmer and then do the following;

1. Get to the root of the anger. Don't react to the sting. React to the cause of the sting instead. You are bound to get more positive results this way.
2. Pick your battles carefully. When you are angry, something you value has been violated. Often times, those things are minor and not worth the hassle over. So, just breathe and ignore. In turn, you conserve energy for the things that matter.
3. Own your feelings. Sweeping things under the rug to present a façade of calmness can lead to a rage eruption of volcanic proportions somewhere down the road. In the very least, admit to yourself that you are angry and look for constructive ways to express your feelings.

Anxiety

Fear activates your survival instincts. It is your body's way of telling you that it wants to live. Experts tell us that without the right amount of anxiety, there is a strong possibility that we will be complacent in how we live our lives. A complete lack of it would cause us to become reckless in our dealings. The instinct to look before we leap would be absent and so we would constantly find ourselves in situations that compromise our emotional and physical wellbeing.

Too much of it on the other hand can paralyze us completely. We would become paranoid about everything and become incapable of enjoying the simplest joys in life. To gain mastery over anxiety, you must first embrace the positives that it brings to you. Now whether your fears are real or imagined, you should never let them shut you down. Instead of reacting to your fear, act on it. Make a conscious decision to do something.

Depression

This emotion forces you to reflect on your pain. There is a general opinion that nothing positive can come from your reflections when you are depressed. In contrast, there are psychologists who believe that this might actually be good for you. This is because in sadness, you are in a better position to analyze what is really important to you than you would in a happier frame of mind.

Bearing this in mind, you can use your sadness to horn in the important things in your life by asking the right questions. The usual self-pity party question of "why me?" does not count. Using questions involving "what" and "how" can help you determine the problem as well as develop solutions to them.

Negative thoughts

This applies to everything on each of these three emotions. The upside to negative thoughts is that it brings your imperfections to the forefront. We may like to think of ourselves as perfect but alas, we are human. Dwelling on those negative thoughts is where the harm comes in from. Instead, embrace those things that you don't like about yourself. Improve on them if you can. But do not let that be the focus of your thoughts. Change your perspective about these emotions that haunt you and then you will be able to rewrite the narrative. This is how you gain mastery over your emotions today.

Day 15

Step Things Up with New Relaxation Techniques

So far, you have practiced meditation to clear your mind, deep breathing to induce relaxation response, and taken on a new outlook on those emotions that were once hanging over you like dark clouds. Accordingly, these techniques have given you a new lease on life, but the journey is far from over. While what you are doing might offer some relief in the short term, you need what I call "booster shots" to get you through to the long term. Right up until this moment, we have been dealing with the things that colored your past and activated those emotions in the first place. Now, we need to start working on habits that will fortify you against what might happen in the future.

You may have an army of psychics that can predict the future for you but we do know that those predictions do not offer absolute certainty. They are all just possibilities, a series of might or might not happen events. The only certainty in life is change. Things are always changing. Circumstances will always evolve. Things may seem bad now, but it will get better and then somewhere down the future, it will get bad again. Of course, situations might never repeat themselves. But, you have to brace yourself because you will be presented with new challenges. The fairytales from our storybooks always end with stories of living happily ever after, yet real life has a different version.

The uncertainties about the future should not force you to live in fear of tomorrow. That kind of behavior is what got you into this mess in the first place. The right thing to do would be to equip yourself with knowledge and habits that will build you up emotionally so that when the time comes, you are better able to deal with the situations and not fall back into the destructive cycle we have already discussed. Unfortunately, there are no spells or potions that can quickly zap us into emotionally stable individuals. But that is all part of the fun. They say that it is not about the destination, it is about the journey. In this case, the process that gets you to becoming even more is vital!

There are many relaxation techniques that are practiced in different parts of the world. Some of them have been in existence for centuries and perhaps are only just being discovered because of the world gradually becoming a small place. What this tells us is that mankind has always been concerned about their emotional wellbeing. Their source of anxiety may have been different from the experiences that we have today, but the threat remains nonetheless. There was a time that the most efficient way to deal with emotional traumas might have involved pills and a trip to the electric chair. Thankfully, those times have changed. Through cultural integration, we are now being gifted with knowledge of how we can manage our emotions and force ourselves to relax in a world that seems to run on constant frenzy.

There are several additional relaxation techniques out there, and I encourage you to take explore them. However, our focus for today's exercise is going to be yoga.

Yoga

Yoga is all about finding your balance and serenity. Through a series of breathing exercises and body movement, you can consciously cause your mind and body to rest. Beyond relaxing you, if you find yourself in an energy rut which typically happens at the end of a long hard day, yoga can relax your nerves and leave you feeling reinvigorated.

Yoga has different poses that offer specific benefits. And because our goal is to help our minds and body relax, we are going to be looking at 5 poses that serve this purpose.

1. The Child Pose also known as Balasana

In this pose, you rest your chest and abdomen on your knees/ thighs with your feet stretched out behind you and your hands in front of you. Let your forehead touch the mat. This pose strengthens your breathing and has a calming effect. Remember to do it on an empty stomach.

2. The Reclining Fish Pose also known as Supta Matsyendrasana

Here you lay on your back with arms stretched out on either side of you at shoulder height. With one leg stretched out in front of you, cross the other leg over the outstretched one moving only the hip and that leg. Turn your face in the opposite direction of the crossed leg and hold position for 30-60 seconds.

3. The Legs up the Wall Pose also known as Viparita Karani

Just as the name implies, this pose requires you to place both legs on the wall as you lie flat on the ground with your arms stretched out on either side at shoulder height. In addition to relaxing you, it functions as a very mild form of anti-depressant. It is usually best for mornings.

4. The Corpse Pose also known as Savasana

All morbid thoughts aside, lay flat on your back with arms and legs apart. Stay still and just focus on breathing. This pose is simple but very effective for inducing rest. It is great for post workout as it soothes sore muscles and helps stimulate blood circulation.

5. The Bound Angle Pose also known as Supta Baddha Konasana

On your back, raise your hands above your head. Let the back of your hands touch the floor and let your thumbs and forefingers connect. And then bend your legs until your feet are facing each other and touching. Hold this pose for 30-60seconds. This pose keeps headaches, panic attacks and muscle fatigue at bay. It is also useful for lowering your blood pressure.

These are all beginner poses and are pretty simple to do. As you grow, you can extend the time period and perhaps explore more advanced yoga poses that offer the same benefits to this. While you are in each pose, you can also do your deep breathing exercises to make the most of things. This would amplify the results that you get. Also bear in mind that this is not a one off thing. It is something that you should practice and get comfortable doing almost every day. While you are at it, you can also research other relaxation techniques like Taichi. Every information you acquire and practice can go on to building a stronger foundation for your emotional wellbeing.

Day 16
Reflect on the Experience

There is a general misconception about communication. We assume that the most difficult people to communicate with are others…as in the people in our lives. But in the true sense of things, communication with ourselves is what we find most difficult. This is because when it comes to ourselves, objectivity is usually missing. If someone other than ourselves were going through circumstances that are similar to our own and we are called to weigh in, we would probably be spot on with our emotional assessment of the situation and perhaps even offer actionable solutions. But when it comes to us, we either run around in circles or worse, crash into brick walls.

This is because we often lack the objectivity required to see things as they are because we are clouded by our own feelings and emotions. To be objective, you need to change your perspective and that can only happen with self-reflection. Now self-reflection is quite different from just simply sitting down at thinking of the situation. Brooding on a situation drags you deeper into the maze of your emotions. Self-reflection on the other hand purposefully analyzes and applies a practical solution. In other words, it is a form of self-assessment. This is a place where you get to be 100% honest with yourself.

In the past, you have needed to put the blame on others so that you could ensure the day. To move forward, that kind of thinking can no longer apply. Whether the blames assigned to the different people is justified or not, it is important that you acknowledge your role in the event. Mind you, this is not about assigning the blame to yourself either. That ship has sailed. This is reflecting on the process that brought you to this point, retracing your steps, reclaiming your power and redefining the impact this experience will have on you. We don't realize how powerful our mind is but all of that is about to change today.

When you are self-reflecting on an experience, you are not going back to the past as a victim or a victor. You are not trying to create and then sell a narrative that you feel will pacify your wounded emotions. You are revisiting this past as an observer and nothing more. Yes, you have lived with the pain and yes, you bear the scars but you are not bound to hold on to those. Revisit the moment or event where you think you lost everything, trace the steps that brought you to that event and then follow up on what happened after the event to where you are today. Again, try not to dwell on the "why" questions. It is harder to get the answers to those if other people are involved. However, if this event itself is something you can classify as self-inflicted, then you can most certainly try to analyze why you did it.

Now, bearing in mind that you cannot change what has happened, you would have to accept the situation for what it is before moving on the next set of questions which would center around how you could have done things differently. The purpose for this line of questioning to determine how you can avoid situations like that in the future. This would prevent you from repeating the same mistake. I have to emphasize here again that this is not the time to assert blames. Acknowledging your role in the event and then assigning blames are two different things. One paves the way for redemption, while the latter breeds guilt and self-destruction.

During this phase, assess your strengths and your weaknesses. This kind of knowledge empowers you to make the right and relevant changes that you need. With this newly acquired knowledge of yourself, if you are ever confronted with similar circumstances, there is a very high possibility that you will make better choices. And the beautiful thing about these choices that you will make subsequently is that they are not rooted in fear or any other negative emotions. But rather, they are being made objectively which would mean that the results would be beneficial for the long term. The lessons acquired will educate the steps that you would take in the future.

Now that you have done your self-assessment in relation to the experience, you can now reduce the impact that the experience would have over you. Let me use a practical example here. I know someone who had been in a relationship for almost 13 years. They met in their early college years and sustained that relationship until they entered the job market. I will call the lady "Laura" because she is the one I know. For Laura, this relationship was her first and only one at the time. And because they had been together for so long, she assumed that this union was going to her happily ever after. She built her hopes and dreams around this relationship only for her prince charming to end things abruptly in what would have been their 13th year together. You can imagine how devastated Laura was. For months, she suffered from depression and panic attacks.

I met Laura during this time, and we began working on turning things around. When we got to this point, Laura noted her fear of rocking the boat in a relationship and how it prevented her from asking the right questions that would have saved her time and heartache. Instead of jumping on the "all men are scum" wagon. Her self-assessment helped her open herself up to new relationship prospects and informed the choices that she made going forward. She took out a year to date herself and in the year following that, she got involved with a pretty decent bloke. Today, she is married and living out her new dreams. The moral lesson here is not that she found happiness. It was the deliberate choices that she was able to make thanks to her objective assessment of her experience. Today, pick up a pen and book and go down memory lane as well.

Day 17

Focus on the Good

Remember that gratitude list that you started some days back? Well, now we are about to step things up. I assume that it is safe to say that you may have heard or come across the "glass half full" expression. This is used to illustrate what a positive outlook and a negative outlook on life are like. They say that the optimistic person would always look at a glass that has liquid in it that is halfway to the top as half full while the pessimistic guy would look at the same glass as half empty. It all boils down to perspective. The perspective we have about life to a large extent would determine our experiences.

Contrary to what we think, our perspective of life is neither genetic nor hereditary. It is a choice that we make and one that we have to continuously make. Sometimes, life's experiences condition us to think and react in a certain way. If you have had a slew of negative experiences thrown at you, it is quite understandable if you begin to develop a fear that some kind of doom or tragedy is awaiting you at every corner. However, even in situations like these, you can make the choice to see things through a brighter lens. Becoming optimistic is the goal, but that is not something that is going to happen over the weekend. It starts with a small but very significant step...seeing the good in everything!

Realists may struggle with this more than pessimists because realists tend to focus on grander things. A realist is not so impressed by the penny that they find on the ground because they think that it might feed their fear of deluding themselves. The sun peeking from beneath dark angry looking clouds is not enough to give them hope about the rains being averted. Those dark clouds would have to go before they would entertain any thought of hope. Whether you are a pessimist, a realist, or an optimist, you have to start training yourself to see the good, no matter how small.

Just to clarify things, this is not to say that you should ignore the bad things or be dismissive of them. It is about getting a balanced perspective. In every situation, there is always a silver lining. Sometimes it is harder to find that rainbow in the midst of your storm but if you keep at it, I guarantee that you will find it. When I was taking this journey during a very painful period in my life, I used to feed my "good sight" with common internet clichés. Initially, they sounded really terrible and unhelpful but as I repeated them, I began to notice positive changes in how I viewed this. I bring this experience up because seeing the good things isn't always about sight. It was in how I reacted to things as well as how I perceived situations.

Focusing on the good things in your life is a deliberate attempt to reclaim hope in a situation that brings you despair and there are very few things that are as powerful as that. Another effective way to focus on the good is to redefine the negative. For instance, if anger is a problem that you are struggling with, instead of hanging on to the negative label that characterizes such behaviors, give yourself a positive spin on things. Choose instead to see yourself as a person who is intensely passionate about things that matter to you and right now, you are trying to figure out how to constructively express your passion in a way that everyone around you can benefit from it. This is not self-denial. But rather, it is a more productive way to help you reclaim your hope and motivate yourself to make the relevant changes.

A study was conducted on the subject of silver lining and it was discovered that 90% of people who were able to convince themselves that their negative traits were strengths were more motivated to work harder to attain the positive attributes of those strengths. This right here is science. Like I said earlier, it is amazing what you are able to achieve when you set your mind to it.

One theme I have repeated throughout this book is the fact that you have to accept the situation for what it is. You cannot go back in time to change what has happened but you can reach into the future to change how it will affect you now. To do this, you need to make some projections. What would you like to see happen? What are the things about your situation that if they changed would make you happier and feel more grateful for life? Now picture yourself in the future with those things and the outcome you have projected. With this in mind, come back to the present. Now, ask yourself, what are the things you think you can do now that would give you the outcome that you desire? Create a plan that would lead you to that point, write it down in clear and concise words and then run with it. This is another way to focus on the good.

These little thoughts of good help you redirect your focus and give you something to look forward to. When we feel like we have nothing to live for, the darkness and the negativity would take over and bring us to the pit. This does not have to be your story. Whether you are redefining yourself, reaching to the future or just feeding your 'good sight," you have to actively make the decision to stay in the light every day. The future is uncertain, but when you envelope yourself in positivity, there is almost no mountain that you cannot climb to get to your destination. It is time to stop letting things happen to you. Get up and start happening to the things around you. It is easy to shrug your shoulders and say life happened but don't. Look into the mirror, shrug your shoulders and say "you happened" instead.

Day 18

Uproot the Negative Sources

There is a Christian parable about a farmer sowing his seeds. Some of these seeds fell on hard soil, so they were scorched by the sun and unable to grow. Some fell on fertile soil and of course they grew, bloomed and bore fruits. And then you have the seeds that fell among thorny bushes. The farmer tried to grow, but the bushes and thorns choked the life out of them and so they withered and died away. Trying to be optimistic when you are surrounded by negativity is akin to planting seeds among thorns and bushes. The negativity would choke the life from the little light and hope you have tried to carve out for yourself leaving you with the darkness.

But like everything else, this too is a choice. You have taken the bold step to redefine yourself and your purpose in life. Now you will have to take an even bolder step to get rid of anything that brings negativity into your life and sometimes that includes people. It is funny how some of these types of negative people in our lives convince themselves that they are only speaking the truth. They use clichés like "the truth hurts" or "the truth is always bitter" to justify the mean things that they say to you. Some people don't even come outright with the mean words. They use snarky comments and backhanded statements to throw you off your game. Today, all of that ends.

It is not your job to try to figure out where their bitterness is coming from (you better believe that they have a source), but you owe it to yourself to look out for yourself first. So, if you have toxic personalities in your life, you are going to have to eliminate them or at the very least tune out their voices. It is very important that you take a very vicious approach to cutting negative people out of your life because the amount of energy required to dismantle the negative impact of toxic words is more than three times the energy required for you to develop a new positive habit. If you choose to tolerate those type of people in the name of maintaining friendships, you would find yourself expending energy in undoing the damage that they do daily instead of living your life. And on top of everything, they are not the only negative voices you are going to have to silence.

The second negative source in our lives is usually found within you. When you have battled with situations that compromised your confidence and left you emotionally battered, it awakens a voice within. The voice of self-doubt. Even when you make giant strides in achieving your goals, you would still hear this voice screaming out from the recesses of your mind telling you that you cannot do it. Sometimes, the piercing screams of our self-doubt can have a paralytic effect on us. This would leave you stuck in murky waters which would then distract you from the other amazing things you could and should be doing. To drown out the voices of self-doubt, you would have to activate another voice. Remember those mantras you have been practicing, you would have to kick things up a notch. Listen to the words that the voice of self-doubt is saying and look for mantras that counter those words positively. The more empowered they make you feel, the better for you.

Outside the voices of self-doubt, you are going to have to banish other negative thoughts that may have been programmed by your beliefs, culture and so on. What you believe in has a very strong hold over you. I have heard the phrase, "a man of conviction is a dangerous man." In other words, because someone like that is firmly rooted in what he or she believes, so shaking this person is going to be as effective as using a regular razor blade to cut through solid steel. Your belief forms a solid wall that is much akin to the steel I used in the illustration. To cut through it, you would need more positive affirmations as well as the redefinition of certain opinions you have held about some things.

You would also need a ton of sheer will power to push through. Today, you will be exerting a lot of mental effort as you attempt to put your life in order. Think of it as preparing your soil for the planting season ahead. If there are habits, materials or images that feed the negativity that surrounds you, it is imperative that you are brutal in eliminating them. Don't let sentiments stand in the way. Somethings or people may be easily let go of perhaps due to familial relationships or some kind of obligation. Perhaps, the source of the toxicity in your life is your workplace but due to financial considerations, you are not in a position to sever ties immediately. In situations like this scenario, you can devise with an action plan to exit at a later time. So, even if you cannot extricate yourself right away, you have something to look forward to in the coming days.

I know I make it sound easier than it actually is but this would make a huge difference in everything. When you let go of anything that might compromise your peace of mind, you are contributing to the creation of an emotionally stable environment that nurtures this new person that you are trying to become. Even more than that, it helps you thrive. As you uproot the negative elements in your life, ensure that you replace them with more positives. Stock up on books that feed you emotionally. Write little positive phrases and quotes and strategically place them around your home and person. Stumbling on them at random moments can inject a much-needed confidence boost.

As you let go of negative friends, connect with people who inspire and motivate you. In this era of social media, you can opt to ensure that your timeline is filled with positive messages by following people who exude the type of content that resonates with you. Constantly remind yourself that you are in charge and you may not control what happens. However, you can control how you react to it and how much it affects you.

Day 19

Bring Positivity to Others

When you have been the recipient of something good, the next best thing is to pay it forward. In the last few days, you have benefited from the wisdom of others and I am not referring to the words in this book. I am talking about the mantras and the positive phrases that you have researched and adopted as your own are gifts from others who came before you. Today, you are going to try and sow back positive seeds into the world that has blessed you. Now this does not mean that you have to start sprouting words of wisdom for others to discern. However, there are things that you can do to get the ball rolling in that direction but first let us find out what this does for you.

If you have never done something selflessly for someone, I suggest you drop this book right now and try it. Beyond seeing the smile on the face of the person whom you are doing the good for, there is just a warm feeling that fills you up. Studies have shown that personal acts of kindness activate a part of your brain that decreases the effects of anxiety. Of course the results are not conclusive, but it is a very promising subject. Still, we are not going to wait until the results from that study are concluded before we act on it. Meeting the need of another human being is a fundamental aspect of human nature and this should be encouraged.

Secondly, doing acts of good draws you out of your own head. It doesn't take much to find yourself preoccupied with the problems that you face. We get so caught up in our own world so much that we forget that there is an entire universe filled with other human beings who are equally facing their own set of problems and even though they are not your responsibility, it helps to show a little empathy. Spending even just 5 minutes as a helpful listening ear might reveal how trivial your problem is in comparison. Don't feel the need to hog the spotlight when it comes to who life has been most unfair to. You may feel like you are the only one in the world, but all you have to do is reach out and you will be amazed to discover that there are so many people willing to fill up your life with love.

As a child, my grandfather gave me an illustration of generosity that stuck with me all of my life. We had gone on a fishing trip and then he asked me to reach into the basket and give him some bait. Just as I handed him the bait, my grandfather held my hand over his and said to me, "givers will always be on top." This image has always played in my mind all these years. When we think of giving, our worry is usually what we have to lose. That favorite sweater, that extra cash or even our time…we tend to think of it as a loss. But in reality, we are gaining so much more. And the more we give, the more we gain.

Giving back to the world is not as complicated as it sounds. And you don't need to go on a venture halfway across the world to be able to give. Charity, they say, begins at home. You can start in your home and then take things to your community. There are lots of ideas for giving and not all gifts have to involve you parting ways with cash. If you are short on inspiration, let my list give you a hint.

1. Volunteer your services:

Look for a cause that you are passionate about and then find an organization that supports that cause in your neighborhood. Most NGO are usually overwhelmed by the demand for the services that they offer so an extra set of helping hands are always welcomed. Offer to serve the organization in any capacity that you can. It does not have to be a long-term thing, so don't worry about making a commitment that you are not ready to accept.

The service you offer could be dependent on the type of organization you volunteered for. Medical NGOs would require medical personnel or at least someone with some medical background and educational organizations would require teachers. So, have this in mind when you make your application.

2. Volunteer your time:

Not all of us are keen on working with other people and if the idea of applying to an NGO puts you off, you can still do your bit for your community by donating minutes and hours of your time for community service. Perhaps the recreational park close to you is being invaded by trash. Get your gear, walk around the park and pick up the trash. You can choose to do this at your own convenience as well.

When volunteering your time, simply look out for opportunities that will show you how best you can use your time to help your community. Even taking the extra time to properly sort your trash at home can be of great benefit to yourself, the community, and the environment.

3. Random acts of kindness

If you are not going to be able to volunteer your time and/or your service, you need to jump on this wagon that lets you just pick sporadic moments to acts of kindness to anyone, despite if it's a known face or a complete stranger.

Giving up your seat for an elderly person on the bus or train, giving a warm and welcoming smile to your new co-worker or giving someone a genuine compliment...these are all acts of kindness.

Today, your task is to perform at least one good deed for someone other than family. Be creative in carrying out your task. Subsequently, make this a daily habit. Put out positive vibes to the universe and watch the universe respond in kindness.

Day 20

Live in the Moment

The present circumstances in your life may not be ideal and living through it might be a painful daily experience for you. But getting yourself stuck in a once glorious past or keeping your head in the clouds of a future that is not certain is not going to make things any better. When people give the advice to "live in the moment," we picture a life that has many good things going on for that person who just seems to be negligent of the "gifts" they possess. But for people who are living through one of the darkest times in their lives, that statement is a heavy burden to bear. It almost seems impossible to do. This is why a lot of people try to escape their lives through drugs, alcohol, and other harmful addictions.

Making the choice to live in the moment despite the tough circumstance surrounding you is a brave and courageous decision that I applaud. It would require more exercise of your will power to stay on track with this decision as there are so many distractions that can offer an escape. And even when you are able to stay away from the distractions, every now and then, you will encounter events that will cause you to become anxious and lead you to worry about the future. These concerns again take you away from the present and all of this can contribute to creating an atmosphere of despair. If you are not vigilant, you could become overwhelmed by it all and lose sight of what is important. Because, no matter how dark things get right now, your bright future is rooted in your ability to cease a moment in your present. And you can only recognize that moment if you are living in it. This is the paradox of life.

The first step to living in the present is to slow down your pace. Today's life is lived on the fast lane. We are always in a hurry to get to our destination. We look for short cuts to getting the job done. We want things to happen at the speed of light. The technology that is being created for this age is designed to meet our need for faster service. The irony is that in our hassle to get to where we are going to in the shortest time possible, we end up running around in circles. We become like those cute little hamsters on wheels. They just pedal and pedal but end up not really going anywhere. This is why they say, "It is not about the destination, it is the journey that counts". Don't be so focused on getting to your office on time that you ignore the important people and experiences on your way there. Hug your partner a little tighter before you head out the door. Give a hearty high five to the kids. Smile and wave at the neighbor as you head to your car. Take in the sights and sounds of the city as you navigate your way through traffic. Your job will still be waiting for you, but this moment slips away forever. Stop and smell the roses, literally and figuratively.

The next step is to be more mindful. What this means essentially is that you have to consciously pay more attention to what is happening around you right now. Life does not happen in reverse neither does it have a fast-forward button. It progresses with each waking moment. Your fears about the future should not disrupt your actions in the now. I am not implying that your concerns are not founded and that you should not plan for tomorrow. But don't get so caught up in those plans that you neglect what is going on right now. Make a deliberate effort to pay attention to the things you are doing now. Even if they are simple mundane activities that you do every day, focus your mind to stay on the task. For instance, when you sit down to have a meal, don't just go through the motions of putting the food in your mouth, chewing and then swallowing. Savor the taste and texture of the food. Celebrate the burst of flavors in your mouth and this may sound like you being extra but it really is just taking advantage of the moments in your life.

Finally, to truly live in the moment, you have to realign your priorities with your present realities. In every stage in our life, our priorities change but not many of us recognize this. What was important for you in your 20s may not hold the same value when you get to your 30s, but we hold on to this anyway. A typical example would be the value we place on our careers when we are single and then still choosing career over the other valuable things in our lives when we get married. This is not suggesting that your career has to be over when you get married and start a family of your own. But it is an undeniable fact that a shift in priority happens. Your family becomes your priority. Failure to do this would result in unnecessary conflicts that take away from the joy of living in the moment. This applies to every aspect of your life. You should give priority to what you place value on if you want to maximize the benefits of living in the present.

Another important factor that can ruin your ability to enjoy the present is keeping a judgmental attitude towards life. We reside in an era where everyone has an opinion about everything, and we all think we are right. To add fuel to an already burning flame, there are several social platforms that amplifies your opinions, so we are always eager to express our displeasure at every turn. The downside to this (among a million on my list) is that we become narrow-minded and intolerant when our myopic beliefs are echoed by strangers around the world. So, instead of approaching a moment with an open mind and open hands, we take on a critical stand thus missing out on the pleasures out there. It is vital to be rooted in our beliefs, to have a voice that represents our values, but it is even more important to live our lives with an open mind. Being open minded is what creates the opportunity for you to enjoy the surprises contained in these little moments that comprise our life's experiences.

Day 21
Letting it all go

To conclude what I know to have been an emotionally trying 3 weeks for you, I am proud that you are now "letting it all go." Not too long ago, you spent the day getting rid of any negative elements in your life, so it does beg the question of "what exactly are you letting go today?" The answer is quite simple. Today is the day that you let go of the pain. Now, this realization offers some good news, right? I mean, no one wants to carry his or her pain around 24/7. If there is a chance to physically exorcise yourself of the emotional pain we feel, a lot of us would sign up for it in a heartbeat. But if we are given the chance to let go of the pain freely, many of us would hesitate. This hesitation is not because we enjoy the pain. It is because on a subconscious level, we have bonded with our pain and this has become our identity. Letting go is one of the hardest things to do, which is why I reserved it for the last tip. But it is also the most significant step to take in getting you to move on with your life mindfully and healthily.

Holding on to the pain from the past and trying to tap into the future is like making omelet with rotten eggs. You have all the ingredients needed for an omelet but putting something that is already contaminated ruins all the taste and flavors that the other ingredients give even though they are in good condition. The only thing you should hold onto from your past is the lessons you've acquired. The pain taught you the lessons, but it is not the pain that will transform your life. It is the lessons. Clutching the pain will just ruin any wonderful experiences you may have going forward. The exercises you have been doing in the last few weeks have been preparing you for this moment. It is scary for sure, but it is also one of the bravest things you can do today.

To help with the scary part, instead of idealizing the pain, how about you put the power of your mind to work by redefining this moment. If letting go sounds a little too hard for you, let us call it the moment that you break up with pain. That sounds a lot better and puts a more positive spin on things. Now, let us get right into the business of it. Pain is not like a tangible thing that you can scoop up with a dustpan and then empty into the trash can. But, there are ways you can still achieve that same effect as you put things behind you with this step by step process.

Step 1: Stop petting the pain

Humans keep pets for various reasons but the most common reason is for companionship. When we feel sad and lonely, we reach out to our furry friends and pet them to make ourselves feel better. We let our pets absorb the feelings and draw on the unconditional love they give us to improve our moods. Many of us treat our pain like pets. Every time something negative happens, we reach for that pain and use it to comfort ourselves. It is not a conscious thing that we do, but if you really want to move on, you are really going to have to stop pampering your pain.

Step 2: Stop making excuses

We know that this pain and bitterness we carry inside cannot bring anything good but every time it comes down to letting go, we start making excuses like "the pain is a reminder of what I have been through." Clichés like that sound like they are deep but in reality, they are just another excuse to retain your baggage. There are other great ways to remind yourself of this experience. Some people get tattoos, some people opt for engraved jewelry, and my favorite is the one where they choose a day in the year to commemorate the battle they fought and the well-earned victory that crowned their bravery. Whatever you choose to do, strive to ensure that you are embracing the right things for the right reasons.

Step 3: Stop playing the victim

We know that this tragic and terrible thing happened to you and that you don't deserve it, but wearing the victim badge just to garner sympathy from everyone is not going to help you move on in any way. For starters, the victim badge cancels out any scenario where you come out as the winner. The only thing it gets you is sympathy and even then, there is an expiry date for the sympathy you are getting now. This fleeting "reward" is not a good reason to cling on to an illusion where pain gets you what you want. This kind of thinking would work against all your effort to move forward. In relationships, you might become mistrustful and manipulative. People may stay with you based on sympathy, but you can only manipulate them for so long.

Step 4: Stop making comparisons

Putting your pain on a pedestal and then using that as a yardstick to define the events that happen to you going forward can make things get ugly really quick. No matter how beautiful you try to make that pedestal seem, it just won't work as long as you have that pain sitting up there. Think of the rotten egg in omelet analogy I used earlier. It doesn't matter if you put the fanciest ingredients in it. Sea salt, Moroccan spices or even the purest form of virgin olive oil cannot change the nasty flavor or smell that the rotten egg would bring to the meal. The same goes for letting pain define your future.

Today, make a conscious effort to let go of the pain. And as you do so, make it a point to forgive all the parties involved. And most prominently, forgive yourself. If you are harboring feelings of revenge, you need to let it go. Letting go does not mean that you are letting the other person off the hook. In fact, it is not really about them anymore. Letting go is about you and your emotional wellbeing. When you cling to a grudge or pain, you give that person or thing power over you. This journey is about reclaiming your power and rising above your emotional battles. No one and nothing should have that much power over you. Let it all go and watch yourself grow.

Embracing the Brand New You

Congratulations! You have made it thus far. I am really excited about the next phase of this journey that you are about to take. If you fell along the way, that is okay. We are not defined by our failures but by our ability to get back up every time we fall. In the last three weeks, you have really put yourself out there. You rode the storm, faced your fears and rewrote your story. You have awakened yourself to your true nature and you have gained knowledge that will continue to serve you for a very long time to come. I am also certain that you have managed to surprise yourself in this period. The revelations about yourself and your experiences in life have opened the door that has led to a more intimate relationship with yourself.

The unveiling of this new dimension to you is a remarkable experience. However, you are not done with this journey just yet. This is literally just the tip of the iceberg. The part of you that has just come up to surface extends deep beneath. As long as life keeps happening, you will need to keep at it. Everything you have learnt and practiced here needs to be repeated on a daily basis until it becomes a part of you. Get yourself to a point where you no longer need to do lists and phone reminders to tell you what to do and when to do it. It should become like breathing. You don't have to psyche yourself or remind yourself to take the next breath, you just do. Don't wait until there is a crisis to start another 3-week routine. Prepare yourself for those moments now so that when (those moments will always come) they arrive, you are in the best shape to take things on and get through it. Situations that would have previously seen you falling apart will now empower you to become even stronger.

As much as you would love this new you and cannot imagine being anyone else (except maybe Bill Gates or Beyoncé), it is essential that you keep an open mind because you will change. Some of those changes are inevitable and it is natural to resist it. But don't fight it for too long. Embrace those changes just as you have taken to this new you. Now while you are high fiving yourself on these milestones you are making, have a care for the people in your life. If the new you manifest this change physically as well as emotionally, it may reflect in your dress sense among other things. Perhaps you were the conservative type who wore muted colors and stayed away from bold graphical prints, you might find yourself being drawn to bright colors and bolder prints. This might be a bit of a shocker to people who know you, especially especially for those who share similar style sense with your previous style preferences. You need to give them some time to adjust to the new you.

Maybe you were the loud and boisterous type who lived an extroverted lifestyle but as you have gotten in touch with your true self, you realize that this is not you anymore. So, you become more introverted. Friends and family who have seen you in your finest extroverted hour would have a hard time reconciling that person they knew with this new person that you have become. You may have to be open to the possibility that they may not be entirely psyched about this new you right away. Don't try to change yourself just so that they can become comfortable with your transformation but don't force this new you down their throats either. Be patient with them and trust that they will come around eventually. As you continue to discover more layers to yourself, you should also do your best to balance the relationships in your life throughout the process. If balancing your relationships appear to be interfering with what you are trying to achieve, perhaps you should have a quick chat with them explaining what you are doing and why you may not be as accessible as you normally would. This quick chat will let them know that you trying to improve yourself and those who really love you can better support your efforts and encourage you to keep at it.

This is a period where you are permitted to be a little selfish. Your mental and emotional health is important. So even after you complete this three-week exercise, make it a point of duty to find time every day for yourself. You are in a better position to love and give positivity if you are able to stock up on self-love and positive energy. It is impossible to give what you don't have. Don't get sidetracked by "distractions." The Internet is a great resource for information, but if you don't make conscious decisions, you could end up being sucked into its endless maze of irrelevant and mindless data.

Teach yourself to practice joy every day. They say that happiness is a choice and given your newfound power in the choices you make, diligently seek out joy in everything that you do. You can do this by starting off each day with the mentality that every day that you wake up to is presenting you with a clean slate. Life will scribble a few things on that slate but the main author is you. And if it turns out that you don't like the narrative that life is giving, grab the pen and rewrite that chapter.

All of these things you are doing is to honor this new person that you have become. Love this amazing person that you are now. Don't settle for anything less than you deserve. Don't let this be a phase in your life. It should be a continuous process. Seek out new adventures, confront old fears…stay evolving. There is so much you have to live for and if you ever get stuck in a similar kind of emotional jam that drove you to this book in the first place, remind yourself of this. You have come a very long way, and there is a long road ahead. But if you can make it this far, you can go even farther.

I am confident in you and in all your efforts to making this transformation, so much so that I urge you to share your personal experience with others. Your story might uplift them and inspire them to claim their own power. Remember, it is in lifting other people that we lift our communities. Just like the many people who have inspired you to be better, you can be the inspirations for others.

On a final note, you do not have to wait until the start of the New Year to implement the changes that you want to see in your life. Every day is a good day and this is enough reason to get out of bed and march your way into your best life. New Year's resolutions are great and all, but new day resolutions are absolutely the hottest self-care trends to try at the moment.

Closing

I want to thank you so much for giving me the honor of including me on your journey. Thank you for letting me be one of the voices in your head that encourages you to be better. Being allowed into your space makes me feel truly blessed and humbled. I am usually eloquent with my words, but in moments like these, I lack the words that accurately encapsulates my thoughts and feelings. Suffice it to say, you inspire me!

It is my earnest desire to see that people are able to build relationships with themselves. There are too many broken people in the world: despite e the advent of the Internet and the wealth of information from technology, there is still not enough knowledge out there to help them heal from their wounds. Many of us have been rendered cripple emotionally and mentally by the tragedies that we have endured. We have gone from living to just surviving. We were made for more than that. I don't just want to live; instead, I want to thrive and I want these things for all of us!

Emotional healing starts from within and there is no surgery as of this moment that can fix that. However, in the face of this seemingly helpless situation, we have been given the power to turn things around for ourselves. The game changer in all of this is choice. What have you decided to do with your life today? Are you going to sit back and take everything that is being tossed your way? Or are you going to stand up and say "enough?" These are the choices that you are confronted with today, and your answer will determine the rest of your life.

I hope that you find the courage to choose life every day. No matter what the rest of the world has said about you, the simple truth is that you deserve better. And while you may have become isolated in your struggles, know that you are never alone. Millions of people around the world share stories that are similar to your life experiences. And many of them have done more than just survive those experiences. They have persevered on top. And the remarkable thing about their stories is that these victories they have didn't come by wealth or a change in their circumstances. It was as a result of a change in their attitude.

They recognized their power and they acted on it. The change did not happen overnight. And the change did not stop the moment they got their victory. It is a process that happens every day and they thrive in the fullness of it. The best part is that they do not have a monopoly on this. You can also rebuild from the loss you have experienced and restore relationships that have been damaged. Tragedy and trauma do not have to characterize your life. Choose instead to characterize those things that have gone wrong. You can transform your life in 21 days and there is no better time to begin this journey than now. For those who have started, I celebrate you in advance. Be consistent, be diligent, and most importantly, be deliberate!

Book #4
Stoicism

The Timeless Wisdom to Living a Good life

Develop Grit, Build Confidence, and Find Inner Peace

Introduction

"It's time you realized that you have something in you more powerful and miraculous than the things that affect you and make you dance like a puppet."
Marcus Aurelius

I remember the very first time I encountered this quote. I was doing some online research for a project I was working on and, by chance, I stumbled on a page with this quote at the very top. I was experiencing one of the lowest points in my life. I was juggling so many projects at the same time and, as you can imagine, I was stretched thin both mentally and emotionally. My bank account was bleeding profusely as the projects took a lot of my money, too. I was tired, but I was too afraid to stop—everything I was doing at that point in time was my identity. On top of that, my dearest friend was battling cancer. If you have ever encountered cancer, you know it takes its toll on not just the person affected, but their loved ones, too. It was a dark, dark period in my life. But when I read these words by Marcus Aurelius, I felt like he'd singled me out in that moment to speak specifically to me. As a typical skeptic, I assumed it was going to be one of those rhetorical things that resonated with you, but never really had any true impact. Still, I was desperate enough to find out more. While I hate to sound cliché about this, I have to say that ever since I took that step, I have never looked back.

Stoicism is nothing like I ever thought it would be and, at the same time, it became everything I needed. And it still is, today. Exploring it took me to heights and depths of myself that I didn't even realize were there. And these were the same words uttered by a childhood friend of mine, who had served in Iraq when the crisis there was at its peak. This was a guy who, when he returned, was a shadow of himself. A lot of us tried to help him and we failed. We were so powerless in the face of what he was going through, it affected our friendship. We fell out of touch for years but in the months following my first contact with Stoicism, I ran into him during one of my travels. I did not recognize him, so he was the one that called out to me. He was very different, but in a really good way. Gone were the sunken, sleep-deprived eyes that had become his trademark. In front of me was a healthy-looking man who appeared happier than I had ever seen him in my life. It was surreal. We chatted for hours and shared our experiences, but one comment he made really stood out for me. He said, "When I came back, I was a broken man. I was barely living, and my pain on a daily basis was a steady ten. And then, the Stoics found me. My pain is still a ten on most days, but my life is richer than it had ever been. Even better than the days when my pain was a one."

This book will not change the circumstances surrounding you. By the time you get to the last page, a lot may have changed, but everything will still be the same. But take this from me: If you open your heart to the truths within, I guarantee the most important change you need to happen will have occurred—and that change will be you.

Chapter One
Stoicism 101

"The whole future lies in uncertainty:

Live immediately."

Seneca

When you hear the words "stoic," or "Stoicism," images of a strict and austere life spring to mind. You think of a life of abstinence devoid of pleasure or any of the good things associated with "robust" living. A person who is regarded as stoic is thought of as stern, unkind, uncompromising, and un-showing of any form of human emotion. It is typically ascribed as a masculine trait, but there are women who "fit" that description as well. In general, society's perspective on the subject of Stoicism, while it is not favorable, is not negative. And when people think of Stoicism in a belief or religious context, the general perception is that it is foreign or belongs to one of these new-age philosophies.

In subsequent chapters, I will go into detail to address the misrepresentation of Stoicism in our times, but I can categorically tell you that Stoicism is not a new-age trend. As a matter of fact, elements of Stoicism are so deep-rooted in our cultures and ways of living that we are not even aware of it. Some of the most popular phrases that have become clichés are actually rooted in Stoicism, or straight-out quotes from the founders of Stoicism themselves. One of my personal favorite is "live in the moment." This not a direct Stoic quote, but it is a paraphrased echo of a popular quote from one of the great masters of Stoicism.

"True happiness is to enjoy the present, without anxious dependence upon the future, not to amuse ourselves with either hopes or fears but to rest satisfied with what we have, which is sufficient for he that is so, wants nothing. The greatest blessings of mankind are within us and within our reach. A wise man is content with his lot, whatever it may be, without wishing for what he has not."

Seneca

Compared to this lengthy quote, the four-word version seems like a stretch but here is another pop culture phrase that is 100% Stoic. "Luck is what happens when preparation meets opportunity." You must have heard this, or a version of it, at least once in your life. My point is, the concept of Stoicism has been a part of the fabric of our society for as long as time itself.

But the conscious practice of it is what has become a novelty for us. That said, what exactly is Stoicism? And is it really relevant for our time and era?

In very simple terms, Stoicism is a way of life that extols the virtue of rooting one's happiness in their own behavior, as opposed to depending on the world as the source of one's happiness. Life is a complicated tangle of events that occur to us in series. These events trigger emotions that range from anger to zealousness. There is no "off switch" that can guarantee these events will never occur. As humans, we often convince ourselves that we will have wholesomeness, happiness, and peace in our lives only when certain events happen.

If you could land that perfect job, or if you could get a raise. If you could make more money, or if you could find that one person that completes you, or if you could have a baby. The list goes on and on. Without realizing it, we postpone our happiness with this kind of thinking. The idea that true happiness can be found in anywhere or anything but ourselves sends us on an eternal quest to locate it. Despite the harm this brings to us, we romanticize these quests, adopting social clichés that have no factual relevance to what we are going through—just so we can justify our choices.

We ascribe titles to ourselves to feel like we are truly on a journey of purpose. The "goal getter" has a set of mantras to keep us on the trail of our holy grail. Modern thought leaders echo our feelings with equal fervor, egging us on to our destinations. And, more often than not, we arrive at these destinations. We get what we want. We snag the trophy. But we're frequently disappointed by what we have. The man or woman of our dreams is not so charming, after all. The promotion we worked so hard for is fast becoming a nightmare. And money cannot really buy you happiness.

This realization does not stop us on our tracks, however. Instead, we simply fall back on old patterns—we just put new labels on them. "Maybe if you had a travel job, or maybe if you set up shop in a niche industry." The biggest maybe of them all? "Maybe if she were taller, or maybe if he looked like your favorite MCM. Maybe if you were a capricorn like your best friend. Maybe, if all these maybes were a reality, you would get a shot at happiness."

We permit the prevalent voices of society to reflect these emotions. We channel those "you can do better, you can be better, or you deserve better" phrases and let them become the voices in our heads. And with that, we hit the repeat button just to end up right back where we started in the first place. There are so many people who go through this cycle of unhappiness without realizing there is no "thing," no person or place, that can give you genuine, lasting happiness. And this is because happiness is not from the outside. It is from within.

You cannot be hypnotized into a state of happiness. Temporary euphoria, perhaps, can work but there is no amount of finger snapping that can suddenly put you in a happy place. Even drugs cannot get you there. Certain drugs may loosen any emotional tethers that keep you in that dark tunnel, but they'll never truly set you free. If anything, this entangles things further, leaving you completely dependent on a drug for any form of reprieve, however temporary.

Stoicism takes you on a journey to self by eliminating destructive thoughts and behavioral patterns that you probably were not aware of. And the beauty of following the Stoic process is that the power is put back in your hands. Let me offer a quick illustration: Three ladies went out on a beautiful sunny day. Suddenly, the clouds darkened and a light rain began to fall. The first lady had anticipated this, and brought out her umbrella and a raincoat. Even her shoes were chosen for the weather. For her, the crisis was averted. The second lady made a poor attempt at shielding herself from the rain, all the while thinking about how her outfit and the entire day is ruined. In her case, the crisis was asserted. The third person thought of her hair puffing up like a puffer fish if the rain touches it, and laughed at the image as she made a dash for cover. She might have gotten a little wet, but in her case, I would say, the crisis was diverted.

So, we have three different people who all had the same thing happen, but their experiences were different. The rain falls on everyone. Your status, your race, and not even your mind can stop the rain from falling on you. In the same way, life happens to everyone. It is your mindset that determines the experiences you will get out of life. Stoicism opens your mind, empowers you for life's journey, and puts you in a position to determine what your life's experiences will be—including how happy you are with your life.

Chapter Two
History of Stoicism

"If one does not know to which port one is sailing,

no wind is favorable."

Seneca

To understand Stoicism, it is important that we travel back in time to the era of revolutionary thinking. A time when the value of a man was determined by the soundness of his mind and the strength of his shield. Stoicism has its roots in Ancient Greece. A lot of experts believe the earliest voice of Stoicism was the great philosopher Socrates who, ironically, is said to have fathered the philosophy of Cynicism, as well. Both philosophies share some similarities, but there are a great many differences between the two. The true founding father of Stoicism is Zeno, who stumbled on the philosophical teachings of Socrates by accident—literally.

Before founding the Stoic school of philosophy, Zeno was a very successful merchant who traveled across the seas from his home town, in what we now know as Cyprus, to many places for trade. One of these places was Greece. On one of his many trips, he survived a shipwreck. Surviving something as terrifying as that puts people in a sober, contemplative state, and I think this was his state of mind when he decided to put aside his business plan and head for Athens. While Zeno was in Athens, he paid a visit to the city's library, and while he was there, he came across manuscripts discussing the great Socrates.

If you don't know who Socrates is, his teachings founded western philosophy. While he didn't do any writing himself, his most ardent students and disciples Plato and Xenophon documented his teachings. The manuscript that Zeno discovered was written by Xenophon, and Zeno loved the writer's portrayal of Socrates so much that he wanted to find and meet a man just like him. Zeno was discussing this with the person who'd sold him the manuscript when Crates of Thebes walked by. The bookseller directed Zeno to him.

Before we go further into the history of Stoicism, it is important to highlight the series of accidents that led Zeno to this point. First, there was the shipwreck. Next was his discovery of the manuscript written by Xenophon, and then, the fortuitous meeting with Crates of Thebes. It is said in one of Zeno's biographies that he famously joked, "Now that I have suffered shipwreck, I am on a good journey." In other versions, Zeno was quoted as saying, "You've done well, fortune, driving me thus to philosophy." This kind of thinking, converting the experiences of one's misfortune into a source of pure happiness, this is exactly what Stoicism is about. Now, back to the story.

Crates of Thebes was a well-known Cynic philosopher and, in his time, Cynicism was fairly popular (not widely practiced, but known) among the people. He was born to wealth but, based on his beliefs, Crates gave away everything he owned to live a life of poverty on the streets of Athens. He ate on the streets, slept on the streets, defecated on the streets, and was even known to have masturbated on the streets. As if this public way of life wasn't bad enough, he was said to be lame in one leg and he had hunched shoulders. So, he was an extreme Cynic who was somewhat disabled, but he was highly respected by the people of Athens. His allure to the people wasn't just because he nobly gave away his wealth for poverty, but the fact that in that bare and simple state, he lived a cheerful life.

One student of his put it this way: "But Crates with only his wallet and tattered cloak laughed out his life jocosely, as if he had been always at a festival."

So well-liked was Crates that people nicknamed him the "door opener," because he could enter any house and was received with honor everywhere he went. He went on to attract a wealthy heiress who gave up her wealth, married him, and joined him in living on the streets. Hipparchia was known to have borne him at least two children. This was remarkable, because the idea of a woman—a high-born woman, at that—choosing to live in that way was abhorrent. But they did, and their marriage worked because of it.

Picture this chance meeting between Zeno and Crates. On one hand, you have this guy who just lost his wealth at sea and is now trying to make sense of his life, in a low emotional state. On the other hand, you have a guy who had all this wealth and looked like he would have been a lot more comfortable in his physical condition if he was wealthy, yet he willingly gave it away. To top it off, he was immensely happy. What an impression this would have made on our young Zeno!

Armed with the manuscript about Socrates, Zeno followed Crates and became an ardent student of his. However, Zeno did not entirely follow his teacher's ways. Zeno imbibed the idea of living a simple life but he believed in modesty, as well. I'm guessing the street life wasn't for Zeno. He studied under other philosophers of his time, too, but Crates had the greatest influence on him. Unlike his cheery and humorous teacher, though, Zeno was perceived to be gloomy and withdrawn.

He chose his company carefully and was not keen on making long, elaborate speeches. He was an earnest man of purpose, and even his death is reported to have reflected this. He was said to have died quoting a line from Niobe's tragic tale, "I come, I come, why dost thou call for me?" Everything had a purpose for Zeno, and this was emphasized in his teachings. He started his teachings in a place called Stoa Poikile, which is where the name "Stoic" originated from. At first, poets who originated from this area were called Stoic but, thanks to Zeno's influence, his followers and disciples were later known as Stoics.

Here was a man on the precipice of his greatest tragedy. He had lost a significant portion of his wealth on a voyage. While there has never been a time when being poor was easy, I believe people in this era likely had it even worse. Poverty was considered vulgar. People clung to their wealth like their lives depended on it. Their sense of purpose, sense of freedom, and sense of happiness were determined by the size of their wallets. We are not so far from this kind of thinking in today's world—the major difference is what we consider as wealth.

Back then, the quality of one's tunic was considered a marker for wealth. The number of fields you owned, and the number of laborers you had on it, were also signs. Even the number of children one had played a role defining one's social status. Today, we look at the number of cars you have. The pricier the model, the more points you earn. Our sense of accomplishment hangs on the number of likes and followers we are able to attract on social media. These are different concepts, but the context remains the same.

The early teachers of that time sought to help people remove the limitations placed on their happiness by wealth or the absence of it.

Chapter Three
Early Stoicism

"The purpose of life is happiness, which is achieved by virtue, living according to the dictates of reason, ethical and philosophical training, self-reflection, careful judgment and inner calm."
Stoic Quote

Given that Stoicism sort of descended from Cynicism, it is understandable that the early practitioners of Stoicism may have had to work harder to convince people that they are different from the Cynics. One famous poet, centuries after the death of Zeno, is reported to have jokingly said in one of his satires that the major difference between a Stoic and a Cynic was their choice of clothing. Given that Zeno was heavily influenced by one of the extreme Cynics of his time (Crates), you can't blame people for making this assumption.

However, true followers understood the clear difference. Zeno, in his teaching, broke down philosophy into three major areas—logic, physics, and ethics. He believed these three things were elemental to achieving complete peace of mind. Zeno was not a man of many words, but the founder of Stoicism wrote many articles on the subject of man's control over his mind and his wanton cravings. Sadly, none survived through time. We have fragments of his statements quoted by other writers, but it is his teachings and principles, as well as his vision for the Stoic society passed on to his students, that gives us his general view of life from a Stoic perspective.

Logic

On the subject of logic, Zeno believed there are four stages a person must go through before he can attain true knowledge. First came perception, or one's impression of a matter. The next stage is the person's acknowledgment of the matter, which Zeno referred to as assent. After acceptance, the next stage on this journey is comprehension. And it is only after the individual has gained full comprehension of the matter that he can really get true knowledge of it. Logic is a broad subject that covers not just the theories of perception and thought, but included rhetoric and grammar, as well. Zeno's thoughts on logic were influenced by one of his teachers at the Megarian school of philosophy in Attica, where he studied under great philosophers.

Now, while the teachings of Zeno started the Stoic movement in his time, certain prominent philosophers may have felt that his teachings, particularly on the subject of logic, were a somewhat watered-down version of what had been taught by some of his predecessors. One man who voiced this opinion was Marcus Tullius Cicero, a philosopher and lawyer who is considered to be Rome's greatest orator of the 1st century. But the life and times of Cicero happened long after the passing of Zeno, and he did very little for the Stoic community. However, Chrysippus, who later took over as head of the school of Stoic, had in hindsight protected the school from such attacks. We will get to him later.

Physics

In Stoic teachings, physics is more than the science of things. It explores nature in its rawest form and identifies the Universe as God. His view was not bestowing humane qualities on inanimate objects. He reasoned that the universe is the whole to which every other part belongs, and that the universe is a divine reasoning entity that advances and extends itself by creating. Zeno believed that universes undergo cycles of formation and destruction, a process which starts with the primary form of the universe—fire. From fire, it becomes air, which becomes part water and part earth. The water then becomes air again before going back to fire.

The interesting part of Zeno's early view on physics is that our souls are all part of the same fire, which is the primary substance of the universe. The differences in our thinking, our status as well as other physical attributes, is a result of the transformation process. At our core, though, we are all the same. And it goes on to tell us that the nature of the universe is balanced. It sets out to accomplish what is right. And, even though our actions and choices might take us on different paths and create alternate routes to our destination, Zeno recognizes the impact of unconditional fate in its design to keep the balance in the face of free will.

Ethics

The subject of ethics is where the early Stoics clearly distinguished themselves from the Cynics. The Cynics held the belief that if a thing is morally indifferent, it cannot be of any value. Therefore, since a house is just a thing to provide shelter, cannot be defined as being good or bad. Nearly all worldly possessions take on the same characteristic, which is why most Cynics disowned any wealth they had. Extremists like Crates lived their entire lives with nothing to their name. Another known Cynic extremist at that time is Diogenes of Sinope. He was said to beg for a living, and his home on the streets was in a ceramic jar.

Zeno, despite his great respect for Crates, did not necessarily agree with him in this regard. He was of the opinion that things that cater to our natural instinct for self-preservation could have some relative value apportioned to them. However, he made it ostentatiously clear that the value provided by these things does not in any way lead us to happiness. Zeno maintains in his teachings that happiness is directly dependent on our moral actions, and no moral action is more virtuous than the other. Our actions are either good or bad.

This kind of thinking resolves a lot of emotional conflicts that arise from the internal debate we have concerning the actions we take. This thought process is crucial to help weed out the unnecessary challenges we place upon ourselves. In a world where we are constantly seeking labels for ourselves, our thoughts, and virtually everything we do, the early Stoic life sought to connect us with the foundation of it all—our sense of reason. Zeno identified four negative emotions, and the three corresponding emotions to these four. Zeno was unable to find any corresponding rational equivalent emotion for pain. So, you have the positive "will" for the negative "desire," "caution" for "fear," and "joy" for "pleasure."

Desire and pleasure are words we don't identify as negative today. However, these are emotions that we typically confuse for joy in our quest for happiness. You desire a thing, seek it out, when you attain it, for a brief moment, you are "happy"—only to realize that this happiness is fleeting. And, because you want to retain this feeling of happiness, you divert your desires to something else and repeat the cycle. Zeno understood this and, even though his time is different from our time, the human interaction and emotional reaction to the world remains a static process. The early Stoics sought peace in their simple way of life while preserving the balance with their natural instincts.

Chapter Four
Modern Stoicism

"It is not what happens to you,

but how you react to it that matters."

Epictetus

In the last chapter, we took a philosophical tour through the years 500 – 200 BC, and even touched on the first century to set the precipice for the beginning of Stoicism. We know the people, logic, and ideas that influenced Stoicism in its earliest years, and we also know that all of Zeno's works were lost. But, after the death of Zeno, how was stoicism able to persevere, evolve, and take root in society? And how relevant is the Stoic way of thinking in today's world? Well, the answer to that is simple—great ideas outlive the people and the times in which they were conceived. That said, in this chapter, we are retracing the Stoic movement after the passing of Zeno and following in the footsteps of his pupils and disciples to more conventional times. Now, I am certain that you came to this book for enlightenment, not a history lesson—but I should point out that sometimes, to get to where you want to go, you have to pay attention to where you have been (especially if you are lost).

And so, for a few more minutes, let us lose ourselves in the city of Athens. After Zeno's death, one of his most devout pupils, Cleanthes, took over leadership of the school. His story was just as tragic as that of Zeno's: He was a boxer of some repute in his early years, but when he came to Athens, he had barely enough money to feed himself for the day. He chose to study philosophy with the greats. First, with Crates the Cynic, but he soon took to Zeno. Cleanthes lived the Stoic life and was considered by many to be a man of character. He made valuable contributions to Stoicism, particularly in the area of physics.

Cleanthes elaborated on Zeno's notion about everything in the Universe being a part of one. He characterized the soul as a material substance, and claimed souls go on to live even after one's death. And on the subject of ethics, he emphasized the role our will has over our emotions. In other words, what Zeno started, Cleanthes completed—and he did this quite literally in some cases. For example, it is a general belief that Zeno was quoted as saying, "the goal of life is to live consistently," and Cleanthes was said to have added, "with nature." This completes the popular Stoic mantra, "the goal of life is to live consistently with nature."

The contributions of Cleanthes broadened Zeno's view of Stoicism but the real game changer came from Chryssipus. I mentioned him earlier, in passing, but now, we will look at his role in this story. Cleanthes may have broadened Zeno's theories, but it was Chryssipus who expounded on them, who crystalized Zeno's thoughts and set Stoicism on a path that influenced the minds of some of the greatest philosophers of the eras that followed, and even right down to this day.

His interpretation of Zeno's teachings did what in modern terminology would be described as setting the Stoic school on fire. For those who didn't grasp the teachings of Stoicism in the initial stages, this guy made it clearer. The practice spread across lands and transitioned into the lifestyles of many people in that time. This laid the foundation for the integration of Stoicism into cultures and religion, even though the people who adopted Stoic principles didn't identify as Stoics. This explains why we hear Stoic quips here and there. In this era, Stoicism transcended just being the "new age" religion of the time. Chryssipus laid out practical principles for daily living. He taught how to get to the root of emotional problems and provided a guideline to help extricate ourselves from the chains we have put on ourselves with our own expectations and ambitions. There were so many voices at that time, but Chryssipus created a cohesion for these different opinions, which probably explains why people accused him of quoting other philosophers in his writings.

His comprehension of the ideologies presented at the time made it possible for Stoicism to gain a definitive stand. His achievements and arguments earned Chryssipus recognition as one of the foremost logicians of Greece, and some even place him above Aristotle. Some proficient Stoics who benefited from his teachings and were recognized are:

Seneca

This is a wealthy poet and philosopher who is quoted throughout this book; he offered practical guides on living the Stoic life. Also, he is one of those Stoics who didn't disavow wealth—on the contrary, he was one of the wealthiest Stoics of his time. This tells us that Stoicism does not despise wealth, therefore embracing the Stoic life does not mean embracing poverty.

Epictetus

In contrast to Seneca, Epictetus was a slave who rose to the ranks of highly respected philosophers. He was born into slavery somewhere in Turkey and had a master who let him study. When he was given his freedom, he went on to teach philosophy. One of the people he influenced was Marcus Aurelius.

Marcus Aurelius

Seneca was known to have gained more wealth, power, and influence for being the tutor for the young lad who later became a much-disliked emperor, but Marcus Aurelius became powerful because he was an emperor and a staunch Stoic, as well. His reign was plagued with wars and troubles and, despite the tremendous power he wielded, Marcus was considered noble, just, and devoid of corruption—proving that a Stoic can have power and still be true to his beliefs.

Modern-day thought leaders who adopted Stoicism includes the likes of Theodore Roosevelt, Robert Louise Stevenson, and Bill Clinton. However, in the centuries that followed the reign of Marcus Aurelius, Stoicism was looked on publicly with contempt and it wasn't until the 20th century that it made a comeback. This return was thanks to the recognition given to Stoicism for its immense contribution to logic and other aspects of science, particularly mathematics.

But, we are not here to discuss the math, physics, and science of Stoicism. We are here to elevate our minds above circumstances in order to attain complete peace of mind. I wanted us to go on this historical journey for several reasons beyond helping us gain an understanding of the origin of Stoicism. I want us to look at the men who founded Stoicism. They were men limited by the science of their time. They were beaten down by life but, despite the tragedies they suffered, they shaped the outcome of their lives and influenced their world by elevating their minds. They didn't just say the words that we have come to appreciate: they lived those words.

Their journey to elevation started with the opening of their minds. And it is time for you to open your own mind. With history out of the way, let us examine the Stoic principles and logic.

Chapter Five
The Stoic Logic

"As long as you live, keep learning how to live."
Seneca

Stoic logic in textbook context is the system of formal logical reasoning that is concerned with the practical application of philosophy designed to help people live better lives daily. The Stoic logic covers every aspect of your life, from sex to emotions and even your social interactions with others. The concept of Stoicism is so encompassing that these principles still resonate deeply with us today, though they have been around since 400 years BC. The founders of Stoicism were so ahead of their time, the advancements made in modern-day technology in the areas of computer science, artificial intelligence, and many others are made possible largely due to the groundbreaking discoveries made by these Stoic philosophers.

More important than the machinery we have become so heavily reliant on is the impact of Stoicism on our lives. According to Stoic logic, when it comes to human behavior, everything we do is determined by our ability to reason. The Stoic logic is about embracing the power of decision making. The world we live in today has sold us on the idea of living off our desires. The bigger your house, the more fulfilled you will be. The more expensive the cars you drive, the more respected you will become. The wealthier you are, the happier you will feel. And so, we are trained to want more. We desire the latest phones, fashion items, and anything else the media sells to us based on the picture they have painted.

However, there is also a school of thought which, like the old school of Cynics, frowns on anything that could add value to your life. Under the guise of religion and beliefs, people are manipulated to discourage the seeking of wealth, power, knowledge, or anything that could put them in a position to be of any kind of influence. This kind of thinking limits them from achieving their true potential and making any kind of valuable contribution to the world. It also makes them more susceptible to the manipulation of others because, like it or not, we need these things to preserve our dignity.

On top of these conflicting views on life and our insatiable appetite for more "things," we are forced to deal with life. We know life is not going to be put on hold simply because you are trying to earn your degree, finish that project, or build that relationship. I watched a movie where the actor says life is like an endless series of train wrecks, with only brief commercial breaks of happiness. Not everyone goes through the same cycles of happiness interspersed with moments of grief. For some of us, the pain comes in short doses, while for others, the pain goes on for longer. And then, you have people who have dealt with pain all of their lives. No matter who you are, just as I mentioned earlier, the rain falls on us all.

People say the circumstances we go through in life shape us and make us better. That kind of thinking can work in certain situations, but what about events that cause senseless pain? In those moments of grief, you are unable to gain a proper understanding of why these things happened to you and how it is meant to make you better. If you are lucky enough, you are able to move forward with your life, but you may remain scarred by the experience. There will always be residues of the pain caused by the event. Those who are not so lucky may enter into emotional warfare that causes them to hurt themselves, as well as those around them. Their inability to make sense of their tragedy plunges them into depression and, until they get to the root of the problem, they will continue to relive this pain on a daily basis. The thinking that your circumstances shape you puts you at the disposal of life. You are left to the whims of these events, like being aboard a ship with no wheel and no captain to steer it—you will drift whichever way the storms toss you. If you are not careful, that ship could end up breaking apart.

The Stoic logic trains you to steer your ship with strength and conviction, even in the face of life's stormy waters. And if by chance the storms you face steer you in a direction you are not going, with wisdom and careful decisions, you can chart your course to take you to where you want to go, or even make a better life for yourself in the place you now find yourself. With the Stoic logic, even in the eye of the storm, you are in charge. Your decisions come from a place of rational thinking—when you are able to think rationally, the choices available to you become clearer.

The founders and major contributors to the advancement of Stoicism are people whose lives and teachings direct us on how to attain perfect peace of mind, even when we are going through hardships. The goal is to get to that place where you can live the good life. Now, what is the good life? We have established that wealth and the accumulation of stuff is not the good life. This can contribute to improving your quality of life, but even with the absence of these things, you can still live the good life. And that is because the good life is a state where we are living in agreement with nature. This definitely does not portend living in our basic state just like animals, because we have the one thing that animals do not possess—the ability to reason.

The good life for the Stoic is where all actions are a byproduct of the application of sound reasoning. It is easy to confuse a true Stoic with one who is obsessed with being in control, because they appear to linger on their thoughts and rarely take action without thinking it through. However, the decision to apply reason to their every action comes from a place where they recognize the things which they cannot control, and instead focus on what they can. With this perspective, you may find they are much more fluid, if not a direct opposite of the rigid impression we have of them. The fluidity of the Stoic allows them to go with the ebb and flow of life without necessarily being subject to it.

When the Stoic logic is narrowed down to the goal of living the good life, it does sound rather simple and uncomplicated, but you would be right in assuming that it is anything but. This is why there are guiding principles to take us through each moment of our lives. In subsequent chapters, you will often see the word "virtue"—this word plays a major role in the Stoic logic. "Virtues," in this context, refer to the things we aspire to be and become.

For those of us who are used to living on the edge between light and darkness—in other words, people who like to stir up a little trouble every now and then—the Stoic path might seem a bit daunting. You may be worried about becoming a goody-two-shoes. However, while you are expected to apply reason to every action, it doesn't mean your life has to be boring. There is plenty of room to have fun and, more importantly, there is plenty of room for you to be better.

Instead of living off cheesy one-liners, use Stoic logic to become the most authentic version of yourself, where there are no compromises in values and moral integrity.

Chapter Six
General Misconceptions About Stoicism

"All our knowledge begins with the senses,

proceeds then to the understanding and ends with reason.

There is nothing higher than reason."

Immanuel Kant

In order to overturn your thinking system, which is critical if you want Stoic logic to be effective in helping you achieve the goals you have laid out, it is important to examine the most common preconceived notions people have about Stoic logic. I talked about a few earlier but here, we are going to be more specific. I will start with the more common ones and build up from there.

1. That Stoicism is too austere

I believe this opinion stemmed from the early years of Stoicism, which was a time when Cynicism was in vogue. The Cynic lifestyle was about renouncing any worldly possession and living a pious life. Although the early Stoic masters made a clear distinction in this regard, it has taken a while for their differentiation to catch on.

It is also quite possible that the absence of a flamboyant lifestyle, typical of most Stoics, may make it seem like they do not have fun or enjoy life. The truth of this is simple: Stoic logic teaches you not to place value on wealth and material things, hence, you are not easily moved by materialism. Rather, you appreciate the contributions made in your life, but this doesn't control your actions.

2. That Stoicism is a religious sect

Again, in the early years, Stoicism had a cult-like following, which probably instigated the idea that it was a religious sect. More than being a religion, however, it is a way of thinking and reasoning. Unlike religions, where you are required to embrace every facet, Stoicism allows you to take certain elements and apply them in a way you see fit.

In the application of Stoic logic, a deity does not dictate your dealings in life. What you eat, how you dress, as well as what you do is dictated by your sense of right and wrong. However, your perspective is not the only factor in the decision-making process. You also have to consider how your actions may affect your relationships with others.

3. That Stoicism means withdrawal from the world

To practice Stoicism, you do not have to quit your day job, sell your house, and take up residence in a hidden monastery. You are not required to contemplate the mysteries of the universe from the silence of a cave, and you most certainly do not need to take a vow of silence just so you can activate the voice of reasoning within.

There are many people, both past and present, who were actively involved in their communities and maintained a vibrant social life, yet were staunch Stoics or, at the very least, practiced Stoic principles. If you need to take some time off from the pressures of life, by all means do so. This is a primary human need. But do not ignore the other primary human need to connect, either. The key is balance.

4. Stoics are emotionless

This may fall under the purview of the first misconception on the list, but I had to separate this from austerity because of its importance to our everyday lives. The average human experiences a variety of emotions. Some of these emotions are very uplifting, while others are soul crushing. On the larger scheme of things, some of these emotions are our body's biological defense against threats to our person.

Choosing to live without these emotional experiences is the exact opposite of what Stoicism teaches. Grief helps you cope with loss, fear keeps you alert for danger, and even anger serves the purpose of strengthening you to protect yourself. The Stoic logic allows you to experience these emotions, but trains you to avoid letting them dictate your actions—even when you are in your most riled upstate, your actions will be guided by rational thought.

Sure, the average Stoic is not going to have a temper tantrum when the waiter mixes up his order. That doesn't mean he wasn't angered by it. He simply chooses to react in a manner that is more productive to the situation. So, if by any chance, you signed up for this because you were hoping to become an unfeeling human, you may need to rethink your options.

5. Stoicism is hard

I think this is more a millennial thing. We are so used to life at the push of a button that going through things that require a process might seem tedious. You want to go into your meditation corner, connect your thumb to your finger, take a deep breath, and exhale all your troubles away.

Stoicism does not work that way. This is a lifelong process. Each day is lived with a conscientious effort to be mindful of everything we do. If you are hoping to correct certain behaviors, build your confidence, and live the good life, you will have to get used to the idea of applying Stoic logic every single day.

6. The practice of Stoicism removes your free will

The Stoic logic embraces the role fate plays in our lives. This essentially means you have to accept your place and station in life. Most people have interpreted this to mean that we are expected to simply roll over and play dead in the face of circumstances—this could not be more wrong.

The Stoic logic advocates people analyze their situation objectively. In the process of analyzing whatever is going on, they are able to truly understand what is in their control and what isn't. This kind of thinking puts them in harmony with the situation, because they have gained insight into the true nature of what they face. And it is with this knowledge that they can take actions that will bring about the most desirable results.

Chapter Seven
Stoicism in Everyday Living

"When you arise in the morning,

think of what a precious privilege it is to be alive –

to breathe, to think, to love, to enjoy."

Marcus Aurelius

Practicing Stoicism in modern times is not so different from being a Christian, a Buddhist, or practicing whatever customs and beliefs are prevalent in your community. It is not a religion, however, it is a way of life. Practitioners simply reflect on the teachings, then try as much as possible to engage their minds with topics and thoughts that offer better choices for their lives. Stoics are more proactive about their day-to-day living—they do not go to bed, wake up, and wait for life to happen to them as they go about their activities for the day. Instead, they do their best to anticipate the challenges of the day and plot corresponding actions to those challenges.

They meditate on the four cardinal virtues of fortitude, justice, temperance, and prudence, and try to envision how they may have to employ each of these virtues that day. This is not to say that they can predict the events of the day. However, they are able to program themselves to better handle the surprises life will have in store for them. The "programming" of the Stoic mind is done by participating in different Stoic exercises, which may include picturing a worst-case scenario for the day. Here, the Stoic thinks about the worst event that could happen that day, then build their mindset to be indifferent towards this tragedy. This exercise is called Hierocles' circle.

This does not necessarily mean that the Stoic wants this tragedy to happen. Obviously, we would rather have good things happen to us. But this kind of training puts your mind in a state where you are able to remove your sense of value and self-worth from the event. If you are like most people, your biggest fear would be the loss of your source of livelihood. With the standard mindset, a loss like that could lead to depression, panic, and other negative emotions that may instigate negative reactions. This exercise helps you eliminate that fear. So, even if it happens, you are able to live above this crisis.

For some people, this kind of thinking may appear morbid, especially if your worst fear is your own death. Often, these fears stop us from living our day-to-day lives. I know of a woman who barely escaped her marriage by the skin of her teeth, due to her abusive husband. With help from friends and family, she was able to bring him to justice and have him sent to jail. It was a temporary victory for her, because his sentencing became a countdown clock that caused her to experience anxiety and panic attacks.

She would jump out of her sleep in a state of fright, thinking that day would be the day her husband would walk free. She couldn't take on jobs, was scared to buy a house, and couldn't even enjoy a simple moment with family because at any moment, her ex-husband might walk through her door. She practiced the Hierocles circle exercise. In those moments of meditation, she dug up every horrible version of her nightmare. Where she was dragged by her hair on the streets, where he murdered her in her sleep—it was gory and, in the initial stages, it was discombobulating.

But she kept at it. In her own words, the visions became less frightening over time until she found herself trying to invent scarier scenarios to amp up the fright level. However, the truth was, she had lived out her worst fears and this opened up a new door for her. She signed up for self-defense classes, not because she wanted to fight but because it helped her feel more confident. She moved closer to her family and opened up more to her friends. The paralysis imposed by fear ceased the moment she overcame her fears. This is just one example of how Stoicism can be applied in your life.

Another relevant benefit of the practice of Stoicism is its ability to help you focus on the present. There is so much going on around us in life—so many passions, so many dreams, so many opportunities and, in the same vein, so many fears. The uncertainty of tomorrow is what drives a lot of us on a fundamental level. The prospect of paying those heavy, recurring bills have us sitting at our desks day after day, working jobs we have no interest in. We settle for relationships that cause us more harm than good, because we are afraid of being lonely.

In situations where we are meant to speak up for our rights, we allow our fears to silence us—but more than anything, we spend our days worrying. We worry about what could have been, what should have been, and what would have been. Some of us worry more about the past. Previous mistakes and actions taken haunt us and prevent us from enjoying what is happening now. Then, you have people who are the exact opposite—they live in the moment, but for the wrong reasons.

These are the people who live only for their desires and passions. They must buy that new fall coat. They must own the latest phone. If everyone is doing it, it must be okay for them to do it, too. It's like pulling beads along a string that has no end. They just keep picking one bead after the other. Never experiencing happiness, never truly enjoying the moment. All they do is want more. This is the bane of living in these modern times. The practice of Stoicism can keep you grounded in the present. Seneca put it this way:

"The greatest blessings of mankind are within us and within our reach. A wise man is content with his lot, whatever it may be, without wishing for what he has not."

You do not need to embrace Stoicism in its entirety. You can take up Stoic exercises that you feel would bring you closer to your goals. Throughout the rest of the chapters, I will share some of these exercises and offer guides to help you integrate them into your daily routine.

Chapter Eight
The Four Cardinal Virtues of Stoicism

"Everything we hear is an opinion, not a fact.
Everything we see is a perspective, not the truth."
Marcus Aurelius

You cannot practice Stoicism without first understanding its cardinal virtues. The origin of these virtues is unclear, but they predate the earliest Stoic teachings. Perhaps going even further back than the time of Plato. If you look on the internet, you may find different variations of the words typically used as the four cardinals. This is because of the difficulty in translating ancient Greek texts to the English language. There is also the conflict of perspective. The only philosophical dictionary known to have survived from the ancient Greek times come from Plato's era, which means the definition is given from a Platonist perspective. Unfortunately, there are no definitions from the Stoic era.

However, given the materials we do have, we are able to gain a better understanding of what the Stoics thought. We will look at each virtue individually:

Phronêsis: Prudence or Practical Wisdom

This is the most important of the Stoic virtues and it refers to our ability to discern good from bad. It is believed that wisdom is the only virtue, while the remaining three cardinal virtues which we will discuss shortly are simply its primary applications. Seeing that wisdom is essentially practical reasoning, I tend to agree with that thinking.

Wisdom is the foundation of all Stoic logic, because you cannot make sound decisions and actions if you have no clear understanding of what is good and what is bad. In this application, good does not refer to what appeals to the senses. The smell of a nice, warm bowl of soup can be very appealing to whoever perceives it, but that does not automatically ascribe the moral value of good to it. The bowl of soup falls under the preferred indifferent category. Eating this bowl of soup will not make you a good person or a terrible person, it is how you go about your pursuit of the soup—whether you steal it or cook it—that is classified as either good or bad.

Wisdom is the understanding of the true nature of good. With this understanding, you are able to ascribe value to different external things rationally. Under Stoic teachings, a wise person is not just someone who can tell the difference between good and bad. For a person to call himself wise, he must be able to offer himself wise counsel. In other words, wisdom is an internalized process.

Dikaiosunê: Justice or Morality

Again, this is an area where we have issues with the direct translation of the word. When you hear justice, you may think this refers to the legal sense of the word, but that definition is simply not enough to encapsulate the true Stoic reference of this virtue. While an aspect of this virtue implies a state where we are obedient to the laws of the land, it goes much deeper than this.

Morality, on the other hand, does not fully encompass the stoic meaning of the word, either. In this instance, we are talking about doing right or, as some people would like to say, living an upright life. If you are the religious sort, you may go as far as calling it righteousness. However, between morality and justice, we can understand what this virtue is about.

In practical terms, justice or morality is the application of wisdom in social interactions. We've established that wisdom is the knowledge of good and bad, and the ability to clearly distinguish between both. It is one thing to know something, it is another thing to act on it. In your dealings with people, justice/morality refers to the wisdom you apply in relating to them. Your respect and treatment of others is not based on their status, gender, or the benefits they offer. Rather, you make a deliberate choice to be fair and impartial.

Sôphrosunê: Temperance or Moderation

In some books, this is referred to as self-discipline or self-control. In life, we are almost always in a constant state of want. And, more often than not, our wants are not always the same as our needs. Our carnality is propelled by what books like the Bible refer to as the "desires of the flesh."

The entire sales force in the world is built on this concept. You turn on the TV to see a nice-looking guy running and, without so many words, you are programmed to think that to get that body, you need to run—and for your running to feel good, you need the shoes he is wearing. This prompting of your desire is so strong that even if you have 10 sports shoes lined up in the back of your closet, you still feel you need this one shoe.

This kind of feeling is amplified in areas of our lives that have to do with gratifying our pleasure impulses. This virtue is all about tempering those instincts that drive our wants. It is, in essence, the application of wisdom when dealing with temptations.

Andreia: Fortitude or Courage

Fear is another prominent driving emotion behind most of our decisions. You find people who work themselves to the bones because they are afraid of not being able to afford the things they want. They sometimes live a stagnant and unprogressive life, deliberately avoiding risks that would propel them forward, even if those risks are supported by their rational thinking or wisdom.

This virtue grants the ability to act on the wisdom you have discerned, even if it is not exactly conventional. Wisdom is fantastic, but without the application of wisdom, it is just another nice thing something thought or said. This virtue is also likened to endurance. But in that sad, long-suffering way that makes you a victim of circumstance. But in an emboldened form that sees you facing down your deepest fears and not acting on them. Rather, you push past it to think and act logically. You can say fortitude is wisdom applied in adversity.

Chapter Nine
The Practice of Misfortune

"Say to yourself in the early morning:
I shall meet today ungrateful, violent,
treacherous, envious, uncharitable men.
All of these things have come upon them
 through ignorance of real good and ill...
I can neither be harmed by any of them,
for no man will involve me in wrong,
nor can I be angry with my kinsman or hate him;
for we have come into the world to work together."

Marcus Aurelius

Optimism is good. Hope is good. Maintaining a positive outlook on life is good. These are vital tools in the world we live in today. But if you want to thrive, if you really want to live the good life and you have found yourself struggling with this, perhaps it is time to throw away the rose-tinted glasses and step into the dark for a minute. For people who have characterized themselves by their ability to maintain a sunny-side-up attitude toward life, looking on the flip side might be likened to them violating their nature, but hear me out.

For a long time, we have been taught to believe in concepts like luck, grace, supernatural blessings, and so on. While some may deny the existence of these things, it would be detrimental to live our lives hoping that one of them (if not all of them) happens to us. The reality is that life is more like a game of chess—it requires strategy and careful planning. To develop and execute a well-thought-out strategy, you need to see the picture from all angles, anticipating the best- and the worst-case scenarios. This may sound morbid, but stay with me.

The "hashtag blessed" movement that is so rampant on social media, as well as in our regular daily lives, is not what it appears to be. That person who seemingly got lucky went through a process you are not entirely aware of. In Stoicism, there is a generally held belief that luck is simply preparation meeting opportunity. Except in most cases, these "lucky" people get into their favored season without any deliberate preparation on their part. Stoics don't stumble into their season. They prepare themselves adequately and, when the right moment comes, they seize it. But how do you prepare for something that is not exactly within your control?

For starters, you have to stop thinking you are just someone life happens to. Obviously, it would be delusional to think you have any form of control over the universe. Remember that boat on the sea illustration I used earlier. There is no way you can dictate the direction of the wind or the movement of the waves, and certainly not the intensity of the storm. However, that doesn't mean that every time your ship is tossed, you lose your position as captain. The wheel is still in your hands—you just need to activate your thinking hat. Here are a few things you can start doing:

1. Get out of your comfort zone.

The general saying, "if it's broke, don't fix it," is a lie that feeds the delusion many of us call "optimism." The reality of life is the constancy of change. If you do not determine the change that will definitely come, the change that comes will determine your fate.

2. Expect the worst but hope for the best.

We have this habit of making decisions based on the best-case scenario while living in fear of the worst. This is the source of anxiety and fear. Instead, develop the habit of taking actions based on your worst fears, living on the hope that the best will happen. This is not to say your fear should guide your actions. The Stoic exercises we will talk about later will clarify this.

3. Be deliberate in your efforts

Each day should not be just another series of meaningless routines. Break patterns, but don't be impulsive about it. Think it through and ensure that at the end of your thinking process, you are able to conclusively establish actions that support what you have discerned.

STOIC EXERCISES THAT HELP IN THE PRACTICE OF MISFORTUNE

1. PRACTICE POVERTY

I can almost picture that one eyebrow shooting up to your hairline as you read this. I mean, after everything I did to convince you that Stoicism is not a vow of poverty, the very first Stoic exercise I share is to tell you to practice poverty. It sounds insane, but in a minute, it will make sense. Comfort is a form of slavery, because it conditions your happiness to the things you have. A loss of those things would result in a major disruption of your life. More than that, it would affect your emotions negatively and cause you to react in the same way. The amount of suicides recorded during America's great financial depression illustrates this.

The practice of poverty involves taking a few days each month to live conservatively, well below your means. During this period, you would eat very little, and ignore that comfy bed to sleep on the cold, hard ground. If you can, dress in your rattiest clothes. Essentially, you should familiarize yourself with being in a state of want. The benefits of this exercise are that it keeps you in touch with reality and helps you get to a place where you can appreciate the things that give you comfort without depending on them as a source of happiness. By so doing, you are able to see those "things" for what they really are. Whether it is your job, your home, or your wealth, the goal is to be able to enjoy them—not be enslaved by them.

2. PRACTICE WHAT YOU FEAR

As humans, it is instinctive to want to get as far away as possible from the thing you fear. Our need to distance ourselves from our fears is so intense that, sometimes, it drives us to the point of denial. We refuse to acknowledge the threat, and the price we pay for this denial can be very high. On the other end of the spectrum, you have people who go to extreme lengths to avoid what they fear most. Either way, we are deprived of living to our fullest potential, because we are being held down by our fears.

I know of someone who came from a family where breast cancer was prevalent. This was the time when the management of cancer did not include some of the medical advancements being made today. This meant there were a lot of deaths from cancer within the family, which led to the women and some of the men living in fear. For the longest time, this woman lived in the shadow of the disease. She bought into the slogan of "living in the moment," but in the worst possible way—she spent money as fast as she could earn it, and rarely made plans beyond the next week.

On the surface, she seemed to be living the life. She was fun, energetic, and a joy to be around. But in her heart, her fears ate away at her. She turned down jobs, marriage proposals, and basically any opportunity that held any future prospects. By chance, she was involved in an accident that almost took her life. Lying in pain in her hospital bed forced her to confront her fear—she realized cancer was not the only thing that could kill her. So, right there, she decided to get screened. She figured if she can survive that accident, she can survive cancer. That's how she became free from her fears.

3. PARCH YOUR IGNORANCE

Have you ever asked yourself why you are afraid in the first place? I have an intense phobia of snakes. I am usually described as calm and collected, and I'm able to maintain this ambiance even under the most intense high-pressure situation. But throw in a slippery, slimy snake, and I lose my cool in the most embarrassing way imaginable. My reaction was unexplainable. It felt like it was something I was programmed to do. One evening, I was watching a documentary, listening to this explorer talk about snakes and his mission to ensure the survival of a certain species. I was stunned that anyone cared enough to do this. But the more I listened, the more I realized that, in their way, snakes are beautiful, too. And yes, a fraction of them are poisonous, but through the eyes of this explorer, I could see their beauty.

My fear of snakes was based on the stereotypical information I was fed all my life. But the moment I replaced that ignorance with factual knowledge, my fear reduced a significant degree. Don't get anything twisted, though—there's no chance of me having a snake as a pet in the nearest future, and I still think that the way they move is super creepy. Still, I'm not as terrified as I once was.

In this exercise, you need to dry up the well of ignorance that feeds your fear by asking the right questions. For example, you might have a fear of losing your job, because of the downsizing rumor you heard. Have a talk with your colleagues and go over your performance to help determine if your fears are valid. Then, ask the tough questions. Is it the loss of a paycheck or the prospect of finding a new job that scares you? The answers you get will give you the confidence to face the future and, most importantly, it demystifies your fear. Because the truth is, the thing that really scares us is not necessarily the thing or event itself, but rather our mind's often exaggerated interpretation of it.

Chapter Ten
The Training of Perception

"You act like mortals in all that you fear,

and like immortals in all that you desire."

Lucius Annaeus Seneca

Anyone who knows me knows I am a big fan of wildlife documentaries. Of course, if given a choice, I would choose my concrete jungle any day, but that is neither here nor there. The point is, wildlife fascinates me. This is how I found out something very interesting about the way lions hunt in the wild—and it is nothing like what we were shown in *The Lion King*.

When lions hunt, whether in a pack or solo, they stalk their prey. They have a selection process for this prey, which could be based on a number of factors like the desirability of the prey, its vulnerability, and so on. And when the lion sets their sights on prey, they keep their focus on it until they sense that the timing is right. Then, they lunge an attack. If this attack occurs where the selected prey is in the midst of other prey, a stampede occurs as the other animals try to get away from the lion.

In the midst of the chaos, you'll see hooves flying left and right, but the lion keeps its focus on the prey it has selected. If you examine clips of these attacks, you will find that in the middle of the chase, other prey likely could have made it to the lion's dinner plate with very little effort, but because they are not the selected prey, the lions miss out on that opportunity. This scenario plays out in our lives, too. We have the things that we desire, and we often pursue those things with a single-minded focus. In pursuit of our goals, many of us develop a tunnel vision, which makes it impossible to see anything except the thing we most desire. And because of this, we tend to miss out on even better opportunities—just like the lion.

This kind of behavior is also prevalent in our relationships. The world has more than seven billion people living in it, and still, we have millions of people who are experiencing loneliness to the point of depression. This is not because of the absence of people in their environment, it is their perception of people that puts up a barrier preventing genuine relationships from forming. To live the good life, it is important to train yourself to see things from the right perspective. When I say the "right" perspective, I'm not referring to good vs. bad—I am simply talking about a view of life that allows you to harness and maximize opportunities and relationships.

This kind of thinking can be applied to our emotions, as well. Today, we live in a world where it feels like everyone is overly sensitive about everything. In modern colloquialism, people are easily triggered. A parent enforcing discipline can easily be interpreted as a form of violation or the abuse of the child's rights. Your decision to support your personal beliefs can be seen as an act of discrimination. And often, we are on the receiving end of that stick. We see ourselves as victims—and sometimes we are—so everything we hear can seem to be a direct attack on our person or our way of life. Social media has become a platform that amplifies voices, whether it is your own voice or the voices of others. And, given the amount of time we dedicate to these platforms, it is not surprising that it seems as though we are constantly in a triggered state.

But, like the Stoic virtue of wisdom teaches us, it is our duty to discern between good and bad and to understand the true nature of things. This can only be done if we train ourselves to see things a little differently. Perception is the force behind creativity. With the right kind of perception, you can create an experience that uplifts and inspires joy, regardless of the negative circumstances surrounding it. Marcus Aurelius put it perfectly:

"Choose not to be harmed and you won't be harmed. Don't feel harmed and you haven't been."

I have outlined a few Stoic exercises you can apply daily to help you train your perception.

1. TURN THE OBSTACLE UPSIDE DOWN

This is an exercise that aims to turn a negative experience into a source of good. It works by taking something you can describe as a huge thorn in your side and looking at how it can become a blessing to you. When I thought of an illustration for this, what came to mind as parents. If you are a parent to a strong-willed child, you understand what it is like to be at your wit's end, where you are on the verge of pulling the hair off your head because you are can't get them to do something as simple as taking a bath. It can be a frustrating experience—or, it can be an opportunity to learn and apply patience. Your crazy boss at work could be a chance to learn people management skills, and your misery at work could present a way for you to find out what makes you happy.

2. CLARIFY YOUR THOUGHTS

Unless you have been living under a rock most of your life, chances are many voices shaped the way you think. The first voices were those of your family, but you also have your friends and peers from school, as well as your teachers who used the books (the voices of others) to impact you. And let us not forget your experiences in life. All these things allow you to look at the external structure of an apple and decide if it is healthy and good enough to eat. However, we also apply these things to our dealings with people, as well as our experiences in life. This serves us to an extent, but it can also become limiting as you develop preconceived notions of how things should be, how people should behave, and so on. Your narrow-minded perspective limits you from enjoying people or moments. To clarify your thoughts, take time every day to isolate yourself from the world. Cast aside any personal opinions you have about people and examine the facts of the situation. This gives you pure insight, untainted by any bias. With this perception, you can alter the reality of your situation.

Chapter Eleven
Keeping the Balance with Eupatheiai

"The happiness of your life depends on the quality of your thoughts."
Marcus Aurelius

If you have never wanted something so badly it affects your ability to sleep at night, I am not sure if I should congratulate you or feel sorry for you. But my thoughts on the matter are beside the point—I simply wanted to draw your attention to the intensity of our passions and how far they can drive us. There is a distinct difference between passion and desire, although we often use them interchangeably. Desire has more to do with your wants, while passions are more of a need. Desires have a more sedentary effect, while passions have been known to start global wars. Why am I talking about this, you may wonder?

he Stoic life, as I established earlier, is not a life devoid of passions. It is my personal belief that it is impossible to be impassionate and stoic at the same, because Stoicism is about being true to your nature and, as humans, we are created to be passionate. Stoicism teaches you to control your passions, and the only way to stay passionate about life without letting your passions control you is to find balance. In the previous chapter, we talked about training your perspective, and this has a lot of great mental benefits. One of them is helping you attain a balanced insight. In a general sense, the exercises discussed herein are helpful, but if your problem is deeper than that, you need exercises that are more focused.

The Greek word for passion describes passion as emotions that are irrational, excessive, and mostly unhealthy. One common example of emotions that may fall in this category is anger. We all experience anger at some point, whether it occurs as mild irritation or a consuming rage. The intensity of your anger is dependent on how triggered you are by the event that brought it on in the first place. The real distinguishing factor is how we react to the anger triggered in us. Some have a passive-aggressive reaction while others may choose to ignore the incident with the hope the anger will go away. But anger never really goes away if you don't deal with it; it just recedes to the background where it continues to build up like the countdown timer of a bomb until, one day, there is an explosive display of rage.

A historical example of reacting to anger in extremity is the story of Alexander the Great, who killed one of his closest friends in a fit of rage. He immediately regretted his actions and was so consumed by grief, he could not eat or sleep for three days. You may not have gone to this extreme to express your rage, but without control, you could do something you will later regret. Emotions like jealousy and greed can also have a devastating effect. The Greeks called all of these passions "pathetic." To control your pathetic, you have to replace them with eupatheiai, which are the exact opposite. A good example of an emotion that can be classified as eupatheiai is joy. Seeing as we cannot surgically remove those negative emotions and replace them with happy ones, there are Stoic exercises you can do to curb your impulses and, in the very least, slow down your reactions. If you find yourself struggling with anger, envy, and depression, there is a strong possibility that your ability to be rational has been compromised. Your mind, in this state, is teetering toward thoughts that promote self-agenda, therefore you are likely to be unbalanced. To level the scales, try the following exercises:

1. Remind yourself that everything is temporary

Nothing in life lasts forever, and this applies to the things that make us emotional in an unhealthy way. Go back to your early teenage years, when you felt that if you did not attend that much talked-about party, you would die. Your parents stood their ground and you didn't attend but guess what? You didn't die. And I can bet that if you had the chance to attend that party as your current self, you would find it pretty lame. My point is, right now, the thing troubling you may seem overwhelming, but in a few days, months, or years, it won't even matter. It doesn't make sense to take actions that could have a lasting effect for something that is ephemeral. Always remind yourself that this, too, will pass.

2. Remember that you are small

Sometimes, our wealth and status in life fool us into thinking we are incredibly important. The world's inability to treat everyone equally fuels this foolery. You may find men and women who are so obviously beautiful, they think their very existence is a favor to the rest of the world. As pride sets in, they may begin to treat people in horrible ways. But the truth is, in the grand scheme of things, we are such a tiny speck that neither our presence nor absence affects life. You may be so wealthy that you have many people whose livelihood depends on you, but you would be terribly mistaken if you think that the moment you walk out of their lives, they would stop living. Anger is sometimes a by-product of pride. Remember the infinitesimal role you play, and you might be able to keep those unhealthy emotions in check.

3. Let history be your teacher

This time, I am not talking about your history—I am referring to the history of great men and women who came before you. Their greatest achievements, as well as their biggest failures, could help you nurture your ambition and, at the same time, humble it. But never use history to justify your actions. If your goals are driving you to the point of unhealthy obsession, a history lesson might be the thing you need to help keep your ambition alive without compromising your values. History is like a kind of mirror and if you look closely, you might find your reflection in the lives of those who came before you. But it also exposes a glaring truth—the actions of people are what outlive them. Egypt had beautiful architectural buildings during its time, but no one remembers who built them. Time can make you obsolete, regardless of your achievements.

4. Be aware that death comes to all

We have established that everything is temporary. All those nice things you want so passionately have an expiry date. Even if you are able to obtain them, ownership of that thing is temporary. Even the life you live can't last forever. So, when you feel yourself slipping into that space where your ambition is overpowering your virtue, pondering on the fact that death is the final end for everything may help you keep your emotions in check. By reflecting on these truths, you able to gradually subdue your patheiai and open the door for your eupatheiai to reign.

Chapter Twelve
Plato's View

"If one has made a mistake and fails to correct it,

one has made an even greater mistake."

Plato

Plato, as you know, was one of the greats. His teachings were studied by early Stoics and even though they disagreed with him on certain things, his works laid a good foundation for some Stoic principles. For the sake of this chapter, we will focus on Plato's view on idealism. Idealism is an aspect of philosophy where reality is asserted as we know it through our own mental construct. In other words, we create our own reality. The word in itself was born from the Greek word *idein,* which means "to see." In broader terms, idealism is meant to represent the world as it might be or as it should be. Don't mistake it for optimism, which is essentially hope in the future success of something. Idealism acknowledges the present state of things, but takes actions based on what the situation has the potential to become.

With this established, let us bring things back to our real-life situation. I am going to use our relationships to illustrate this. We typically have a firm idea of how we would like each relationship in our lives to play out. These relationship ideals are what form the basis for our expectations. We want our partners, friends, family, and even perfect strangers to think, act, and behave in a certain way. Having ideals and expectations for relationships are good, but if these ideals are drawn from the wrong place, you are simply setting up yourself up for failure. Let's talk about romance.

For years, Hollywood and romantic writers have told us what love is meant to be. Ladies want to be swept off their feet, and men have been programmed to look for that damsel in distress. We all enter into relationships with these expectations. But then, reality shows us a different side of things. Men are so busy trying to be providers that they have very little time to attend to the emotional needs of their partners. The only thing they are on the lookout for is an obvious sign of distress, which would prompt them to step in and show off their manliness. Women, on the other hand, are no longer waiting to be rescued—they have become much stronger. While there are now fewer scenarios where they are in distress, their emotional needs remain very high. Not a lot of men recognize this, so you often find women who are emotionally unfulfilled in their relationships.

The ideals fed to us by Hollywood make it difficult to pay attention to the things that really matter, like how our partners resolve conflict, how they handle rejection, and the quality of our communication. Instead, we focus on sex, material gifts, and everything else glamorized by the movies we love. So, when we meet prospective partners, we see them through rose-colored glasses that make them appear perfect. Our instincts may warn us of certain things that seem off, but we typically prefer to cling to that idea of perfection rather than face the problem at hand. It is like a woman walking into a designer store to buy a nice pair of size 12 red shoes, but leaving with a size 8 green pair and hoping that by the time she gets home, it will magically transform into what she really wants. This sounds ridiculous, but this is what we do in most of our relationships.

The Stoic approach to resolving this is to first draw your ideals from the right place. There are many books and resources that talk about relationships and offer tips on escaping the hurdles most couples will encounter. They may sound like the right place to draw your relationship ideals from; however, you must remember one crucial fact. Every relationship has its own DNA. Any resource you find on the subject can only offer a single perspective, so you need to go somewhere that gives you a bird's eye view of things. And one person that really teaches us to do this is Plato (and now you know why I mentioned him in the beginning).

Plato's view is referred to as the view from above because when you channel it correctly, you are able to see everything at once. This helps reorient your judgment of people. It also humbles your assessment of the situation, which is very handy if you are the type of person who hears a hello from a prospective partner and immediately starts hearing wedding bells. Identify your priorities in a relationship with this Stoic exercise that help get that bird's eye view:

Try to see everything at once

This is tricky, as we have a tendency to be short-sighted. Even though you have trained yourself to think long term, your objectives may be your own self-preservation. And, on the universal scale of things, that kind of thinking in itself is short-sighted. To see everything at once is to look at things from every angle that you can explore. When Marcus Aurelius described Plato's view, he put it this way:

"Whenever you want to talk about people, it's best to take the bird's eye view and see everything at once – of gatherings, armies, farms, weddings and divorces, births and deaths, noisy courtrooms and silent spaces, every foreign people, holidays, memorials, markets – all blended together and arranged in a pairing of opposites."

The world, they say, is now a global village and to an extent, this is true. But seeing the world through these "lenses" narrows our perspective on life. Say, for instance, you are dealing with the negative opinions of others. We give credit to these voices and limit our potentials to these criticisms because we feel these opinions are important.

Take a moment to silence the voices and think of the boisterous life going on around you. The endless chatter, the cycle of life, the simple mundane activities of people—do these negative opinions influence or affect life in the tiniest bit? No. Sure, the words might hurt, but they are like paper planes thrown at a rock. They can only make an impact if you amplify the sound. This overhead view gives you a perspective that reveals the grandness of the universe and downplays the illusion of people's individual roles within it. Essentially, other people's opinions aren't really that important.

Chapter Thirteen
Memento Mori (Remember Death)

"It is not death that a man should fear,

but he should fear never beginning to live."

Stoic Quote

One of the Stoic exercises I talked about earlier had to do with remembering that death comes to everyone. Memento Mori aims to take that concept a step further. More than just being a symbol for change, this seeks to initiate reflection of one's own mortality. I once read a relationship book that brought readers deeper into the recesses of the male mind. The goal of the book, essentially, was to help women understand how men work, and to use that information to manipulate men into giving them what they want. Many of the things discussed in the book are things I would agree with, to an extent, but I am also of the opinion that while those things may be true, they are not right.

One topic that stood out was the idea that a man's worth is determined by his job. In other words, if a man loves his job, it's likely this man would love himself, and vice versa. My disagreement is the fact that we ascribe this quality to a specific gender. This is a generation and a time when a person's worth is determined by the substance they possess, regardless of gender. That is not to say that this kind of thinking started today; in fact, this has been prevalent throughout the ages. Preferential treatment is given to those who have more. If you are at the receiving end of this preferential treatment, it is easy for this power to go to your head.

I can see you sitting on your chair and judging some political figure for doing exactly this but, you see, the fingers point back at you—this abuse of power is not limited to the elite. We perpetuate this behavior in our corners of the world, as well. How have you behaved since you got that promotion at work? Have you taken advantage of your position at the expense of others? There is a reason they say, "power corrupts, and absolute power corrupts absolutely." In the same way they say, "money amplifies the character of a man." So, if you had an issue with ego when you were barely getting by financially, coming into wealth is only going to make that character flaw even more noticeable. When we get this kind of power, we start to feel invincible. We start thinking we are exempted from the law and that certain things don't apply to us. This is very dangerous, because you may start acting recklessly. And when you are reckless, you are at risk of self-destructing. This is why when seemingly normal people land a position of power or wealth, they just "lose" it.

However, it is critical that I mention here that neither wealth nor power is evil nor good. This is a Stoic perspective, and no one illustrates this better than Marcus Aurelius himself. This man was one of the most powerful men in an empire that was considered one of the most powerful in the world at the time. The kind of power he wielded can only be described as that absolute power, which is famous for corrupting those who possess it. Yet Marcus was humble, fair in all of his dealings and a man of true strength of character. Proving that it is possible to be powerful, wealthy, and still be a force for incredible good. And, while it may sound like I am talking about some fantastical character straight out of a Marvel comic, I assure you there are regular people like that in our day-to-day lives and no, they were not born that way—it requires immense self-discipline on a daily basis. The exercises we talked about can help you in the area of curbing excessive unhealthy behavior, but if you find yourself making reckless decisions that endanger you and those around you, or perhaps your ego is competing with the universe, you need a healthy dose of humility.

In Stoicism, for every virtue we seek, there is a corresponding vice that you need to uproot. The objective is to replace vice with virtue. Now, you and I started this journey because you want to live the good life. We have defined what the good life is from a Stoic perspective. One crucial element of this life is maintaining harmony with the universe. I did this quick trip back to the beginning to bring us into focus, because humility is something many of us struggle with. I have heard people question the purpose of humility. We think it is a quality that keeps us in the gutter with people we consider undesirables. But without humility, you may never be able to get out of your comfort zone. For too long, we have identified fear as the primary reason many of us want to stay where we are, and yes, fear can hold us back. But ego is what makes you stagnant. When you start to think you know it all, you have it all, you create chains that anchor you to that spot in life. To break those chains, spend your mornings meditating on scenes guided by the following thought processes:

1. See your death vividly

I read about a group of early Stoics who would occasionally hold a feast in the presence of a corpse. This is insane, just as the thought of seeing your death, but only if you are missing the point. And the point here is to find the answer to this question. How big is your ego going to be when you are six feet under? Nobody looks at a corpse and marvels at its intelligence or how wealthy it was. The best quality that can be attributed to a corpse is that it looks "restful," and not even the artistic skills of the best mortician can change this. Despite the commonly-held belief in an afterlife, your influence over the living ceases the day you die. The effect of death on the body of a rich, influential person is exactly the same on that of a poor nobody. Death, which is the conclusive end of all things, pays no attention to things that make you think that you are better than everyone. Instead of pondering on those superficial things that feed your ego, meditate on your death and recognize that, in the end, none of those things matter—everyone meets the same end.

2. Acknowledge that tomorrow is not guaranteed

If you are one of those people who loves to procrastinate, meditating on this could help you be more proactive. If you are also struggling with your relationships, this meditation exercise can help bring things into perspective. We have a tendency to take things for granted. We abuse the grace of waking up to see each day. We don't appreciate those in our lives, because we take their presence for granted. What would you regret the most if you died right now? If you can do something about it now, do it and stop putting it off. Tell those you care about how much you appreciate them.

Chapter Fourteen
Recognizing Limits

"Life is like a play: it's not the length,

but the excellence of the acting that matters."

Seneca

The serenity prayer was written sometime in the 30s and has become a very important mantra for anyone seeking to correct certain behavioral patterns. And while it has Christian origins (the original version was written by a theologian), it does have a lot in common with something Epictetus wrote in his time. If you are not familiar with the serenity prayer, here it is:

"God, grant me the serenity to accept the things I cannot change,

Courage to change the things I can,

And wisdom to know the difference."

Epictetus, on the other hand, wrote:

"Make the best use of what is in your power, and take the rest of it as it happens. Some things are up to us and some things are not up to us. Our opinions are up to us, and our impulses, desires, aversions—in short, whatever is our doing. Our bodies are not up to us, nor are our possessions, our reputations, or our public offices, or, that is, whatever is not our doing."

The words are different, but the implied meaning is the same—despite the fact that one was written a few centuries BC. It is a high-pressure world we live in. The pedestal for success is really high and because success is obscenely celebrated, we feel even more pressure to achieve more. For every industry, there is a standard and, sadly, these standards are mostly unrealistic and unattainable—still, that does not stop us from reaching for those things. Beauty, for instance, is now defined by having high prominent cheekbones, thick pouty lips, and perfectly arched eyebrows. We see these beautiful models in magazines and on television, and use them as a yardstick to define our beauty.

I think it is either we chose to be ignorant or we simply do not pay attention to the fact that these so-called beauties attained that perfection with the help of a makeup artist who has artfully sculpted the face of the model with the tools at her disposal. And, in the areas where the skills of the makeup artist fall short, professional photographers used light and shadows to play up the model's best features. And where the photographer was unable to attain perfection, there was the graphic artist who used technology to airbrush out any flaws. In other words, what we have adopted as the yardstick for beauty is the product of a group of people whose goal is to sell a product to you. Except that you end up buying both the product and their concept of beauty.

The same process applies to body image. We buy into an unrealistic idea of perfection and almost kill ourselves, literally, to attain it. As kids, we were programmed to go to school, get good grades, graduate at the top of our class, and take on high-paying jobs to cater to a high-profile lifestyle. As if that was not stressful enough, you still have to make time to have the perfect love life, get married, and create that ideal home where the kids are well-behaved around the clock and your partner adores you 24 hours a day. Failure to attain any of these activates conditions like depression, poor self-esteem, and a general negative outlook on life.

The reality is, going into life with perfection as your expectation is setting yourself up for disappointment. There is no such thing as perfect. While there may be moments that are perfect, they are just a fragment in time. If you spend your days obsessing over the things you want to happen, you will miss out on those glorious perfect moments, and your life may seem like a series of sad events—even when you succeed in certain areas, your victory would taste like ashes in your mouth because you cannot get over your emotions long enough to appreciate and celebrate your feats.

This exercise helps you shed the burden of these stressors so you can connect with what is really important. By recognizing what lies within your control, you are able to productively channel your energy and resources into activities that will significantly improve the quality of your life.

1. Be naked with yourself

I mean this literally and figuratively. When was the last time you stood in front of a full-length mirror to look at yourself? Stand naked without any shape-wear, makeup, or wigs. Don't suck in your tummy, tilt your head for a better angle, or try to cover up any flaws. In Stoicism, we are taught to accept ourselves as we are. You may buy into the general logic that justifies our personal discrimination against ourselves with the need to become a better versions of you. However, this logic fails to deliver any value if you are unable to appreciate yourself as you are. While your body may not match up to the current dictates for the perfect body, you still have a lot of things to appreciate about the body you have. As you do this exercise, you also have to remind yourself that trends fade. For women, there was a time when the skinny body was the rave of the moment, and that transitioned into the era that directed their perfection lenses to the more voluptuous body type. You have to try to not take trends too seriously, because your body is going to serve you for the rest of your natural life.

2. Ask the right questions

Stress has received a lot of bad press for being the harbinger of heart diseases, blood pressure problems, and myriad other chronic illnesses. Stress has been known to stem from our physical, emotional, or mental participation in activities that take us outside our comfort zone. While stepping out your comfort zone is essential for growth, the transition process is not always easy. When you find yourself in highly stressful situations, take a step back and ask yourself, what do I have control over? What can I actually do about the situation, and should I really do it? The answers may help you determine what is up to you and keep you from obsessing over what isn't.

Chapter Fifteen
Journaling

"Leisure without books is death, and burial of a man alive."
Lucius Annaeus Seneca

We have all heard this at some point. As a child, I used to view this exercise as the most important way to deal with my emotions. As I grew older, read more, and generally attained more knowledge, I have come to see journaling as one of the most effective non-confrontational ways to deal with emotions. I arrived at this conclusion long before I became aware of the great Stoics who, as it turns out, agree. Before I go any further explaining how this plays out in our lives and what Stoic teachers had to say, I would like to dispel the notion that journaling is a feminine thing. Many of us assume journaling to be a "dear diary" moment, and Hollywood's biggest ode to masculine journaling is the *Diary of a Wimpy Kid* which doesn't do much to remove the gender stigma attached to it. In reality, strong historical figures like Albert Einstein, Charles Darwin, Leonardo da Vinci, and Thomas Edison were known to keep journals. So, do not let the idea that journaling may be emasculating stand in your way.

In Stoicism, you are expected to start the day by visualizing the outcome (for me, this is one of the coolest Stoic exercises), and end the day reflecting on everything that has happened. It may sound nice to just sit down with a nice glass of wine and go over the events of the day, but if you really want to do the whole deliberate living thing—which is what Stoicism is about—you are going to need to whip out a pen and a notebook and start writing. I appreciate that some of us have the memory of an elephant and can remember even the most minute details, but journaling helps you gain a broader view on things. But that is not the only benefit of journaling:

1. It provides an outlet for your emotions

One of my childhood friends who struggled with anger was able to control her outbursts and improve her relationships with others through journaling. Whenever she felt triggered, rather than lash out—which was her typical reaction whenever she felt this way—she opted to pour all of her feelings into her journaling. At first, it was like a painted board of raw emotions. But as she evolved, she realized that she started writing more constructive descriptions of her emotions, which gave her a more objective view of the situation. Her anger never disappeared entirely, but she was able to react less aggressively.

2. It helps promote self-awareness

Certain things about yourself will come to light when you start journaling, and it may surprise you. For instance, there might be situations that upset you that you have been struggling to deal with. But because you are dealing with the symptoms and not the root cause of the problem, nothing appears to be working. And, most times, you are unaware of this. Journaling connects you with your inner-most thoughts and, while the whole picture may not show up with just one night of journaling, you will get the answers you need with consistency.

3. It helps push you towards your goal

Nothing makes your vision clearer than writing it down. When you have all these things you want to do and achieve but life keeps throwing hurdles and challenges, it can end up distracting you if you are not focused. Writing down your goals gives you clarity of purpose, and when you have a strong sense of purpose, you are able to strategize effectively towards achieving them.

I could write a whole book on the benefits of journaling, but it makes sense to stick with these for the purpose of this book. Writing a journal is just one half of the equation—reading it is the other. To enjoy the full benefits of journaling, you have to imbibe the habit of both writing and reading what you wrote. It can be a bit tedious, seeing as you are the author and you certainly know what you put in your journal. However, the objective of this exercise is to gain a deeper insight into what you do and why you do it. To help you get maximum benefits from this, here are a few things you can do:

1. Pick a subject to write on

You have the freedom to write about anything that is going on in your life, but you gain more from the experience if you narrow down the subject. You could start with your thoughts and hopes for the day, and how you intend to go about achieving your daily goals. Or, you could decide to write about your last emotional incident. Talk about your reactions and why you think you reacted that way.

2. Use your words

Your journal doesn't have to compete with the latest bestseller on the market. You don't need to fill it with an impressive lineup of hard to pronounce words just so to seem smart to the reader (which most likely is only you). This is an intimate moment with yourself, and does not need to be embellished. All you need is honesty. This is another opportunity to be naked with yourself. Use the words you are most comfortable with, and just let them come to you. Also, don't worry if you are barely filling out a page the first few times. That, too, will come with time.

3. Don't read to criticize your work

Chances are you are going to find a lot of cringe-worthy moments when you go through your journal. Perhaps it was the way you reacted to something, or some previous misconception you had about a person or situation. Either way, you are going to find some not so proud moments. Embrace those flaws and view them as an opportunity to grow and be better. That said, obsessing over a few "I's" you forgot to dot and the "t's" you forgot to cross is a total waste of time. Save that attitude for school projects or communications with employers and clients.

4. Chose specific times for journaling

If you are the type of person who is able to concentrate in the middle of chaos, kudos to you. For the most part, journaling requires quiet time and space where you are able to spend time alone with your thoughts and feelings. But the right time is dependent on what you want to achieve. For instance, you might journal at the start or end of the day if you want to be consistent in pursuing your goals. If you journal when you feel emotionally triggered, your objective is to exercise control over your reactions.

Chapter Sixteen

Premeditatio Malorum (The Premeditation of Evil)

"We should every night call ourselves to an account;

What infirmity have I mastered today?

What passions opposed? What temptation resisted?

What virtue acquired?

Our vices will abort of themselves if they be brought every day to the shrift."

Lucius Annaeus Seneca

This is another one of those exercises that might sound morbid or creepy when you take it at face value: You are expected to anticipate the very things you are subconsciously hoping will never happen to you. I can even understand why, even though people respected the early Stoics, they were more comfortable keeping them away from their homes. But if you sit down and consider this topic for a minute, it starts making a lot of sense. The good life is about having a healthy balance. Keeping your focus on only the positives instead of planning for what you have tagged as the "bad stuff" makes you ill-prepared for those situations, which often eventually come whether we want it or not. Granted, it never fully plays out the way we envisioned it, but it happens nevertheless.

One truth of life we are never willing to accept is that bad things happen to us even when we have worked hard to earn the good things of life. In fact, I cannot think of any person (with a heart) who would walk up to someone experiencing a tragedy and say they deserved what they are getting—even if the person facing those hard times is incredibly cruel and generally disliked, we still do not wish the worst on them. If we feel this way about people we do not like, it is easy to imagine how we would feel about ourselves and those we love, especially when our self-preservation instincts set in. And, if I am being honest, there is nothing wrong with wanting the best for yourself—but you would be doing yourself a great disservice if you do not brace yourself for the worst.

If the name of the exercise bothers you, instead of calling it the premeditation of evil, think of it as a safety drill. Almost every public building in any civilized society has a safety drill, which usually consists of a series or sequence of routines that are meant to be executed in the event of an incident that threatens the safety of the building or the people in it. For these safety routines to be developed and perfected, the people who set it up had to anticipate something terrible that could compromise safety. That is not to say that they were actively hoping for terrible things to happen. In fact, you can see they are going out of their way to make sure that tragedy does not happen. But they recognize that a change to the safety status of the building is inevitable, and rather than twiddle their thumbs, they put safety measures in place. Often, they will even go further to get the personnel to reenact potential threatening situations and then play out a routine that would keep everyone safe.

This is what this exercise is about. We already know that the only constant in life is change. So, even if we live in this fortified bubble that makes us feel safe and cocooned away from anything that might harm us, the wise thing is to appreciate what we have been blessed with while preparing for the event that might take all those things away. Now, just because you are anticipating the negative things does not mean you should go into full apocalypse mode. For as long as mankind has existed, we have always lived in fear of that gloomy day when the whole world would be consumed in one swoop. Some say it will be some sort of natural disaster of huge proportions. Others say it will be a religious phenomenon separating the good from the bad. While the world has had its fair share of natural disasters, it has survived through the ages. In essence, this should not be your worry. Life's hurricane affect each of us individually, at different phases in our lives.

Seneca has this to say about premeditating evils:

"Nothing happens to the wise man against his expectation… nor do all things turn out for him as he wished but as he reckoned—and, above all, he reckoned that something could block his plans.

"

What he is saying, in essence, is that this exercise helps you prepare for anything that might disrupt your plans, while helping you figure out how to use those disruptions in your plans to your advantage. So, whether you make a loss or a gain, you are well prepared for it. How exactly do you go about this exercise?

1. Rehearse your day

Start your day by visualizing every aspect of it. Think of what would happen to your loved ones if you suddenly suffered a tragedy. Would they be taken care of? Let's say you have a presentation to make at work. What would happen if there was a glitch with the computer system—how would you be able to deliver excellently, despite the setback? What if the client doesn't like what is being pitched? Do you have a backup plan? Go over every important event that might occur throughout your day.

2. Practice being calm

In the face of calamity, we tend to lose our wits, but expending our energies this way is an unproductive waste of time—this does nothing to change the situation. Part of this exercise aims to help you come to terms with the alternate realities of your circumstance. While it is not guaranteed that those things will come to pass, you should still prepare for them emotionally, mentally, and physically. Face down your fears by accepting these possible realities and plan accordingly.

3. Take action

Wallowing in thoughts of what might or might not happen after you have made your projections is unwise. Instead, make concrete plans and create a "safety drill" of your own that factors in the contingencies you have put in place, just in case some things don't go the way you have planned. However, keep Seneca's quote at the back of your mind. Even with your exquisite and well-thought-out backup plan, things may not play out exactly as you wish—but your visualizations make you better prepared for the unexpected.

Chapter Seventeen
Amor Fati (Love Fate)

"Accept the things to which fate binds you,
and love the people with whom fate brings you together,
but do so with all your heart."

Marcus Aurelius

Fate is a dangerous concept. The idea that certain events in our lives are predestined to happen is something we all struggle with. It makes us feel powerless in our bid to change the events that dictate our daily experience, and even when we come to a place of acceptance, we do so with dejection, sadness, and a "why me" attitude. Now, when I am talking about fate, I am not referring to what you had for breakfast—no, you were not fated to eat cereal this morning. Things like breakfast are within your control because you had a choice in the matter. A diagnosis of something you dreadful that you least expected, that is fate. Winning the powerball lottery on your first attempt also involves the hand of fate. Basically, anything that happens to you without your choice in the matter is fate. Although there are exceptions, fate does not need your permission.

In line with today's double-standard custom, we tend to celebrate fate when it favors us. We don't question the abundant blessings we receive, even when we know we did not do anything to earn or deserve it. The moment things go awry, however, we get upset. These ill-fated setbacks drive us into an emotional downward spiral that we may never truly recover from. Many of us have made several attempts to fight fate. This rebellion sets us on a path that clearly has no end, yet we totally commit ourselves to it in the hope that, somehow, we can thwart fate. After wasting so much time and energy, we come to a place where we finally give in and surrender—except more often than not, we come to this realization a little too late, or after we have wasted so much time and resources trying to avoid what should have been embraced from the beginning.

Now, I'm not saying you should roll over and play dead when something you did not predict happens to you or the people you love. That would be ridiculous advice. But a scene from a very popular medical TV series often comes to my mind when I think of fate, and I believe that this is the best illustration for the point I am trying to make.

In this scene, there was a single dad who came to the hospital with his terminally ill daughter. This ailment was diagnosed from the time that this child was a baby and they had been managing her care ever since. However, the child suffered a major health crisis in this scene and according to the doctors, there was nothing else that could be medically done to improve things for her. In fact, they did not think she would make it through the night. The concerned dad understandably refused to accept the damning verdict. Instead, he raced out, leaving his daughter in the care of physicians while he made a mad dash to spring for a cure. He was out of money, out of time, and out of ideas, but he was willing to try anything that could offer the possibility of saving his young daughter's life. Naturally, it was heartbreaking. For a parent, it is instinctive to want to protect your child and he just followed his instinct, but in doing so, he nearly missed out on a moment he would never have been able to forgive himself for missing. So, if this moment was important to him, why was he out there fighting it? Because he did not embrace fate.

We are groomed to expect miracles, and while miracles are known to happen, they also fall within the realm of things we do not control. You cannot manipulate a miracle, just like you cannot manipulate fate. But in embracing fate, you don't take on the dormant role, even though it may feel like it. The reality is, your acceptance actually empowers you. Marcus Aurelius put it this way:

"A blazing fire makes flames and brightness out of everything that is thrown into it."

The fire is your potential. Obstacles, challenges, and fate's whims are the things that are thrown into the fire. Your decision not to embrace these things will not stop them from happening to you. As a matter of fact, you might see the embers of your potential burning out faster because you are unable to bring yourself to a place of acceptance. Seneca, who was a slave, a cripple, and later became one of the most influential men in Rome, put it this way:

"Do not seek for things to happen the way you want them to; rather, wish that what happens happen the way it happens; then you will be happy."

I have a few mental exercises that will help awaken a mindset within you that embraces this Stoic philosophy:

1. Be balanced in your thinking

When things happen to you, good or bad, train yourself not to react emotionally. While your instincts may be self-serving, they don't always serve a higher good. Think rationally and objectively, and let your actions be guided by this. During your thinking process, assess the situation by weighing in on the dangers and risks that threaten your objective. Ask the right questions that would provide solutions to those risks you listed out, then act accordingly.

2. Get comfortable with being uncomfortable

Since you have accepted that you cannot change what has happened, ask yourself how you can make it work to your advantage. This exercise is particularly good for people who have suffered some kind of trauma. Tragic as it was, it has already happened. There is no going back, no undoing, and certainly no forgetting. But you have a choice: accept it and redefine your experience, or fight it and let it control your experience. You've heard the expression, "If life gives you lemons, make lemonade." This just means to make the best of your situation. I remember losing a close friend of mine and, yes, his death was painful. I was racked with grief and couldn't function for days. But as I reflected on his life, I came to the realization that I could either celebrate his life—which was glorious—or wallow in his death. I chose life, and even though it still hurts to not have him here, I can find joy in the knowledge that I was privileged to know this amazing person.

Chapter Eighteen
The Power to Enforce Change

"It is the power of the mind to be unconquerable."
Seneca

If you read the Christian bible, you'll be familiar with the one story that strikes me as a modern Stoic. This happened during one of the teachings of Christ, who was generally disliked by the Pharisees and Sadducees—essentially the spiritual and philosophical thought leaders of their time. But Jesus was not necessarily afraid of them and his words explained why the son of a carpenter stood fearless in the face of their threats, anger, and accusations. To paraphrase, he admonished his followers not to be afraid of the person who can harm them physically; instead, they should fear the one who can harm their souls. This is a not a religious book, but I draw inspiration from great thought leaders and, in his time, Jesus was one of them. What he said was absolutely powerful and empowering at the same time.

The mind is the singular most powerful weapon mankind possesses. It is not your ability to wear the finest robes that separates you from primates. It is not your muscle that makes you more powerful than a full-grown lion, which is known to be a strong and fierce predator. It is your mind. If you groom it right and feed it right, it can put you in an untouchable position in life. It is not as though life doesn't happen to you. On the contrary—when your mind is being exercised the Stoic way, it would appear that you experience life even more than the average person. Your mind is the key to unlocking the true powers of the universe and, most importantly, the process of opening your mind is in your hand. Our concept of universal power fluctuates between Pinky's [from *Pinky and The Brain*] comical attempt at following his master's orders in their bid for world domination, and the eternal intergalactic battles between humans and other species. I don't blame people for thinking this way; I blame Hollywood. According to Stoic teachings, we are all a part of the universe and attaining universal power simply means you dominating your own corner. And when I say dominate, I am not referring to the fleet of cars in your garage or the exquisite private jet sitting in your hangar, or even the mansions you own on every continent. All those things are nice to have, but it is possible to own all these things and still not live the good life, much less dominate your universe.

Generally, life is very hard, even for those who seem to have everything they need to deal with its complications. Applying the principles of Stoicism helps you work with the tough hand life deals us on a daily basis. The most puzzling thing for me when I first came across the concept of Stoicism was the fact that, on paper, it sounds so simple. I mean, all you are expected to do is sit in your house and think about things, and then let the rest happen. But when it comes to application, it is a very complicated process. I think the most challenging thing for anyone is the fact that you have to unearth and discard patterns of behavioral and thinking processes that have been entrenched in you for decades. You have been taught to expect and plan for the good things in life. We know that we don't want bad stuff to happen, so we don't plan for it at all. Then, you have this principle telling you to sit down and think of everything that could go wrong before the sun goes down—and not only that, you are expected to plan for those things.

Every single Stoic principle is something that goes against the grain of our upbringing, and this is why it is going to be an uphill task. You are going to have to work extra hard to push the heavy barrel of your mind to the top of that hill. It is an extremely hard battle, but it is also a very rewarding experience when you are able to get yourself to the top. However, the battle does not end when you get there—it is only when you reach the top that you realize there are more hills for you to climb and, in true Stoic tradition, you cannot afford to get too comfortable with the hill that you have just conquered. You are going to have to roll up your sleeves and take on the new challenge. With each new hilltop you reach, you make an advancement in your life.

Another thing I find particularly fascinating about the Stoic teachings is that your experience, your process, and your journey is a personal one. Even if you are married with kids and have a huge, close-knit extended family, Stoicism is a lonely road. That barrel-up-the-hill process is one you take alone. You can draw insight from other people, just as we have drawn from the great Stoic philosophers I mentioned in this book. You can inspire others the same way others have inspired you, but no matter how close you are to a person, this is something you experience solo.

For people who have never ventured out into anything on their own, this can be a scary process, but power is not something to be afraid of. Especially since this is not the kind of power you wield over people, but over your experiences in life. If you have struggled with confidence issues, it is likely you have let the voices of others control your thoughts and actions for so long that your own has been put on permanent mute. You know how you feel, and perhaps what you want, but the voices of other people in your head automatically disqualify you, so you timidly sit back and let life just do its thing. By recognizing the truth—that these voices don't matter and that their opinions do not control the outcome for you—it is possible to block them out and gradually empower yours which, in truth, is the only relevant voice for your journey.

You can draw strength by echoing the words of thought leaders who support your goals but, at the end of the day, it is your voice that will help your mind create the experience you want. In the same way, if you have dealt with loss, you can find joy in the realization that death is not the finality of life. If you change your perception and see things from Plato's perspective, your mind can convert that experience into one that births a new beginning for you, and as many people as you would want to be affected by it. The founder of Alcoholics Anonymous turned his struggle with addiction into a program that has impacted and continues to impact the lives of millions globally. This is the power of your mind.

Chapter Nineteen
Stoicism in Cognitive Behavioral Therapy

"If you really want to escape the things that harass you, what you are needing is not to be in a different place, but to be a different person."

Lucius Annaeus Seneca

Sometimes, the depths we have sunk to in life make us pray fervently for a clean slate to help us start over. The truth is, even if you are given a clean slate, without truly addressing the problems at hand, you would likely end up creating the exact same messes you are trying to run from. The issue, then, is not the slate that we are praying for, but ourselves: the things we do, the things we say, and the way we act—these are the main problems that need to be fixed. Unfortunately, we do not have a reset button we can press when we start experiencing glitches, and then just get back with the program. But if you think about it, it really is not unfortunate such a button does not exist. If Thomas Edison had pressed the reset button after every one of his scientific failures, he would never have been able to become the inventor we recognize and respect today. He told us of his many failed experiments, but we don't remember him for that. In fact, his errors helped him upgrade his experiments. In the same way, the mistakes you make as a result of your behavioral tendencies don't necessarily define you. And, like Edison, you can upgrade. In a few minutes, you will find out how.

Cognitive behavioral therapy, or CBT, basically involves making a conscious decision and a deliberate effort to correct certain behaviors that are having a negative impact on your life and slowing down your performance in the area of achievement. CBT is not restricted to specific behavioral patterns—just isolate the patterns you want to replace and apply the Stoic principles. Before we get into the nitty-gritty of this, you should know that this is something that will require deliberate efforts on your part. Stoicism is generally discussed as philosophy, but it has a very strong therapeutic effect because it focuses on reframing the mind. Epictetus was said to state that, "the philosopher's school is the doctor's clinic." The teachings of Stoicism have both a preventative and proactive approach in CBT, and at the core of this is emotional resilience training—key in replacing bad behaviors with good practices. Rather than simply responding to instincts and reacting to emotions, you are taught to take a step back, evaluate your emotions and, most importantly, gain a better perspective of the situation.

There are three core areas that need to be influenced by Stoicism in order to set you on the path that effectively helps you correct your behaviors, and that is exactly what we are going to explore in the chapter. These core areas are your thoughts, your will, and your actions. Pay attention to each of these, because it is almost impossible to make any genuine progress if you are experiencing a setback in one aspect. Take what you learn here and apply it with wisdom.

YOUR THOUGHTS

They say that out of the abundance of the heart, the mouth speaks. In other words, what you say is a byproduct of what you have been thinking. The same thing goes for your actions. Your thoughts control your view of the world and how you perceive the people around you, and it is from the seat of your thoughts that your interpretations of life's experiences are transmitted. The things you do are dictated by what you think. For instance, if you find yourself reacting in anger every time someone uses a certain word or phrase, that reaction is simply a projection of your thoughts on that word or phrase. If you react to emotional crisis by overeating, it is because you have convinced yourself that the food helps.

The foundation of Stoic principles involves replacing vice with virtue, and this applies to what you think about, as well. Then, you need to consider how you think. Many of us make the mistake of thinking after we have taken action, and this impacts our behavior. To set your thoughts on the right path:

1. Feed your mind with materials that promote positive thinking. If you must read something that contains negative elements that could compromise your emotions, be objective in your assessment of it.

2. Ask questions. Just because things have always been done a certain way doesn't mean this is the right way. Take Plato's view of the situation: see everything from all angles and make your assessment from this perspective.

3. Manage your thoughts effectively. With so many things fighting for our attention, it is easy to get distracted. Use a journal to help you stay focused on your thoughts. Journaling also helps you isolate problematic thoughts that fuel negative energies.

YOUR ACTIONS

In our default setting, we react more than we act. Certain reactions are instinctive, but some are habits we have established over a long period of time. If you were ever physically abused, you may feel defensive if someone enters your physical space. This is an instinctive reaction. To correct instinctive behaviors, you have to start laying the psychological foundation, first. Start by getting to the root of the problem—in this case, deal with your vulnerability to let other people in.

To correct habitual behaviors, you need to make a deliberate decision to implement actionable steps. For instance, if you find yourself sleeping for less than four hours each night, you need to look at the things you do that take away from your sleep time. Things like your phone habits, bedtime routines, and even diet could play a role. When you have found out what is hindering your sleep, take the necessary steps to correct it. The key here is to act out your plans and make observations as you go along.

In order to effectively change the way you do things, you must do the following:

1. Think it through

You should not wake up one morning, snap your fingers, and decide you are going to change the way you do things. Often, you end up crashing out or losing interest long before you achieve your goals. Say, for instance, you want to lose weight. Don't just jump on the nearest treadmill or sign up for the first diet program you get your hands on. Think a little deeper. Why do you want to lose weight? Want kind of weight loss program is suitable for your lifestyle? These questions will help you get started on the right action plan.

2. Have a clear vision

It doesn't matter how noble your intentions are—without a vision, you are most likely going to get distracted or worse, fumble your way through the dark in a bid to reach your goals. Get a journal and write out what you hope to achieve with your actions. This helps you monitor your activities and can also serve as a source of inspiration that will motivate you and push you towards your goal. Remember, in order to change your habits, you have to be more deliberate about the actions you take.

3. Be consistent

To create sustainable lifelong habits that are beneficial to you and those around you, you are going to have to be consistent. The best athletes in the world carry out a routine series of activities on a daily basis. This training can be brutal for the average man, but for the athlete, excellence requires sacrifices, and sacrifice demands commitment. You cannot do something today, then ignore it and come back to it in the hopes that you can hit your goals. Stoicism does not work that way, and if you really want to use it as part of your CBT training, you need to discipline yourself to be consistent and persistent.

YOUR WILL

You have your actions on one end of the spectrum and your thoughts on the other. Your will is like the mediator between the two. For your thoughts to be translated into actions, you need your will. There are times when you may feel you cannot go any further, or that your goals are no longer worth the sacrifices you have to make to get to there. It is your will that will keep you in the game, so to speak. Your level of consistency and your ability to remain persistent even when you don't feel like it can be attributed to your willpower.

Wanting or wishing to do something is very different from having the willpower to actually do it. To muscle up your willpower, I would recommend practicing the Stoic exercise of training your perspective. Flip the script by viewing the obstacles that threaten your ability to go through with the process as an opportunity to transform yourself. When athletes compete, they are confronted by opponents who appear stronger and more physically suited for the challenge as well as those who look weaker and less likely to win. But you don't see them back out of the race simply because they worry that their counterparts could defeat them. And, at the same time, they don't get cocky because they think they are better than their opponents. They simply enter the game with a focus on their own performance.

In the same way, when you step into the field of life, you have to keep your focus on yourself. When the negative thoughts and physical challenges come to distract you, stop fighting it off or giving in to your fears. Instead, see this as the opportunity that it really is and use it to fire up your ambition to be better.

Chapter Twenty
Stoicism in Pain Management

"He who is brave is free."
Seneca

Anyone who tells you that pain is just a state of mind should be smacked in the head—or better still, sent to a labor ward to watch a woman give birth to a child. Pain is a reaction to physical, mental, or emotional hurt. And it is a perfectly natural process. However, with the implementation of Stoic principles, you can control the intensity of the pain you feel, as well as the extent of the damage it may cause. It is a very difficult concept to accept, but it is not as foreign as we think. We have heard stories of brilliant people who work with intelligence agencies and are trained to withstand the most gruesome forms of torture without breaking. People who work in the military, air force, or navy are rumored to undergo similar pain management training in the event of their capture. Now, we are not going all gung ho on this like people who work with government security agencies, but there are some kinds of pain that do need to be managed.

For this topic, I will be discussing the two major types of pain that we experience: emotional pain and physical pain. In my opinion, all pain stems from these two types of pain, and if you can equip yourself to deal with it, you are in a better position to deal with all of the other stuff. But before we get into it, there is something you need to bear in mind. Pain is not your enemy. Don't make it your mission to seek out ways to numb yourself. There is a reason your body and mind were built with pain receptors. They can help you recognize your limits. Without those pain receptors, you run the risk of hurting yourself beyond repair. Without pain, you lose the ability to function like a normal human being. In a world that glorifies superheroes, we may aspire for a life where we live beyond the reach of pain. But if you look closely, you will see that your favorite heroes hurt, too. They do not live beyond pain; they have simply learned to live above it. Embrace your pain, and when you do, you will reclaim the power it has over you.

PHYSICAL PAIN

Don't let anyone tell you that the pain you are feeling is all in your head. We all experience pain at different levels. My six could be your two and your 10 could be someone else's five. This is not something to get into a competition over. It is just one of those realities that you are going to have to embrace. That said, there are several techniques that can be used to manage physical pain without relying on medication. These practices date back millennia. Women employed these techniques to help them cope with the pains of labor. Obviously, women have a lot of pain relief options for this now, but in the past, all they had was a cloth to chomp on and some mind games to get them through it. I am not even going to try and compare the pains of a woman in labor to anything, because I have been told that unless you are going through it, you are not going to understand it. Instead, I will use a more relatable kind of pain. And I found that in one of the greatest emperor that Rome had ever known: Marcus Aurelius.

Now, here was a man who suffered from chronic stomach ulcers, which prevented him from eating certain foods and eating at certain times. He was also known to experience chest pains and had issues sleeping. It is hard to accurately diagnose what Marcus was going through, but suffice it to say that he was in an incredible amount of pain, which he lived with for most of his life. His resilience has been attributed to his Stoic training. In a few short steps, you can build your own mental resilience towards pain.

1. Don't judge the pain

We have a tendency to identify pain as bad, but when you do that, you develop a knee-jerk response to it that can distress you even more. So, step one is to step off the judgment box. As I pointed out earlier, pain is not your enemy. Neither is it your friend. Detach your judgment of the pain from the experience of it.

2. Change your perspective

Pain does not really harm you in the stoic sense, as it does not hurt your morals. What affects you, though, is how you react to it—and wallowing in pain is considered a negative reaction. So, if it is not truly harming you in the areas that matter, can it really hurt you? The answer is no—not unless you let it. In other words, pain requires your permission to truly cause harm.

3. Stay in the present

There are two things you need to consider when managing your pain. The first is your perceived ability to cope with it, and the second thing is your perception of the pain's severity. If you think the pain is too great and you cannot cope, chances are your anticipation of the pain will heighten the pain itself. Stop panicking and get your mind to relax. Stay focused on each moment, because each moment will get you through the next.

These Stoic techniques help build your mental resilience as well as your endurance level. You can pair them with physical pain-relief methods like focused breathing and meditation exercises. Other things you can do to complement your efforts include journaling your pain. We know of the physical travails of Marcus Aurelius because he wrote about his experiences. This gives you a better understanding of what you are dealing with. The more understanding you have, the better equipped you are to cope with it. Medical experts also recommend maintaining a healthy lifestyle, which includes less alcohol, more exercise (which release endorphins, the body's natural painkiller), and a balanced diet.

EMOTIONAL PAIN

If you thought measuring physical pain was difficult, the complicated nature of emotional pain will leave you very confused. Saying that we are all genetically wired in different ways is stating an obvious fact, but this plays into how we handle our emotions, as well. We react to emotional traumas differently, and sometimes, our reactions to these traumas can limit our ability to function as a human being. I have had days when getting out of bed seems to be the most tasking thing I can handle. People suffering from depression may reach a point in their emotional pain when living no longer seems like a viable option. People whose emotional pain was triggered by a physical trauma describe themselves as being stuck in the place of their trauma. For them, life seems to have stopped from the very day they experienced that traumatic event. They feel frozen in time, burdened by the pain and trapped in their nightmare. This is the extent of the damage that can be caused by emotional pain.

It is very possible to experience excruciating emotional pain with no physical evidence. You can mask your pain with a smile, and that is what makes it more dangerous than physical pain. On the flip side, there are emotional pains that can manifest physically. I have heard of medical cases where the patient's emotional distress presented as a heart attack. The doctors were able to address the emergency and patch the patient up, but there are no pills or surgeries that can help you deal with the pain that is inside your head. However, if we adopt the Stoic principle that urges us to change our perspective, we can see this as a huge advantage. For starters, the absence of pills to help you get rid of your pain means that you can step into that void and be your own pill.

Being in a state of emotional pain means you are no longer in harmony with your true nature, and we know how important it is in Stoicism to maintain that balance. The obvious solution would be to restore that balance and get you back in tune with nature. Kick start the process by doing the following:

1. Accept the reality of your experience

I am not talking about amor fati or loving fate here. I am referring to the fundamental Stoic principle that tells us our experiences are neither good nor bad. Rather, they fall into the category of one of those indifferent things that are not regarded as a vice or a virtue. It is a neutral external factor that can only harm you if you let it. Yes, what happened to you is tragic and painful, and you would love for that fact to be recognized, but dwelling on it only amplifies its hold over you. This is the reality you need to awaken yourself to.

2. Recognize the limits

When we think limits, our first thought is ourselves and the boundaries that we must be conscious of. But the events around us also have their limits. They can trigger distress, cause significant pain, and temporarily create a disruption in your life—but that is as far as they can go. However tragic it was, it cannot truly harm you. Ultimately, you have the power to shut it down.

3. Take Plato's view as your stand

I love William Blake's poem, *to see a world*. When I think of Plato's view, the first verse of this poem is what comes to mind.

"To see a world in a grain of sand

And a heaven in a wildflower

Hold infinity in the palm of your hand

And eternity in an hour"

Don't narrow down your entire life's journey to this single painful moment. You have an amazing life ahead of you, and it only takes a shift in focus from the present pain to the powerful possibilities that life has to offer for you to acknowledge this. Life can take you through several twists and turns, but there is no single moment that defines you. You are the one who defines the moment.

Chapter Twenty-one
Stoicism in Growing Emotional Intelligence

"He suffers more than necessary,

who suffers before it is necessary."

Seneca

If there is anything that Stoicism does, it is that it gives you a stronger sense of self. You gain a better understanding of your strengths and your weaknesses, and understand why you act the way you do. Certain traits and behavioral patterns that you exhibit will begin to make more sense as you explore this journey into yourself. More than that, you also enjoy the benefits of this process, which includes heightened confidence. A better understanding of self also goes a long way in helping you improve on the relationships in your life. However, I feel that one of the most important benefits of consistent practice of Stoicism is the insight it gives you into the feelings of others.

As the world transitioned from small, local communities to a giant global village, I think we lost touch with each other. We have become so engrossed in ourselves and in our lives that we could literally be surrounded by hundreds of people and still feel as though we live on an island that is on a planet on the dark side of the universe. Family events that are supposed to be about connecting turn into a silent communion, where the ritual involves peering into our phone screens for long hours at a time. Even intimate dinners are not spared this treatment. We no longer talk to each other, we simply talk at each other. And it is much easier to reach the person next door to you via their social media handle than by calling out their name.

When it comes to conflict resolution, our emotional intelligence is so poor that it affects our ability to see any side of the story beyond our own. Even the dissemination of information has followed the same suit. There was a time when the integrity of the journalist or writer mattered more than the stories they were telling. Before any story was published, it had to be vetted and thoroughly investigated. The truth is what was shared in the media. These days, people are more interested in making money off their stories. Sensational stories have been known to draw attention, and when you are able to draw attention, you draw the money. Therefore, priority is being given to vapid stories propped by sensational headlines, done without proper verification or investigation. And we can't place all the blame on the media—we are just as quick to share those stories with the people in our networks. And sometimes, these stories we share are so salacious and damaging for the people involved in them, but we don't give it a second thought before we spread the word.

To become emotionally intelligent, we need to apply every single Stoic principle you have learned. For starters, stop acting without thinking your actions through. When you take the time to consider every angle of the situation, your views, their views, as well as the truth, should be addressed objectively. Apply the concept of premeditation of evil to others, as well. Think of how your actions could negatively affect them. Is it worth it? Take this approach to life. Another Stoic principle that could help improve your emotional IQ would the reframing of perspectives and emotions. I cannot emphasize enough how much this has helped me in my relationships, especially in heated moments when I feel exasperated by their actions.

Our relationships with people are most vulnerable when we feel slighted or hurt. And this can happen more often than we anticipate, because another marker of the times we live in is that we have become sensitive to things that do not really matter—and, at the same time, desensitized to the things that should be important to us. We find ourselves arguing about things that have no real bearing on ourselves and walking on eggshells when it comes to topics that could shape our lives. Reframing your emotions gives you a new perspective and can make you more tolerant. Being tolerant of other people's views, behaviors, and beliefs comes from a place of emotional enlightenment.

Emotional intelligence is also reflected in how far you can push people. In our work relationships, one of the biggest issues we have—especially as leaders—is the inability to accurately assess the potentials of your colleagues. We either underutilize or over-utilize their skills. The concept of boundaries and limits is foreign to us, so we end up with employees and colleagues who are frustrated. Applying the principle of understanding limits, you are able to identify the pressure buttons of the people in your workplace, and with that information, you better understand their limits and are able to delegate tasks that motivate them enough to want to keep at it, but are still tough enough to keep them on their toes. In situations where you are unable to please people no matter what you do, using the love of fate, you can embrace the animosity in the environment and empower yourself to excel. Again, with the right perception, those challenges can be sharpened into the very tools that will bring about your advancement.

You should keep in mind that having emotional intelligence does not necessarily mean people are going to automatically like you. The objective is not to become the most liked person in the room—it is to ensure you are able to have uncomplicated and untangled relationships that are, at the very least, founded on truth and mutual respect. It is a point where the value you ascribe to people is not based on their net worth or their status in society. The same respect you accord the CEO of the company is the same respect you accord the janitor. In other words, you are not superficial in your dealings with people.

On a final note, when you use Stoicism to grow your emotional intelligence, you are able to enjoy the benefits of having people in your life without depending on them as the source of your happiness. This is a mistake we make a lot. We buy into the Hollywood notion that we need someone to complete us, and every potential relationship sets out with the goal of filling up the missing holes in our lives. The truth is, you cannot outsource your happiness. Enjoy your relationships without putting the pressure of fulfilling your happiness on them.

Chapter Twenty-two
Stoic Exercises and Practices to Get You Started

"Until we have begun to go without them,
we fail to realize how unnecessary many things are.
We've been using them not because we needed them
but because we had them."
Lucius Annaeus Seneca

Most Stoic exercises, in practice, require meditation. You are to meditate on the ideas and philosophies of Stoicism so as to absorb them into your system and make them a part of you. If you have not inculcated the habit of meditation, this is something that you need to get into today. Meditation only requires your time, a quiet space, and a journal. It also requires consistency in your daily mediations. Now that we have set the tone for a Stoic lifestyle and given you an in-depth look at how Stoic principles can impact your daily living, here are a few final pointers to get you started. These are simple exercises that are more suited to a beginner, or someone seeking to reconnect with their Stoic roots. To grow and attain further enlightenment, I urge you to expand on this list. If you have been able to successfully keep at this list for at least six months, I urge you to read more books on the subjects. Books that offer excerpts or teachings based on the writings of Stoic greats like Marcus Aurelius are an excellent place to start.

For setting goals:

1. Take a pen and a notebook and write out your vision. It could be a vision for your family, your career, or even your home renovation. Don't try to raise any mental barriers, don't look at anything you feel might impede your success. Imagine that you are on a race track, with no competition on either side of you. It is just you, the empty track, and your destination. Fill those pages with your visions of the future, with no holds barred.

2. After clearly writing out your vision, use a separate sheet to write out the things that could potentially stand as obstacles—things that would either slow down your progress or threaten your vision entirely. Don't feel threatened by these obstacles. They are basically there to help you see where you should expend your energies and resources.

3. Chart the best route to achieve your goals, factoring in the obstacles you have foreseen. Ask yourself what you must do to reach your destination. If your goal is career advancement, what are the relationships you must build at work to help with that? What new skill set do you think would be relevant for the position you are aspiring for?

For growing your self-esteem:

1. Define what self-esteem means for you at this point. Would that be a more fit and healthier version of you? Or would you like to be more fashionable? Perhaps you want to be more assertive in your dealings with people. Whatever it is, write it down in clear words. If you are not sure how to begin, start your sentence with "Confidence for me means...." Complete it with exactly what you want. Try to write five or six sentences that center around what you want.

2. Objectively assess what you want and evaluate what is attainable and what isn't. Ask yourself what factors are within your control and what factors are not. Perhaps your goal is to have the body of a famous superstar. Look at your body and ask yourself if it is really achievable. If not, opt to be healthier, instead—perhaps your goal could include losing a specific amount of weight.

3. Before you create an action plan that will lead you to your goals, start a love relationship with yourself. Write out the qualities you love about yourself, as well as qualities other people have appreciated in you. No matter how small or insignificant you think that quality is, write it out and start falling in love with yourself. Look at how well your body, your character, and your personality has served you and the other people in your life. Embrace that—and only when you are comfortable with that should you advance to creating a plan to become the most confident version of yourself.

For becoming more generous or giving [philanthropy]:

1. Start this process by meditating on your perception of other people. In order to become more deliberate with the distribution of your wealth—be it time, money, or knowledge—you have to first start thinking of people as an extension of yourself. As long as people remain strangers to you, you will be unable to care enough to genuinely become concerned about their well-being.

2. Look at the tethers that bind you to your possessions. We are typically unable to give because we have formed unhealthy attachments to the things we own. Remind yourself that nothing is forever. You may never fit into that shirt you are holding onto, so why not give it to someone

who can benefit from it right now? Also, apply some meditation of evil in this process. If you were to suddenly lose everything, how well would that serve you or the people around you? This helps you detach yourself from the things you own. Enjoy the benefits they bring you, but don't attach any value to them.

3. Gift someone without prompting. If, at first, the process feels weird, you can start by giving those closest to you a gift. It could be a quick phone call that just focuses on their well-being, where you listen and offer the support they need. Find out how they are doing, what is going on in their lives. Spend a few hours with your grandparents. Do the odd chore around the house, or just sit down and chat. Volunteer at your local soup kitchen. It may feel a bit strange, initially, but keep at it on a monthly or weekly basis. Saying hello to a random stranger and paying them a compliment are also daily or weekly tasks you could assign yourself.

Chapter Twenty-three
Taking Ownership of Your Life

"Most powerful is he who has himself in his own power."
Seneca

If you have spent your life blaming the rest of the world for any perceived injustice, you might never be able to make any real progress. Yes, what has happened to you may have been cruel and unfair, but the power that the person or persons in question had over you ended the day or the period in which they inflicted that hurt or trauma. The moment you stepped outside of that, the power reverted back to you. And, right now, I am not referring to the general talk about the negative energy that surrounds one's inability to forgive, although that does have its own type of emotional poison. I am talking about subjecting yourself subconsciously to hurt over and over again. Except this time around, you are holding in your own hands the weapon that is inflicting the pain.

Throughout this book, the underlying message has been that the ultimate power to transform our lives and to live the life we desire is in us. And all you have to do is reach out and take that power. Of course, to do it the Stoic way, your first hurdle would have to be overhauling the years of thinking patterns and behaviors that you have learned throughout your lifetime. This process is not easy, but it is not complicated, either. In a few paragraphs, I am going to go over certain thinking pillars that you will need to break down so these new principles you are trying to imbibe can inform the decisions that you make. This is not a complete list, but it covers the basics. As you evolve, you will make new discoveries. Include those discoveries in your own list.

1. You are responsible.

When we hear a phrase like that, we think in terms of obligations and duties. We think of specific tasks that fall within the purview of what we feel is our "job description." In this new life, being responsible goes beyond your daily chores or the duties assigned to you in your role as a wife, husband, parent, friend, or employee. It means you are the main agent for everything that happens in your life. This is huge, especially if you have always believed that everything that has happened to you up until now is the work of divine power. But here is the truth: That divine power still exists and, in the grand scheme of things, there are events that have been designed just for you. However, you are the one who defines those experiences. So, if you want to explore your full potential, you need to accept that you are the one responsible for the choices, actions, and experiences in your life.

2. You should expect the terrible stuff to happen to you.

Put this way, it does sound like a horrible thing to say, but these are some of the things you are going to have to psychologically prepare yourself for. When you face the future, don't just look for the white fluffy clouds, the pot of gold at the end of the rainbow, and the unicorn. There will be dragons and darkness and things we would rather were not there, but denying their existence will not make them cease to exist. Instead, see these things as necessary tools to fast-track your process to living the good life. Your power lies in your ability to use both the good and the bad stuff to your advantage.

3. Your idea of what is good and what is bad is skewered.

There are true virtues, as you have learned, and there are also vices. But what is classified as good or bad are actually known as either preferred indifferent or disliked indifferent. That awesome job you love so much is a preferred indifferent, and losing that job would be defined as disliked indifferent. That job has benefits that, to an extent, help you maintain your dignity as it pays your bills, keeps you fed, and clothed. So you would rather have a job than not. However, it does not affect your virtue because if you were to lose it tomorrow, you could still find happiness. In other words, a lot of the things you have held close to your heart as the things that defined your life and well-being are actually just positive contributors. They are placeholders for the real thing, until you are able to get to that place where you understand the true value of your own thoughts. Your power or sense of self-worth is not in the things you desire.

4. Your experience is essentially what you permit.

This goes along the same line as you being responsible, but I had to create a separate section for this because many of us have been through experiences that our peers cannot even begin to imagine. And often, we feel these experiences justify the pain we live with daily. We make mistakes that come with grievous consequences, and we cannot get past the pain we have caused others. So, we feel that by punishing ourselves, we can in some way atone for them. These are lies that we tell ourselves to help us feel better about what has happened, but the feeling is temporary, and we continue this cycle of self-hurt. The things that people have done to you have no power over you. Just like the mistakes that you have made have no power over you. This is a concept that you will struggle with, especially if you the voices around you have been echoing your thoughts. Embrace fate, and everything that has happened, and you embrace your potential to be more.

I can write 50 books on the Stoic principles, and Seneca himself can rise up from his grave to mentor you on this very subject, but if you are unable to admit these basic truths and accept the powers that come with them, there is a distinct possibility that you will not be able to live out your full potential, much less reach the goals of being more confident, living more consciously, and enjoying the good life. There are no walls, no barriers or persons that can stop you from living your best life. As they say, the only person capable of standing in the way of your success is you. And that is because you hold the ultimate power.

Closing

I would like to leave you with these wise words from one of Stoicism's greatest masters, Seneca:

"Let us prepare our minds as if we'd come to the very end of life. Let us postpone nothing. Let us balance life's books each day... the one who puts the finishing touches on their life each day is never short of time."

We typically live our lives trying valiantly to postpone our meeting with death. We want to live forever—a noble concept, but leaves us with the fear of tomorrow. Among a group of friends, the subject of mortality came up. I found out that a lot of us are more enthusiastic about the afterlife. We hold onto the prospect of going to heaven and, obviously, nobody wants to make their bed in hell. We talked about living a life on earth that makes us worthy of heaven. One of our more mischievous companions asked the question: if the proverbial trumpets rang out today and the call to all saints to go to heaven was made, would you willing leave everything behind and answer that call?

A deadly hush fell upon the table. This was followed by a loud clearing of throats and uncomfortable laughs. Not one person was ready to face death, even after they had just portrayed heaven as this wonderful place. You see, there was no questioning the existence of heaven or hell—that was not the real issue. The issue was that many of us are tethered to earth, despite our pious affiliation and devotion to heaven. There is nothing wrong with that, either. Only that, for a group of people who are clueless as to when death will inevitably come, we sure take living for granted.

The Stoic way of living prepares you for the inevitability of death while ensuring you live your life to the fullest. The uncertainty of tomorrow should not stop you from living now, and just because you are living now doesn't mean you should not pay any attention to tomorrow. Live right, with the people you surround yourself with. Do things that give you a sense of purpose, in that you are playing your part in the universal scheme of things. Take everything life arms you with and turn it into a bestseller that will be your life. That is what this book is all about.

Epictetus described life as "hard, brutal, punishing, narrow and confining, a deadly business." Stoicism is meant to help you make sense of your journey. With it, you'll find strength in the face of adversity, discover the opportunities in your obstacles, and attain a perspective that sees you rising above your pain.

Book #5

Public Speaking

Speak Like a Pro

How to Destroy Social Anxiety, Develop Self-Confidence, Improve Your Persuasion Skills and Become a Master Presenter

Preface

Have you been called upon to speak at an event recently and the thought of doing it is giving you sleepless nights? Are you looking to make your mark in the world of public speaking but have no clue where to begin? Whether you are speaking as the best man at your friend's wedding, leading a presentation by your team at the next board meeting or speaking to an audience of eager people, this book, *Public Speaking: Speak Like a Pro; How to Destroy Social Anxiety, Develop Self-Confidence, Improve Your Persuasion Skills and Become a Master Presenter* is just what you need.

Delve into the core issues that could be affecting your self-esteem. Get practical tips on how to deliver your speech and overcome your social anxiety with the wealth of information made available in one accessible platform. Unlock the amazing potential within you in quick and easy steps. In this book you will find:

- Tips on getting you out of your comfort zone
- Effective ways to define yourself as a public speaker
- A guide to creating a winning strategy for your presentation no matter the occasion
- How to dress like a professional public speaker
- Tools that will help you succeed in your presentation
- And much more!

The average public speaker earns as much as $104,000 annually in the US. The guys in the upper echelon of that statistic have annual earnings that go as high as $300,000 within the same timeframe. In essence, this is a profession that is valued by a lot of people and if done right, it can get create a sustainable income that can set you up for the rest of your life. But the road that takes you from where you are to the point where you are raking in a six-figure income annually is paved with obstacles that not many books or public speaking resources have addressed.

This book, Public Speaking: Speak Like a Pro; How to Destroy Social Anxiety, Develop Self-Confidence, Improve Your Persuasion Skills and Become a Master Presenter, provides you with a wholesome perspective on becoming a public speaker that is effective, practical and insightful. The objective of this book is not just to make you a public speaker, but one who is bold enough to stand on any stage and share their truth with their audience. Your fears should not have the power to impede your dreams. Reach into yourself and unleash your full potential with this book one page at a time. Don't let that incredible talent that you have go to waste. Turn over to the next page and begin the next chapter of your life!

Introduction

I remember the first time I got on stage to speak. I was only six-years-old and I was meant to be a very mean tree in a school play. The key to skillfully playing that part lied in me wearing a scowl for most of that scene and delivering my line (just one line) perfectly. I attended all the rehearsals. I practiced my line. I was going to crush it on that day. After wearing my costume, my teacher called me the cutest mean tree ever. I was convinced that I had this locked down. But when the time came to deliver, I completely froze. Even now, I can see the whole thing playing out before me in slow motion. First, the tree costume suddenly became too hot for me so I became sweaty and fidgety. I heard some people in the audience laugh (perhaps thinking it was all part of the play) and this agitated me even more. Poor Billy (who played the prince) didn't notice how unstable I was as he walked right into one of my extended roots and then tripped.

Billy survived the fall. I didn't survive the humiliation. Stories about my "epileptic" stage antics were pedaled throughout the whole school and it felt like everywhere I went, people mocked and made fun of me. Thankfully, my parents moved us to another city which meant a new school, new friends and a clean start. But the new environment did nothing to assuage my growing paranoia around people. Every time I was asked to speak to someone, even those I was familiar with, I would clam up and start sweating profusely. My father thought it was an age thing so he assured me that as I got older, those feelings would pass. They didn't. Things only intensified to the point that I was living as a total recluse. This was the lowest point of my life. It has been over two decades since that incident and my life has undergone a complete 360. I am now an author, speaker and a successful businessman.

So how did I go from James the hermit to this person who loves and lives for the spotlight? People shouldn't be able to change that drastically, right? Well, wrong. I am living proof of that and I am excited to share my journey and my process. It started with my first job as an independent telemarketer for an insurance company. The job suited me because my interaction with people was limited to phone conversations. All I had to do was cold-call people and make a pitch. I know that people hated getting those calls but I actually enjoyed it because I was the one making that call. This led to a pretty interesting discovery about myself...I am an incredible salesman. Underneath that painfully shy exterior was a guy with an amiable personality and a voice that made people feel at ease. It was like discovering that I had this superpower.

Subsequently, I was called in by my superiors to take on more responsibilities, one of which was to speak to a team of telemarketers and share my success tips with them. Oh boy! I was immediately transported back to my nightmare moment on stage. There was no way I was going to willingly put myself through that horror show. However, my supervisors were not having it. I had one month to prepare for that speaking event. In my head, that meant I had one month to get my affairs in order and move to another city. If my budget could afford it, I wouldn't have minded moving to another country altogether. When I got back home that day, I shared the news with my dad. I also told him what I planned to do. He simply nodded just like all the wise dads I knew and then asked me a single question: "How long are you going to keep running, James?"

This question prompted a flashback to my high school and college years. Every time I was assigned speaking tasks, I ran away from them. I didn't see it as running away at the time. But as I stood there with my dad, those memories came to me in flashes. It was like a montage in a very bad movie. I knew I had to stop running and that moment seemed like the perfect opportunity to begin. I was terrified. But I started by doing some research on public speaking. I found a few courses that promised to transform me into a prolific speaker in a month if I had at least $500. At my age and money bracket back then, it was like asking me to pay millions. Obviously, that route wasn't going to do it for me. I had to comb through hours of videos and articles on the subject for information on public speaking. A lot of it was vague or written to sell a product or service. None of it delved into the subject completely.

I went through this process for weeks and by the time the day for my speaking event came, I was maybe 35% ready. I would like to say that I went through that event like a boss and totally nailed it but no, that was not the case. Nobody fell on the stage that day and even though I was drenched in sweat by the time I was done, I made it through with a semblance of my dignity intact. However, in the notes I made after the event, I compared my performance there to mowing a lawn. I just kept droning on like a lawn mower and chopping through my points in the same manner. It was bland, boring and uninspiring. There were a lot of cringe-worthy moments but I had one big takeaway from it: It heralded the beginning of my public speaking career.

More than eleven years later, I have worked on a lot of projects that involved me speaking on stage in front of peers and colleagues. I still get hit by stage fright every time I get close to the stage but getting over my fears and climbing on stage anyway has gotten easier with each try. If you are reading this, there is a part of you that identifies with my journey. You have a gift that needs to be shared with the world but your shyness, anxiety and lack of self-confidence have enabled your decision to keep to yourself. I am going to ask you the same question my dad asked me: How long are you going to keep running?

You have the chance to step out of your shell and there is no better time to begin than now. Before you flip to the next chapter, here are tips on how to use this book successfully:

1. Take your time to read through each chapter and process the information. Diligence—not speed—is required here.
2. Make side notes as you study. This helps you assimilate better.

3. Complete the exercises at the end of each chapter. They nudge you gently out of your comfort zone.
4. Put the information that you get to practice. Practice is the key to perfecting your craft.
5. Maintain a positive outlook. This feeds your esteem and fuels your determination to see this through to the end.

I want you to succeed and I am not alone in this. If you pay attention, you will find a lot of people who are in your corner rooting for you. To succeed, you have to remember that this is not a leisure read. It is about taking action, and your first assignment is to flip to the next chapter. See you on the other side.

James Williams

PART ONE
THE BATTLE WITHIN

CHAPTER ONE
The Introvert's Bubble

"You never change your life until you
step out of your comfort zone;
change begins at the end of your comfort zone."
Roy T. Bennett

Living in Your Comfort Zone

We all have that space where we are the most authentic version of ourselves. In this space, there is no room for doubt, worry or fear. The world fades out the moment we enter this place and we experience a sense of calm. This place is known as our bubble and in this bubble, things happen effortlessly. The bubble is not always an actual place. It could be certain things or activities or even related to time. This calmness we experience within our bubble is not just random. And the things we have psychologically tagged as our comfort do not really give us the sense of calm that we think it does. For example, people whose comfort zone is linked to food might be inclined to think that the food is what makes them calm when in reality, they are simply projecting the emotions that they crave onto the food.

Your couch may be the space you have chosen as your comfort zone. Its cozy and plushy seats envelop you in a welcome embrace every time you sit on it. The proximity of the couch to all your favorite things like the TV, the coffee table which also houses your favorites snacks and books (and let's not forget, the remote) are just one of the many things that make it seem as though the couch gives you everything you need to feel emotionally comfortable. But the operational word here is "choose." You "chose" that couch. In essence, your comfort zone is a place of your choosing that feeds what psychologists refer to as an anxiety neutral position.

It is a very good feeling to be in your comfort zone but let me break down the actual cost of your "rent" if you choose to remain in your comfort zone. When your anxiety level is neutral or minimal, your stress level comes down and this is because you don't have to deal with any crisis, any uncertainty and you are obviously more in control. With the absence of these things, your performance level is steady. If a comparison was done between your performance level in your comfort zone and when you are out of it, there would be a startling difference. Imagine we have drawn up a line chart to show the differentiation between your performance levels in and out of your zone. Now let me describe what it would look like.

The lines from the "in zone" performance would be a perfectly straight line that doesn't deviate or fluctuate. The numbers would be below the radar but it holds steady. The lines from the "outside zone" performance would be the opposite. It would be on a wavering line that ascends and sometimes descends. The more you push past your comfort zone, the higher you ascend. I did say that the line sometimes ascends and descends but what is interesting is that no matter how low it descends, it does not get below the steady line that is your performance when you are in your comfort zone. What is the point of all this? Well, I will get to it in a second.

Introverts have a propensity to stick to their comfort zone. And this affects their ability to speak up in public. I know because I lived in one for years and it wasn't until I pushed past that zone that I got to discover some of the potential I have. However, I have also observed that introverts are not the only ones who operate from this place. A lot of people (possibly you included) are in a place in their life where they are just generally comfortable. Your current skills and talent are celebrated, you have a job or run a business that ensures all of your needs are taken care of and you are surrounded by the people you trust…so this begs the question, why would you need to take a risk at doing something that you are not really good at? The answer is change. I will discuss this extensively in subsequent chapters but let me put it into perspective here.

Change is one of those inevitable things in life. It will disrupt life in your comfort zone and if you are not prepared for it, you will be deeply affected by it. The only way to get ahead of change is to step out of your comfort zone and push past your limits. Since you are reading this book, I am pretty certain that the assignment that is taking you out of your zone is public speaking. This is the reason you are terrified. Not because you are terrible at it or you are worried that you would be terrible at it. You are just being pulled out of your comfort zone. Stop fighting it. Just take a deep breath and embrace the challenge. Today, you are leaving your comfort zone. Next challenge? Figuring out where the real battle is.

The Fictional Friend or Foe

Back in high school, there was this girl I was so into. She was smart, incredibly beautiful and best of all, she was really nice to me. We took a few classes together where we sat and exchanged love gazes (and yes, this is a thing) all throughout. Our houses were on the same street so we sort of walked home together every day after school, which wasn't really far away. We didn't talk much, as I was painfully shy, but she seemed okay with it. She didn't say much either but she always looked at me with a smile. One day she didn't walk back home with me. I thought that was strange but then I saw her girlfriends, Leah and Sophie, waiting behind so I assumed they had one of those girlie events lined up. You can imagine my horror when I came to school the next day to hear the news that my Gina was dating quarterback "jerk face" Derek. I was shattered and heartbroken and listened to a lot of sad music for months.

That story I put up there was all in my head. Gina and I were never dating. Sure, we lived a few buildings apart—hence the walking home together part—but it was never really "together." She walked a few steps ahead with her friend and a cousin. Gina smiled generally at people because she was just a nice person naturally. And in truth, she probably only smiled at me once or twice. I just recorded it in my head and played it over and over again until it seemed as if she smiled at me all the time. Which leads me to the point I was trying to make. I made up that entire relationship in my head. I really liked Gina but there was no way I was going to talk to her, much less do anything about it. So, I created a fantasy relationship built on little snippets of reality and I actually ended up with real heartbreak for it.

Many of us make up this fictional battle in our minds and we react in fear to this make-believe battle we have going on. This is one of the main internal struggles we have when we are being called to speak in front of a crowd. Before we even get on stage, we imagine the reaction of the crowd. It doesn't matter if you are going to be speaking to your peers, a group of people you already share some similarity with or strangers. We picture that disapproving face in the crowd. We hear the mocking laughter and the crude jokes that are being made about us while we are even speaking. Sometimes, we even go as far as picturing an electrical malfunction that sets the podium on fire and sends the crowd into massive fits of laughter. The humiliation of all this cripples our courage and causes us to panic. But like me and my fantasy high school girlfriend, all of this is in our head.

The real battle is not facing the crowd of people who are hell-bent on your humiliation. The real enemy, in this case, is you. As humans, we have been gifted with an active imagination and this gift can be used in one of two ways. You can either use your imagination to fuel your dreams or empower your nightmare. In this case, you are using your imagination to force yourself back into your comfort zone, and we have already gone over what happens there. Some of you might say, "Oh, this happened to me in the past," but it is not happening to you right now, is it? No. You are just making up another excuse to justify your fears. The most powerful weapon in the arsenal of a public speaker is not their oratory skills or their great sense of style (although these are important too). It is not the absence of stage fright or their great people skills. It is their ability to harness the power of their imagination in their favor.

American athlete Michael Strahan is quoted as saying, *"We're our own worst enemy. You doubt yourself more than anybody ever will. If you can get past that, you can be successful."* I agree with him 100%. In the battle within, the enemy that we must face down is ourselves. Stop promoting theories that amplify your fears. Instead, make yourself your ally. This may require unlearning certain habits you have picked up over the years. A few pages down, you will get the full scoop on how to do this. For now, let us shift the focus from negative thoughts to finding positive reinforcements.

Finding the Right Connections

In a bid to get me to make more friends when I was younger, my mother invited her friends who had kids to come over. Either that or she would take me by hand to their houses for a visit. As expected, I was always reluctant. Not because the other kids were not nice or welcoming. It was just that being around them even made me more aware of my shyness, which worsened my anxiety. I never acted out or anything but my mother would always find me sitting by myself in one corner. She would sigh and say to me, "No man is an island, James; you need to be around people." I heard this phrase a lot as I grew older and at first, I thought it was all about just having people around you. Perhaps you could go as far as putting the "friend" label on some of these people.

I thought that our connections with people were mainly about our outward interaction with them until our dog, Jojo, died. Stay with me on this. I know I started with the sad kid on the playground and now you have the sad kid whose dog died. I have a point I am trying to make here. As you can imagine, Jojo's death affected me badly. I was sad for a long time and my mother encouraged me to write about my feelings in order to get through it. Reluctantly, I did. And I remember the words I wrote.

"Jojo never said a word to me. I did most of the talking and even then, he never gave any indication that he understood the words I said. But Jojo was my best friend in the world and we had a special connection..."

I wrote a lot of other things after that but it wasn't until a couple of years later when I was going through my stuff that this last sentence really hit me. Friendship is not about the people you have around you but about the connections that you make. No matter how much of a recluse we are, this is an important aspect of our nature; call it a biological programming that craves this connection. Some of us find it difficult to make those connections with human beings so we bestow it on either animals or inanimate objects. I know people who are deeply connected to their faith and a few who find this connection in their jobs. Why is this connection important and what does any of it have to do with public speaking? You see, the connections that you make in life have a way of bringing out the best, or sometimes the worst, in you. The deeper the connection, the greater the effect. Right now, I am not merely focusing on our connections with other people. I am looking at the things in our lives that influence our behaviors.

There is a lot of depth to this subject and I don't want to bore you with the details so I am just going to skim the surface and give you the low down on how this impacts your ability to speak in public. When we connect with something, we plug into it psychologically in a way that allows said thing to influence our thoughts and thus, our behavior. Take Jojo for instance. This dog brought out a side of me that not many people got to see. His antics, though frustrating at times, turned on the fun part of my brain and got me laughing like there was no tomorrow. Losing him affected my ability to turn that part on again.

Your paranoia about speaking in public can stem from the fact that you have absolutely no connection to anything that turns on that part of your brain. For me, my connection was activated by my love for my job as a salesman. That whole process where you meet a person, speak to them about the product or service that you are selling and then convince them to make a purchase was such a rush. I didn't identify public speaking with this connection I had with my job at first. When doing the research for my first public speaking assignment, I understood on a basic level that there was a link between making sales and public speaking. But when I personalized it by establishing that connection, it opened up a whole new universe for me.

What opens you up to people? What is that subject or topic that the second you start talking about it, you suddenly fall into a rhythm that is calm and comforting and you can ride that wave forever? Is it the work that you do? Or the people that you work with? How can you connect that with what you are about to speak publicly on? When you find the right connection, you will find your voice. And when you do find your voice, it is time to let that bird fly free.

Taking Your Freedom in Leaps

So far, we have talked about three major internal issues that could impact your road to public speaking even before you set a foot on that part. These are deep-seated issues that may take months or years to change. This can give you pause and I understand why. We live in an age where everything is done rapidly. So it makes sense that we would want our transformation to happen overnight too. Well, let me burst your bubble right there. That is not going to happen. Not if you want a result that is sustainable throughout your years. Because this is not something that is exclusive to helping you become a better public speaker. If done right, it can help you become better at so many other things.

However, just because the process is going to take long does not mean that you should defer your public speaking assignment or goal until you think you are "fixed." Even if you have an assignment tomorrow, I urge you to follow through with it. It may not be your best performance but it will get you closer to your goal. The objective right now is to take things one step at a time. Before we move on to the next chapter, we are going to review the highlights of what we have talked about, and then you will also have a few simple tasks that you can carry out today to help nudge you in the right direction. These tasks are not one-off things that you simply cross off your to-do list. They help you build habits that will help you grow.

That said, here is what we have learned so far:
- Our comfort zone is where our performance level is at its lowest.
- Change is what spurs our growth.
- Self-doubt, more than anything, is what brings us down.
- The greatest tool in public speaking is one's imagination.

- To be a great speaker, you need to find your connection to what makes you want to speak in the first place.
- Transformation does not happen overnight. It starts with one deliberate step at a time.

Your tasks:

1. Say yes to an invite to a social event at least once every month.
2. Have a conversation with a perfect stranger every week (a few strings of sentences count).
3. Pick out five things or persons you have a connection with. They must be classified under the stuff you either like to talk about or who/what you like to talk about things to or with. Write out why and how they get you to talk.
4. Do a little research on some famous public speakers. Who do you identify with the most and why?
5. Include something very different in your routine today. Do that every other day, and you must not repeat these exercises.

CHAPTER TWO
CROWDED SPACES

"Wild animals run from the dangers they actually see and

once they have escaped them, worry no more.

We, however, are tormented alike by what is past and what is to come.

A number of our blessings do us harm,

for memory brings back the agony of fear

while foresight brings it on prematurely.

No one confines his unhappiness to the present."

Seneca

Social Anxiety 101

In the previous chapter, the primary focus was on the internal conflicts that impede our ability to speak in public. In this chapter, we are going to be looking at external factors that can stand in our way.

My aunt, who was a devout Catholic, was often fond of saying, "A sinner runneth when no man pursueth." Basically, some of the things that we fear the most are grounded in our imagination more than the existence of the actual thing or event that scares us. For people who suffer from social anxiety, the boogie man is often the crowd. And if you are going to move on to becoming an excellent public speaker, you are going to have to move past your fear of crowds. This is easier said than done and I know because I have been down that rabbit hole and let me tell you, it is not pretty. In order to defeat one's fear, you must first understand it.

In very succinct terms, social anxiety is a form of stress brought on by interacting with people socially. A lot of times, people confuse social anxiety with being shy. We all experience an unpleasant reaction when we are thrust into a social situation, especially if you are going to be meeting new people for the first time. It gets even worse if you are expected to speak to or address these new people that you are meeting. Our pulse becomes elevated, our palms sweaty and we experience this sinking feeling in our stomach. This is all perfectly natural. However, the difference between normal stress experienced when we are in those social conditions and social anxiety is that you can push through the normal stress. But social anxiety completely paralyzes you.

It is so intense that it has been classified as a mental disorder. So, if you find yourself unable to function in any way when you are in a social setting, chances are you are suffering from Social Anxiety Disorder and it is very important to see a doctor about it. Now, this recommendation does not mean that your dreams of public speaking are a foreclosed issue until your doctor says that you are better. I am saying that the first step to eliminating it is seeing a doctor. There are several reasons why people suffer from social anxiety and the degree to which they experience it can be influenced by a number of factors. For starters, there is a biological element to it. Having a relative who suffers from Social Anxiety Disorder increases your risk of having it. If you have a history of abuse, especially if this abuse started at an early age, your risk doubles.

In some cases, certain insecurities we have about ourselves can trigger an attack. If those insecurities are physical or visible, it gets even worse. It could be an ugly scar, a birthmark, or perhaps the sound of our voice. We feel that these attributes make us stand out in a very loud way and that people would not approve of this difference. So we anticipate their judgment and this puts us in an anxious state. For those who experience this intensely, they would rather not put themselves out there for that kind of judgment anyway.

Whatever the case, the road to recovery starts with acknowledging the existence of a problem and then taking an introspective journey that will take you to the root of the problem. For people who have gone through some kind of psychological trauma in the past, there may be a lot of unresolved emotional issues. Working with a trained psychologist can help you get to a place where you come to terms with what has happened and then release the burden of holding on to that memory. You may also need to undergo some behavioral therapy that would help retrain your instinctive reaction to certain situations. This way, your body does not have to go through the fight or flight response every time you are confronted with situations that trigger your memory.

People whose Social Anxiety Disorder stem from a biological proponent, like having the portion of their brain that controls fear function in hyper mode, may need medical treatment to get that under control. This again requires consultation with a doctor. Now if your anxiety is a result of some form of insecurity or low self-esteem, you can speak with psychologists to help you come to terms with who you are. And if it is something that can be fixed, it would not hurt to meet with someone who is qualified to do so. Just remember, they can only fix what is on the outside. I have seen cases where people had these insecurities about certain parts of their body, got it fixed perfectly, but they still battled with their insecurities. It becomes like that phantom limb that doctors talk about.

You cannot get to the point where you can comfortably speak publicly without first overcoming any form of social anxiety you may have. This is a delicate process that might open up some deep emotional wounds but healthy healing is what would follow afterward.

The Dreadful Cycle

Having looked at what social anxiety is, I want us to look at its impact on public speaking beyond the physical symptoms that we talked about. We have explored the *what* and touched a little bit on the *why*. Now we will go into the *how*. As a child, one of my favorite moments with my dad happened when we were in the garage together tinkering with stuff. It could be an engine, an electrical device or whatever my father got his hands on. The objective was to pull it apart, understand how each of the different pieces worked and then put it back together again. More often than not, the stuff that we put back together didn't quite function again the way it was designed to. It either got the "Williams Upgrade" or ended up making weird noises while doing what it was designed to do.

For us to successfully "upgrade" a device, we would have to thoroughly understand the role that each part had to play in the process and then figure out how it did what it did. Then we would have to break the cycle. It was either we took something out entirely or we took it out and replaced it with something better. When it comes to emotional trauma, I use the same approach. Anxiety, as with most emotions that happen in the extreme, go through a cycle. This cycle is made up of a series of events that take you from point A to point B and sometimes up to point D before bringing you right back to point A again. And then the process continues. The starting point for this cycle is the mind. There is no emotional angst we face today that does not first begin in the mind. There are external factors that can set things in motion but long before those things happened, the mind played its part.

When an event happens to you, the emotion you feel as a result—whether good or bad—is registered in your mind and identified with that event. That memory and the feeling that induced it is locked in your mind with certain markers that could be sight, sound or smell. This is why a specific scent can take you back to your childhood. Amazingly, this registered event does not have to be a firsthand experience. It is possible that you witnessed something that locked that event in your mind. It is also possible that you were told of an event that was so emotionally intense that it locked itself in your mind. And then you have the case where you made up an experience and somehow convinced your mind that it is a real possibility, that it also locks that false memory. I told you before—the mind is a very powerful tool.

Now that your mind has locked this memory, the next sequence in this cycle is the event that triggers the memory locked away in your mind. In this case, it is the crowd that you are trying to interact with. The crowd itself is not the problem. The problem is the way your brain interprets what it is seeing because your mind is feeding it information based on the memories unlocked. For social anxiety, the memory unlocked is usually linked to unhealthy relationships with people. Whether this memory is real or projected, if it is unpleasant, the brain interprets the social situation as a threat. When the brain senses a threat, it goes on alert and your natural preservation instincts kick in. Essentially, the signals being fed to your body are telling your impulses that you are not in a safe space and you need to get out of there.

These signals manifest as increased heart rate, problems breathing and muscles tensing up among other signs. These symptoms can amplify the information reaching your senses. An innocent laugh or smile at something general might seem as though it is targeted at you. A person walking towards you may seem like they are making a threatening advancement. This brings you back to your mind, where the whole process is put on repeat. All of these things happen very fast. The point when you walked into the room to the moment that you are virtually hyperventilating can happen in a matter of seconds. As the cycle repeats, the emotions experienced hit you like waves. Each one more intense than the last until the situation either escalates or you are removed from that moment completely.

For some people, the anxiety kicks in the moment they walk into a room full of crowded people. For others, getting on stage is what triggers the attack. Understanding the sequence listed here is key to creating solutions that will help you break free, and this is where we are going to next.

How to Break Even

In the first section of this chapter, I laid a lot of emphasis on the importance of consulting with a specialist to help get you over your social anxiety. That has not changed but that is just the first step. You need a doctor for many reasons, with the primary one being to get a proper diagnosis and possibly the root cause of the problem. Follow through on their treatment and management plan.

For people whose social anxiety falls within the mild to moderate spectrum, you may need to take a more proactive role in managing your anxiety problems. For starters, experts believe that what you have is related to performance anxiety. This is related to social anxiety but related to your performance than just being in a social setting. If this is the case, then this is good news. Performance anxiety, also known as stage fright, is very common and it is suffered by millions of people all over the world. You are not alone. As a matter of fact, your favorite public speakers suffered from performance anxiety at some point in their lives. One of my favorite examples is our country's most appreciated president, Abraham Lincoln.

Despite the rousing speech he gave at Cooper Union in New York, Abe was terrified of speaking in front of a large crowd. His fear was so great that he turned down an opportunity to speak at an event that would have taken his political career to the pinnacle. His note on the subject alluded to some anxiety issues. Of course, he went on to become one of America's greatest, but that required him stepping up to the challenge. Other famous speakers who had similar issues are Joel Olsten, Thomas Jefferson and even Warren Buffet—who was rumored to have been unable to get up and say his own name in class.

Now that we know who they are and how prolific they are at speaking, it is difficult to reconcile this image of them with the ones who were scared of speaking. But history paints a clear picture for us. But what speaks loudest to me is the fact that if they can overcome their performance anxiety, so can you.

To break the dreadful cycle of performance anxiety, you are going to have to first start with your mind, which controls all of the sequences in the cycle. The memories that trigger your emotions, which go on to activate certain impulses, need to be replaced. If you had a tragic stage experience, you cannot just forget that it never happened or delete it from memory. That is not how this works. However, you are going to have to take your focus away from those memories. Remember what I said earlier about the power of your imagination.

Darwin's experiment on the subject is a perfect illustration of this. He pressed his nose against a glass cage that held a poisonous adder within. When the snake struck at his nose from inside the cage, Darwin jumped back even though he knew that there was no way that the snake could get to him. In the same way, we are aware that the crowd we are about to speak to are not going to harm us. However, we instinctively react as though they would. So, stop seeing the crowd as your enemy and the stage as a kill zone. Instead, picture them as people who share your concerns and interests, because they do. If not, why else would they be coming to hear you speak? You have something to say that they would like to listen to so embrace the opportunity and just go ahead and say it.

I have mentioned a lot here in trying to explain the *how*. So I decided to simplify everything I have said in actionable points:

1. Stop running away. You need to face your fears head-on. It may require every ounce of discipline in you to do it the first time, but it gets easier over time.
2. Be prepared. There are very few people who can give great speeches at the drop of a hat. All those carefully and artfully delivered stage performances required hours of rehearsals, at least.
3. Focus more on your speech and less on the crowd. You cannot do anything about the crowd anyway.
4. Have more confidence in your abilities.
5. Be positive.

Get Ahead and Be Heard

It is said that when Thomas Jefferson spoke during his public speeches (he gave only two of them throughout his eight-year tenure), he spoke in very low tones that required you to strain your ears before you could hear him. Mahatma Gandhi was the same way too. But they did not let their voices get drowned in the sea of people they had to surround themselves with. What they did instead was keep their words concise but very effective. Not everyone has the gift of gab, however, when it comes to public speaking, it is better to keep your message succinct yet impactful than to drone on endlessly.

As we go further into this book, we will learn the very art of public speaking itself, but not before overcoming the fear of speaking in public. Also, if you are going to wait for a time when you no longer get anxious about speaking before actually doing it, you are never going to do it. This is because those jittery feelings caused by anxiety never really go away. It has been almost a decade since my first speaking assignment but I still get sweaty and shaky right before I go in front of the crowd. And I have been a public speaker on more than fifty occasions. The only difference is that the fear is not as paralyzing as it used to be. You just have to embrace the fear, don't let it envelop you. Put your feet down and tell yourself that today, you are doing this.

And on that note, here is a summary of what this chapter has been about:

- Social Anxiety Disorder is a mental disorder brought on by the stress of being in a crowd. Performance anxiety is a form of social anxiety associated with stage fright or speaking in front of a crowd.
- Social anxiety is very common but it is treatable, manageable and very possible to overcome.
- The messages that you feed your mind will determine your reaction in a social situation. If you feed yourself messages linked to fear, you will react in fear.
- Deferring your public speaking to a later date when you might feel more comfortable will only prolong your torment. It is better to bite the proverbial bullet now.

Your tasks:

1. Speak to a doctor about your anxiety. You may not get a fix for it right away but the knowledge that you are doing something about it can be very reassuring.
2. Take up the habit of meditating at least thirty minutes a day. This practice will teach you how to get your body to relax even when you are under pressure.
3. Find a mantra that you can repeatedly say to calm yourself in stressful situations. It could be a phrase, words of affirmation or confidence boosters. I like "Hakuna Matata."
4. Every morning, look at yourself in the mirror and give yourself a compliment. It might feel awkward at first but that feeling passes in time.
5. Maintain longer eye contact with people. For strangers across the room, a three-second gaze is fine. For people you are having a conversation with, try as much as possible to maintain eye contact. Don't glare. Don't stare.

Maintaining eye contact helps you build confidence in your social interaction skills, and we will get into more on confidence-building in the next chapter.

CHAPTER THREE
BUILDING BLOCKS OF CONFIDENCE

"Wouldn't it be wonderful
if you fell so deeply in love with yourself
that you would do just about anything
if you knew it would make you happy?
This is precisely how much life loves you
and wants you to nurture yourself.
The deeper you love yourself,
the more the universe would affirm your worth.
Then you can enjoy a lifelong love affair
that brings you the richest fulfillment from inside out."
Alan Cohen

The Lies We Tell Ourselves

Growing up, we were taught to see the wrong in telling lies to other people. There was always honor in telling the truth. The reason that was given to us most of the time was that it made it difficult for people to trust you if you had a habit of telling lies. Lying is a self-preserving trait and this is not something you are trained to do. It just comes to you naturally. This is why a three-year-old would tell a bald-faced lie. The main objective of lying is to give a narrative that serves our purposes and interests best. If lying becomes a habit, then it becomes a serious problem and there could be some psychological angle to that. Lying is so complicated because it never really just ends with one lie. It grows from one tiny untruth in a giant entangled web of lies that entraps the person telling the lies and I find this very interesting because when lying is involved, it is not just the person lied to that is affected.

As a matter of fact, lies affect the person who told the lie even more. And I am not referring to the late-night visit from karma that most people believe delivers judgment to those who have erred on the wrong side of humanity. I am talking about the impact on the psyche of the person perpetrating the lies. If you have ever been on the other end of the stick, you would know how much it hurts to realize that you have been lied to. In other words, when a lie is being told, both the person lying and the one being lied to end up getting really hurt. This hurt may not surface right away. In fact, you may even realize that you have been lied to but on some instinctual level, you sense it and that causes the hurt to linger and fester, leading to a very precarious relationship at best. Knowing all of this, I would like you to ponder on the next question I am going to ask. What happens when the person being lied to and the person telling the lies are one and the same person?

There are lies we feed ourselves and sadly, not many of us were prepared for the consequences of this. The bigger problem with the lies that we tell ourselves is that the lies are usually not anything grand. They are small pieces of information that we assimilate in small doses over a long period of time. In other words, we do it without even realizing what we are doing. Sometimes, the lies are a reflection of what society tells us. We are tagged by culture, status, race and even gender. We then wear these labels and let it define our potential. When your ability to perform is characterized by the label that you wear, you will face a more internal struggle in your bid to succeed. Some people may argue that labels help give you a better understanding of yourself. I agree with those people, but to an extent. You see, unless you are the one giving yourself the label, instead of just adopting the one placed on you by society, you will always end up shortchanging yourself. What do I mean by this?

Let us assume that your parents have tagged you as "painfully shy." They saw certain traits and behaviors that you exhibited when you were much younger and then identified it with shyness. From that point onward, this is the information they reinforced. If they were meeting with friends and you hesitated to socialize, they would immediately apologize and then emphasize the message, "We are sorry, but our boy is incredibly shy." You probably heard this a lot in social settings and you internalized the message. As you grew older, you personalized that message. Your excuse for the awkwardness you experience when you socialize is excused by your "shyness." Your acceptance of this message is so wholesome that you characterize everything that you do with the label. So, when the opportunity comes for you to speak in front of your peers, without giving much thought to what it entails, you play the label tag and wriggle your way out of it.

Lies like these act as a barrier to your growth. Abraham Lincoln's excuse was that there was an illness that ran in his family that prevented him from speaking in public. Imagine what would have happened if Abe just threw his hands up and embraced the limitations set on him by this illness. He would probably have lived a regular life without anything out of the ordinary setting him apart from the men in his era. But we are privileged to know what he evolved to become and it is impossible to picture Abraham Lincoln as anyone less than the phenomenal person he was. The lies that we tell ourselves only serves to amplify our fears and increase doubt in our abilities. Telling yourself that you cannot speak in public is only there to protect yourself from the possibility of failure if you attempt to. It is you telling yourself that you are not qualified for the task. Let us look at the implications of this.

Life in Rocky Places

Have you ever seen a flower blooming on a plant that is growing through rocks? It is incredibly beautiful and at the same time mind-boggling. I look at it as a miracle because under normal circumstances, that plant is not meant to be there. For a plant to grow, it needs soil, light and water. Rocks have very limited amounts of those which is why you don't see plants thriving in such places. But then you have extraordinary situations like these where nature decides to defy the odds. The plant in question did not just grow out of a rocky spot. It thrived, bloomed and became a thing of beauty that is admired. As exceptional as this story is, the main message is that nothing is impossible if you put your mind to it.

I don't know the kind of environment you were born and groomed into. It could have been a rocky spot that did not offer the essentials you needed to thrive. Either that or your environment was a rich and fertile soil that offered you everything that you needed to succeed in life. Whatever the case, here is one glaring truth: Neither of these environments listed can cause you to fail or succeed in life. The only thing they can do is either make it harder to succeed or harder to fail. And this is because the key ingredient that determines how far you go in life is what you feed yourself with. And this brings us back to the lies that we tell ourselves. Imagine the kind of conversation that plant must have had with itself in that dark, dry and lifeless place where it took root as seed. It must have heard the message that only plants in fertile soil can grow. The rocks must have told it to give up because there was very little sun and water that came through. Still, the plant did not internalize those messages even though they accurately reflected the reality of the situation on the outside. To thrive, it would have had to look inward for resources to draw on. I believe that if the plant looked inward and found the same hardness on the outside reflected inside, it would have folded up and died.

But it didn't. Instead, it found an oasis on the inside that made it resilient to the external dry conditions. The growth may have been slower than that of its peers but the moment it broke through to the surface, that process sped up. At this point, the outside world began to conform to what was already on the inside and the result was a flower that was as distinguished as a piece of stunning art. Let us bring it back to your present-day dilemma with public speaking. If you want to unleash the potential on the inside of you, you need to stop paying attention to what you are being fed by your environment. Maybe you are looking at your inexperience on the proposed topic, your supposed shy nature, your speech problem and so on as the things that limit your ability to succeed. Focusing on these things automatically places parameters on what you can achieve and how far you can go. Instead, focus on your goal.

Make it your business to manage your conscious mind (aka your inside voice) and remind yourself that you can achieve the success that you desire in public speaking. Those other issues we talked about might slow down your process or make it that much harder for you but the determining factor at the end of the day is you.

Building Pillars with Stones

We all have our respective struggles in life. Some of us are very good at disguising our pain. Others wear their hearts on their sleeves. Whatever category you belong to, recognize that the struggle is real. However, also remind yourself that your success is equally real. You may have had to deal with social anxiety, stage fright, poor self-esteem and lack of faith in your abilities to get to that spot where you can comfortably speak from. Whether this is your first time or thousandth time, there are hurdles that you have had to or will have to overcome in order to make your mark. The purpose of this chapter is to guide you to that place where these hurdles can become the foundation on which you build your claim to success.

Now that you are aware that you are at the helm of your affairs and not necessarily a victim of some biological or psychological factor, you cannot afford to sit on the sidelines. You will need to make conscious efforts to first let go of some "truths" that you have believed in. Broaden your horizon with your mind. I have a piece of painting in my home that I consider to be one of my most valuable purchases and this is not because of the amount of money I had to put down for it. It is what it symbolizes to me. The artist in question is an Indian man who was born without any function in his arms. Using his feet and mouth, he is able to create such incredible art. Every time I look at the painting, I am reminded of the possibilities.

Possibilities are not always born from the availability of what you need to succeed. It is birthed at the point when you make up your mind to follow through on achieving your goals despite the stones that life has thrown at you. At that point, instead of letting your weaknesses cripple you, you let them inspire you to be greater. When your fears and doubts are screaming the loudest and telling you that you can't, you turn up your voice in your head and yell back that you can. The moment you can do this, your success script is born.

Regaining and Retaining Your Crown

If at this point you are unable to tell yourself that you can do this, I would suggest you stop reading further and go back to the beginning of this book and start all over. I am not saying that your fears would have disappeared or that you have zero doubts about yourself. Because they will always be there. And if for some reason you have no fears or doubts, I would say you should go back and read chapter one because it definitely sounds like you are back in your comfort zone. At this point, you should still feel some pressure about the next step that you are about to take but at the same time, you should be able to say that you can do this.

Reclaim your crown by positively affirming your abilities and keep the crown thereby tuning out the voices of doubt. There are no pills that can get you to this point. And there is no amount of time spent on the psychologist's couch that can fix this. This is a choice that you have to make 100% on your own. All the things I have said here can only inspire you to take that next step but without you actually taking that step, you are always going to be on the other side of the line. We have one more hurdle to cross before going to the next part where we actually start preparing for public speaking. But it requires you to admit to yourself that you can do it. Still, need a little push to get you closer to the line?

Here is a recap of what we have learned so far:
- The words that you tell yourself have a more powerful effect than anything anyone else can say to you. You need to start "watering" yourself from the inside with positive words.
- The only reason you cannot speak publicly is that you have told yourself that you cannot.
- Nothing is impossible the moment you put your mind to it.
- You control the limits of your potential. You can only perform as good as you think you can perform.
- Positive affirmation is one way you can take the challenges that life tosses your way to build your success.

Your tasks:
1. Picture yourself performing on stage. From start to finish, let the entire experience be positive. Meditate on this image at least once a week.
2. Write out in detail how you would like to see your performance as a public speaker. Place this written article somewhere accessible and read it out loud every day. Modify it as you grow.
3. Think back on your life and find an experience that sees you overcoming a challenge. It does not have to be anything grand. If you have been following through on the tasks assigned to you in the previous chapter, you should have something on your list. If not, get to it.
4. Ask three people in your circle who know you on some level to list out your qualities and your "weaknesses" on two separate sheets. Study that list and figure out how to play them up in helping you achieve your goal. Don't internalize the perceived weaknesses; instead, empower yourself with them. For instance, if someone says that you are withdrawn in crowds, rephrase that to mean that you like to observe your environment.
5. List three qualities that you have and how you think those qualities have served you in your job, in your relationships, and in life generally.

The final chapter in this section reflects on the journey we have taken so far and puts us in a mental headspace that challenges what we have accepted as the status quo. We enter into the minds of champions and find out what makes them tick.

CHAPTER FOUR
ELIMINATING OBSTACLES

"The biggest obstacle you will ever have to overcome is your mind. If you can overcome that, you can overcome anything."

Unknown

Emotional Roadblocks

This quote here brings to mind a quote that I heard from an unlikely hero. I am one of those adults who enjoy kiddie's entertainment. You can say that at heart, I am still very much a big kid. Some of my favorite heroes are not from Marvel or DC Comics. They reside in either Dream-Works or Pixar animation studio and right now, the guys from *Kung Fu Panda* are the best. In the latest series, there was a part where one of the characters tells his students "before the battle of the fist comes the battle of the mind." I can attempt to set the premise for this statement but that would lead to a whole different book and we both know that you didn't sign up for that. Besides, given the title of this subject, I think we already have more than a fair idea of where I want to go with this. But hold that thought for a moment. Let us leave the kids arena and step into a wrestling or boxing arena.

Have you noticed that before a fight (I am not a big fan of those by the way, but it makes for an excellent illustration), the people fighting against each other are put in the same room in front of a small audience where they get to talk smack to each other? For the event organizers, it is a great way to promote the show and make good sales. For the audience and anyone watching, it is great entertainment and an incentive to watch the fight. For the fighters, their objective is different. Somewhat sinister, some may say. For them, this smack talk is a way to get inside their opponent's head and throw them off their game. Before the battle of the fist comes the battle of the mind.

Now let us bring this back to you. Going on stage is where your "battle" will happen, but the fight begins long before you step onto that stage. And as I am sure you probably know by now, the person you are fighting against is you and that is usually the toughest fight because you know all of your emotional weak spots, and so when you get into a "smack talk" session against yourself, you knock yourself out before you step into the ring. A typical smack talk between two people usually targets each other's weaknesses. What happens in a smackdown is that you have these two parties making fun of things are sometimes very personal to the opposing team. Now in your situation, you are not making fun of yourself (although some of us use humor to criticize ourselves), however, you are doing a very good job of undermining your abilities. Say for instance you have an issue with the way you pronounce certain words; when you are having that internal smack talk with yourself, every insult or negative comment you have ever received concerning this flaw is amplified and made the center focus. This becomes worse when you are put in a situation that requires you to use this thing that people have made fun of you for before even getting yourself ready to go on stage.

In general, every insecurity that you have ever faced will get its time in the spotlight and in the game of minds, this would make you even less confident and less willing to go on the offensive. It would seem as though you are putting yourself out there for other people to judge when in reality, the only person doing the judging is you. These negative comments are able to weigh on you because of your emotional connection to them. To help you overcome your emotional hurdle, I decided to take cues from the king of smack talk since we are on the subject. If you are a fan of trash TV, you may have come across something called "Yo Mama." It is a form of smack talk where people make dumb jokes about their opponent starting with "Yo mama." I used to think that there was no strategy to it and that it was all about having the best punch lines. But I was wrong. Imagine this. You have a situation where one person is confronted with a personal jab that is made into a joke and everyone laughs because it's a very good joke. And then the person at the receiving end of that joke doesn't take it personally but instead, they turn it around and make a comeback with it, sometimes knocking out their competition in the process.

Then you have the other person who hears this joke made about something that makes them feel insecure and they feel crushed by it. In this situation, they are unable to see past the intention of the other person and so they get out of the game earlier than they should. The difference between the two of them is not just in how they reacted to the jokes made about their insecurities. It is how they heard the joke. The first person saw an opportunity in those insults, and they used it to get their comeback, whereas the second person didn't. It is the same thing when you are having a mental smack talk with yourself. You need to detach yourself emotionally from whatever you are holding against yourself. Look for a loophole in it and then make yourself come back with it.

With the new information you have just received, let us go back to the hypothetical insecurity you are having with the way you talk. Chances are, you are worried that when you get on stage, your speech defect would become obvious. Rather than talking yourself out of the game, think of it as an opportunity to educate the people around you on the problems of speech defect. What this kind of thinking does for you is it helps you recognize those things you consider as flaws and accept them. And don't just accept it as a weakness. Look at how you can make it your strength. In this hypothetical scenario, your strength would be a firsthand knowledge about something a lot of people are ignorant about. By taking this perspective, the stage no longer becomes an arena to showcase your weakness. Instead, it becomes a platform that would frame your strength. I guess what I am trying to say in all of this is that first of all, you need to embrace your flaws. That is the first emotional battle you need to overcome. If you embrace your flaws, no one can use them against you; not even yourself.

Criticism and the Critic

When it comes to criticism, I feel like the art world is the best place to use as an illustration because artists are faced with a lot of criticism for the work that they do and yet, they somehow exceed the expectations of their critics and excel in their game. An example of one such artist is the great Pablo Picasso. When Picasso first showcased his art technique to the world, he received a lot of backlash for it. Some people even went as far as describing him as demonic and his drawings as something otherworldly. Many of those people didn't think he would make it far in the art world. But he did and today's generation references him as probably one of the greatest. And his critics? Well, let's just say their claim to fame is the words that they used to describe his art, which doesn't reflect well on their legacy at all.

When you are confronted with an opportunity to speak in public, the second emotional hurdle you would have to overcome is criticism. In this regard, first, we have ourselves to blame as we are own worst critics. And then you have criticism from second parties. But in my opinion, the criticism from second parties is not really important at this point because what they say is usually an echo of what you think. Besides, there are constructive forms of criticism that build you up. So, this brings us back to you. It is your responsibility to stop yourself from falling into the trap of critics. You have to get to the point where you understand that this is not about you or your performance. You are not getting on stage to be judged even though it feels like it. Standing in front of a group of strangers feels as though you are opening up yourself for those on the other side to criticize but this is far from the truth. You have to change the perspective on this if you want to get past the problem of criticism. People who come to hear you talk are there to take something away from what you say and the only time they will criticize is when you get on there and don't say anything. Even at that, you would still find people who would consider your silence a very vocal statement.

The bottom line is that you can't control what people are going to think about you and so why would you want to waste your mental resources on what might or might not be said? If someone like Pablo Picasso, whose art is highly sought after today, could get criticized for his work, I would say that we are all fair game. So, for this segment my advice is this: Rather than stay preoccupied with the opinions of other people, focus on your craft. Focus on what it is you are going to say (we will get into that in subsequent chapters). This is how you overcome the hurdles associated with criticism. Now I know this is not easy and this is exactly why I used the art world as an illustration. In art, perfection exists but perfection is based on perspective. You have heard the saying one man's meat is another man's poison? There will always be opposing views on everything. It doesn't matter how good you are, there will still be people who won't value what you do. Even the person that is rated as the best public speaker in the world would still have a sect of people who would think that they are worth nothing. In conclusion, accept the fact that some people are not going to like you anyway, however, you are not getting on stage to be liked. Focus on your objective and when the criticisms come after you are done, remember the lessons from the previous segment and roll with the punches.

The Power of Imagination

There was something I learned very early in life and this is thanks to the relationship I had with my parents. They instilled in me an appreciation of this fundamental truth and I have taken this truth with me in everything that I do. It is very simple, really, and I am sure that at some point in your life, you may have heard it. The truth is this: You are a product of your imagination. In order words, if you can think it, you can be it. If you cannot think it, you cannot be it. It doesn't matter how educated you are. It doesn't matter how connected you are. You can only be as powerful as your imagination. If there is anything I have tried to establish from the beginning of this chapter up to this point, it is the fact that the mind is where nearly everything you experience is created. If you are going to imagine negative things, you should expect to have negative experiences. If all you can picture at this point in time after everything you have learned so far is how you are going to go on stage and be terrible at it, my dear friend, it is guaranteed that you are going to be terrible.

This is how influential your imagination is. Now if you picture yourself getting on stage and doing excellently well, chances are this is going to be a reality for you. However, your work does not stop at imagining the results. There has to be some work that goes into ensuring that what you envision becomes a reality, and that is what the rest of this book is about. I want to get you to that point where you're completely psyched about being on stage. Don't focus on rating your performance (at least not until after you are done). All that can do for you is to slow you down. The idea of using your imagination to fuel your performance is not about getting 100% on your score sheet or the applause that you get. It is about getting on the stage and enjoying the experience. When you enjoy the experience, it doesn't really matter what other people think about your performance. Now if you combine your expectation for your experience with the practical preparatory guidelines which we will get to later in this book, you increase the odds that people are going to enjoy seeing you stand on stage this way. So far, everything I have talked about has had to do with the reorientation of your mind. I want you to get into the space where you have the winner's mentality. So, here is what you should take away from this segment: You don't have to have the best punch lines. People just need to see that you are up there and having a good time, and you start that process by picturing yourself there.

Satisfying Your Fears

Staying in line with the theme for this chapter, there are a few questions I want you to ask yourself. Questions like what is the worst thing that can happen to you on stage? What is the craziest, most insanely, out of this world thing that can happen to you on stage to ruin your public speaking experience? The sooner you can find the answers to these questions, the faster you can move past your fears. The concept of satisfying your fears is not about focusing on the negatives. The fact is that oftentimes, the things we fear the most are the things that we have not really thought through. It is like the boogeyman. We have this vague notion of this entity and we don't confront this vague notion. Instead, we just accept the reality of its existence. But then when you actually face it head-on, you realize that there wasn't any reason to be afraid in the first place.

This is what it means to satisfy your fears. Ask yourself those questions you are not comfortable with and ensure that you get the answers. Are you afraid that when you get on stage the light is going to fall down on you? Or maybe you fear that your clothes are just somehow going to magically disappear? These sound like silly questions, but you will be surprised by how these silly questions shape our fears. So, today, right now, take a sheet of paper and ask yourself what exactly are you afraid of and do your best to be honest with the answers because it is from the answers that you get the solution. When your fears are satisfied, they lose their hold over you and when they no longer have a hold over you, you become free. And in this case, you are free to be the best public speaker you can be.

This chapter was about helping make sense of the emotional struggles you have and giving you a little insight into the consequences of your thoughts because yes, the things that you think about can shape your experiences. In this recap, we are going to focus on the four major emotional obstacles we face and how we can push past them:

- You undermine your abilities by focusing on your weaknesses. To win on stage, you must first win the battle of the mind. Embrace your flaws.
- Your fear of criticism can get the better of you. Keep your focus on your efforts instead of trying to predict the opinions of others.
- Your expectations for your performance on stage sets the tone for everything. Expect great things.
- Fears have a paralytic effect. Free yourself by confronting those fears.

Your tasks:

1. Write a vivid description of what you imagine your stage experience would be like. There are only two rules for this. The first rule is that you don't limit yourself in any way. No matter how silly you think a concept might be, if you want it to be a part of your stage experience, include it. An example would be you imagine that your hair on stage would be perfect as that of a movie star. It doesn't matter if you have hair or not, just include it as part of the experience. The second rule is that no form of negativity is allowed. You cannot include any negative element in this narrative of your stage experience.
2. Make a list of all the possible things you think can go wrong on stage. This list should be written in a question and answer format. So, instead of imagining what you think will go wrong, ask yourself a question about it. For example, instead of saying "I am worried that the lights will go off," ask yourself, "Why would the lights go off when I'm on stage?" And then you try as much as possible to answer those questions. After you are done compiling Q and A, the next step would be to evaluate these fears.
3. Look at the questions and then deliberate on them. Decide on if a fear (phrased here as a question) is in the same category as the boogeyman or if it falls within the realm of possibility. Beside each question, write down your conclusion on the subject. If you think it's valid, indicate that. If not, write the word *irrational* beside it. This will help you sort your fears into categories.
4. Read through this list every single day leading up to the day you have to get on stage.
5. For the questions that you feel are valid, create an action plan on resolving them.

PART TWO
SETTING THE STAGE

CHAPTER FIVE
UNDERSTANDING THE WHYS

"Your preparation for the real world
is not in the answers you've learned,
but in the questions you've learned how
to ask yourself."
Bill Watterson

Find Your Purpose

Now that we have pushed past some of the internal struggles you are having, it is time to start asking the tougher questions and taking a tougher stand on things. Before this chapter, I would say that we have been taking baby steps to lay the foundation for the next stage. And now, this is the point where you ask yourself questions like, "Why are you doing this, anyway?" There is a huge difference between wanting to do something and understanding why you have to do that thing. And that difference is the motivating factor that will get you through the stormiest parts of this journey. We know that life will always come with challenges and with this topic, I am not only referring to public speaking. This is something that applies to every area of your life as well.

The crazy thing about these challenges, in my opinion, is that they are not meant to derail you or take you off the path you think you are supposed to be on. As a matter of fact, I think they are meant to propel you forward because the challenges you go through in life is what helps you define the reason why you are even doing it in the first place. Now let us bring this back to public speaking. I find it hard to believe that you're going up on stage to just check one item off your bucket list. In theory, it might be a cool idea, but why did it even make it on your list anyway? That question is for you to answer if that is your situation. For every other person, I would say that any reason that does not resonate deeply within you is not enough to keep you going, especially when the challenges come (I guarantee that they will). If you understand why you have to do something, even though this is not exactly something you liked in the first place, you stay motivated to do that thing.

I remember when I was a very young lad, my father was very involved in a community project that helped young people get jobs. There was a weekly event that he was in charge of and he used to have me tag along with him. I hated it because we had to wake up early to get to where we were going to in order to get the resources that we needed to use later in the day for this weekly event. This was a big challenge because these locations were on opposite ends of the city. On one end, you had the resources and then at the other end, you had the event. And my dad only had this day of the week to do it because he had to work full-time every other day. I, for the most part, hated it and you can't blame me—I didn't understand why I had to be involved in it anyway. It is not like my dad and I had any special bonding moments during the course of it (or so I thought). I always looked at it as something my father wanted to do and it didn't help that my mother called it my father's pet in that down-the-nose way only mothers can. But despite the challenges associated with pulling each weekly event off, I never saw it slow my father down in any way. He never missed a week and he was, as far as I can remember, always on time. It was almost as if with every single challenge, he was more inspired to do it. On the morning of one of those event days, he woke me up and as usual I grumbled and complained. Then I got it into my head to ask him this pertinent question: "Why don't you ever get tired?" His response was simple but very profound. He said, "Because of Tim and every other Tim that is out there."

Now the Tim story comes with a lot of emotional baggage for my family, especially my dad, so I am not going to go into that here. However, I remember his response because his vivid description of his purpose immediately got me to understand why my father remained dogged about his work. I bet every time he had to drag himself out of his bed on a day that he should have been resting, the mental image of Tim would flash through his mind and he would be up in a flash. Public speaking is not something you should do for clout or to impress some people. Not unless you are okay doing it that one time. But if you want to make a life out of this and go far, if you really want to surmount the challenges ahead, you have to understand why you were doing it and when you understand the *why*, the challenges in front of you are not going to be enough to stop you.

Moving with the Crowd

Before I get into this segment properly, I would like to comment on how many contradictions there are in life. On one end, you have people who tell you that it is important for you to be an individual. They say don't roll with the crowd. And then on the other end, you have people who say the voice of the people is the voice of God so when the crowd speaks, you just have to listen and go with. It is hard to discern what applies best in this scenario, especially if you are still struggling with a lot of personal issues within yourself. If you haven't defined yourself and you still get into that place where you do not appreciate the value that you have to offer to the world, it is hard to decide if you are going to stand by yourself or just blend into the crowd.

When you are going for public speaking, this is one of those cases where we need to apply a little bit of both—and by both, I am referring to your individuality and the opinions of the crowd. The fact is this: People are coming to hear you talk and when hard-working people take the time out of their day to come and listen to you, chances are there is a message they are hoping to get out of what you say to them. Now, I don't know what platform you are going to be doing this public speaking thing on; maybe it is a work project or perhaps you want to hone in your skills at being the master of ceremonies at events. It could be something as simple as making a best man speech at your friend's wedding or maybe something a little more complex like your first foray into the political field...whatever your reasons are, you have to bear in mind that the crowd is there for a reason and if you are unable to carry them along in your message, you will lose them.

That said, I also don't believe that you should pander towards everything that the crowd wants. I have a background in marketing as you probably know, and there is something I learned from my mentor in the field which is very key in executing a successful marketing campaign. We are taught that oftentimes, the customer doesn't know what they want. At least not until you pitch it to them. I feel like it would make sense to apply that wisdom here. Your crowd may be coming to your event with one thing in mind, but there is a way you can pitch your individuality to them that would get them to become interested. So now you see why I say you have to toe the line between having a little bit of your individuality on display and catering to the needs of the crowd. In subsequent chapters, we will look at how you can move the crowd but before we get to that point, this is where you lay the foundation by focusing on how you want to get the message across using the two essential ingredients for public speaking: your individuality and the people's need.

The Truth Vs Your Truth

After deciding on how you want to pass the message across, the next important thing is to focus on what the message is going to be about. You know how they say that there are two sides to every story? In the same way, when it comes to public speaking, there are multiple perspectives. However, until you understand the complexities of this, there are two perspectives that matter the most. The first one is the truth. It is always important that when you get on stage, no matter how unpleasant it is, you much share that truth for what it is. If not for any reason, do it for the sake of your integrity. When you go on stage and speak in front of a crowd that is a bell that cannot be un-rung, you have to ensure that every word that you put out there is supported by the truth. If you are trying to find the courage to speak the truth, you must first start with the assumption that the people you are talking to are going to be very intelligent. If you have paid any attention to political debates, you would see that candidates come well-prepared with facts and figures.

People are not just going to come to the event and swallow everything that you say hook, line and sinker. You have people who are going to take notes, people who are going to analyze everything that you have said and most likely they would want to implement it in their own lives. Now if parts of what you have said or everything that you have said is untrue, you jeopardize their chances of success and undermine your own integrity. This is not a track record you want to set for yourself. In the news, we have heard of who has made an income of selling lies to the public— and some of them have been very successful at it too—but at the end of the day, their lies caught up with them. Then on the other spectrum, you have people who have maintained their integrity in the trade and still amassed a fortune in the process. That said, our objective here is not the wealth that comes from playing in the field. In general, it is said that a good name is better than riches. This speaking opportunity you have been given would put you on a platform that can elevate you to a global stage. It will bring opportunities that will transform your life. A lot of changes will happen but the one thing that should not change is the integrity associated with your name. And this brings me to the second perspective: your truth.

Now in the application of the truth that you're going to share with the crowd, I am very sure that there are personal lessons you learned along the way. As a public speaker for whatever purpose, it is important that you infuse these personal experiences with the truth that is either already out there or that you just discovered along the way. This gives you authenticity and if you are true enough to your person, it will connect you better with your crowd. Please pay attention here, as this is a big deal. Most people may not want to identify with the truth that you put out there but if you stay in that truth and you are authentic in it, you would be able to sieve through the crowd of wanderers to find the exact kind of crowd who you want to share your ideas with. People think that having a large crowd is a testament of your success as a public speaker but in reality, it is the number of people in that crowd who you are able to impact successfully that speak to your achievements. And I believe that the kind of people that would fall in that category are those who connect with you. They are the ones who would be keen on implementing those ideas that you share. So, in conclusion, stay on course with the truth and by all means maintain your authenticity in sharing that truth.

Define Yourself

Have you ever sat alone in the dark and asked yourself, "Who am I? Why am I here? What is my purpose?" I think at some point in our lives, we have all had what the world describes today as an *existential crisis*. In this state, we question virtually everything about us. This is good. Except that when you are having an existential crisis, you are not exactly operating from the right frame of mind. So, the answers that tend to come up stem from fear, anxiety and sometimes loss. To answer the question of who you are, you need to step away from the circumstance. Because, if you let yourself be defined by the circumstance surrounding you, you would fail to achieve your full potential. There is so much more to you than your experiences and if I know anything about life, it is the fact that experiences change according to the state of your mind. This is why certain things that caused you so much pain some years ago can be laughed at when you look back on them now. So if your experiences are going to define you, it means that you are essentially whatever you are experiencing at a specific point in life. This would be very sad because it would mean that there is a chance that we are described by a sum total of our failures, our successes, our shame, and our glories.

This is not how I picture each person. I feel that we have a lot more to offer. And as a public speaker who is bent on speaking the truth and only their own truth, you need the strength of character in order to pull that off. Strength of character comes from being rooted in the true version of yourself. You can only be the true version of yourself if you take the time to reflect on these questions that we asked at the beginning of this segment and provide answers that are outside whatever experiences you are having at the moment. This may be a lot to ask, but in the task segment of this chapter, I have given a detailed step-by-step process on how you can define yourself.

Remember, confidence doesn't come from knowing all the answers or being liked by everyone. Confidence comes from knowing the right answer to the question of: Who are you? Answer this question and there is no stage that would be too big or too small for you.

To wrap up this chapter, let us go over the highlights:

- Connect yourself with public speaking by having a clear understanding of why you are doing it. It doesn't have to be something grand. But let it be vivid enough to get you off the couch and onto the stage anytime you are called.
- The winning combination for winning the crowd over is saying what they want to hear and doing that the way that only you can.
- Maintain your integrity by speaking the truth. Showcase your individuality by being authentic.
- Define your personality and then use this personality to connect with people.

Your tasks:

1. Start by identifying your passions. Write out a list of things that you would be more than happy to do even if you were not getting paid for it. Set this list aside.
2. Make another list of things that you wish you could do and you feel that if you did them it would make you happy.
3. Create an action plan on how you can do those things and give yourself two weeks to follow through on this action plan.
4. At the two-week mark, look at the things you have checked off this list and the things that you haven't. The things you have done, write out how they made you feel. The things that you haven't, write out why you didn't follow through on them.

5. Now sort the things that you have done that you actually enjoyed and would love to progress on, and add them to the first list that you created for this task. For the things you haven't done, file that under a "curiosity" folder.

The answers that you arrive at will provide clues to your personality. They may not be related to public speaking yet but as you continue to grow this list, you get a better knowledge about yourself. When you know yourself better, you develop a healthier relationship with yourself and it is from here that you can confidently answer the questions of why, what and who. In the next chapter, we are going to take the focus away from you and put it on the subject that you plan to speak on. Brace yourself!

CHAPTER SIX
CHOOSING YOUR FIGHTS CAREFULLY

"Choose your battles wisely. After all, life isn't measured

by how many times you stood up to fight.

It's not winning battles that makes you happy,

but it's how many times you turned away and chose

to look into a better direction.

Life is too short to spend it on warring.

Fight only the most, most, most important ones, let the rest go."

C. JoyBell C.

How to Decide on the What

Before we go any further into this topic, it is important that we acknowledge the journey that you have taken so far. Double up on the accolades if you have been following through on all of the tasks given in each chapter. By appreciating how far you have come, you are able to mentally empower yourself for the journey ahead. And even though you feel as if you have regressed in certain areas and have not quite gotten over your fears, don't let that deter you. As for fear, I don't know if you have heard this being said, but I will go ahead and share this with you. Courage isn't the absence of fear but the choice to go ahead and do what needs to be done anyway. In other words, *that* fear is always going to be there. The only difference is that over time, it will become easier to overcome. From the moment you are invited to speak until the second you get off the stage, you will experience that jittery feeling that makes it seem as though your legs have become jelly and your stomach is sinking. But with each speaking engagement, you become even more experienced at ignoring them. With that assurance, let us tackle our next task for the day.

Now, this particular chapter is another very important step in this journey because this is where you get to decide on what you are going to verbally put out there on stage. People underestimate the amount of work that goes into preparing for a speech. When we see our favorite public speakers do their thing on stage, because of their excellent elocution and smoothness in delivery, many of us (myself included) assume that this is something that comes naturally to them. But the truth is the best speeches are well-thought-out and rehearsed days, if not months, in advance. I don't know of many people who go on stage and "wing it," as they say. Not unless you are a professional and even the professionals take that time to practice. Earlier on, we used political debates as an illustration, and I am going back to it again because I feel like this is the most brutal form of public speaking and if you can get it right here, you can get it right with everything else.

When you look at political debates, you see these candidates arguing their points with each other, but what you don't get to see is what happens behind the scenes. Before the date for the actual debate, there are several reenactments of the debate and the goal is to get the candidate to that point where they can speak comfortably about possible issues that might be brought up. They want to be able to argue their points while ensuring that their opinions get heard. The people coaching them through these mock debates emphasize the importance of sticking with the facts while showcasing their personality. You may not be going for a political debate but if you want to excel as a public speaker, you have to imbibe the same practices. Take your time to plan your speech and then rehearse it as often as you can.

Chances are, you have already been given a topic to work with. If that is the case, the best way to lay a foundation for an interesting speech is by conducting thorough research on the topic. Remember, integrity is important, therefore it is essential that the truth is infused in your narration of the topic. The next step would be to combine the facts that you now know with your experience. In a situation where you have not been given a topic but just a general theme, what you want to go for, or rather, the first question to ask yourself is, "What would I like to talk about?" In making your decision, you have to bear in mind that whatever topic you choose must stay in line with the theme of the event. In formal settings, keep your topic on issues relevant to the kind of organization hosting the event. For informal occasions, you may want to update your speech to include trendy news relevant to the occasion. Then you have to figure out how you can align this thing you're talking about with the theme. I recommend that you start out by focusing on your area of expertise. You will always have firsthand knowledge on the subject and information that is most likely not common knowledge for your audience.

Pay Attention to the Seasons

I am fairly certain that you know that I am not referring to the weather. The world that we live in today is a very sensitive place. There are so many social issues that have risen up to the surface that the level of political correctness one must master will make you feel like you are walking around on eggshells or worse, an emotional minefield where a single verbal faux pas can cause a catastrophic backlash with enormous repercussions. In sticking with the truth, you also have to be sensitive to the social consciousness of your environment emotionally and mentally. And even if you are speaking at a place where you feel the social consciousness is behind the times, you have to remind yourself that with the presence of technology, it has torn down the walls that once separated nations. News travels at the speed of "now." You may be speaking to a local audience without realizing that you have been put on a global stage. You do not want to go viral for the wrong reasons. Now I know that this may feel like added pressure but instead of looking at it that way, think of it as a way to make you even more equipped for your speech.

Your awareness of the seasons would give you a better connection to the people in your audience. The fact is, times have changed…a lot. People are thinking and feeling things a lot differently than they used to in the previous centuries. I know that throughout this chapter and in the chapters leading up to this point, I have and will continue to emphasize on sticking to the truth for the sake of integrity. But my focus on this segment is to open you up to the real nature of the truth, especially in these modern times. We have heard it said quite often that truth is a bitter pill to swallow. This is true and delivering the naked truth on certain occasions will not get you any extra points. Rather, it can set you up for total failure, which is not good, especially if you want to make a living off public speaking. So, how do you navigate this murky terrain and come out without a smudge to your name?

First of all, you must have a good understanding of the times that you are in. The issue of gender, sexuality and equality should be factored into the truth that you are telling. You cannot carry on the same narrative of the past and expect the present to comply. Secondly, you must realize that the truth is not finite. There are different perspectives on the same subject and the truth depends on the view where you are taking your standpoint on. So, ensure that you factor in as many perspectives as possible in the narration of your truth. What I am trying to say is that you need to be delicate when you deliver your truth. Be empathetic to the people and the emotional atmosphere of your environment. Say, for instance, you are delivering a topic that is related to a science project. Factor in the views of some people who may be concerned about the potential damage that this science project can cause the environment. Come up with a view that would still deliver on the truth and facts of what you want to talk about, but at the same time make an attempt to address the concerns raised by other parties. It is imperative that your speech is inclusive. Use your voice in telling the truth (remember the part about being authentic) but try as much as possible to avoid statements that would make certain parties feel excluded. Because if you fail to do so, not only will your speech be interpreted as offensive, you also put a cap on the growth potential for your target audience. The fine art of developing the kind of speech that can be appreciated in today's climate can be compared to that of the performance artist who has to walk a tightrope across a long distance while juggling as many objects as possible at the same time. It is difficult, but it can be done.

One thing I feel I must warn you about is being guarded about becoming too politically correct that you lose the ability to make any impact with the platform you are standing on. Some experts hire professionals to do the speech writing for them and then they have another team who would go over it and accede to the contents of the speech. If you can afford to have this many people on your payroll, this is a genius solution. If not, my rule for this is very simple. I try to answer these two questions correctly:

1. Am I trying too hard to be liked than I am trying to share practical solutions?
2. Is this courting controversy or putting too much airbrush on the truth?

The best place to be in answering this question is somewhere in between.

Creating a Winning Strategy

You have to remember that the goal here is to win. And when I say win, I am not referring to a medal of honor that would be given at the end of the stage because there isn't one. Neither is it to get off each stage with the loudest applause (although it would be totally cool if that happened too). The goal is to overcome your fears, get up there on stage, hold the crowd in your sway (even if it is for all of five minutes) and then get off the stage knowing that you have accomplished all four and can do it all over again if you are called to do so. I would say that we have gotten the first part locked down. Those tiny insecurities whispering reasons why you can't and shouldn't must be silenced and replaced with the voices telling you that you can. Among those voices, your voice must be the loudest. Arm yourself with daily affirmations designed to fire you up from the inside for the tasks ahead. Choose words that resonate deeply with you. At first, it may sound a little unusual coming from you. To get myself comfortable with positive affirmations, I started up by listening to or watching videos of my favorite celebrities doing their Monday morning motivation speech. There are some that are so upbeat that you suddenly feel like a lion at the end of it. Look for what works for you and roll with it.

The strategy for getting up on stage is simple. Just do it. The second your name is called up on stage, don't freeze and certainly don't think about it. Just get on there and every single thing that you have been practicing will come to you. You may even surprise yourself with a few tricks that you had no idea you knew. To hold your crowd in sway, think of yourself as the magician and your speech as the act. You must have the killer introduction, several parts that are clearly broken down to take your audience from one point to another and then the grand exit.

Let us start with your introduction. Some public speakers like to start off with humor (we talk about this a few chapters from now) and some like to start with very dramatic facts. I have known speakers who start off with a compressed biography on themselves. Choose the one that you are most comfortable doing. Humor does not have to be of the same quality as what you would expect on Comedy Central, but it should be able to tease a smile out of them. Unless you have perfected the art of comedic timing, I would not recommend going for those classic jokes where you pause for the crowd to laugh. I made that faux pas once and there was dead silence. However, I was prepared for that too. After a second or two of no laughs, I simply went on to say, "What a tough crowd. Obviously, no one came here for the jokes so I will just get right into it." This elicited some small laughs and I just moved on. Now, I make it a routine. I give a dead joke and then make some fun about nobody laughing and just get into speaking. If you are going for dramatic facts, start off by stating statistics that are not related to the subject you are discussing and are not commonly sourced for. Even if they are, you can switch up your perspective by interpreting those statistics in relatable terms. So, instead of saying "Out of 100 million people, only 10 million people brush their teeth at night," you can try saying "Out of the ten people sitting close around you, possibly only one went to bed with fresh breath." This immediately brings their focus to the topic and stirs up a personal interest in the subject.

If what I have talked about seems a little too dramatic for you, it is okay to just start with a very, very short biography about yourself. It can be just three sentences and if it was written down in a book, it shouldn't exceed three lines. Also, remember that your introduction should match the theme of the occasion. The next should be the subject matter of the speech. Don't give a long drawn out statement that you read word for word. Divide it into segments and discuss on each point. You can have little notes and cue cards containing major points. If your presentation is being done with a projector and screen for your audience to look at, even better. List out your speech in bullet points on the screen and throw in an image every now and then. It keeps them visually engaged. At the six to ten minutes mark (it depends on the duration of the speaking event for me), I throw in some humor. I like to use funny cartoons or images that look odd, hilarious and out of place and when the crowd laughs or snickers, I chime in a fake "oops" and then tie it into the rest of the presentation. I try to finish ahead of time so that I can ask questions (if the event allows) and I usually have small souvenirs with me. Any audience member with the right answer gets a souvenir instantly. It is a fun way to keep my people entertained and gives me better vibes when I get off the stage. Find a routine that will work for you, practice it and nail it.

Bracing Yourself for Conflict

The statement "expect the worst and hope for the best" used to be something that scared the life out of me. I don't want to expect the worst. I want only the good things to happen to me. My sentiment towards this statement is even amplified when I think of public speaking. But this was before my experience with public speaking. After my first successful stage debut (you read about my earlier disaster), I realized that the more prepared I was, the better my experience on stage. This was all fun and good until I had a Q and A segment added to one of my public speaking events. This was while I still working at the marketing firm. I was not ready to field the kind of questions that came at me that day on the stage. It felt like it was a personal attack. Most of the questions were from disgruntled employees who felt that I was now representing the company since I was speaking for them on stage. It was, of course, unfair of them to attack me that way but in hindsight, if I had come on to the stage better equipped, I would have been able to field those questions in a better and more appropriate way.

It doesn't matter how nice, warm, creative or inspiring you are, there are still people who will come at you with questions that will throw you off your game. You cannot prevent that by attempting to be even nicer, warmer, more creative or more inspiring than you already are. The only way to combat it is by anticipating the resistance thereby anticipating their questions and preparing your answers beforehand. Try as much as possible not to take some of these questions personal, as the resistance is not always directed at you. In some cases, the people in the audience may have some preconceived notion about you and in receiving your message, they filter it through the lens of that notion they have about you and respond in that manner. In some other cases, perhaps, the problem has more to do with the message than it does with your person.

Whatever the case, don't try to explain their actions. Instead, do your best to bring the focus back to the message that you are trying to get across. And in the event you are asked a question that you absolutely have no idea how to respond to, you can either deflect or admit to not knowing. The problem with deflecting is that you could miss out on a learning opportunity for both yourself and the person who asked the question. And I would only recommend deflection in cases where the question asked is inciteful and hateful. But if it comes from a place of genuine curiosity, you could tell the person that the question that they asked is very intriguing and that you would love to have the time to explore that train of thought even more. Go a step further by asking them to reach out to you via your professional email address so that you can share your findings with them. Chances are, with a response like this, you would win over more people to your "fan base." In a situation where the conflict is not expressed at the venue, you will find some people going online to express their displeasure. Again, do not take it personally. If it is not harming your reputation, I urge you not to give it a second thought. If there were constructive criticisms made, look at them carefully and learn from them. This is a learning process for you. Try as much as possible to learn, adapt and evolve.

After completing this chapter, I arrived at a not-so-startling conclusion. You cannot please everybody no matter how hard you try. The best you can do is to ensure that you please the majority and that majority should include yourself, the organizers of the event you will be speaking at and a larger part of the audience. If you can do this, you should be fine. That said, let us look at how I arrived at this conclusion based on the lessons from this chapter:

- In deciding on what to speak on, you have to ensure that the topic, whether given or chosen, is the truth wrapped around the theme of the event or vice versa.
- Be sensitive to the emotional climate and guard your words diligently.
- Have a strategic plan that would take you from the point of your stage fright to the point where you exit the stage. Use affirmations, speech plans and stage presence in building a winning stage routine.
- There will always be something negative that certain people will say. Recognize that the goal is not to be liked by everyone but to deliver excellently in your public speaking.

Your tasks:

Do these tasks before any public event:

1. Identify the nature of the event you will be speaking at. Get specific details.
2. Find out as many details as you can about the kind of people that would be coming for the event. Information like age, gender, ethnicity and so on will play a key role.
3. Relate the details from one and two with your expertise and your experience.
4. Brainstorm on at least five different topics that fit all the information listed above and draft your speech around them. The more prepared you are, the lesser the chance that you would be taken off-guard.
5. Practice your speech for at least two hours every day leading up to the event.

CHAPTER SEVEN
LOOKING THE PART

"All fashion brands are about looking good.

Being Human is also about doing good.

And you can do good by the simple act of

slipping into a t-shirt or a pair of jeans."

Salman Khan

Addressing Your Dressing

When you get on stage to talk in front of the crowd, you get just the one chance to impress and you know what they say about first impressions lasting longest. Your window to create an impression is only about ten seconds (this is for a very generous crowd) and if you get it wrong, in the minds of your audience, you might end up spending the rest of your speech trying to make up for that poor impression (if that is even possible). It doesn't matter how intelligent, smart or articulate you are. It doesn't even matter if your speech was written by the great Steven Spielberg himself. There is very little you can say in ten seconds or less that would instantly impress your audience. However, you are aware of the saying that a picture is worth a thousand words, right? Well, your dressing can speak several volumes about your personality and what people can expect to hear from you.

Now, I am going to try and get you to be comfortable with this topic because I feel like a lot of introverts have this mentality that putting effort into your dressing, especially when it is not even something you are comfortable in, is somewhat pretentious. I know this because, like most introverts, I am more comfortable in my own skin (and by my own skin, I mean my favorite t-shirt from college paired with cargo pants and a pair of multi-colored socks). But seeing as the world does not qualify this as classy, it is hard for me to feel comfortable when I am dressed in anything but my comfy wear. To come to terms with this, I had to learn some hard truths about dressing. One of them is the fact that comfort makes you feel good but it does not in any way mean confidence. And my objective when I get on stage is to exude confidence and to achieve this, it was important that I understood that comfort is for my comfort zone and confidence is for the stage.

Confidence is the currency that buys you the "consideration" of your audience so if you really want your speech to make a lasting impact, you cannot afford to wear the regular flip-flops, t-shirt and jeans. However, this doesn't mean that decking yourself in designer duds from your head to your toes is going to score you major points either. Especially if the designer gear is not put together in a way that makes it visually appealing. You would be amazed by how your appearance can distract people from the beautiful message you are trying to get across. So, before you head off to the nearest clothing store, the first thing you need to do is to start with the basics. Start with what you like to wear. I already know that the jean and t-shirt look is a classic favorite but it comes off as super casual, and even if you are speaking at an informal event, it still wouldn't make sense. Not unless you do an upgrade on the look you generally prefer. An upgrade does not necessarily mean a big budget or total discomfort.

The reason I vote for going with an upgrade of what you like to wear is that it gives you the comfort that you crave while at the same time giving your audience a better representation of yourself. So, what exactly does an upgrade look like? Let us assume that your favorite outfit combo is a pair of denim jeans and a t-shirt. The upgrade for this is totally doable regardless of your gender, age or the type of event. There are two looks you can aim for with this. The business casual vibe for that casual affair and then the complete professional look for that formal event. First, for the semi-casual or business casual look, let us start with your jeans. They must be fitted and in a dark shade to nail the business casual look. Anything less than this would take you farther away from the look. Pair with a button-up shirt and a jacket in a color that contrasts nicely with your jeans. Both must be fitted too. To complete the look, wear formal shoes. This would mean court shoes for the ladies and the derby, brogues or oxford for the gents. The shoes should be in a shade of black, brown or navy. For the head to toe professional look, gents can throw in a tie and ladies should keep the color combinations white, black and blue. Do not try to pull off the monochrome look with denim. It rarely ever works. This is one of those times that you should play it safe.

If you want to ditch the denim look entirely but still keep things within that comfort range, swap your jeans for khakis or slacks. Today's design options have found a way to get your slacks to transition between an active lifestyle and formal wear effortlessly. There are so many options. At the end of this chapter, you should be able to decide on what the best possible look for you would be and how you can avoid making a terrible fashion statement on stage.

Style Mistakes to Avoid

Welcome to Style 101 for public speakers. If you consider yourself a fashion guru, don't skip to the next chapter just yet. I may have one or two fashion tips that will go on to improve your stage experience. We have established that while the streets may be your daily runway, the podium where you do your public speaking is anything but that; as you will come to learn eventually. It is where your performance as a public speaker will be judged. If the information you put across with your outfit does not match what you are trying to say, you can be certain that most of what you say will not be heard. And now I know I said earlier that we should pay less attention to what people think about us. However, this doesn't mean that you should arm them with the tools with which they can use to judge you. That said, here are a few fashions don'ts for a public speaker.

1. Thou shall not show skin

The stage is not the platform for you to showcase skin in any way and this is not a gender-based type of instruction. It goes for everyone. The only thing that should be showcased is your talent and your wit. So ditch those cargo pants, shorts and any type of shoe that will reveal your toes. For ladies, your dress or skirt should be below your knees. Now, this is not a backdated 1940s instruction. It serves a very practical purpose. There is a possibility that the podium you will be standing on to deliver your speech might be very high. A very short skirt would give the people sitting down at least a few feet from you an unexpected view that neither you nor they bargained for. In my opinion, it is better to wear an outfit that prevents this than to deal with the outcome afterward.

2. Thou shall not dress casually

It doesn't matter if the event you are speaking at is being held at a beachfront in Hawaii. The rules of engagement remain the same. The best you can do is to tie in the theme of the event into your outfit to ensure that you do not stand out terribly and look like you are not "playing with the team." This is what accessories are there for. You can stick with the basics with your main outfit and then use a few accessories like ties, scarfs or hats (if the occasion calls for it) to expand on the details.

3. Thou shall not be insensitive

You can make a statement with what you wear. That is why they call it a fashion statement. And now more than ever, it is important that you pay attention to the kind of statement that you are making. For instance, getting on stage wearing a mink fur coat is a loud statement to animal lovers that you don't care about the pain and suffering that animals have to go through for your outfit to be made. Not only that, it is quite distasteful. You may not share the same sentiments with animal lovers but you shouldn't have to throw it out there in their faces, especially not on a platform that is as public as this either.

4. Thou shall avoid bold colors and loud patterns

I am of the opinion that it is very hard to put on bold colors and loud patterns without looking like a clown and I am sure that there are a lot of people who would agree with me. There are certain colors that do not belong on stage or in front of the public unless you are going on stage as an actor in full regalia. For a more professional feel, it is best to stick to muted colors, as they help to tone down your personality. Another thing that muted colors can do for you is to prevent a situation where your outfit distracts your audience from what you are trying to tell them. Muted colors are colors that fall within the white, black, dark blue, brown and grey spectrum.

5. Thou shall not go on stage in a rumpled outfit

If you would rather do your laundry, do not skip out on ironing your clothes. They make you appear shoddy, disorganized and irresponsible. Remember what I said earlier about letting your clothes speak for you. Don't take any chances with the perception you want your audience to have about you.

How to Dress Like a Pro

Now that we are done with the list of don'ts, it is time to focus on the dos. Essentially, if you want to look the part of a public speaker, these are the things you need to do to get you started:

1. Pay attention to your grooming

There is nothing wrong with sporting a beard; not even a long one at that. But you have to keep them clean and trim. The caveman chic look was a great look for Shaggy from *Scooby-Doo* but it is more likely to get you mentally booed off the stage. Ladies, this is not the time to put glitter on your eyes and amp the color volume in your makeup or hair. Keep it simple yet elegant. Most nudes will go well for the occasion. If you are feeling daring, try a pop of red on your lips.

2. Give hygiene your 100%

It is odd that I am talking about hygiene since I think I am addressing a group of adults. Nevertheless, it must be done. Have a shower before you go anywhere on stage. Brush your teeth and do the flossing too. Use a nice deodorant and don't forget to trim your nails. Your outfit for the speaking event should also receive the same treatment. You would be amazed by the difference something as simple as this can do for your whole look.

3. Go easy on the accessories

Accessories are meant to accentuate your look. They bring it together and give it an overall finished look if they are done right. Bold statement pieces like jewelry look great on the gram and can get you on a centerfold spread of a fashion magazine but they do not belong on a stage when you are speaking. Go for simple understated pieces that have an elegant look. Also, do not try to wear more than one accessory at a time. It makes your outfit "busy" and in fashion speak, that is not something that you want anyone to use in describing your look. Finally, if you want to follow the fashion trend, that is great but go for one trend at a time. If all of this sounds a little too complicated for you, just keep it simple. My general rule is until you are able to hire a professional stylist, stick with the fashion basics. It is hard to go wrong with that.

4. Dress for the occasion

We already established that public speakers should go for the semi-casual or purely formal look and then integrate certain pieces into their attire to tie into the event. But when I say dress for the occasion now, I am focusing on the theme of your speech. For instance, if you are going to give a speech relating to success in a specific field, it is important that you look the part. People should be able to look at you and get the success vibe off of you. I remember coming across a viral image of a young man who was giving a YouTube lecture on how to get 1 million views for your videos when he only had videos with a little under 600 views. I think the irony of it is what made the poor guy famous. If you are going to reach success, you must look the part. Now I must emphasize here that success does not necessarily mean that you have to rock designer outfits from your head to toes even if you can afford it. You would make better use of your money if you combine the pieces that make up your total outfit in a well-coordinated manner.

5. Infuse your personality into your style

With the list of dos and don'ts provided here, it is easy to lose yourself in the process and end up looking like a factory-made version of other public speakers. Having your own style in the mix helps you stand out from the crowd and also makes it feel more comfortable being on stage. Just because you want to be perceived a certain way shouldn't mean that your personality should be muted.

Complete the Look With a Good Finish

Most fashion magazines would tell you that you need great accessories to complete a look. As we have already talked about this, what else could I have to say on the subject? Fashion is more than just the clothes you wear. It matters how you wear them. You can get all the clothing tips from the best stylists in the world and have the best designers do their best work on your outfit but at the end of the day, if you fail to wear it right, you could end up giving the wrong kind of impression. And to wear it right in this business, you need to nail your posture. You can improve people's perception of yourself with the way you stand, sit or gesticulate.

Your competence in certain circles is determined to an extent by how you carry yourself, and this may seem unfair especially since you know that you are probably one of the few people who can do what you do excellently. But again, it is that mind translation thing. People are prone to judging a book by its cover and despite the numerous warnings that preach against this, the societal standard for assessing a person's capabilities is based on the first impression. This emphasizes the need to pay more attention to not just the way you dress but to how you wear your outfit as well.

To project confidence and competence, you need to maintain an upright position. Keep your head up and for men, ensure that your chest is not closed in. Dragging your feet on the floor when you move connotes laziness while unnecessary gesticulations can make you seem more nervous than you actually are. You may not feel confident about your performance on stage but there is no reason to see this. If they do, they may not have confidence in what you have to share with them. Recognize that you have important information that could potentially make a difference in their lives and it is your obligation to ensure that you do not give them any reason to question the validity of what you are trying to say.

So, after complying with the basic fashion principles and compiling an excellent speech, the next thing to do is to walk the talk…literally. Let your walk exude the confidence that you need to make it work.

Fashion is more than the clothes that you wear and it is essential in establishing yourself in the minds of people. You can use it to your advantage or set yourself up for failure with it. I vote for using it to our advantage and I am sure that you would agree with me too. That said, let us look at the main points from this chapter:

- Comfort and confidence are two different things. You dress for comfort at home but dressing for confidence is what you should aspire to when it comes to your stage style.
- Make a statement with your fashion but it is important that you are making the right statement for your brand.
- There are general rules in fashion to help you keep your look stylish and socially acceptable. However, your style is also an expression of your personality. Don't forget to include that in your overall dressing.
- The wrong posture can give a wrong perception about your competency and confidence. Ensure that you master the right posture.

Your tasks:

The primary objective is to help you define your stage style and to do this, you need to complete the following tasks:

1. Do a current assessment of your closet and using the pointers in this chapter, determine what outfits you feel would be stage-worthy and put them in a separate pile.
2. Create a "look book" consisting of stylish outfits that you strongly admire. You could keep your focus on public speakers or expand your search to include actors, legal professionals or any person whose formal style strongly matches what you aspire for.
3. Using the look book, evaluate the pile of clothes you have selected in step one and try to get them to match the various looks you have selected.
4. If what you have does not match the looks you want to create, make a shopping list to accommodate what you need.
5. Continue to build on what you are working with. Most importantly, every other year or so, switch things up. While there is nothing wrong with sticking with the same style if it works for you, you can quickly get stuck in a comfort zone. Be a little adventurous but don't go overboard with it.

PART THREE
GOING FOR GOLD

CHAPTER EIGHT
THE ART OF PUBLIC SPEAKING

"You are not here to merely make a living.

You are here in order to enable the world

to live more amply with greater vision

with a finer spirit of hope and achievement.

You are here to enrich the world and you impoverish

yourself if you forget this errand."

Woodrow Wilson

Qualities of a Good Public Speaker

There is a public speaker who is most suitable for a specific situation but then there are distinct qualities that put you in the same league as the big guys. It is not by the number of Instagram followers that you have or the number of events you are able to book annually, or even by the amount people spend to book you for an event. Those are the perks that come with building a solid brand for yourself and requires the right combination of publicity, hard work, consistency and possession of certain qualities that I will be discussing very soon. These distinguishing qualities are sometimes innate talent that is built on over time with training and practice. However, it is very possible for you to move from where you are right now to become good in your craft by honing in on the following skills:

1. Connecting with your audience

All of your tasks and training right up to this point would not serve you well if you are unable to connect with your audience. They are the reason you are on that stage in the first place. To connect with your audience, you have to first understand that being there is not about you even though they have come to hear you speak. It is about them. You are the speaker but rather than segueing into a long, drawn-out monologue, you have the responsibility of making it seem like a dialogue without the other parties doing it. In the next segment of this chapter, I give a detailed breakdown of this quality and a short example to help you get started. It may not immediately turn you into a crowd whisperer, as the charm switch that you need to turn on is unique to each crowd. Still, we will cover the basics to help you do more than just get by.

2. Being a master storyteller

In every chapter of this book, I shared a little story about myself and found a way to tie it in with the theme of that chapter. This is not because I am a person who just loves to share stories about myself. This is a deliberate attempt to:

a) Stop you from being bored
b) Make the concept more relatable to you
c) Prove that this is not something that was lifted off some other person's page but an actual experience

Storytelling humanizes your idea and paints a picture that your listener or audience might find more conceivable. You may have the best theories and the greatest solution for a problem in this century but if you cannot get people to understand it, it will always remain a theory. A good public speaker must master this. So, when you share, create or look for a story that best illustrates your ideas.

3. Voice modulations

Before you continue reading, take a minute to read a few sentences of this book out loud in a slow voice without any inflections. Disregard the commas and any other punctuation marks. If possible, record this on your phone. You will observe that you sound uninteresting and if you keep at this for at least twenty minutes, your own voice would have a snooze-inducing effect on you. In a crowd, this effect is multiplied and you don't want that. Voice modulations help you build on the two points listed above. You are able to give your speech a semblance of a conversation which is essential to keeping your audience engaged. Master this and your storytelling will take on a new dimension. Think of the narrators in a movie. The emotional inflections in their voices help you connect with the story even though you don't see them.

Charming Your Audience

A public speaker shares their ideas with an audience. A good public speaker shares their ideas with an audience and holds them in their sway. There are so many distractions in today's world. The advent of the mobile phone makes it that much more difficult to compete against them for the attention of your audience. There are simple strategies you can employ to get and sustain the attention of the crowd, whether it is a small presentation with a handful of people or a stage delivery with a large crowd.

1. Come with a message that would surprise your audience

The Internet provides a wealth of information and there is a very strong possibility that a significant number of the people in your audience may have more than an average idea of the topic you want to discuss. If you stick to the general information, you might end up feeding them with the same boring stuff and that kind of recycled information can earn you a few minutes of their time. After that, you may have a tough time regaining their attention.

2. Use a language that they understand

You want to impress your audience and I get it. But don't use bogus words that sound impressive without the ability to convey the true meaning of the words or the message you want to get across. For instance, the word I want to use in describing the true state of your audience if you choose to use big words in your speech is *discombobulated*. But don't you think it sounds a lot better and keeps you on track with this article if I replaced that word with *confused* instead? Stringing a few sentences together using big words could make it difficult for people to follow your train of thought, and even if they manage to scale through the first few minutes of your speech, there is no guarantee that they would keep this up throughout. Stick to simple and easy-to-understand words.

3. Get off the stage

Just because you have been set up on a podium shouldn't mean that your movement is restricted to that space. The entire room is your stage and as long as the movement does not interfere with the audio, there is no reason you can't do your thing from where the crowd is. This makes you seem accessible and when people feel this way about you, they become more open to your ideas. And when people are more open to whatever it is that you have to tell them, they pay more attention. It is really that simple.

4. Be flexible

For a novice public speaker, I can understand why you would want to create a script for your performance and stick to it. But if you observe several yawns a few minutes into your speech, it may not be working for your crowd. In this case, you may have to flip the script. If you were too upbeat, you may have to tone it down a little bit. If you are taking it slow, you may have to increase the tempo. And in some cases, you may have to veer completely off course (we talk about this in the next segment) and get the crowd buzzing in excitement before you bring them to the topic in focus.

Showing Your Witty Side

You do not have to be a comedian to get your audience rolling in laughter. And while it would be great to hear that glorious sound, the objective for public speakers is to inject some excitement into the room and in so doing, keep your audience engaged. For someone who is just overcoming their natural tendencies to be shy, it is a very daunting prospect to get on stage and amuse a crowd. From my personal experience, you can get the crowd moving by doing nothing more than being yourself. You have different options on using your wit to create a humorous moment. I am going to list a few ways you can do this. Go with what comes naturally to you. In fact, with practice, you may even discover a technique that I did not include on this list and this is one of the things that makes the remarkable journey you have embarked on that much more interesting.

1. Tell a story

We all have that embarrassing tale that we have lived through. Narrating that experience with a few exaggerated details can turn out hilarious. Sample this story with a small crowd and observe their reaction. If it is what you hoped for, embellish it a little and tell your audience. Be sure to include every funny detail you can recall into the narrative. However, it is important that you pay attention to the kind of crowd you are sharing this story with. An audience from your workplace who are there to witness a presentation where you pitch your ideas to them might not appreciate a joke about your escapades at the club. To avoid a situation where you might offend a race, gender or religious belief, it is safer to stick with narratives that are self-deprecating.

2. Give an activity that your audience can carry out

This may not immediately cause anyone to go into a laughing fit but at least it would get your audience moving. However, only do this if the crowd is not much and if you feel that the energy levels are dropping. From my personal experience, this works very well during training. I split my crowd into teams and come up with group bonding activities that pits them against each other. The competition gets them fired up. For a small crowd of people who are just meeting each other for the first time, at the start of the session, I ask everyone to fill out a card and drop it in a box. The instructions on the card ask them to tell two truths and a lie about themselves. About twenty minutes into a one-hour session, I pick three random cards, call out the names, read the contents of the card and then ask the audience to guess the truths and the lie. This takes about five minutes and then we get back to the session. It creates an atmosphere of familiarity and eases the tension in the room.

3. Tell a joke

Now, this right here requires timing, gesticulating and timing (again) to get the desired results from your audience. You might hear the same joke from three different people and have three different reactions to the joke and this is because of how the joke is told. Sure, when the same joke is told over and over again by the same person, it loses its humor. But when some other person does it and with flair too, you find yourself laughing even if you know exactly how the story ends. The key is the technique. You have to know when to smile, when to wriggle the eyebrows, where to screech and where to throw in the punch line. To successfully pull this off, you need to practice your joke. For those of us who find it difficult to get through our own jokes without first laughing our heads off, this bit might be difficult. However, if you have a knack for this sort of thing, this might be the best weapon in your arsenal.

Elocution

I think that this builds on the point I made earlier about using a language that your audience would understand. The emphasis, in this case, is on more than just the use of big words. The objective is to ensure that you are able to communicate concisely and clearly to your audience. So, matters like the clear enunciation of your words, the variance of your voice pitch, and the use of body language are thoroughly examined.

Enunciation: This is your ability to speak clearly and pronounce words in a manner that is understood by your audience. For people with speech defects like having a lisp or stuttering, there are speech therapies designed to help you navigate the difficulties associated with your condition. I, for one, am of the opinion that there is nothing that can stand in the way of you attaining your dreams. With hard work, commitment and consistency, you can turn your biggest disadvantages into a platform that sets you up for the future that you desire. If English is not your native language and you are speaking to an audience that is comprised mainly of English speakers, a speech training class might help you with the enunciation. Make friends with your dictionary. Learn new words every day and practice the proper tenses where those words apply.

Pitch variation: To maintain a certain mood in your crowd, your voice decibel must not rise or fall below a certain level. If you go above, you start to appear as though you are screaming the words at your audience. That may work if you use it on a particular word to create emphasis about something you want to illustrate. Use it sparingly and even then, you have to time its use properly. If your voice note dips too low, you become inaudible to your audience. Maintain this note for too long and you might as well pick up a violin and play a slow accompanying tune that would lull your audience into a deep sleep. At the same time, keeping the same pitch throughout your speech can quickly become monotonous. This could instigate the same sleep-inducing phenomenon as keeping your voice too low.

Body language: Your facial expressions, as well as the movement of your body parts, can clue people in on the state of your mind. Without saying a word, your facial features and body language can tell anyone if you are frightened, excited or just plain bored. If the words that come out of your mouth say one thing and your facial expression says another, anyone listening to you may have a hard time connecting with the words that you say. The gestures that you make on stage help add character to the words that you say. If you are giving a presentation and you stood perfectly still without a single movement or facial expression, you would look absurd. The same thing would happen if you use wild gesticulations. There has to be a balance between both extremes to keep the audience engaged and to effectively communicate with your audience.

A public speaker is a performer of sorts. They are not expected to use theatrics in the delivery of their role but there are techniques employed by stage performers that would prove very useful for a public speaker. Master these techniques; you will dominate the stage and keep your audience in your thrall. Remember, consistency in practice can make a difference. But that is not the only thing that we picked up from this chapter.

To become a good public speaker, you must work on developing and mastering certain qualities. You should connect with your crowd, craft your stories masterfully and learn to control the rise and fall of your voice pitch.

To win over your crowd, you need to keep your content fresh. Use words that your audience would understand and be ready to change things at a moment's notice to accommodate the atmosphere of the crowd.

To showcase your wittiness, you only need to be yourself. Find out the unique aspect of you that people connect with the most and use that to your advantage

Finally, communication is everything. Your clothes, your confidence and your platform mean nothing if you are unable to get the right message across. Learn the technicalities of speech and practice daily.

Your tasks:

1. Learn at least three new words every day. Your learning of these words should include the meaning, the correct use in sentences as well as the correct pronunciation of the words. The richer your vocabulary, the more articulate you become.
2. Practice four to five jokes before your next speech. Choose jokes that are appropriate for the event where you will be speaking.
3. This one is more of a suggestion than a task; consider taking a class in elocution or speech training. There are several online options.
4. Watch and take notes of the techniques of other public speakers. This is not so that you copy the way they do things exactly. This is to inspire you to do things a little differently from the usual.
5. Do exercises on facial expressions. The more exaggerated, the better. Your audience should be your mirror. Start with anger, curiosity and then keep going. The more expressions you master, the better your stage performance becomes.

CHAPTER NINE
MANAGING YOUR STAGE

"I'm about as monolingual as you come, but nevertheless, I have a variety of different languages at my command, different styles, different ways of talking which do involve different parameter settings."

Noam Chomsky

Movement for the Stage Novice

You may not be inclined to agree that your presence has more to do with performance than anything else but this is just one of those facts you are going to have to accept. There is an existing relationship between you and your audience. The audience may play dormant as the observer, but there is an unspoken dialogue that ensues and mastering your movement on stage can help you take charge of that conversation and lead it in the direction that you want it to go. Earlier on, we talked about confidence and body language. These are essential attributes that will help you make better use of your stage. Knowing how to move on that stage in the next step to maneuvering the stage to your advantage. I will start you off on the basics. Over time, the rest of it will come naturally to you.

1. Be deliberate in your actions

Every movement you make on stage should appear deliberate. Pacing the floors of your stage aimlessly would give negative feedback on your competency; random movements with no visual purpose would highlight your nervousness. Obviously, shuffling your feet among other unnecessary hand or foot movements is out of the question. A trick I like to use is to imagine that I have an invisible small cage around me restricting my range of movement. So, where my arms would extend out in a very wide gesture, I am consciously made to narrow my movements. This makes it appear less random and more deliberate.

2. Let your movement portray your message

If the speech you are giving has a motivational tone to it, the way that you move on stage should reflect this. Now, what do I mean by this? A motivational message is meant to inspire the listener to take action, right? Well, your movement should convey a sense of urgency to your audience that demands action. There should also be a lot of positive reinforcements using hand gestures. Let me give you a tiny but significant gesture that has a lot of impact in terms of the use of space and communication. When you point your index finger, you automatically create a focal point. Point it downwards, and you convey time (now, present, this moment), point it forward and your message takes a tone of responsibility (you are assigning responsibility). Point that same finger upwards and it can be interpreted as denoting authority.

3. Know where everything is

This has a much more practical function. You need to know where everything is in order to enhance your performance. This means that you have to arrive at the venue on time...perhaps while the organizers are still setting up so that you know where the equipment you might be using is going to be located. You don't want to get on stage and start fumbling around with the projector or trying to figure out where to put down any of the props you might need during the course of your presentation.

Speaking and Being Heard

There are many fancy tools these days that are used to make public speaking a much more impactful experience for both the audience and the speaker. But no tool is more powerful than your voice. Learn to control it and half your battle is won already. During a regular conversation, your voice takes on a regular tone. This way, you can be heard by the peers with whom you are having a conversation with and you don't need to increase your voice and make any extra effort to enunciate your words. On stage, the game is a little different. Not only do you need to project your voice, but you also need to enunciate your words carefully. To make matters worse, there is a very strong possibility that fear might make your voice sound a little coarser and hoarser than it naturally is. This is why you would find some people suddenly battling a coughing fit when they get on stage in an attempt to clear their throats.

To prevent this, here are some things you can do:

1. Take things slower

Trying to rush your words can seem as though you are trying to talk past the hot potato in your mouth. Your words are not clear and your pitch tends to be a little higher. Take a deep breath, exhale and then pace yourself while speaking. This will keep you within audible range and give your listeners an impression that you are knowledgeable on the subject. Speak slow, be loud (but not high pitched) and speak clearly.

2. Eat something before your presentation

Given the tension you feel in the pit of your stomach before you go on stage, some people worry about eating. The general fear is that they might throw up on stage. Except in very extreme cases, there is a slim to none chance of that happening. And contrary to how you feel, a light meal can go a long way to improving your performance on stage. I try to eat a high protein meal at least two hours before I get on stage. Not only does it make me feel energetic, I feel more alert.

3. Avoid cold things

A nervous sweat brought on by a nasty case of stage fright might have you reaching for iced water, but this can only make your voice coarse and thus make your stage experience worse. Warm water, lemon drops, and honey are excellent if you are already battling a sore throat but used on the regular, you can expect that your voice would be crisp and clear which is perfect for public speaking.

Turn Up the Drama

I did say earlier on that being on stage as a public speaker is somewhat like being a stage performer. You may not be theatrical but there are theatrical techniques you can employ to enhance your performance and engage your audience. Even if you are going to be reading your speech directly off a piece of paper, you still need to be able to know when to look up at the people you are reading it to. We already talked about being too monotonous in the delivery of your speech. The dramatics I am referring to here doesn't mean that you suddenly have to include pantomimes in your routines. It is about improving your sense of timing. A dramatic pause can create tension in a room so thick that as they say, you can cut through it with a knife.

To turn up the drama, you just need to do the following:

1. Talk confidently

Injecting confidence into your voice even though you don't feel that way can bring a massive dose of drama to your presentation so that even though you are talking about quantum physics to a group of high school students, they would want to listen. It can take a lot of practice but if you keep at it, it will eventually come to you effortlessly.

2. Keep it short and sweet

People have a very short attention span. Waiting until the last minute to reveal your card might not work. Stir the drama by doing a quick introduction and then launching straight into the subject matter. This keeps your audience interested in what you have to pitch and sustains them to the end. Prolong things for longer than five minutes into your presentation and your big reveal may not even matter.

3. Don't complicate things

If you find yourself trying to explain your point five minutes after you made it, you probably have not done a good job in explaining it. Being dramatic in public speaking has little to do with complication. If you are speaking to people about makeup, there is no need to use terms specific to people in the aviation industry. You just end up confusing them. Use relevant colloquial terms to connect with your audience, convey your message and command their attention. Because at the end of the day, that is what the drama is all about.

Using the Stage for One

In acting, an actor would have to consider the presence of other people on stage and do his or her best to ensure that everyone gets their day in the spotlight. For a public speaker, you only share the stage with the idea you are hoping to get across. Other than that, the stage is really about you. Whether it is a big platform or a small podium, do your best to own it. Before you get on stage, you will be given a time limit. Do everything you can to ensure that you stay within this time limit and try not to think of it as a limit. For me, I like to think of it as a slice of time given to me to digest however I want to. Since most of my public speaking has had to do with training, I focus on driving my point home in that timeframe. To do this, I like to give bullet point presentations. This makes it easier to assimilate. I almost never use up my entire time, as I am more interested in interacting with my message than having them react to my message. I feel that if they interact with my message better, my point is driven home faster.

Set your own agenda for the time slot allocated to you and work that to your advantage. And most importantly, remember to have fun with the entire process. There is no rule that says that you can't. And if everything is looking a little too tedious for you, the next chapter breaks down how technology can be used to make your life that much easier. But first, to recap the contents of this chapter, let us go over what we have learned so far:

- Your movement on stage sets the tone for the kind of communication success you will achieve with your audience.
- Eating an hour or two before your presentation can keep you energetic and help you sustain an even tone of voice throughout. Starving yourself has the opposite effect.
- You need to employ the use of theatrical techniques to sustain the interest of your audience.
- The stage is designed for you to use as you will. Decide on your objectives and plan towards achieving them within the timeframe that you are given.

Your tasks:

1. Besides making a name for yourself as a prominent public speaker, what are your objectives? Specifically, what do you expect to happen to your audience every time you get on stage? This will help you plan effectively.
2. Record yourself speaking. Listen to it, assess your performance and point out areas for improvement.

3. Practice your regular speech and a compressed version of this speech. This frees you up to be flexible if your time is suddenly cut short. This way, you can still have an impactful session with your audience.
4. Think of three possible questions that your audience might ask that will throw you off your game. Draft fresh and inspiring responses and then practice those responses.
5. Draft a response to a question that you may not have an answer to. Let the response be as fresh and inspiring as possible and then rehearse this also.

CHAPTER TEN
THE TOOLS OF THE TRADE

Fools ignore complexities. Pragmatists suffer it.
Some can avoid it. Geniuses remove it."
Alan Perlis

Coach Your Speed with Teleprompters

Technology is designed to make our lives easier and it is no different when it comes to public speaking. You can spend hours on end trying to rehearse a speech to help improve your stage performance and appear more authentic than choreographed to your audience. But what happens when you are called on to make an impromptu speech with not enough time to practice? Do you give up and miss out on an opportunity or do you step up to the challenge? Without enough practice, you may not feel confident to take the challenge, and this is where technology comes in. A teleprompter helps you in situations like this. Instead of keeping your head buried in the written speech on your paper, you are able to look up and deliver your speech. The teleprompter is actually quite popular in the oval office and in newsrooms, but it can come in handy on stage too.

Besides helping you with speech prompts, it can also help you with the precision of your words. I should point out here that while prompters are handy, they are best used in situations where establishing a connection is not as important as ensuring that the right message is passed across to your listener base, which may include more than those currently present in the room with you. That said, practicing your speech with a teleprompter can help you with your voice modulation and correct enunciation of your words. However, to avoid any awkward situation, you have to ensure that:

a) You have a printed version of the script. As with all machines, teleprompters can be problematic. If it suddenly goes off on you, you want to ensure that you are not frozen up in the middle of your speech.
b) Use cues to help you make the speech seem less robotic. Your teleprompter shouldn't have to mean a boring speech from start to finish. Infuse some excitement into your time slot by cueing yourself on the prompter to tell a story, a joke or engage the crowd in an activity.
c) Set the pace for the teleprompter. Certain prompters can only display a few lines at a time. If you don't set the pace, when you speak too slowly you get left behind, and if you speak fast there will be too many awkward silences. Rehearse the script at least once to

give you an idea of how you want the timing to be like. Always remember, you take the lead.

Speech Training Apps

There is no law against improving your speech. As my dad always says whenever he gets an opportunity to learn, "I may be really good at what I do but there is always room for improvement." Speech training helps you become more articulate as a speaker and goes a long way in helping you perfect your craft. Thankfully, you can get these trainings right on your mobile device. These apps have a collective goal of helping you improve your public speaking skills but they do this differently. You may have to sample a few to determine what would work best for you. For this reason, I am going to highlight three of those apps. Not because I think that they are the best but because of the uniqueness of how they go about helping you become better as a public speaker.

1. The Simulator

Apps that fall in this category are designed to get you acquainted with the idea of speaking in front of a crowd by simulating the effect of a crowd. You may find the experience limiting, as an app can only do so much, but it does help you get over that initial fear and help you focus on your speech. An app that falls in this category is the **public speaking simulator** designed for iOS.

2. The Coach

These apps listen to your speech and offer pointers for improvement. Grammatical errors are corrected, practical tips for improvement are offered and areas where you sound repetitive are highlighted. While the focus is more on the technicalities of the speech than the delivery itself, it is a first step in helping to improve on the quality of your speech. The **Ummo** app is a good example of an app that can be grouped under speech coaching apps.

3. The Voice Tutor

After nailing the speech, you want to make sure that you get the delivery right on the money. It helps with issues like learning to pace yourself properly in terms of word flow and speech rhythm. "Pro Metronome" is an excellent app for this purpose. And this is available for both Android and iOS devices.

Compliment Your Presentation with Visual Aids

Typically, public speakers have had to rely on their gift of gab to paint a picture so vivid that it becomes etched in the minds of the audience. With the technological advancements of this age, you can use actual images to buttress your point. Using PowerPoint as a visual aid is an excellent tool. However, because you are going to have to divide the attention of your audience between yourself and the crowd, it becomes imperative that you take the lead and take the attention of the crowd where you want it to be at any point in time. Try these few tips to make a seamless transition:

1. Do not include your written speech in your presentation. This would only end up making the board the total focus at the speaking event. Instead, put bullet points with amazing facts on the board and then expatiate on them as you scroll through each slide.

2. Use more imagery and fewer words. I believe that this is pretty self-explanatory. The idea is to get your audience to have fun with the session no matter how serious. At the very least, you want them to be engaged. Images do a good job of complementing what you are saying.

3. Keep the board interesting. Just because I said stick to using more images and fewer words doesn't mean you should go and complicate things with graphs, charts and mind-boggling figures. Save those for information that you can share with your audience after the presentation.

Timers to Keep You on Track

Timing is key in succeeding at public speaking and it is important that you utilize the time that you are given for maximum impact. Practicing your speech with a consciousness of time would ensure that you are able to effectively break down the information within that timeframe and as you master this, your confidence in your ability is being nurtured in the process. There are special devices designed for public speaking, but you can simply use your phone or even your wristwatch to get the ball rolling. Phones can sometimes interfere with the audio system so they may not be a good idea when you are on stage. But for practice, the stopwatch and timer features come in very handy. Some event organizers will install a timer that is visible from where you stand but not to the audience. Pay attention to it. This timer displays different colors to indicate when you are approaching your time limit and cue you in on when to wrap up. I do not advise that you wait until the last minute to wrap up. Give yourself at least five minutes to spare so that you don't feel hurried when you leave the stage. It speaks volumes about your competency, especially if this is a very formal setting.

In conclusion, technology can be your best friend. But you have to understand the basics in order to key into the benefits that a lot of these technology platforms would offer you. For starters:

Be clear about what you want to achieve and then look for technology that can support your goals. It would not make sense to go for the tech first because it mentions a few things related to what you want to do in the description. It is like going to buy a red shoe from the store in the hopes that it would become black. Before you subscribe, be sure that you are clear on how it would help you achieve your goals

Nothing can take the place of practice. No matter how efficient technology is, its level of efficiency is determined by how prepared you are.

Understand that even under the best circumstances, the unexpected happens. All of the careful planning and preparation you are putting into your next public speaking event is admirable but don't go in thinking that everything is going to go according to plan. Hope that it does but if it doesn't, this is one of those times that you are going to have to roll with the punches and learn from the experience.

CLOSING

"All is well that ends well."

William Shakespeare

There are no short cuts to attaining greatness and I believe that this book clearly illustrates this. The roads that you have taken so far and the places that you will have to navigate emotionally to get to the place that you desire will take you farther and farther away from who you used to be, and that is a good thing. You started this journey in your comfort zone and I am certain that in that time, you have undertaken at least one task that challenged your comfort. Public speaking can be easy or difficult. This depends on what angle you are looking at it from. This book was not written to resolve that debate. Rather, it is meant to give you a head start in running towards your goals.

The tasks written here are not one-off things that you can simply do and cross them off your to-do list. This is something that you are going to have to wake up and do every day, and decide to follow through on your promise to yourself to be better. I can talk this way because I have been exactly where you are. Desiring something so badly yet too afraid to seize it even when it is being presented to me on a platter of gold. Obviously, we know that you are not getting this on a platter of gold. You are going to have to work hard to earn every progressive step you make on this journey. There will be blood, sweat and frustration but that is what will make this all the more fulfilling when you make your way to the finish line, which would be on that stage as you exit to the sound of roaring applause. Of course, I am aware that you are not doing this for the cheering of the crowd, but it would not hurt if people acknowledged the greatness in you.

And even if the crowd has yet to recognize the greatness in you, I want you to recognize it because I am aware of it. Seeing as I have never met you before, how did I come to the conclusion that you are a great individual? For starters, the mere fact that you can dare to dream is an excellent indication. Secondly, seeing as you purchased this book as a next step to achieving your dreams tells me you have made up your mind to pursue your dream. If that doesn't speak to your greatness, I don't know what will. Your unique struggles with emotional issues like anxiety and absence of confidence in social settings even makes your ability to dream of becoming a public speaker that much more daring and interesting. They say that the only limitations we ever experience are in the mind. You have made the choice to break free from anything that will hold you back—and I salute that courage.

Silence the voices that question your fears and keep pushing until you break through. Thankfully, this is a field that celebrates your individuality. You just have to work up the courage to put yourself out there and own the space that you are given. If you need extra motivation, just bear in mind that the world is in dire need of innovative ideas and lending your voice to that process can bring us closer to developing the solution that might change the lives of people forever. I thank you for your time and consistency. And now, I look forward to seeing the many great and wonderful things you will do. Stay fresh, stay vibrant and most importantly, stay winning.

Book #6
Self-Discipline Mastery

Develop Navy Seal Mental Toughness, Unbreakable Grit, a Spartan Mindset, Build Good Habits, and Increase Your Productivity

Introduction

Would you listen to a businessman and author who has failed a hundred times and has failed miserably at that? Should you?

Well, you should.

You see, there is wisdom in listening to mistakes and failure, and you learn vicariously through the experience of others. By doing that, you get to improve a lot faster than I ever did.

Imagine setting up business after business only to see them fail. Imagine lacking the knowledge, making the mistakes, and then relapsing into a muck of failure complete with self-loathing and total lack of discipline.

What does it take to get over that?

The answer for me was my self-discipline, grit, and mental toughness that I developed over the years. And in this book, I outline not just the mistakes I made but how I bounced back from them using the lessons I've learned. But I didn't make that transformation on my own.

I learned from countless mentors and coaches so that I could go back into my little mouse wheel and strive once again for success. A lot of them were from countless hours of reading and researching the most disciplined and successful people in history.

It took a lot of practice and perseverance to develop a shift in mindset. I drew from all of that experience when I wrote this book. It is a collection of thoughts, ideas, practices, personal experience, and coaching from some of the most disciplined people on earth.

Was it easy to try and regain self-control and muster enough willpower?

It was never *easy*. But the journey back to self-mastery and the friendships that I made along the way have made it all worthwhile. I have learned to apply mental fortitude and self-discipline in business, family life, and now in writing as well.

This book is my way of giving back to everyone who may have lost their way too—just like me. The lessons and practices here from mental toughness to meditation have helped me accomplish things that I never imagined I could.

If you immerse yourself in the principles that I have learned and outlined in this book, you will also learn how to put everything on the line and strive for the goal like there's nothing left to lose.

May the information here be a powerful guide for you as it was for me.

Chapter 1: The Science of Self-Discipline, Motivation, and Willpower

"Discipline is the bridge between goals and accomplishments."

(Jim Rohn)

Do you want to enhance your self-discipline, increase your willpower, and improve self-motivation? One of the secrets to achieving all of that is to develop habits and willpower. Experts say that these are two important keys to every accomplishment that has been measured in the modern world.

Habits and Willpower: Engines behind Change and Progress

Willpower is the thing that drives us to save for our future. Habits, on the other hand, establish patterns that lead to success and progress. These principles drive us to keep on working even if we don't want to or when we don't feel like it.

It is our willpower that makes us say no to that cigarette, no to that whiskey, and no to that extra helping of cake. It is willpower that makes us hop on that treadmill, report to the gym, and be patient with a wayward child.

When willpower fails, our self-discipline fails. Where willpower pushes us to go on the right path, our actions become habits, and our habits determine what we ultimately can achieve.

The Energy/Strength Model

Willpower, habits, self-discipline, and motivation are all interrelated. They are also subjects that have been studied extensively [1] by psychiatrists and other experts as well. When it comes to self-control and self-discipline, one of the reigning theories is called the energy model, or strength model [2].

According to this model, the brain is viewed as something akin to a muscle. And just like any muscle, it is seen as one that also has a limited amount of strength. It has limits just like any other part of the body.

Can this energy source of the brain be depleted? Yes, it can be depleted via mental exertion. That means no one is disciplined all the time. Every human being will act without discipline every once in a while.

Can Self-Discipline Be Enhanced?

Again, following the energy model, the answer to the question of whether self-discipline can be improved or not, the answer is yes, you can build self-discipline and self-control [3]. Of course, not everyone agrees with the energy model. However, everyone agrees that one can increase in self-discipline with practice.

The next question now is, how do you master, or at least improve, self-discipline? Here are a few tips that you can start with. We will go over more ideas and strategies later in this book.

Forgive Yourself

Sometimes people lose motivation for change simply because they beat themselves up for past mistakes and foibles. Remember that even with all your best intentions and your best effort, you will at one time or another fall short.

All well-laid plans will fail at some time. Remember that it doesn't happen only to you—it happens to everyone. If you fail, learn to acknowledge that fact. Pick yourself up and move on.

One of the ways to learn how to acknowledge past faults and get over them is to practice mindfulness. We will go over mindfulness and how you can use it to overcome shame and guilt due to past mistakes in chapter 3 of this book.

For now, understand that you will have to learn to forgive yourself before you can move on to better things. Self-discipline also involves forgiveness of oneself.

Pay Yourself First

Paying yourself first before anyone or anything else is a powerful motivator. If you don't, then you will get the impression that all your hard work just passes by without you noticing. Paying and rewarding yourself first gives you something to be excited about.

It doesn't have to be a big reward. It can be as simple as a dessert that you have always wanted. It can be a little quiet time that you promised yourself a long time ago. Sometimes you can reward yourself by spending time with friends and family.

Anticipating a reward can be a powerful tool to motivate you to stay the course. It can be something that you can use to obsess about the process that you are going through. You are not only going to think about the changes that you are making, but you've also got the reward in mind as well.

Make a Backup Plan and Plan for the Worst

Again, we mentioned earlier that everyone fails, right? So what do you do? You create a backup plan. A technique that you can use to boost your willpower during trying times is what psychiatric experts call *implementation intention* [4].

In simple terms, it is a plan that you can implement whenever you are faced with an anticipated difficult situation. It is a backup plan that you have prepared for the worst-case scenarios that you can imagine.

For example, you want to lose weight, and you are following a low-carb diet plan. What's a possible worst-case scenario? Here's one—you went out to have dinner with your friends. Unfortunately, all the food that's on the menu is unhealthy and rich in carbohydrates.

What do you do?

Before you dive into that scrumptious chocolate cake, you should have made your preparations for such an occasion beforehand. You pack a favorite low-carb snack, and while having the meal with your friends, you just order a nice low-carb drink—worst case, it will only be water, but tea minus the sugar or sweeteners should be fine as well.

While in the diner or restaurant (or wherever it is you went to eat) you planned to focus on having a great conversation with your friends. And that is how you planned to overcome the temptation to break your low-carb diet.

Realign Your Beliefs

Studies [5] show that the amount of willpower that you have is deeply rooted in your personal beliefs. If you believe that you have very little control and a limited amount of willpower, then that will be your truth even though you can summon more, but you just weren't aware of it.

The secret, of course, is to change your inner conceptions. Change how you see yourself, and your true potential and worth will eventually increase. Think along the lines of Napoleon Hill's famous statement:

"Whatever the mind can conceive and believe, it can achieve."

Your beliefs have a huge impact on your behavior, according to a 2007 study published in the *Journal of Applied Social Psychology*. If you want to increase mental toughness, self-discipline, and have unbreakable grit, you need to realign your negative beliefs and limiting beliefs and form positive and empowering beliefs.

Here are a few tips on how you can do that:

1. **<u>Identify Your Feelings</u>**

How do you feel about a certain task or a goal? For instance, do you feel confident that you can make a million dollars in the next three years? How do you feel about losing weight and trimming down to two clothing sizes in the next six months?

The first step is to identify these negative feelings. These feelings contribute to limiting beliefs, and you must identify them first before you can change the negative belief associated with that feeling.

2. **<u>Accept Your Feelings</u>**

You can't deny your feelings. You experience them, and therefore they are evident. However, you should also realize this truth—your feelings are not permanent. You can feel sad one moment but then feel happy, the total opposite, a few minutes later.

By that same token, you may feel that you can't hit this month's sales quota. However, that feeling can also change to you can—especially after closing your next sale. Then you will begin to see the possibilities and change how you feel about yourself and your capabilities.

3. **<u>Replacing Old Realities with New Ones</u>**

As your feelings change, you change your perceptions. You experience what Stephen Covey calls a *paradigm shift*. Paradigm shifts don't have to be huge and world-changing. They can be small but significant, like saying no to that extra helping in a buffet.

When you do that, you begin to understand that you already have the capacity to lose weight and stick to a diet plan. When you close the next sale, you begin to see that this is something that you can do.

You change your paradigm, you change your reality. In effect, you change how you see yourself, and you change how you see the world. Your positive experiences are not the only source of positive or reinforcing beliefs—you can use the experiences of others and concepts that have been taught or shared with you as the basis and evidence for positive feelings and beliefs.

4. **<u>Repeat the New Truths That You Have Discovered</u>**

Where you used to tell yourself that you can't do it, tell yourself that you can. Use the evidence that you drew upon in step number three to reinforce your new beliefs. You need to repeat and reinforce these beliefs, especially when you experience setbacks and failures.

It will take some time, but you will realize that every failure is but a proverbial stepping stone toward success. Failure is part of the process. Remind yourself of your new truths.

By realigning your beliefs, you slowly feed your self-confidence. Your improved self-confidence improves your mindset and contributes to your level of mental toughness. You begin to understand that despite your failures, you are an achiever.

Eat Often and Eat Healthy

Unless you intend to practice intermittent fasting, it should be a priority to eat healthy and to eat often. Research [6] suggests that the resolve and willpower of people go down when their blood sugar levels go down.

Do you notice that your ability to focus and concentrate is greatly diminished when your stomach is growling? You need to fuel up if you want to increase your resolve to do what is needed, but remember to eat healthy always.

Work on Small and Simple New Habits

Complex habits will be harder to develop. The solution is to choose simple and easy habits and build on them [7]. For example, do you find that working out in the gym for two hours is just way too much?

You can resolve that by reducing your workout time to 15 to 30 minutes. Another alternative is to work out at home. If you have trouble getting enough sleep, don't aim for the full six to eight hours at first. Start by sleeping 15 minutes earlier than usual. You can increase the number of minutes until you get to the full amount of sleep you wanted to get.

By working on small and achievable habits, they eventually add up to bigger habits. Smaller habits require smaller disciplined steps that are easier to achieve. Small achievements help to reinforce your self-confidence.

In the next chapter, we will go over what mindset is and how you can shift your mindset to gain more self-discipline.

Chapter 2: Shifting Your Mindset

"Once your mindset changes, everything on the outside will change along with it."

(Steve Maraboli)

A standard textbook definition of the word *mindset* goes something like this: it is an established set of thoughts and attitudes that have been selected and held by someone. In psychology, a person's mindset is that belief or set of beliefs that guide the way people handle situations [8].

That last definition above was by Dr. Gary Klein. He further explains that our mindsets help us do things and determine things. For instance, with our current mindset, we judge whether we are looking at an opportunity or not.

Our mindsets can be self-defeating, but they can also be progressive and beneficial. Self-discipline is, first and foremost, strongly tied to one's mindset. Your attitude toward something will determine whether you will pursue a disciplined approach about it or not.

If you want to be more disciplined and have more self-control, then you need to change your mindset.

What Is a Mindset?

Professor Carol Dweck of Stanford University popularized the idea of mindsets in 2006. She contrasted people's beliefs about the source of their abilities. She observed that when people have a fixed mindset that they have innate abilities.

This can be a dangerous situation because when they encounter failure, their mindset is challenged, and so is their self-esteem, so their self-confidence is also called into question. Such an experience can make people doubt their true potential.

Dweck, on the other hand, pointed out that there is a fixed mindset and a growth mindset. A growth mindset is very different. It is a point of view that you are adept at improving your capabilities. It is the attitude that accepts mistakes and expects continuous growth.

With that type of mindset, failure is nothing more than an indication of what people need to work on. There are other key differences that she pointed out in her research.

For instance, people with a fixed mindset tended to go out and prove themselves to others. When someone would suggest that they have made a mistake, they would take a defensive stance. They also tend to measure themselves using their failures as the decisive factors.

People with a growth mindset tend to be more resilient. They don't mind making mistakes, and they are often better at persevering. Thus, they are more motivated and usually are more of a hard worker.

Note that these aren't the only types of mindsets. There are others. We just used these two to point out the contrasting facets of different mindsets.

Now, as you can see, some mindsets can be beneficial, and some mindsets can be detrimental. If you want to progress, be more disciplined, and become more successful, then you need to experience a shift in mindset.

Changing Your Mindset

Here are the steps necessary to trigger a shift in one's mindset:

1. Accept your mistakes and learn lessons from them

A truly successful person can readily make a list of his failures. They can be an open book and tell you right then and there how and where they failed and made mistakes. They can also tell you exactly what lessons they learned from those failures.

If you want to learn how to shift your mindset to a more progressive and growth-centered one, then one of the first things you should learn to do is to accept that you have made mistakes along the way.

In my efforts at growing businesses, I remember making all sorts of mistakes from hiring too many personnel, spending too little on advertising, not paying attention to order flows, not listening to customers, and many others.

From the many setbacks that I experienced, I learned a lot of valuable lessons. Mistakes can be a powerful teacher. An entrepreneur that is open about blunders is better able to cope with difficulties because they have growth as their primary centers.

I have learned how to get up from the failure, analyze where I got it wrong, and then lead everyone to better opportunities. The better you are at handling losses, the better you will be at shifting mindsets.

2. Set small goals

Sometimes we get so busy doing the daily grind that we lose sight of our goals. At times we focus too much on the large long-term goal that we fail to measure our progress. We sometimes are fooled into thinking that we aren't progressing and that we aren't capable of a mindset shift.

Take the time to sit down and break down your large long-term goal into smaller short-term goals. Set these goals on a timeline and try to achieve them one at a time. When you accomplish a small goal or mini-goal, go out and celebrate—not too lavish, but enough to remind you that you are already progressing towards that much-awaited mindset shift.

For instance, if you want to shift from the "I am a bad salesman" mindset to the "I'm the greatest salesman" mindset, you don't have to wait until you have made a million-dollar sale.

You can set mini-goals along the way and use them as stepping stones to reach your overall goal. Here are some achievable mini-goals that you can set on the way to becoming the best salesman that you can be:

- Contact the first 100 people and get rejected 100 times
- Find your first three leads
- Get your first seven leads
- Sign up your first 21 people
- Get rejected 200 times
- Convert your first customer from your accumulated leads
- Convert five more leads into customers
- Make 30 new customers
- Get your first three repeat orders
- Get your next ten repeat orders
- Get your first 100 leads/200 leads/300 leads
- Reach up to 100 customers
- Hit your first $1,000 sale (you can set the figure that you want)
- Make your first $3,000 sale
- Achieve $5,000 in sales in one month (again, the figures are all up to you)

You set the mini-goals that you would like to achieve. If you are a writer, then set mini-goals like writing a 300-word article each day, your first newsletter, completing one chapter in your new book each month, or maybe writing a blog post each week. If you want to be more disciplined when it comes to working out, then you can start by committing to go jogging for five minutes each day. You can then slowly work that up to ten minutes two weeks later, and then up to fifteen minutes the following month.

3. Learn to find inspiration from any source

No one has a monopoly on genius. Take some time each day to find inspiration even in the small things. It can come from your employees, your next-door neighbor, and even that irritating landlord.

Read blogs, watch motivational videos, read self-help books, attend webinars, listen to podcasts, and take part in master classes. To truly gain a shift in mindset, you should immerse yourself in the views of others and learn to pick up golden nuggets of wisdom that can be useful to you.

Your point of view won't change unless you expose your mind to insights and ideas from other people. Your mindset won't shift unless it has something to shift into, ergo finding ideas and inspiration from coaches, professors, and other experts in their respective fields.

4. Practice meditation

In the next chapter, we will cover mindfulness and mindfulness meditation. Meditation is a great way to flex your mental muscles, so to speak. Think of meditation as a tool that you can use to calm your mind and stretch your mental faculties to new limits.

If you want to try meditation for at least ten minutes a day, then I recommend that you download the Headspace app on your phone. The first ten days are free, and it will give you a good introduction to meditation. You can also read more about mindfulness in the next chapter.

5. Find three positive changes each day

You think you're not growing or progressing? You might be surprised to find that you are actually going through a lot of positive changes each day, and you just never knew it.

These changes can be ones that are happening (or have happened) to you personally or to someone you know or someone you're associated with. It can be changes that happen in your home.

The goal is to train your mind to see the bright side of things. One day you will notice that even the negative and bad events in your life were actually for your benefit.

6. Accept these three truths

This one is from an executive friend of mine who is quite successful. She says there are three truths you should learn to accept in order to help you embrace a shift in your mindset.

The three truths that she was referring to are:

1. Life is short (so let things slide and don't worry or fuss about things that may offend you)
2. Time is precious (spend it wisely and delegate as much as you can)
3. Your ego will always need to be tamed (it will take time to learn humility)

Remember that change is inevitable. In fact, in many instances, change is good. Your mindset is an ever-growing thing. Embracing that growth is equivalent to embracing your progression.

Why Changing Your Mindset Builds Self-Discipline

Your mindset is your own set of thoughts, beliefs, and attitudes that you have selected for yourself. If you want more self-discipline, you need to change your attitudes and point of view.

If you used to think that work is something unpleasant, then you should change your mindset and start seeing your work as a means of getting something better in your life.

Changing your mindset changes your attitudes towards losing weight. By seeing weight loss as something achievable, then you gain enough grit and mental toughness to avoid binge eating.

Chapter 3: Building Good Habits and Breaking Bad Ones

"If you are going to achieve excellence in big things, you develop the habit in little matters. Excellence is not an exception, it is a prevailing attitude."

(Colin Powell)

Maybe you have heard somewhere back in the day that it takes 60 days to form a new habit. Perhaps you may have heard of a different theory—and this one's shorter—that it takes 21 days to form a new habit.

Sometimes there are longer days like the 20-80 theory, and sometimes they say it takes 24 or 25 days to form a new habit. Well, that is an old science that has since been debunked.

It's not that they are not completely true. It's just that their data isn't as complete as we have it now. Studies on habit formation have grown in the past decade, and we now understand them better than we did years ago.

What experts are saying now is that there is no fixed time frame for anyone to form a new habit. It is different for everyone. According to a study [9] published in the *European Journal of Social Psychology*, it ranges from 18 days to 254 days.

The same study points out that there are 66 days to form a new habit. Well, that is the average. That is also why some theorized that it takes that long. However, that is only the average rate.

It doesn't follow that everyone needs 60 days or so. Some people may even require less, which is why some say you need 25 or 27 days to form a new habit. If you dig into the details, it takes 66 days (on average) ***for a new habit to become automatic***.

What it means is that you may already have formed a new habit before that prescriptive two-month time frame. The actual time to form the habit will rely on different factors. Sometimes it has something to do with the person wanting the new habit, and at times the new habit you want to form will affect your success rate.

We'll go into the details a little later on.

The Little Habits That Make Up Your Day

Whether you realize it or not, you already have lots of habits that you perform every day. A habit is an automatic behavior that we all do without thinking. We may not even remember creating these habits.

Here are a few routines you might want to check just to see which ones are already habitual:

- Which shoe or sock do you put on first, the left one or the right?
- How do you put your kids to bed?
- How do you feed your pet dog or cat?
- How do you take your dog out for a walk?
- When putting on a shirt, which sleeve do you start with?
- How do you wash your hair?
- How do you water your plants?
- When you mow the lawn, where do you start?
- What exercise do you start with?
- How do you start your day at work?
- How do you go shopping for essentials?
- How do you do your laundry?
- What's the first thing you do when you get home from work?
- How do you brush your teeth? How do you put toothpaste on your brush? Where do you start brushing?

The list goes on, and before you know it, you already have a long list of habits that have become a natural part of your routine. Almost everything is a habit from how you sit at your work desk to how you sit on the couch to watch Netflix.

It also includes how you react when you see your friends or how you respond when your boss sounds angry or upset. We carry out these habits without thinking about them, and we only notice them when we pay attention—like putting them in a list.

Ivan Pavlov and Classical Conditioning

Our understanding of habits, classical conditioning, and everything else connected to them started with the theories and discoveries by Ivan Pavlov [10]. Believe it or not, it all started with studies related to saliva.

Pavlov won the Nobel Prize for his work on medicine in the year 1904. But his work started as an experiment to figure out how much saliva a dog would produce as a digestive response—totally unrelated to behavior and habit formation.

Long story short, what he discovered then formed the foundation of our understanding of classical conditioning. Pavlov found out that a dog would salivate to food, but a canine would also salivate to the footsteps of the pet owner or even the sound of the bell that announced that food was being brought to him.

The initial stimulus was the food, and the resulting behavior was the dog salivating. But then he added a second stimulus—the sounding of a bell. So each time food was being brought to the dog, a bell was chimed.

The dog would salivate and then receive the food. Pavlov then removed the first stimulus—the food. And then he would just ring the bell to see if the dog would salivate as much without the presence of the food.

The result was that the dog still salivated to the sound of the bell minus the food. You get the same response with the associated stimulus.

But you might think that hey—we're smarter than dogs, right?

Of course we are. But just like our canine friends, we humans are also creatures of habit. We also have that stimulus–response process going on within us.

Here's a classic example.

A smoker habitually lights a cigarette as soon as he sees one. The first stimulus is seeing a pack of cigarettes—it doesn't have to be his. It may be just a cigarette shown in a commercial on TV or a billboard, or even someone else who happened to be in the same smoking room as he was.

When he sees a cigarette, he would reach for his own cigarette and light it up. Now, a second stimulus can enter any time. A good example of that is boredom. Let's say a man is a smoker who is waiting for his girlfriend to get off work.

He's been waiting for an hour (he didn't know his girlfriend was doing overtime work). He's already bored, and then he sees a poster of a cigarette—of course he reaches for one and lights it.

Now, this happens several times. He gets bored exactly while seeing a cigarette. He lights it. It will eventually turn into a habit that every time he gets bored he has associated that boredom to lighting a cigarette.

This happens a lot, and it happens to everyone.

It doesn't have to be about lighting cigarettes. It can be for any habit that we form.

The Three-Step Loop in Habit Formation

Charles Duhigg and other researchers, such as BJ Fogg, for instance, have identified a three-step pattern when it comes to habit formation. They call it by different names—well, each author does.

For instance, Duhigg calls it the Cue, Routine, Reward cycle, or process. On the other hand, others would refer to it as the three Rs of Habit Change. Well, whatever they choose to call it, just remember that they're all referring to the same thing.

I'll just use the 3 Rs because it's easier to remember. So, what are these three steps? They're the following:

1. Reminder
2. Routine
3. Reward

Reminder: This refers to the trigger or stimulus that solicits a behavior (remember Pavlov's experiment?). This trigger or cause is Duhigg's first step called the cue—well, it's pretty much the same thing. Just remember that the reminder or first step is something that will solicit a reaction.

Routine: This refers to the actual behavior that you do in response to the reminder or cue. It can be any action that you take as long as it is your response to the stimuli, cue, or reminder (again, remember they're the same thing).

A routine, therefore, is any behavior that we automatically perform every time we get a trigger or stimulus. This routine can become something that we do without even thinking about it.

Reward: The reward phase refers to the benefit that we gain from doing the behavior as a response to the trigger. Something doesn't become a habit without any reason to repeat doing it again.

The reward, in effect, reinforces the behavior as a favorable response towards the stimuli. In Pavlov's experiment, it is the food that represents the reward after the dog behaves favorably in response to the stimuli (the bell, footsteps, etc.). The dog's behavior (salivating) is reinforced by the reward and thus etching the entire routine into the mind, and it becomes a very powerful memory.

Well, it's actually more than a powerful memory. That is because if repeated enough times, it already becomes a habit. After the routine has been rewarded, everything cycles back to step 1—every time the reminder is provided, the mind automatically moves to step 2 and then step 3 in the process.

How The Three-Step Loop Works

Here's a very common and very simple example of how this three-step loop works. This cycle happens to everyone—as long as you own a phone, you may have already fallen for this cycle.

Phase 1: Phone Rings Either Text or Call (The Reminder or Trigger)

Now, this is a very common trigger. When people's phones ring, what's the very first thing they do instinctively? Yes, they reach for their phone. It doesn't matter where it is; we all reach for that phone, albeit instinctively.

It can be in our pockets, our bags, or on the bedside nightstand while you're fast asleep. When that phone rings, you reach for it. The question is: why are we mercilessly under the influence of these phones and are compelled to react?

We react because we have been conditioned to react to it. In short, we have formed the habit of answering phones promptly. We will drop everything else just to answer the said phone.

So, what serves as the trigger or cue?

Your smartphone or iPhone employs two or three cues to grab your attention. It uses a visual cue—it lights up even in the dark, it then displays the caller (a picture or maybe just a phone number), it will then create an auditory cue—it will ring, and finally, depending on the settings you choose, it will also vibrate, which is something that you will feel in case you have the phone in your pocket.

It uses a multi-sensory cue that can snatch your attention if you are not careful.

Phase 2: We Answer the Call or Text (Routine or Response)

The next phase is almost inevitable. Well, there's a way to break this habit, but we'll go over that later in this chapter. We grab our phones and answer it (text or call) sometimes automatically.

It would appear as if we have no choice—but we do. Have you ever experienced being in the middle of an interview, and you forget to put your phone on silent mode, and then it rings? Almost like some kind of lightning instinct, you forget that you're in the middle of an interview (or a business meeting or something where answering your phone is considered rude), and you almost reach for it to answer the darn thing.

But then you remember where you are and what you are doing so you just turn your phone off. It's not that the phone has any power over you, but it's just that you have made it a habit to answer your phone right then and there without question.

Phase 3: You Find Out Who It Was That Called/Texted You (The Reward)

This is the satisfaction that you get out of reacting to your phone. You can call this some kind of feedback loop. When you are satisfied during phase 3, it feeds your desire to repeat the process from the beginning.

You can compare it to a powerful reminder or memory that's telling you to answer the phone next time it rings because, according to your previous experience, you get the satisfaction from that call or text.

Experts posit that all habits that we form—whether they are complex or simple ones—follow this same three-step cycle.

Big Actions vs. Small Specific Actions

Here's an interesting question: which actions that we decide to make have a better chance of becoming a habit? Experts say it is the small specific actions that we do that have a better chance of becoming a habit.

What you need to do is to make your target habit as specific as possible. For example, let's say you made a resolution to exercise more this year. Does it ever happen? It doesn't, right?

The reason behind that is the fact that this decision to make a new exercise habit is too general and vague. If the actions you decide upon fall in that category, then they will become less likely to be adopted as a new habit.

Select your target action/habit to be as specific as it can be. In this example—exercising—you can differentiate your actual target habit like this:

- I will put on my running clothes and go on a quick jog as soon as I get home each day from work.

That is specific enough. Here's another way to formulate your newly selected habit:

- I will go on a walk every Monday, Wednesday, and Saturday morning until the following Christmas.

What You Can Do: Pick a habit. If it is too general, then specify what you want to do and when you should do it. Specify how frequently you are going to do it and how exactly you will do it. You may also create a plan on how you can get it all done.

Easy and Simple Actions vs. Complex Actions

If the planned or selected habit is too complex, chances are it won't be converted into a regular habit that you will have on your list. Other than being specific about the habit, you shouldn't choose complex habits.

For example, setting up a home gym complete with all the state-of-the-art exercise equipment and weights that you can find won't get you exercising. You'll just end up wasting a lot of money on a home gym system.

On the other hand, the very simple reminder of putting your running shoes by your bedroom door where you are sure to see it as soon as you change your work clothes is a sure reminder and trigger to your mind that you should go out to run.

What You Can Do: Pick simple habits. Remember that you can use small habits to remind you of other habits. One thing can lead to another. The simpler the habit you select, the better.

Physical Actions vs. Mental or Emotional States/Decisions

Some people think that they can make it a habit to choose to be happy no matter what happens. And then they get depressed. I have seen that happen to friends of mine. They thought they could will themselves into happiness and positivity.

The chances of success of that endeavor are very slim at best. But here's a better way to do that. Select a habit that requires any physical action that will result in making you happy.

This one, I have tried myself. I remember back in the day that I used to have fun playing tennis. So I decided that maybe I could try playing it again. All I did was bring out my old tennis racket and placed it right by the door.

That way every day I saw the old tennis racket. I didn't pick up on tennis right away, but the constant reminder because of that racket eventually allowed me to go out one afternoon to play tennis.

It happened now and then at first. But then it became something fun and then a little while later I was regularly playing tennis during the weekend all over again. Habits take time to form, but simple and actual physical actions tend to get remembered a lot better than just saying it or trying to keep things inside your head.

Okay, let's use a simpler example. I'm not very good at remembering things, so when I try to get groceries or have stuff that I need to do on certain days, I tend to forget a thing or two—and that would eventually make me upset at the end of the day.

My first solution to this problem was to take five minutes each morning and try to remember everything that I need to do. Of course, that never worked.

My second solution (which I tried a day or two later) was to buy a small notebook—one that could fit in my pocket. Along with that I also bought a pen to go with the notebook.

All I had to do was to write down all the stuff I needed to get and do on that day each morning. I also had to keep the notebook with me all day. And it worked.

Every morning I would update my list. The mere presence of the notebook was a reminder to me that I had a list. Whenever I had the chance, I checked out my list and got things done without missing an item.

Using Visual and Auditory Cues

Again, this goes back to the mobile phone analogy that we covered earlier. Auditory and visual cues create a conditioned response. Let that be a rule of thumb: if you want a new behavior to become a habit, then make sure to practice it with auditory or visual stimuli. We will go over the details about this a little later in this chapter.

Building Habits That Stick

Plato once said that "We are what we repeatedly do. Excellence then, is not an act, but a habit." The key to making an action a habit is repetition, according to that quote from the ancient philosopher.

On the outset, repetition might get the initial emphasis on everyone's mind. However, if you think about it, there is another underlying principle that Plato was trying to highlight.

You see, you can't just keep repeating something religiously without another guiding principle behind it. The true principle that will push you to keep repeating something over and over again until the action becomes ingrained in you is called *discipline*.

This is true of actions that aren't always pleasant—like fasting, exercising, restraint, and others. The immediate reward isn't always there, and you may get discouraged along the way as you try to repeat the actions associated with these goals.

That is why habits can sometimes be hard to build. In our day-to-day life, we will have a lot of distractions that can set us off our desired path. Here are five tactics that you can do to make new habits that will stick with you for a long time.

Tactic #1: Mini-Goals and Micro Quotas

Studies show that setting smaller goals can help people change their lives for the better [11]. If you have a huge habit in mind—like losing weight, for instance—you can break it down into several smaller habits (aka goals).

For instance, you can break it down into:

1. Work with a fitness coach every Saturday morning
2. Try intermittent fasting twice a week (Tuesdays and Fridays)
3. Reduce sugar intake by implementing a low-carb meal plan

By going through this goal-setting process, you will be better able to transform new behaviors into habits. Smaller goals are more realistic, and the more specific they are, the easier they are to convert into a habit.

These mini-goals will serve as your micro quotas. In other words, they represent the minimum amount of work that you have to do. It's like breaking down a huge task into smaller, doable tasks.

Every time you hit a micro quota, it gives you a sense of accomplishment. It is a self-rewarding system that encourages you to move forward and to keep repeating the task or action.

You can set these mini-goals or micro quotas daily, weekly, bi-weekly, or some other frequency that suits your needs.

Now you might be wondering if this really works. You need to look no further than writer and app developer Nathan Berry. He made a simple goal every day, and it was a commitment that changed his career.

What commitment/goal was that? It was to write 1,000 words every day. It is a tough grind, right? He made that goal back in 2012 and it skyrocketed his career. It empowered him to earn $30,000 in just a month and a half [12].

It was a mini-goal that eventually led to the accomplishment of a much larger goal. And it started with just a little habit of writing a thousand words each day.

Tactic #2: Use Behavior Chains

One of the techniques that experts have found to be quite useful in making habits stick is using behavior chains [13]. It's a very easy concept. You don't have to be taken aback by the term—it just sounds fancy.

The idea is that one behavior or action can lead to another. It makes use of physical contextual cues to remind a person of something that he or she has to do. This goes back to placing, or even hanging, your running shoes right at the door so it's the first thing you see when you walk in.

It reminds you that you should go out for a run or jog as soon as you get home. Here's another thing that worked for me. I purchased a small green bowl along with a smaller spoon.

Every night before going to bed, I would put all of that on the breakfast table on top of a placemat at the chair where I usually sit for breakfast. What it did is that every morning when I rush to prepare my breakfast cereal and milk, those things would remind me to practice portion control.

That way, I don't overeat during breakfast. Doing that until it became a habit eventually contributed to achieving my weight loss goals. Determine a small behavior or habit that you can do to achieve a bigger goal that you want to achieve.

Tactic #3: Visualize Your Goal the Right Way

You may have heard of dream boards and visualization exercises where people try to envision what they want to achieve. They may even create a pinboard and add to it anything and everything that they want for themselves.

These are visualization techniques that are designed to help you achieve your goal. However, some people are more successful in using them, and others aren't. Why is that? This is true of habits as well.

For example, if you want to visualize yourself as being able to end a smoking habit, sometimes that visualization is not enough. The same is true for other things like a brand new car, being physically fit, being financially free, and others.

You see, it is one thing to visualize what you want and take five minutes each day to do it. However, if you do not visualize the reason why you want that change to happen, then there is an essential part of the entire vision that is missing.

The reason why you have that vision should also be part of the vision as well. Going back to our example, if you envision yourself quitting smoking in six months, you should include in that vision why you want to quit.

Studies show that visualizing results alone is not enough [14]. It may even prevent you from breaking a new habit or starting a new one. So don't just visualize what you want, envision why you want what you want.

Other than the why you should also envision how you will attain it. Let's say you envision yourself making a million dollars in the next two years. Well, don't just imagine yourself with a brand new car and a paycheck with that much money.

Envision how you're going to do it. Studies from UCLA have shown that this is a more effective way to acquire a new habit and to realize a goal [15].

Visualizing and planning helps you stay focused on the new habit or goal that you want to achieve. Itemizing each step that you need to take reduces the anxiety that may come due to being unsure of what you ought to do and how to determine if you're progressing or not.

Tactic #4: Take Away Excess Options (Don't Overplan)

Research shows that having too many options when forming a new habit will deplete your mental energy [16]. The same study also points out that making repeated or multiple decisions also have the same effect.

Even if those decisions are small or mundane, they will add up and eventually take a toll on your mental faculties. So, how do you reduce the number of decisions that you have to make?

The solution suggested by experts from the Harvard Business Review is to turn the mundane and daily decisions that we make into routines [17]. Former US President Barack Obama used this strategy by just wearing gray or blue suits.

He said, *"I'm trying to pare down decisions. I don't want to make too many decisions about what I'm eating or wearing because I have too many other decisions to make."*

So how do you put this into practice? Here are a couple of ideas:

- Pack the same lunch every day for a week (just change the menu every week) so that you won't have to think about what to eat at lunchtime.
- If you have too many shoes, then just pick two or three that you really like and then sell the others in a garage sale or give them away to charity.
- Don't go to the lunchroom or the vending machine down the hall so you won't be overwhelmed by the snack options—pack your own healthy snacks before going to work.

Note that by simplifying your choices, the better the chances that the new behavior will become a habit.

Tactic #5: Don't Give Up When You Screw Up

Do you beat yourself up inside when you make a mistake? Don't do it. Remember that each mistake is a lesson learned, and it only wafts you closer to a much-desired outcome. Think along these famous lines from Samuel Beckett:

"Ever tried, ever failed. No matter. Try again, fail again. Fail better."

Take note that new habits that you form are such fragile things. That also means you should remove any possible obstacle that may lead you astray. Do you find yourself abandoning ship when you slip up the first few times?

Some people doubt themselves and think that they can't get the new habit into their system when faced with failures every now and then. Remember that each failure is a lesson, and if you scrutinize how you failed, you can identify the factors that led to that failure.

Fine-tune the screwup. Find out where you made the mistake and then try again. Don't give up.

Now you know how to grow into good habits; in the next section of this chapter, we will go over how to get rid of bad habits.

Why Habit-Building is Essential to Self-Discipline

Remember that discipline can be built on the small habits that you do every day. Micro quotas, behavior chains, visualization, simplifying goals, and a positive attitude are small habits that contribute to the establishment of better discipline.

To be a better-disciplined entrepreneur, you should acquire habits like learning a new subject or skill regularly, reading an entire book each week, being on time for appointments, networking on purpose, and finding ways to improve customer relationships.

How to Quit Bad Habits

Your good habits will help you live a better and more disciplined life. You will have more self-control if your habits are truly beneficial. But what if you have bad habits? How can you break them?

We'll go over the answers to that question and several tips along the way in this section of the chapter.

Top 10 Bad Habits

Figuring out what the top 10 bad habits are shouldn't be that difficult. Just pull up your browser and Google it. Here are the top results that I was able to find recently. Some of the results were kind of surprising.

Here's what I got (your results may be a bit different though):

- Alcohol
- Procrastination
- Smoking
- Watching TV (I was like—really???)
- Picking your nose (ugh!)
- Swearing
- Biting fingernails
- Drinking lots of coffee
- Overeating
- Playing with hair
- Worrying about things
- Late-night snacking/raiding the fridge
- Skipping breakfast

Okay, so my list is slightly longer than ten items. Note that I didn't arrange them in any particular order. I just typed them as they appeared on my search results. I had no intention of ranking them from 1 to 10.

Also, I didn't put drugs on the list because it is an addiction, and it is more than just a bad habit. Well, I guess we can remove smoking and drinking from this list, but only if they are chronic conditions that one is already experiencing.

Breaking Bad Habits

In this section, we'll go over the different methods that you can use to overcome bad habits. You can try the tips that I will mention below chronologically, or you can just pick the ones that you think are much easier for you. Note that I have arranged them in a bit of a logical order.

Identify the Reward

Remember that it was mentioned earlier when we discussed the three Rs of habit formation that every behavior that becomes a habit will have a reward associated with it. The reward reinforces the behavior, which is why it becomes habitual.

If you are nurturing a bad habit, that means you are receiving a reward for that habit. There will be a reward somewhere in some way. From behavioral psychology, we understand that habits can either be rewarded or punished.

When a behavior is rewarded, it is reinforced and may become habitual. But if a behavior is punished, then it is curbed and has a slimmer chance of becoming a habit. Rewards reinforce, while punishment reduces the chances of having that behavior repeated.

For instance, if you are a smoker, identify the reason why you smoke. What do you get out of that behavior? A lot of people smoke because it is their way to release the tension and stress that they are feeling.

When you overeat, your reward could be the taste of the food. If you have a bad habit of putting tasks off (procrastination), then your reward could be the extra free time. Identify the reward.

After identifying the automatic reward that you get for your bad habit, the next step is to decide whether to get a punishment for the habit or to remove the reward you're getting for that habit.

Punishment vs. Reward Removal

After identifying the reward you're getting for that bad habit, you have the choice of either removing that reward or just punishing the bad habit. The idea is to cut the cycle habit formation so that the bad habit won't get reinforced.

Note that this will require a certain commitment from you. You need to commit to either impose a punishment every time you do that habit or take away that reward that you are getting every time you experience a relapse.

For instance, if you are trying to lose weight and then you overeat (i.e., your bad habit) you can impose a penalty which takes away the satisfaction (i.e., the reward) of the bad habit—let's say that you commit to not have dessert until tomorrow at lunchtime or for 24 hours.

But in case you decide you want to impose a punishment for the bad habit well, here's a suggestion. Next time you overeat, then you should go on a 15-minute workout session.

Replacing the Bad Habit

Bruce Lee, the renowned martial artist and actor, once said:

"Empty your cup so that it may be filled; become devoid to gain totality."

What does that mean? It means that if your mind is already preoccupied with something, then don't expect that you will be able to fill it with something else.

The same is true when you want to learn a new habit, but a bad habit is getting in the way. What you can do is to get rid of the bad habit first and then replace it with a good one.

You are then hitting two birds with one stone. You are breaking a bad habit and getting a new and better one. The first step was to identify what reward you are getting from your bad habit—e.g., stress relief, great taste in your mouth, etc.

What you need to do is to find a replacement habit that also gives you the same or equivalent reward. It's like getting all the good out of your previous habits minus the side effects.

So, for example, your habit is that you put off your tasks for later (i.e., procrastination). The reward you are getting from this is that you get a few extra minutes to yourself to get some peace and quiet before tackling a very difficult task.

What replacement should you use? Here's a good idea—use a Pomodoro Timer. Using a Pomodoro Timer (also known as a tomato timer), you can set a very realistic work schedule that allows you to take plenty of breaks in between tasks. That way, you have more chances to do something enjoyable and reduce the tensions that your work may be having on you.

Tell a Friend

Telling a friend about a habit that you want to obtain already imposes a possible punishment or penalty for not achieving it. If we don't follow through and our friends know about it, then we are punished by the shame of failure.

Of course, the shame of it all isn't a powerful motivator. However, it may be quite effective for others. But there is another benefit that you can gain from telling others.

If you tell your goal habits to your friends, then you gain the support of the people who care. Let's say that you tell your friends that you intend to break your bad habit of swearing.

You may have times when you're so pissed off and your friends are around. Before you blurt out your next cuss word, they can give you that warning look. It's a little check and balance that you get, and because you have friends around you that are there to help you, you can slowly but surely curb the instinct to swear.

Another way to make this work is to find a buddy who also has the same problem who may also want to stop just like you. So let's say you want to quit drinking beer. Find a drinking buddy who also wants to quit.

You will then hang out, and in case either of you feels the urge, you can call one another or just send out text messages. You can then go hang out for a no-beer get-together. If someone relapses, there shouldn't be any mocking involved.

You go out and encourage each other in case a relapse happens. The support system you get from friends and buddies helps to reinforce you through the ordeal of getting rid of the bad habit. They help you get over relapses and get you on the right track again.

Friends help to reinforce your motives to stay self-disciplined. Sometimes we all need a helping hand.

Small and Big Rewards

Rewards have a huge impact on our brains. The first thing you should do when you put off a bad habit is to reward yourself. Experts suggest that you shouldn't restrict the rewards to sporadic big-time rewards.

For instance, you want to break the bad habit of living an inactive lifestyle. You can schedule a reward, such as a brand new set of gym clothes, after working out in the gym for four weeks. But four weeks is a long time, and you might end up relapsing within the first week.

What you can do is set up small rewards every time you go to the gym. You can get a protein-rich meal after gym time. Well, you need the protein anyway so that your body can recover from all the exercise that you just did.

Make a reward schedule. Use small rewards for smaller achievements, and then after a set period of time, you can schedule a big reward.

Is It a Habit or Is It an Addiction?

Now, here is a serious question. At one point, you will have to identify whether your bad habit is either just a bad habit or is it already an addiction. Because if it is already an addiction, then you will need some direct medical intervention.

Knowing the difference will help save you from a lot of frustration. Examples of addictive habits include gambling, alcohol, and smoking. Note that these habits are very difficult to break.

To determine whether you're dealing with an ordinary habit or a full-blown addiction, please answer the following question:

If I break this habit, will it cause any changes to my physique and my mentality?

Why answer that question? When you go through the process of breaking an addiction, you will undergo withdrawal symptoms. These symptoms are physiological and very noticeable. Here are the symptoms to look out for:

1. Vomiting
2. Nausea
3. Sweating
4. Shaking

You may need the help of a professional to break an addiction. It will require more than just your effort to get over one. If that is the case, please see immediate medical help.

Breaking Bad Habits to Improve Self-Discipline

Bad habits impede self-mastery, and they are hindrances to self-discipline. To increase your productivity and achieve better self-discipline, you must get rid of any bad habits that you may have picked up along the way.

How to Practice Delayed Gratification and How to Overcome Temptations

One of the most powerful ways to gain impulse control and to improve self-discipline is to practice delayed gratification. What is delayed gratification, and how can you use that to increase your self-mastery? We'll answer that question and more in this section.

What is Delayed Gratification?

Delayed gratification involves the ability to wait for any given amount of time before you can get what it is that you want [18]. Delayed gratification can be a bit difficult for some people, while others have the ability to do it whenever they want.

If you want a more technical definition, here's a brief one:

"Delayed gratification is the ability to postpone an immediate gain in favor of greater and later reward."

Imagine this scenario. You're at a party with your friends, and they bring out all the delicious-looking and nice-smelling scrumptious food. Unfortunately, you're trying to lose weight.

You have two options—give in and enjoy all the food with your friends or just pick the healthy options and stay on your diet and still enjoy the company of your friends. It is the gratification of your senses versus your willpower to stay on a diet.

If you manage to just stick to the salads and maybe a few carrot sticks, then you still get to enjoy the company of friends and eventually lose weight, which is your long-term goal. Does that mean you will never get to enjoy tasty party food ever?

Of course not—you will still get to enjoy that kind of food, but not today.

Your satisfaction with being able to eat like a king will be given to you the day you hit your fitness goals. Once you create a good habit of exercising and eating healthy, you can allow occasional "cheat days." You are essentially delaying the gratification of your senses until that day when you achieve what you want to achieve.

Now imagine your reward if you stay away from the party food this time around: you will be in better shape, look great, and you can occasionally allow yourself to eat more of the great food without feeling guilty and still look great while others look on in envy at your figure.

Now the question is, will you trade what is right before you now for what you can become and have in the future?

And that is basically at the heart of delayed gratification.

It All Began with a Marshmallow

Our understanding of delayed gratification began with the Stanford Marshmallow Experiment. You may have seen videos about this experiment on YouTube, or you may have seen the video as part of an ad on TV.

This experiment was conducted back in 1972 by Walter Mischel. And this is how the experiment went:

- It all began by bringing a child (sometimes two) into a room with a table at the center and a chair to sit on. A plate with a marshmallow was placed in front of the child.
- After placing the treat where the child can see it and, of course, reach for it at will, the researcher would then make a deal. The deal was that the researcher was going to leave the room and return some time later.
- The child (or children) is allowed to eat the marshmallow if they wanted to. However, if the child waited, then the researcher will bring another marshmallow—sort of a reward for waiting.
- Now, here's the catch. If the child ate the first marshmallow, the deal is that the researcher won't give another marshmallow.
- Some of the kids played with the marshmallow until, eventually, they gave in to the temptation. Other kids grabbed the marshmallow as soon as the door closed behind the researcher. Some kids were able to refrain from eating the marshmallow, and thus they were given a second treat.

The researchers observed the kids as they grew up and found that those who were able to control themselves fared better later in life. They even had better SAT scores. This experiment and the said video with the kids became quite popular back in the day.

Of course, that was only the initial study on the theory of delayed gratification. There were follow-up studies too [19].

What the researchers back in the 1970s discovered then led to a whole new understanding of the power of delayed gratification. There were other follow-up studies conducted on the same children who participated as well [20]. These and other studies also helped us understand the factors involved in delayed gratification [21].

Practical Benefits of Delayed Gratification

You don't have to participate in any science experiment just to see the potential benefits of delayed gratification. You can already imagine how it might help you out if you just practiced a little more self-control.

Here are a couple of examples:

- An example of practicing delayed gratification is when a student commits to finishing all his homework first before watching Netflix. Once all of that is done, the student can watch Netflix for the rest of the day. All the important tasks get done, the student can expect to get better grades and have more time to enjoy his favorite shows.
- By choosing not to use your credit card to buy the latest iPhone, you practice delayed gratification. You take on a disciplined approach instead by putting some money aside so you can pay for it in cash.

The practical application of this principle is that you choose to be disciplined first and put distractions behind you. In effect, you are choosing between the easy way out and the hard but more rewarding way.

What Determines Your Ability to Practice Delayed Gratification

Before you can better practice the principle of delayed gratification, you should first understand the factors that contribute to your capability to do it. As it turns out, your experiences and the environment have a huge impact on your ability to forego immediate satisfaction (i.e., delayed gratification).

Researchers from the University of Rochester replicated the marshmallow experiment but added a very important detail [22]. Other than the marshmallow, the kids were either given stickers or crayons as well.

The researcher then promised to give more or better crayons or stickers. Some of the kids were made to wait in vain, and the researcher never fulfilled her promise of more/better crayons or stickers. But some of the kids were given new crayons/stickers a few minutes later.

After that came the marshmallows. Researchers found out that the kids who had negative experiences with the researcher (she never fulfilled her promise of more/better crayons or stickers) were more likely to be unable to practice delayed gratification compared to those who experienced the researcher fulfilling her promises.

Researchers found out that they could sway a child either to practice delayed gratification or not depending on their initial experience with the researcher. If they found out that the researcher was reliable, then they would be more willing to wait and not eat the marshmallow that was on the plate before them.

What researchers learned here is that the ability to delay gratification is not an inherent trait. No one is born with this ability to discipline themselves in such a way. Sure, some are better than others at first. But it only proves that people can learn it. It can be influenced by one's experiences and also the surrounding environment.

Each child who participated in this experiment learned two things:

1. They have the capability to wait for a better reward
2. If they waited for a later gratification of what they wanted, then the end result is worth it

How to Get Better at Delayed Gratification and Overcoming Temptations

The good news is that anyone can get better at delayed gratification. That also means that anyone can get better at resisting temptations and practicing self-control. Just remember that everyone has the ability to do it.

Here are some of the things that you can do to improve:

Start Small

Make the new habit very easy to do so that it is impossible for you to say no. For example, if you hardly exercise, then make it a habit to do jumping jacks every day in the morning for only two minutes—no more, no less.

You want to cut back on drinking soda and sweet drinks? Then make it a habit to skip drinking sodas only on Mondays. You want to start a writing habit but have no gusto to write an entire novel? Then start by writing three-sentence blog posts every day. Keep doing it until it becomes habitual.

Start small. Once you have made that into a habit, then move on to bigger things. At least now you know that you have the power to exercise delayed gratification.

Find Out What is Holding You Back

There was a time when I defined myself as a person who hated working out. I thought I was destined to become out of shape forever. That was until the time when I realized that I needed to live a healthier lifestyle.

I spoke to a fitness coach who was wise enough to probe through my excuses. We found out that I didn't hate exercising. After some serious introspection, the real reason why I didn't like working out is that I didn't feel comfortable about exercising in public.

The thought of seeing other fit and muscular guys outperforming me at the gym frightened me. The bottom line was that I was embarrassed at how I looked being flabby and all.

The solution that was suggested to me made sense—work out at home. I started with yoga videos. Eventually, after a few months, a free yoga class was offered in school, so I went there.

I was able to attend that class because I thought to myself, *At least I'm exercising with people I know*. The gym was different because the people there were all strangers to me. From school yoga I was able to transition into the gym after being comfortable exercising with and in front of other people.

The secret to all of this was finding out the real reason why you can't do what you were supposed to. Dig deep into your excuses.

Expect to Fail and Create a Plan When You Fail

"You're not good enough to be disappointed"—that is from strength and conditioning coach Dan John. When you are new at something, do you think you're already good at it so much that you ought to be disappointed when you fail at it?

Of course not—that means you shouldn't get disappointed when you experience failure since you're not even that good at delayed gratification. Expect to fail. You should expect that you will give in to temptation.

What you should be doing is to prepare a plan to pick yourself up when you do fail. Here are a few ideas:

1. Forget about deadlines; set schedules instead and monitor your progress.
2. Focus on building your new you (i.e., how good you are at delaying gratification) and don't stress out about how fast or slow you are progressing.
3. Never miss two times in a row. What this means is that you may fail once in a while, but once you are aware of the failure, you will want to avoid repeating the same mistake in a row. This prevents you from forming the habit again.

Focus on the Process Not the Performance

Here's a strategy used by the great Jerry Seinfeld: make a commitment to do something that will require you to practice delayed gratification. It can be anything from not having dessert at lunch to not drinking soda. Anything will be great.

Now, print a calendar for that month and hang it by a mirror. Or tape it on the wall right next to the mirror. That way, you see it every day. Each day before you go to bed, mark that day on the calendar with an "X" if you were able to meet your commitment to delay gratification.

After you've been at it, you will notice that you will have some X days on that calendar. Next time you try it, here's what you're going to do—each day, when you've achieved marking an X on that calendar, try to create a chain of Xs.

You were able to do it on Monday, so try your very best to succeed so that you can put an X on Tuesday, and so on. Create a chain and then try not to break the chain. Just focus on making the chain longer and maintaining it.

Don't worry about how well you did. What matters is that you were able to do it. If it is about exercising every day, then don't worry if you only exercise for five minutes or two minutes. The important thing is that you exercised.

Focus on not breaking that chain. Keep at it until whatever commitment you made has become habitual.

Sturgeon's Law and the Pareto Principle

Sturgeon's Law is named after science fiction author Theodore Sturgeon [23]. He coined the saying, "Ninety percent of science fiction is crud, but then, ninety percent of everything is crud." Back in 1951, he called it Sturgeon's Revelation, but everybody just called it Sturgeon's Law instead.

A simplified version of what he said is, "Nothing is always absolutely so." If you prefer having numbers in it, then just stick with the 90% of everything is crap.

Now, the idea behind Sturgeon's Law is similar to another maxim called the Pareto Principle, which is also known as the 80/20 rule—the law of the vital few. A simplified definition of the Pareto Principle is this: 80% of the effects that anyone produces are derived from 20% of the causes.

The Pareto Principle is named after Vilfredo Pareto [24]. Pareto observed that 80% of the wealth of Italy only belonged to 20% of the population. People have observed this to be true in many things as well, such as:

- 20% of input produces 80% of output
- 20% of a product's features produces 80% of its usage
- 20% of all the workers produce 80% of the results
- You only watch 20% of all the channels on cable TV, and you spend 80% of your total viewership on those few channels

As you can see, the only difference between the Pareto Principle and Sturgeon's Law is the percentages. But essentially they mean the same thing. The next question is, what do they have to do with building good habits and breaking bad ones?

The lesson here is that you should focus on the 20% (Pareto) or 10% (Sturgeon) that made a difference in your resolve. Sure, there were times when you failed, but there were times when you succeeded in maintaining a new habit (or breaking the old bad one).

Now, when you focus on the 20% or 10% that brought you the best results, it doesn't matter how much you failed. Focusing on the details of that 20% or 10% will help you produce 80% or 90% of the results later on. Study and analyze the factors that came into play for your small successes and then put them into practice.

With all of this in mind, in the next sections of this book, we will go over four essential habits that you can work on that will help you stay motivated and practice better self-discipline.

Essential Habit #1 – How to Build and Stick to a Workout Plan

If you're anything like me, then one of the hardest parts of any workout plan is showing up for gym time or getting on the road and start jogging. We sometimes think of a billion reasons why we can't go work out on any given day.

Here's an interesting strategy that you can implement to make things work for you when you work out. Here it is—make workouts a no-brainer. Studies show that it takes an average of 18 to 66 days for a habit to stick [25].

You can get that done a lot better if you turn your workouts into no-brainers. Eventually, after a good amount of tries and fails, you will put everything on autopilot.

This chapter goes over several strategies on how you can be more disciplined in your workout. The habits that you pick up from a disciplined approach to your exercise routines can also be used in the other things you do from day-to-day.

Keep It Short and Consistent

Here's a rule of thumb: it is better to have a short gym session each day than to have none. If you don't have much time, then make quality workouts instead of quantity. Ask your gym instructor about HIIT or circuit training instead.

By keeping your routines short, you can be more consistent and disciplined about your workout. It is easier to maintain discipline and consistency about smaller and simpler things. You don't need to allocate huge chunks of time to your exercise routines, and you get a sense of fulfillment because you're getting things done.

Break Things Up

Life can get hectic, and it can happen a lot. So, you can't have a 30-minute workout that day. What you can do is to break up your total workout time into three 10-minute workout chunks. You can do it this way—have 10-minute workouts before breakfast, lunch, and as soon as you get home.

That way, you achieve your goal of working out 30 minutes a day. The same can be applied to other tasks. If you have a financial report to complete, then break it down into smaller doable chunks or subtasks and get things done one subtask at a time.

Be Accountable

Exercise with a friend and agree to meet up at the gym or park (or wherever you two talked about) and go there at the set time. That way, you're also worried about not disappointing your friend. As an added bonus, you also get some quality time with your friend, which makes the routine feel enjoyable.

It will make you more disciplined because you will feel the added responsibility since you agreed to do things with someone else.

Add Variety

Doing the same thing over and over gets boring; you eventually lose focus. It's hard to stay disciplined about something if you lack focus. To get your mind back on track, you should add variety to the things that you're doing.

Try out new things because even the latest and hottest workout can become boring eventually. Try some new cardio each week, follow it up with some yoga, and maybe do some Thai boxing somewhere in your schedule. Try different things to keep you interested and motivated.

Have Fun

People like to keep doing something fun, right? Making working out fun will keep you interested and focused.

Don't be the serious grouch at the gym. Have fun working out with friends. You can turn part of your workout sessions into a kind of contest. You can even post leader boards about who can do the most reps or lift the most weight.

Essential Habit #2 – Maintain a Healthy Diet

Everyone knows that 80% of weight loss has more to do with your diet than exercise. Eating healthy doesn't only help you lose weight, but it also ensures that you have more energy during the day.

It also helps to boost your mood, and a healthy diet reduces your risk for chronic disease and reduces brain fog. However, despite all of these benefits, a lot of us still have problems maintaining and sticking to a healthy diet.

Here are some suggestions that will be helpful at staying disciplined about dieting. Making a diet stick is one of the biggest tests in self-discipline. Those who are truly disciplined about their eating habits have better mental clarity because they are healthier.

Start with Realistic Expectations

Studies have shown that when people are pressured to lose weight, they tend to fail eventually. Your plan to eat healthily will backfire when you get a lot of pressure to get results fast. Research even suggests that when you feel this pressure that you will have a higher tendency to drop out of any kind of weight loss program within a year [26].

The better alternative is to set realistic expectations. Talk with your fitness coach and set your expectations straight.

Clean Up Your Pantry/Fridge

It should be obvious that it is difficult to stick to a healthy meal plan when you are surrounded by temptation in the form of unhealthy food. The simple solution, of course, is to do an inventory of your fridge.

Clean it out. Remove the unhealthy snacks, treats, and food options. Give them away to charity or to a friend who may want them. Next, make a new grocery list full of healthy food options and then go out and buy them.

Here are some foods that nutritionists have recommended to help reduce brain fog:

- *Cocoa* – boosts overall brain power, improves memory, and helps you concentrate
- *Nutritional Yeast* – rich in B Vitamins that improves overall cognitive function
- *Turmeric* – rich in curcumin, which reduces cognitive decline
- *Spinach* – rich in lutein, which can prevent cognitive impairment

- *Eggs* – loaded with lots of choline that enhances cognition and memory
- *Avocados* – rich in Vitamin E, which has been shown to slow cognitive decline

Schedule a healthy diet meal plan. Make sure that the recipes are tasty and include recipes that you love. Being more disciplined in your food choices translates to better discipline in other aspects of your life. Best-selling author and life coach Stephen Covey explains that smaller victories translate to bigger and more fulfilling victories.

Find Out What Really Motivates You

You have to write down your goals. You may even have employed a vision board. If that is the case, then make sure to include a vision of yourself having that healthy figure.

You can even include a picture of all the healthy food that you want to eat. Write down the reasons why you want to eat a healthy diet. You can make a collage out of your vision or dream board and take a picture using your phone.

Every time you feel discouraged, or you are tempted to eat unhealthy food, then you can look at that photo and be reminded of the reasons why you wanted to eat healthy in the first place. You can even use it as the wallpaper of your phone so that it is the first picture you see when you answer a call or send out a text message.

Having a clear-cut goal will motivate you to keep going. Even if you fail sometimes, your goals will keep you committed and disciplined.

Skip the All or Nothing Mindset

Do you often think that your diet is ruined because you had some ice cream or you gave in to your cake craving? That is an all or nothing mindset and isn't going to help you.

The same is true when it comes to work and your goals. Do you call it quits when you fail to close that sale? By skipping the all or nothing mindset, you keep going despite your failures.

Everyone makes mistakes, and just because you failed that one time it doesn't mean that you have already ruined your diet—or you're a failed entrepreneur.

Forgive yourself on the spot and pick up where you left off. If you have reached your maximum calorie intake for that day because of that ice cream, then just go on with the rest of the day. Resume your diet immediately and let bygones be bygones.

Change Your Diet and Exercise Plan at the Same Time

When you try a new diet, it should be complemented by a new exercise plan. Studies suggest that when you make this tandem, your chances of success will improve since both of these changes tend to reinforce each other [27].

When two habits reinforce one another, your chances of maintaining both habits increase. *Here's an example. You want more consistent results at work—let's say you want to make it to work on time every time? Then make it a habit to get enough sleep each night so you can wake up early and refreshed every morning.*

You can also complement that with food that can help you wake up better each morning, such as apples, eggs, dark chocolate, red meat, and spinach. Making healthy food choices is a display and practice in better self-discipline. These are habits that help you become more disciplined.

Have a Healthy Snack in Your Pocket Always

Keeping a healthy snack on hand will help you avoid buying unhealthy snacks from the vending machine (or anywhere you usually buy them from). That way, when you get hungry or when you're tempted by unhealthy food options, you have something to munch on. This practice helps you stick to your health and fitness plan.

One of the best ways to stay disciplined is to avoid temptation. Are you tempted to put things off and procrastinate? Then find something that can take your mind off the temptation, like a photo of your kids or maybe a dream vacation you're saving up for. Keep it on hand so that you can be reminded of better things and resist the enticement.

Plan Ahead When You Go Out or Travel

Sticking to a healthy diet plan is easy when you're at home. You have all your healthy food options there. However, you can't say the same thing for restaurants or diners, especially when you're on the road traveling to some distant point in the country.

When you have to travel, then you should research the restaurants that serve healthy food options that you will find as you make your journey. Plan your trip so that you will make stops at those restaurants, bars, stores, or diners.

And just to make sure, in case you can't find any place that serves healthy options, then pack your own snacks and meals.

Start Your Day with a High Protein Breakfast

Starting your day with a high protein diet will reduce the chances of getting hunger pangs or cravings. Note, however, that your breakfast should be well balanced but should have more protein.

Protein takes longer to digest, and that means you will feel full for most of the day. Studies show that doing this might even help you keep your blood sugar levels steady [28]. You also tend to avoid overeating for the rest of the day as well [29].

Remember That It Takes Time to Change Your Eating Habits

How many years have you been on that unhealthy diet of yours? Was it five or maybe ten or so years? Do you think you can change that in a week? The answer is no.

It will take time before you can replace unhealthy eating habits with healthy eating habits. A lot of times, those old habits will creep up on you. And that's okay because that will happen from time to time.

What's important is that you get back to your healthy eating habits as soon as you can. Give it as much time as it needs. The important thing is that those little changes are piling up, and you are getting healthier steadily and surely.

Being healthy and making healthy food choices improves mental clarity. Your ability to focus diminishes when your brain doesn't get the nutrition it needs. Adding foods that help to reduce brain fog to your diet helps increase mental focus.

Essential Habit #3 – Sleep/Wake Up Early

Do you hit the snooze button first thing in the morning? Let me guess—you also have a zombie routine to go with it too. Getting up in the morning is usually one of the first challenges that we face.

Sometimes you just want to stay in bed just for once in your life. Sometimes you just want to get over that sleepy feeling early in the morning so you can get your day started with a lot more energy and enthusiasm.

Chances are if you feel that way most mornings, then you may be sleep-deprived. That might also mean you need to do some tweaking concerning your sleeping routine.

The good news is that there are things you can do to help you sleep well and wake up early with a lot of energy to begin your day.

Deciding to wake up early is a test of your self-discipline. By choosing to get enough sleep, sleeping early, and waking up early, you practice self-discipline first thing in the morning. You begin your day with a disciplined start.

Admiral McRaven explained that the simple act of waking up early in the morning and making his bed improved his productivity. This habit radically transformed his life.

Signs That You May Be Sleep-Deprived

Here are some of the telltale signs that you may be sleep-deprived:

- Excessive yawning
- Increased appetite
- Brain fog
- Excessive daytime sleepiness
- Fatigue
- Lack of motivation
- Irritability

Note that if you experience two or more of the symptoms mentioned above, then you may be having quality sleep problems. Being sleep-deprived is a huge factor when it comes to waking up early in the morning.

Why Is It Difficult to Wake Up in the Morning

There is more to it than just loving your bed and hating the morning. Taking medication, certain medical conditions, and lifestyle factors can sometimes make it really difficult to wake up in the morning.

Other than being sleep-deprived, there are other possible causes for why you may be having a hard time waking up in the morning. Here's a partial list of possible causes:

- Chronic pain
- Medications such as muscle relaxers, beta-blockers, and antidepressants
- Circadian rhythm sleep disorders
- Depression
- Anxiety
- Stress
- Sleep deficiency
- Sleep apnea

How to Wake Up Early in the Morning

Now there are several things that you can do to help you wake up early in the morning. However, do take note that if you do have sleep deprivation problems and other disorders, then you might need some medical intervention to address this problem.

Improve Bedtime Routines

One of the first things that you can do is to improve your routine before going to bed. If you're not doing this already, then you are, in effect, sabotaging your efforts to wake up better in the morning.

Things, like using your phone or taking caffeinated drinks, can disrupt your sleeping patterns. Cellphones emit blue light that prevents people from getting to sleep. Caffeine is a substance that will keep you alert and, of course, prevents you from sleeping.

To sleep better, you should avoid using your phone an hour before you go to bed. You should also avoid taking caffeinated drinks at a later part of the day. Here are other things that can disrupt your circadian rhythm that you should avoid:

- Drinking alcohol before bedtime
- Taking too many naps during the day
- Drinking coffee or any caffeinated drink six hours before going to bed

- Looking at screens that emit blue light before going to bed (includes phones, laptops, tablets, etc.)

Make sure to avoid these things to improve your bedtime routine. You can also sleep with the light turned off or dimmed. Use a lampshade on your bed stand to reduce the amount of light in the room when you sleep if you find it hard to sleep in the dark.

Move Your Alarm Further Away

The snooze button is truly tempting, isn't it? Getting a few more minutes of sleep can sometimes be very irresistible. But if you do that, you will just get fragmented sleep, which won't do you much good anyway.

So, here's a little suggestion—keep that alarm further away. We usually put it on the bedside table, but that is still too close for comfort. I suggest that you move your alarm all the way to the other side of the room. Place it on a chair away from your bed if you have to.

If you do it that way, then you will be forced to get up from the bed and walk over to the alarm. Sometimes that is all that is needed to get you started first thing in the morning.

Exercise Regularly

People with chronic fatigue syndrome may find it very beneficial to exercise regularly. Research suggests that it can increase energy levels, reduce fatigue, and it will also help them sleep better [30].

It can also help people sleep at night and wake up better in the morning, especially for those suffering from depression, anxiety, insomnia, and excessive sleepiness.

Get Some More Sunlight

Sunlight regulates our circadian rhythm. A healthier circadian rhythm will improve the quality of your sleep, which in turn helps you wake up earlier and with more energy in the morning.

The goal is to get some sunshine first thing in the morning. The sun does not just boost your energy levels, it also gives your mood a much-needed pick-me-up. You can also make it a morning routine to open the blinds as soon as you get up from bed.

Other than that, you can also make it a habit to take a morning walk. Another thing I suggest is to take your morning cup of coffee and enjoy it outside under the early morning sun.

But what if it is a cloudy day and the sun isn't out? The best thing you can do in that scenario is to just turn on the lights in the house.

When All Else Fails

Let's say you tried all suggestions and you still have trouble waking up early in the morning. On top of that, you also notice that you have sleep disorder signs as well. So, what do you do?

In that case, you may have to talk to your doctor and ask for a referral so you can see a sleep specialist. A sleep study can help to diagnose your sleeping disorder. This might be necessary to help you resolve symptoms of morning fatigue.

Some of the known sleep disorders include restless leg syndrome (RLS) and chronic insomnia. The type of treatment will also vary depending on the condition that you will be diagnosed with.

A sleep specialist might provide you with any of the following treatments:

- Surgery for obstructive sleep apnea
- Behavioral therapy
- A breathing device to help you stop snoring
- Melatonin therapy
- Prescription drugs for RLS and other sleep aids

By addressing the causes of sleep depravity, you sleep better and wake up better each day. Being refreshed at the beginning of the day sets you up for making better choices and a more disciplined approach to the rest of your day. You can't be mentally tough if your mind can't beat the call of your mattress.

Essential Habit #4 – Work Smart: Eat the Frog

When you hear the term "eat the frog," it can be one of the weirdest things that you will ever hear in your life. But it is one of the biggest habits that you can develop, especially when it comes to working smart.

Where Did That Phrase Come From?

The man that came up with that phrase is no other than American classical author Mark Twain. His original statement was this:

"If it's your job to eat a frog, it's best to do it first thing in the morning. And if it's your job to eat two frogs, it's best to eat the biggest one first."

No, he didn't mean to gross us out when he said that. But this is what he meant. The frog represents the worst or the most unpleasant thing you have to do during the day. It can be anything.

You hate doing that thing so much that it could be the first thing that you will procrastinate on. Simply put, what Mark Twain is suggesting is that we should prioritize the worst task on our to-do list. Well, that is giving it a more modern twist and interpretation since the concept of a to-do list wasn't available in his time.

Which is Your Biggest Frog?

As it was explained earlier, a frog represents a task that you have to do today. Now, we also mentioned that this task is the worst one that you have to do today. Well, it's not necessarily the worst thing you have ever done or will do.

When we say worst task, we mean that it is one of the most important tasks that you will have to do that day. It may be important, but it is the one among all those really important tasks that you will most likely put off.

If you can put it off until tomorrow—never mind how important it is—you will do it. You will procrastinate doing it. It can be anything from slides that your boss is waiting for, it could be a dreaded phone call that you have to make, a doctor's appointment, that annual physical, breaking up with someone, or it could be a deadline that you need to beat.

The Rationale behind the Frog-Eating Habit

Why do you have to do the worst item on your to-do list first? There should be some form of benefit behind it. Other authors and productivity experts have caught up on the idea or principle of eating the frog first [31].

One of the most well-known authors to follow suit is Brian Tracy [32]. His book *Eat That Frog,* which was published in 2006, is now a classic. He paraphrases Mark Twain slightly by saying that you should "eat your frog," which is pretty much what Twain originally meant to say.

Tracy explains that the best leaders and top executives are the ones that have made it a habit to tackle the major task first thing each working day. It should become a routine habit if you want to achieve the highest levels of productivity and performance.

Launch yourself into that major task and muster the discipline to get it done before everything else. Turn this into a daily habit, and you will have done more than any other person in the office every single day.

Too Many Meetings

Tracy notes further that one of the biggest flaws in many organizations today is that we have so many meetings. It's like we are addicted to meetings. It doesn't matter which organization you're looking at.

It happens to small businesses, medium-scale enterprises, large multimillion-dollar businesses, churches, non-profit organizations, BINGO clubs, and other organizations. We all do a lot of talking and make a lot of great plans, but only a few are getting the job done.

Dive! Dive! Dive!

The secret, Tracy explains, is to make it a habit to get into action immediately. The first thing you should do when you get into work mode is to identify your biggest frog. And within the next five minutes, you should hack into it until it is done.

No Shortcuts

Anyone who has ever cultivated this habit of eating the frog first will tell you that there are no shortcuts. You will fail to do it some days, but you just have to keep doing it every single day until it becomes a habit.

One thing they promise, though, is that when you make it a habit, this "eat the frog first principle" can be addictive. You get the most difficult task done first thing each day, and then you're all set for easy street the rest of the day.

One last thing is that at the end of the day, you should identify the frog for the following day and make a note about it that you will see as soon as you step into your work zone. That way you save time—you no longer have to sit around deciding which one is your biggest frog each day. You just dive into it as soon as you arrive at the office.

Essential Habit #5 – Mindfulness

You may have heard of mindfulness as a kind of meditation, but it is actually more than that. Yes, there is a meditative part to it, but it is also a state of mind and a habit. Apart from helping you learn to sharpen your focus, it also has a lot of other benefits.

What is Mindfulness?

Jon Kabat-Zinn [33], the man who popularized mindfulness in the West, described mindfulness in the simplest way—he described it as:

"The practice of being aware."

Note that mindfulness and mindfulness meditation are two separate things. Mindfulness is a day-to-day practice, while mindfulness meditation is a type of meditation.

Although, do take note that Kabat-Zinn also describes mindfulness as a type of meditation. The two terms get interchanged a lot, I know. Mindfulness meditation has more to do with what Buddhists practice known as *samatha*—but that is a whole different topic in itself.

You'll see the difference as we go over the details in the discussion below. For now, you can think of mindfulness as a habit, and mindfulness meditation is, of course, a type of meditation—but you get the same benefits from both.

Mindfulness is the practice (or habit) of purposefully putting your attention and focus on the things occurring in the present moment. You take everything that is happening in stride and do not apply any judgment, and accept events for what they are.

Some say that this is one of the key elements for anyone who is in search of true and lasting happiness.

Studies have shown that if this practice is done correctly, it has the power to reduce anxiety and stress [34]. It can also reduce that feeling of being overwhelmed, and it will help you to appreciate all the things that are happening around you.

You live from one moment to the other fully and wholly. It has enabled thousands to navigate an ever-changing and chaotic world. Many are using it today to help them overcome and cope with a hectic and sometimes insane schedule.

How Can You Benefit from a Mindfulness Habit?

We have already mentioned a few benefits of being mindful. We'll go over several more benefits that might convince you to adopt such a behavior.

Benefit #1: Prevents Overthinking and Anxiety

One of the symptoms of anxiety is the tendency to overthink things. When you start worrying over anything, your brain will begin to exercise a vice-like hold on such a thought. That is why sometimes it is very hard to let go of such worries.

In my experience, when I worry about something, I enter into what is known as a *thought loop*. I go through all possible bad outcomes—especially the worst-case scenario I could come up with. And then I play that back over and over in my head until it consumes me.

This isn't something healthy or useful. Going through a thought loop won't stop or prevent the terrible imagined events from happening. According to one study, people who practice mindfulness tend to reduce this frequency of rumination [35].

Another study suggests that those who practice mindfulness are able to reduce feelings of stress and anxiety [36].

Benefit #2: Improves Performance, Concentration, and Memory

Having the habit of concentrating on the task at hand improves your overall performance. It empowers you to concentrate on one thing at a time. You can learn to focus on something solely and not get distracted.

That also has another benefit; it improves one's cognitive ability. Experts are currently using this practice as a method to help people who have mind-wandering tendencies. According to research, students who practice mindfulness learn to pay attention to everything both inside the classroom and in their personal lives [37].

According to another study, it is possible that mindfulness meditation can aid in the thickening of the cerebral cortex [38]. The cerebral cortex is that part of the brain that is responsible for learning, concentration, and memory.

Benefit #3: Cognitive Flexibility

Are you easily affected by comments, news, music, media, and other things happening around you? Do you quickly react to negative criticism? If you usually find yourself losing control when something bad happens, then maybe a mindfulness habit can help you, according to one study [39].

Benefit #4: Alleviates Stress

Mindfulness as a practice and a habit can shield you from the chaos and complexity of life in our modern society. It's a buffer that you can use—you focus on what's in front of you, and your mind doesn't wander off to the worries and insecurities presented to you through your everyday experiences.

Benefit #5: Improves Sleep

Note that mindfulness meditation is a very relaxing activity. It helps people find peace and quiet in their lives. By doing this type of meditation before bedtime, people have found a way to improve the quality of their sleep.

According to one study, mindfulness meditation increases the mind's relaxation response [40]. It facilitates better control over one's autonomic nervous system—that part of your brain that is responsible for relaxation and better awareness.

Those are the top 5 benefits of a mindfulness habit. There are others, of course, like increased pain relief, promoting better mental health, improving one's sex life, fostering happy relationships, enhancing creativity, reducing the incidence of burnout, and boosting academic performance, among many others.

How to Practice Mindfulness Now

You don't have to be an expert to practice mindfulness. You may already have practiced it at least once before. Do you drive a car? Do you remember the first time you took a driving test?

Were you totally focused on driving and paying attention to the examiner's instructions? You were totally aware that the test examiner was watching you, trying to see if you were using the mirrors properly and how you handle the vehicle.

Of course, you're not expected to make small talk, but you will have to communicate with the examiner from time to time. If the weather was bad that day, you would have to tell the test examiner that you're slowing down due to weather conditions, but you were still paying attention to how you were driving.

There are other moments when you had to concentrate really hard and you were instantly super focused. You had a heightened awareness of what was going on. If you play sports, then you may have already experienced this state as well.

Now, imagine having that level of focus instinctively. You can toggle into that state at will and forget all the worries and just get things done fast and efficiently.

Here are simple steps that you can follow to practice mindfulness as a habit. After the next section, we will go over some mindfulness meditation exercises so you can practice mindfulness as a habit.

Step #1: Allocate a space and choose a time for mindfulness practice

You will need to allocate some time and a special place to practice mindfulness at first. But when you get the hang of it, you will be able to enter a mindfulness state at will. For now, dedicate both time and a place where you can do mindfulness exercises.

Dedicate a few minutes of your time each day to practice mindfulness. It should be a time when you're not rushing or when the house is peaceful. When I first did this, I set my alarm early enough so that I woke up 30 minutes ahead of everyone else in the house.

That gave me time to brush my teeth, prepare some coffee, and get comfy. I didn't ask Alexa (yes, I bought one) for any flash briefings since I had the tendency to get depressed because of the news.

I also set up a portion of the living room—a little corner by the window where the kids don't usually go to frolic and play. It has to be done in this special place so as to help trigger your mind that it is time to relax and calm down.

You can choose any time of the day you want to do your mindfulness exercise. You can do it first thing in the morning or when you get back home from work. Some practice it 30 minutes before going to bed at night. The choice is up to you.

You also get to choose how much time you want to practice mindfulness. I suggest that you start with five to ten minutes at first. And then you can extend it to 15 to 20 minutes. Now set your alarm for five or ten minutes—or whatever length of time you intended to allocate to mindfulness.

Next, after setting the time and place, go to that place at the appointed time, and sit down. Relax.

Inhale and then exhale. Repeat this until you feel calm.

Step #2: Focus and choose to do so despite distractions and challenges

It will take some effort to focus on what you are doing while you're sitting in your special space for mindfulness. Your thoughts will wander about your problems, the mistakes you made in the past, and a lot of other things that will try to grab your attention.

At this time, choose to focus on what you are doing—sitting down and trying to relax.

Inhale and then exhale—repeat this while you're seated there.

Step #3: Allow yourself that time to do nothing

Make a conscious effort to focus on what you are doing—you're sitting. You're trying to relax. Try to empty your mind and just enjoy the peace and quiet as you sit down in your special place.

Think about this—the past is long gone, and you can't do anything about it. The future is unknown to all of us, so why worry? The only thing you have absolute control over is the present. That is what you have complete control over right now.

Remember that this is a moment for your mind to recharge. Just sit there and empty your mind. Leave your worries behind. Try not to think about your problems.

Inhale and then exhale—repeat this while you're seated there.

Step #4: Try not to look at the clock

You will be tempted to look at the clock or check your phone from time to time. If you can rearrange the furniture, make sure that your back is turned away from the clock. Place your phone at a distant table, counter, or another surface. Trust that your alarm clock will go off at the designated time.

Inhale and then exhale—repeat this while you're seated there.

Step #5: Pay attention but don't judge and let it all pass

Notice that while you're trying to relax, your thoughts, memories, and feelings will creep into your mind. As you sit there looking at the wall and other things around you, a lot of things will trigger your memories.

You will recall conversations, things that you have said, experiences that you are proud of, and things that you have done that you regret to this day. What do you do when all of that crashes on you like an avalanche?

The answer is to let it all pass. Just observe how you feel and how you react to them. Try to relax and let all the things that grab your attention pass away.

Inhale and then exhale—repeat this while you're seated there.

Step #6: Acknowledge your self-judgments and self-doubt

It is okay to have judgments—we all judge. And in fact, we even judge ourselves. But don't let your judgments about your failures or successes overwhelm you. Some of your self-judgments may even be so harsh to make you beat yourself up.

Sometimes self-doubt will also creep into your thoughts. You will judge yourself as unworthy, not worth it, undeserving, you can't do it, you're too weak, you don't have the willpower, or some other poorly assessed judgment of your character.

Don't do it. Don't allow judgments and self-doubt get the best of you.

Note that self-judgments are just like thoughts—they will come along, but then they will pass and fade away. They are not permanent. **Act like a quiet observer**. Listen to those self-judgments and then watch them fade away. Don't get caught up in them.

Step #7: Return to the Present

Now, this is the key here. All mindfulness exercises and all forms of mindfulness meditation will teach you that you need to redirect your attention back to the present. That in itself is at the core of being mindful that is being in the moment.

If your mind wanders, then forgive yourself and go back to focusing on what you are doing—trying to relax, inhaling, and exhaling.

If you begin to doubt yourself, then allow your doubts to fade, and then focus once more on your relaxed moment. Inhale and then exhale. Relax.

Do the same when a memory comes to mind. Acknowledge it and then allow it to fade. Finally, go back to the present. Breathe in and then breathe out.

Mindfulness Meditation Sample: Body Scan

The following is a simple mindfulness meditation exercise called the body scan. This is one of the first meditation exercises that you will usually be taught if you decide to get a meditation coach.

The body scan meditation will only take three to five minutes. Some people enjoy this exercise so much that they spend anywhere from 20 to 45 minutes. It's a great way to calm your mind and regain your focus.

You can do the body scan while sitting in your dedicated space for mindfulness practice, or you can do it while lying in bed. It's up to you which place you would like to do it.

Some mindfulness practitioners who can already do mindfulness exercises anywhere can do this exercise while sitting on the bus, while having a short coffee break at work, or while enjoying a nice afternoon sitting in the park.

But I would recommend that you do it in your dedicated space first. You will be applying most of the steps as it was described earlier for mindfulness exercises. For this meditation, I would suggest that you read the script below and record yourself.

You can record your voice using your phone as you sit in your special space. Once you're done recording, sit, relax, inhale/exhale slowly, and then hit play.

If you're ready, here's the script (no need to mention the numbers). Read slowly and don't rush:

1. Sit in a relaxed position.
2. Lie back until you feel comfy.
3. Close your eyes.
4. Take five deep breaths
5. Now, inhale slowly and deeply
6. Next, exhale slowly. emptying your lungs of all the air inside
7. Inhale deeply and slowly again
8. And then exhale deeply and slowly again
9. Repeat this slow and steady inhale and exhale pattern three more times
10. Keep repeating this breathing pattern until I tell you to open your eyes
11. Pay attention to how your feet are lying on the floor
12. Try to feel the weight of your feet as they press on the floor
13. Notice how your feet feel as they are pressed against the floor
14. Follow that sensation and then trace the sensations of your legs from your feet all the way to your knees
15. Notice how your knees feel
16. Bring your attention to your buttocks and the sensation that you feel as your bottom is pressed against the chair or bed
17. Breathe in and breathe out slowly
18. Feel the sensations that your hips are sending to your mind.
19. Trace the sensations going up your back all the way to your neck.
20. Notice the weight of your shoulders
21. Focus on the sensations that you feel in your arms as they gently lie on the surface of the chair or bed
22. Next, focus on the sensations being felt by your hands. Are your hands tense? Then release the tension in your hands.
23. Go back to your shoulders, neck, and throat. Notice how they feel.
24. Breathe in and breathe out. Relax.
25. Go up to your jaw and pay attention to how it feels. Is it tense? Then release the tension in your jaw. Relax. Breathe in and then breathe out.
26. Pay attention to the sensations that you are feeling on your face and head.
27. Do you feel any tension there as well? If there is any tension, then release and relax.
28. Breathe in and breathe out.

29. Count slowly from one to ten.
30. Now, open your eyes.

At the end of this exercise, you can go back to your regular breathing pattern. Let the feeling of calm and peace linger. You can even just sit in your chair or lie on the bed a minute or two more just to bask in the peace that you have just experienced.

Now, off you go to the rest of your day.

Chapter 4: More Actionable Tips to Build Self-Discipline

"Failure will never overtake me if my determination to succeed is strong enough."

(Og Mandino)

Do you need to reward yourself for becoming more motivated? When we try something new or try to form new habits, we are usually faced with discomfort. Sometimes we just want it to end, and so we throw in the towel and quit.

Is there a way to get rid of the discomfort of trying to obtain new habits? But maybe the discomfort is the key to your success, and you just didn't know it. In the previous chapter, we covered a lot of tips and tricks as well as habits that you can use to increase your level of self-discipline.

In this chapter, we will go over more of those tips that are also equally actionable. The topics we will discuss cover different facets of our lives. By doing so, we get a more well-rounded view of ultimately attaining self-discipline.

That One Simple Trick That Will Boost Your Motivation to Do Anything

Is it hard to stay motivated to do something? Yes, it is difficult. You wouldn't be reading all the way to this chapter if it was easy. Some might even say at this point is that what they thought they knew about motivation and self-discipline is wrong.

We have all been there—when we were excited about a new goal or habit that we want to achieve. We felt motivated, and we even believed that we could get it done. Maybe we made some progress along the way and that still kept us motivated.

But then we hit a proverbial wall.

There is a point when we can't keep moving forward. In short, there comes a point when we get stuck. So what do we usually do when discouragement gets in the way? We quit. And that's it.

Sometimes it all turns into a vicious cycle where we set a new goal, get excited and worked up about it, we try and fail, get some success, and then hit that wall again and then quit.

So, how do you get over that barrier? Why is there a barrier there in the first place? What's up with that wall?

Beating the Traditional Model for Motivation

There is a traditional model among researchers when it comes to our understanding of self-discipline and self-motivation. So what's the traditional model? Well, you're actually very familiar with it.

That model is the one that involves providing incentives to someone so that they will pursue a given course of action. It's like the carrot and stick method. You know how people used to make donkeys move forward? Tie a carrot at the end of a stick and hold that in front of a donkey (or some other animal), and it will keep chasing after the carrot.

Sometimes incentivizing works, but the magic of that method will have limits. Even the lure of an incentive or reward has its limits. Some researchers tweaked this model a little bit.

For instance, experts from the University of Pennsylvania say that how you deploy or provide the incentive can affect the recipient's motivation. This is from a study that they conducted [41].

That study suggests that people fear the loss of something more than we crave for rewards. The participants of that study were split into different groups. One group was promised to get a certain reward in dollars if they could make 7,000 steps each day.

They did the opposite with the other group. The researchers gave the monetary reward immediately to the test participants. But the deal was that the researchers would take away a certain amount from the money each time participants failed to reach the goal of 7,000 steps.

So who do you think were able to follow through with their commitment? If you guessed that it was the second group—the ones that were first given the reward—then you are right.

It would appear that the fear of losing the reward was bigger than any incentive of getting a reward. That might sound useful in certain applications, but it isn't exactly the one that you will want to use when it comes to self-motivation.

The other limit to that approach is that it is still the carrot and stick method. Whether you give the reward in advance or you give the reward after, it is still the old model. And as time goes on, the lure of the reward or incentive will fail to motivate or even spark the interest of people.

Working with the Science behind Motivation

If you want to improve your motivation, then you must first understand the science behind it. Studies show that your brain tends to deplete its glucose stores every time you exert any form of self-control [42]. That includes times when you try so hard to stick to a goal, try a new habit, or even when you just try to push yourself to get things done.

However, in another study, students were observed as they underwent an adaptive learning program [43]. The study suggests that our ability to learn, remember, and stay motivated tends to increase over time.

Do we get tired due to continuous effort? The answer is yes. But we can stay motivated to continue if we use short, frequent bursts of activity instead of one continuous nonstop effort.

That One Simple Trick

Here's how you can use that scientific discovery to stay motivated to achieve a certain goal or obtain a new habit. This latest study shows that motivation and self-control doesn't decrease.

It's just that the brain just doesn't want to focus on that task that you have been doing for the last several hours or so. Your brain will want to maintain a balance and thus try to pull you away from that task so you can tend to other essential things as well—food, sleep, emotional support, etc., that you may already be neglecting due to continuous effort.

The same study suggests that after a minimum of 30 minutes performing the same task, your brain will want you to switch to something else. This has been identified as a kind of survival instinct. The more you switch to different tasks, the better.

To hack this natural phenomenon, you should break down the new habit or task into several different chunks. Each of these sub-tasks should contribute to attaining the complete and original goal.

So let's say your goal or task is to complete a web page project. You can break it down into several sub-tasks such as:

- Article writing
- Page design
- Marketing
- Graphics
- Interactive features
- Social media features
- Videos

To stay motivated to finish the said task on time, what you should do is to assign 30 minutes for each of these tasks. You can do article writing for 30 minutes and then take a quick break.

But when you get back, switch your task to video content creation. After that, take another break, and when you get back, do some page design or marketing. If you vary your tasks from time to time, you can stay motivated and complete the entire project at the end of the day without feeling spent.

This same technique can be applied to habit-building and other goals that you might want to work on.

Move Towards Discomfort – How Discomfort Builds Character

You may have heard a preacher say at the pulpit or over the TV that pain and discomfort builds character. Well, don't worry. This next tip won't be so preachy. But there may be some golden nugget of truth to what pastors and preachers have been saying there.

Believe it or not, studies suggest that the more you live an easy and carefree life, the more it gets worse for you. The fact is that enduring tragedy and facing hardship is actually something good.

Discomfort, Pain, and Chaos Builds Character

Everyone endures pain and hardship at one time or another. It's part of the human experience. They bring about emotional upheavals but guess what—they can also bring about positive change.

We can come out of these difficult times with a newfound vision, greater strength, and better motivation. It is also a very basic human instinct to protect or shield ourselves from negative and painful experiences [44]. It's a survival instinct—you feel pain when you touch something, then you remember instinctively never to do it again.

You can also see this second hand when parents protect their children from getting hurt. Sometimes they can be overprotective and not allow their kids to run around or play on the playground.

However, getting your knee scraped or scratched during playtime is natural. It can even help a child learn and develop a lot faster. Children will encounter different attitudes while playing with other kids. You don't need to overshadow them all the time—allow them to experience varying attitudes, and some of those attitudes may even be offensive or perhaps even hurtful.

But expect your child to learn how to cope with difficult circumstances like that. It will become a life lesson that your child will learn.

A Paradigm Shift

What I'm asking you to do here is to go into a paradigm shift. Embrace discomfort and understand that it takes a little of that to increase your capacity to achieve and stay disciplined.

You can compare this idea to how our muscles work. If we don't use our muscles, atrophy will take over. Instead of growing strong, our muscles will grow weak and skinny. But if we use them during workouts, we'll get muscle pain. But that is how the muscle will grow—the growth happens after the pain.

Intermittent Fasting

You might be prompted to ask how intermittent fasting helps you become more disciplined. The answer is simple—it takes a lot of willpower to say no to food, especially when you're feeling hungry.

By choosing to fast and skip meals, you improve your self-mastery. You will become better able to resist the temptation of eating unhealthy food. This allows you to practice restraint and self-control, which you can apply in other decisions that you have to make.

Apart from that, intermittent fasting also brings you a lot of other benefits as well.

If you want to fast track healing and lose weight, then you should try intermittent fasting. Intermittent fasting is one of the trending ways people are losing weight today. However, it isn't easy. It is a health and fitness trend, and it is backed by actual science [45].

Intermittent fasting is not easy. It requires a lot of discipline and commitment. It will be difficult to practice during your first few weeks. You will feel the hunger pangs that will make you want to get something to eat. But if you learn to get over the initial challenge and strive for self-mastery, you will learn that you have better control over hunger and the temptation from sugary and unhealthy foods.

Do take note, however, that before you try it, you should first consult with your doctor. Some people who have certain conditions may be prohibited from trying this weight loss regimen.

Studies have shown that intermittent fasting has a lot of health benefits [46]. It may help people heal faster and live longer. But it may also be one of the most difficult habits that you will be doing in your life.

Intermittent Fasting: What It Is

Intermittent fasting is not a diet, but it is an eating pattern. In this eating pattern, you will have some fasting periods and also some eating periods as well. There are no specifications as to what food you're supposed to eat.

Again, remember that it is not a diet. There are different patterns or types of intermittent fasting too.

Intermittent fasting isn't new. Everyone goes on a fast every day. Why do you think we call the first meal of the day as "break-fast?" It literally means to end one's fast.

Let's say you have dinner at 7 pm and then go to bed. You then have breakfast at 7 am the following day. Guess what you just did? You had a 12-hour fast. You didn't eat anything.

Fasting is something incorporated within many religions too. But we're not going to push any form of religion here. We're just interested in this eating pattern.

Methods of Intermittent Fasting

I did mention that there are several types of intermittent fasting. We won't go into detail about them, but I will prescribe only the simplest and easiest methods in this list:

1. **The 5:2 Diet**: You are to consume only 500 to 600 calories on two days each week. That means you will fast for two days, but these are not two consecutive days.
2. **Eat Stop Eat Method**: This method will require you to go on a 24-hour fast. For instance, you will start fasting after dinner at 8 pm. The next meal that you will be having will be dinner the following day. This is a tough way to fast, I know.
3. **16/8 Method:** This method gives you only an eight-hour window to eat during your chosen fasting days. It can be noontime to 8 pm, 10 am to 6 pm, etc. Simply put, you fast for 16 hours and eat within the remaining eight hours, ergo 16/8.

Intermittent fasting drastically reduces your calorie intake, which, of course, has massive weight loss results. It isn't the easiest weight loss system to try and stick to.

I recommend the 16/8 method, and I do it twice each week. You don't need to go on an intermittent fast every day. It is the easiest of the three methods described above since you have a good enough amount of time to eat and get nourished.

Note that during your fasting days, you are allowed to drink water. It is not a total fast without food and drink.

Note that there are other intermittent fasting methods that I didn't mention here. There is also meal-skipping, alternate-day fasting, and then there is the warrior diet. For now, stick to the three that I described above, and I highly recommend that you try the 16/8 method if your doctor gives you the go signal.

Remember to **check with your doctor first before you start fasting***.*

How to Stick to an Intermittent Fasting Regimen

Since intermittent fasting can be the toughest thing that you will be doing in your life to date, you will have to exercise a lot of discipline and self-control. The first few fasting days will be a test of your resolve and willpower. If you get over the first week, you will gain more self-control and discipline. Here are a few tips to help you stick with it.

- Eat nutrient-dense foods during fasting days. This includes foods that are rich in minerals, vitamins, and other nutrients as well. Eating those foods will help keep your blood sugar steady. You should eat a balanced diet during fasting days as much as possible.
- Season meals generously with herbs and spices. These food options are low in calories, but they help to enhance the flavor of your food.
- Eat high volume foods and food that has high water content such as melons, grapes, raw veggies, and popcorn.
- Eat more food that is rich in healthy fat, fiber, and protein. These are foods that are more filling and take longer to digest. They make you feel full longer, so you experience fewer hunger pangs.
- Avoid exercising or any other vigorous activity during your fasting days.
- Don't obsess about food during your fasting day. Don't read cookbooks and don't watch infomercials and cooking shows.
- Drink lots of water during your fasting days. You can also have herbal teas and other drinks too that are calorie-free.

Intermittent fasting teaches you to be more disciplined by saying no to food entirely on different occasions. When and how long you fast depends on the type of fasting regimen you want to employ. Through intermittent fasting, you regain control over your impulses and obtain more self-control. You become better able to resist the impulse to binge eat and become more disciplined about your food choices.

Cold Showers

Believe it or not, cold showers are quite beneficial to our health. It's not the most fun thing to do, but you can reap the benefits like:

- Improved metabolism
- Endorphins
- Improved blood circulation

What Are Cold Showers?

Cold showers are showers that you take where the water temperature is set to below 70°F. Now, that is cold, mind you. Experts refer to it as a type of hydrotherapy or water therapy.

The thing about it is that it isn't new. People have been doing cold showers for centuries and have noted the health benefits that they get out of it. The goal of the ancients who did cold showers was to condition their bodies; thus, they became more resistant to stress.

Benefits of Cold Showers Proven by Science

Research suggests that cold showers can help ease anxiety and depression [47]. This is because taking a cold shower can increase your endorphin and serotonin levels. These are the feel-good hormones. Increased endorphin and serotonin levels improve brain function, improve drive, increase mental energy, and help you to stay focused. With more mental energy and focus, you can stay disciplined throughout the day.

Studies also suggest that cold showers may be beneficial to weight loss [48]. This is due to the fact that taking a cold shower induces your body to produce more brown fat—the type of fat that is readily used by the body as energy. It's the first body fat to go and get burned as an energy source.

A lot of athletes today have incorporated cold showers into their training regimen [49]. They take advantage of the healing potential of cold showers and how it reduces inflammation, which is exactly what they are looking for during training.

Another study suggests that taking cold showers improves the way the body fights off common illnesses [50].

It's Not a Cure-All

Cold showers are not a cure-all, and they are not for everyone. If you are taking antidepressants or any mental health medication, then taking a cold shower may not be a good idea.

If your immune system has been compromised because you got sick rather recently, then you might want to forgo taking cold showers for now until you get better. On top of that, it will also take some effort to get used to taking cold showers.

How to Make the Cold Shower a Habit

Here are a few personal tips from me if you want to make taking a cold shower one of your lasting habits. Remember that it is not going to be easy, but it will be worth it.

1. **Don't rush, ease into it**. It will be very uncomfortable at first. So don't rush. If you can't take the cold any longer, then stop.
2. **Start with warm water and finish with warm water**. I would suggest that you start your shower with warm water. And then you slowly reduce the temperature until it goes below 70 degrees. Take a cold shower for a minute or two and then gradually increase the temperature until the water is warm enough for you. When you're used to it, you can do longer cold showers.

3. **Work your way to five minutes.** You can start by taking 30-second cold showers. Then work your way to one minute. After that, two. The goal is to work your way to a five-minute cold shower.
4. **Don't eat a heavy meal before a cold shower.** Eating heavy before a cold shower inhibits your body's blood flow. And it's not fun to have a belly full of food and then someone blasts you with really cold water.
5. **Start showering your face and neck.** That way, you won't feel the blast of cold water all over your body. This helps you get acclimated to the cold water.
6. **End your shower with something pleasurable.** I have always found that taking a hot cup of coffee or maybe chocolate can be quite a delight. Studies confirm that this method can help make it turn into an actual habit [51].

100 Days of Rejection Therapy

The story of Jiang Jia and his experience of getting 100 days of rejection is a classic example of how rejection can make you fearless. He resigned from a six-figure income working in a Fortune 100 company.

He quit that job because of an investment opportunity. But the plan backfired on him, and it left him with nothing.

He then discovered a game called Rejection Therapy. This game challenged people to look for rejections in their day-to-day lives. He tried it in the hopes that he would gain the ability to face rejections. He called it 100 days of rejection therapy.

Benefits of Rejection Therapy

1. **You will learn rejection-handling skills like flexing a muscle**: The more you get rejected, the less painful it becomes. You also get to work outside your comfort zone. The bottom line is that you get used to rejection; you don't take it personally, and it doesn't affect your mood.

2. **You will realize that it isn't really about you.** You no longer take rejection as something personal. People reject you because of their current circumstances at the moment, or maybe they were just not in the mood that day.

3. **You will learn to take risks.** Rejection therapy will teach you to take risks. Sometimes you will find the biggest opportunities after being rejected time and time again.

4. **You will learn how to turn a rejection into an opportunity.** Rejection is a painful experience; that is why a lot of us run away from it and then go into a corner and lick our wounds. Jiang says that rejections can have an upside and that if you can handle it well, you can find opportunities even while other people reject you.

There is no other way to get better at dealing with rejections than to find ways to get rejected. In my experience, it helped me get better at closing sales. I wasn't the best salesman—not by a long shot—but rejection therapy helped me learn how to close more sales eventually.

Here's what you can do. Make lots of requests every day and give people a chance to say no to your requests. Now, to reduce the pain of rejection, just remember that you're just trying to reach 100 rejections.

Turn everything into a countdown from 100 to zero. Be happy and celebrate when you reach 30 rejections, 50 rejections, 75 rejections, and finally 100 rejections. Write down your thoughts in a journal after experiencing each milestone on this list.

Building Routines

Gretchen Rubin once said: *"What you do every day matters more than what you do once in a while."* Your daily habits and routines, no matter how small they are, have a larger impact on your well-being than large, elaborate, and extravagant experiences.

Are you constantly looking for ways to make your days transition more smoothly? If you're anything like me, you will want to have more stability in your day. What I found out is that establishing routines helped me stay focused on what is important and allowed me to make time and space for my family.

That's one of the secrets to how I was able to maintain a healthy work-life balance.

Routines create consistency in everything that you do. They help you manage your time a lot better—well, you just put a lot of things on autopilot. You just have to deal with a few random things here and there.

Routines also encourage people to build habits and become more disciplined. However, if you're not careful, your routines can be more of a hindrance. This can happen if you're not mindful of it (remember the lesson in the previous chapter about mindfulness?).

In this chapter, we will go over a step-by-step plan so that you can create your routine mindfully and stick to it.

How a Routine Will Make You More Disciplined

I used to think that a routine was something that was beyond me. I was the type of person who preferred a degree of randomness in my day-to-day life. If I get too repetitive in the things I do, I lose focus and tend to become less productive.

Needless to say, I thought routines were mundane and boring. I also thought back then that I didn't have the gusto to follow through with any plan. I couldn't stick to an exercise plan, and I couldn't follow a lesson plan or an outline for a talk or presentation.

However, a few years going forward, routines have given me the stability I need to get creative. It has placed a lot of stability insomuch that I can creatively and efficiently do random things that can produce the best results—like writing this book, for instance.

One of the areas that I started with was my morning routine. It was a self-care habit that I have neglected for a while. But since learning how to make it a routine, I felt better and more empowered because my morning routine got me set up for the rest of my day.

Through routines, I was able to set up habits and add them to my routines. That helped me become more consistent in many aspects of my business. Having a routine allowed me to see that there is order in the things that I do—I learned I can be more organized!

As it was also mentioned elsewhere in this book, a routine will reduce the number of decisions that you will have to make on any given day. This is especially important on very busy days.

Downsides That You Should Know About

Do routines have downsides? It depends on the routine. Routines are like habits—there are bad habits and good habits. Just like that, there are bad routines and good routines.

Back in the day, I had this really bad routine. After coming home from work, I would just throw my keys on that little bowl on a cupboard where all the other keys in the house were in. And then the first thing I would do after kicking off my shoes was to go straight to the fridge and grab a drink.

The next step was to go to the couch and watch TV. The remote was somewhere on the couch—it was always there somewhere because I did this routine every day for about a year. I would sit there in front of the TV until I fell asleep.

That routine, of course, made me miserable. The house was unkempt, I gained weight, and I got depressed. That was an unhealthy nightly routine or after-work routine. I ended up isolating myself from my friends because I used the TV binging as a way to escape my troubles.

Some would argue that having a routine would stunt personal growth. And I agree—a bad routine will stunt your personal growth. But I also disagree because a good and mindfully selected routine will produce better personal growth.

A healthy routine has helped me get out of negative patterns. It also helped me prevent boredom from setting in, and I was able to get over burnouts.

How to Create a Healthy Mindful Routine

Here are the steps that I found were helpful when establishing a routine. Feel free to add to these steps in case you think you need to get something else done in between before moving on to the next step.

1. Choose the Type of Routine You Want to Have

This step is obvious. Some routines are for the mornings after you get out of bed, some can be done at night, and some during the midday. Some routines are for work or, more specifically, to get you into work mode.

Some routines are for creative people. Artists may have their routine before they write songs, create music, or in my case, before I sit down to write a book. Athletes also have routines before practice and before going to work—aka the actual game.

Sometimes the best routine is the one that you have been doing all this time. In my case, I prepare a cup of coffee before I sit down in front of my laptop to write. I also set the early morning hours from 5 am to 7 am for writing.

I play my favorite playlist in the background too. That's my "get to work" music there.

And that is how I set my mind to get into work mode. Pay attention to the little things you do before you do something. Chances are you have the beginnings of an actual routine already there for you.

All you need, therefore, is to pick up on it and get started.

2. Set Your Motive

Now, you may want to set two to three minutes to do a mindfulness exercise when you're just starting out. You can do a body scan, or instead of a body scan, you can just do a mindfulness exercise to become more aware of your surroundings.

While you're at it, take that time to decide what you truly intend to do with this routine that you are about to engage in. Later on, after the routine has become more automatic, you can just skip this step if you want.

3. Start the Motions and Edit as You Go

After affixing your purpose and motive for that routine, then go for it. Start with full intent. Does it have to be a complex routine? Well, it's all up to you. I like to keep it simple so that I could get it done quickly.

But if you want to make it as elaborate as you want, then go ahead and do that. Whatever suits your fancy will work. Just make sure that you edit your routine to your needs and liking.

Try not to copy someone else's routine. Remember that these routines are personal, but if you think a part of another person's routine will help you stay focused and disciplined, then why not just incorporate that into your own routine, right?

4. Select Routines for Different Activities

You can have different routines for different activities in your day. Create a routine for different tasks so that they will become automatic to you.

Chapter 5: Dealing with Burnout the Smart Way

"Burnout is what happens when you try to avoid being human for too long."

(Michael Gungor)

Your ability to stay concentrated on a given task or goal will be negatively impacted if you are experiencing burnout. It will impede your progress when you're striving for self-mastery, and it will be very difficult to maintain a level of discipline.

If you are having problems coping with stress in the workplace, then you may be at risk of burnout. Burnouts can be quite challenging since they can leave you unable to cope with the demands of life.

I know, and I have been there. It affected my family life, and it definitely hit my work performance hard. I'm telling you, it's not just some random stuff that you come up with in your head. A burnout will feel as real as anything.

You feel empty and exhausted, and it may even be accompanied by physical and mental health symptoms too. But what is a burnout and how do you deal with it? You don't want it in your life, but at some point you will experience it and you will have to deal with it.

We'll cover the nature of a work burnout in this chapter. We will also go over some powerful tips and strategies that you can do to cope with it as well. A lot of the tips I will provide here has helped me get back up to my feet after having several burnout episodes in my life.

What is a Work Burnout Exactly?

According to the Mayo Clinic, job burnout is a special kind of work-related stress [52]. However, they also point out that it is not a medical diagnosis. What that means is that it isn't exactly a condition like depression.

It's not on the same level. But burnouts can still hit you hard. It affects people so much that experts recognize them as a type of occupational hazard [53]. The ones who are most susceptible to this experience are those in professions that require people-oriented contact.

If you're in human services, health care, customer service, or even in education, then you are highly susceptible to work burnouts. Any job description that requires a level of emotional and personal contact with others is included.

So, how do you define work burnout?

Burnout can be simply summarized in one word—exhaustion. This isn't like the regular exhaustion that you feel when you get tired after a hard day's work or after you went out for a run or lifted weights at the gym.

Three Types of Burnout

Experts have identified three different types of burnout syndrome. Dr. Christina Maslach, the one who formulated the Maslach Burnout Inventor, has identified them as the following:

1. **Organizational Burnout**

This is a type of burnout that is caused by poor organization. It can also come out of any extreme demands on your time. Another possible cause of this type of burnout is getting unrealistic deadlines at work.

Having these things will give you that feeling that your employment status is in jeopardy. Other than that, these conditions will also make you feel inadequate and that you aren't hitting your organization's goals all the time.

2. **Interpersonal Burnout**

This type of burnout is caused by getting into difficult relationships. This can happen in any of your relationships, both personally and professionally. If you are experiencing this, then a boss that is too aggressive can add to all the stress that you are already experiencing.

Having co-workers that intimidate or challenge you also adds fuel to the anxiety that you may already be experiencing. A spouse (or partner) that doesn't seem to appreciate you will make you feel unloved or unappreciated and may also contribute to interpersonal burnout.

3. **Individual Burnout**

This is a type of burnout that occurs on a personal level. A huge part of this type of burnout is the negative self-talk that people often do to themselves. Sometimes when you have set a rather perfectionist standard for yourself, it can also lead to this type of burnout.

Some people experience a certain level of neurosis when they experience an individual burnout. This can often lead people to a belief that all the things that they do can never be good enough even though they have already accomplished much.

Different Modes of Measuring Exhaustion and Burnout

Burnout is exhaustion that is physical, mental, and also emotional all at the same time. It is something that you will eventually go through after getting continual exposure to a lot of stressful situations.

Exhaustion from a researcher's point of view is measured differently, of course. When identifying the cause of burnout, you need to determine whether you're dealing with cognitive weariness, emotional exhaustion, or just physical fatigue [54]. That is the standard for the Shirom-Melamed Burnout Measure.

Another way that researchers measure the type of exhaustion that one may be experiencing is through making a distinction between psychological exhaustion and physical exhaustion [55], which is how the Copenhagen Burnout Inventory evaluates a person's condition.

Exhaustion also has a lot of other dimensions, and they are measured by other burnout measures/standards. Some experts check a person's enthusiasm in his or her job, levels of guilt, efficacy, adequacy in the workplace, and indolence.

These are all different measures, but they all boil down to one thing—when you're burned out, you are exhausted in more ways than one. Because burnouts are heavily caused by stress, psychiatrists Gail North and Herbert Freudenberger have classified burnouts as a type of stress syndrome.

A Short History about the Concept of a Burnout

Long story short, a burnout zaps out the joy in your life, and it will haunt your family and personal interactions, your friendships, and it can have a negative influence on your career. It happens after working long hours, getting upsetting news, having a sick family member, school or work safety issues, and other possible causes.

We'll go over the causes later on.

The word "burnout" was coined in the 1970s by Herbert Freudenberger [56]. He described it as a condition that involves a severe amount of stress. This highly stressful and prolonged condition then leads to an equally severe emotional, mental, and physical exhaustion.

If you have experienced burnout, you know that it is a lot worse than any regular kind of fatigue. If you're going through one, you will find it challenging to deal with your day-to-day responsibilities.

Your productivity will hit rock bottom. Your relationships with loved ones and friends will suffer. On top of that, you will find it increasingly more difficult to deal with the stress that happens in life.

Who Can Get Affected by Burnouts

Have you ever felt like you have nothing left to give? Have you ever experienced feeling that fear of leaving your bed and you just don't want to get up in the morning when your alarm rings?

That may be a sign of burnout coming along. It will come with a feeling of hopelessness, and then you develop a rather pessimistic outlook in life. Now, here's the scary part—a burnout never goes away on its own, and it can affect anybody.

If it is left untreated, it will lead to other medical conditions. It can develop into depression, and it can also contribute to diabetes and even heart disease.

As it was pointed out earlier, some people are more susceptible to burnouts. Here's a partial list:

- Parents
- Business executives
- Doctors
- Nurses
- Any first responders to emergency situations
- Customer service representatives
- Technicians
- Cab drivers
- Waitresses
- Construction workers
- Office staff
- Front desk staff
- Any professional that is tasked with helping others

As you can see, any job that requires any form of direct interaction and providing service to others is a trigger for this type of condition. One study even suggests that you don't have to be at the forefront of emergency care to rapidly experience a burnout.

Even being a father or a mother caring for a child can put you at risk for burnouts. In fact, parents, business executives, and even doctors are on the same level of potential risk for this condition [57].

Note that you don't have to be a kind of service personnel to experience burnout. Anyone can experience it given certain conditions. We'll cover the contributory conditions and factors in a later section of this chapter.

Be Aware of the Burnout Signs: Some Important Q&A

The following are the signs and symptoms of burnout. If you experience two or more of these signs, then you know that you are at risk of one coming up real soon. Take some alone time and ask yourself the following questions:

- Am I experiencing bowel problems, stomach aches or other stomach problems, unexplained headaches, and other physical symptoms?
- Have I experienced changes in my sleeping habits?
- Do I use alcohol, drugs, or even food just to make me feel better? Do I use any of these things just to feel numb about the things happening in my life?
- Am I experiencing any form of disillusionment from my current job?
- Do I feel dissatisfied with the achievements that I have had at work?
- Do I find it hard to concentrate?
- Do I lack the energy to be productive as consistently as I used to?
- Am I irritable when interacting with clients, customers, and even with my co-workers?
- Do I have trouble getting work started?
- Do I have to drag myself to work all the time?
- Have I become critical of my workmates or even my superiors?
- Have I become more cynical nowadays?

If you answered in the affirmative to two or more of these questions, then you have the definite symptoms of burnout.

In my case, I only noticed that I was having a burnout when my sleeping patterns changed. I often try to stay up late at night rushing to complete a project, only to fall asleep on my desk and struggle to stay up.

I ended up sleeping two to three hours a day. I then felt dissatisfied with my work—it's work that I have been very good at, and I've been doing it for more than five years. I was snapping at my family and I couldn't stand my co-workers.

If you are experiencing burnout, I strongly suggest that you talk to your doctor immediately. And I do mean immediately. You may get a referral to work with a psychiatrist or some other mental health provider, especially if your doctor suspects that your burnout may be related to depression.

List of Psychological Symptoms You May Experience

- Frustration
- Emotional numbness

- Cynicism
- Easily angered
- Absenteeism
- Loss of purpose
- Low commitment to one's job role
- Negative attitude towards co-workers
- Fatigue
- Lack of creativity
- Difficulty concentrating
- Low mood
- Feeling listless
- Detachment
- Anxiety
- Generalized aches
- Feeling really exhausted

List of Physical Symptoms You May Experience

- Muscle tension
- Susceptibility to flu, colds, and other common ailments
- Difficulty sleeping
- Disrupted sleep cycle
- Hypertension
- Gastrointestinal disorders
- Headache

Now, we'll go over the more serious symptoms in the next section of this discussion. We'll cover that below.

Key Symptoms That You Should Look Out For

Here are the key symptoms that can help you identify whether you're already experiencing burnout or not:

1. Exhaustion

This is usually one of the early signs that you will experience. When we say exhaustion, this is the kind that leaves you completely depleted. It's not just an emotional or mental kind of exhaustion—this one is accompanied by actual physical symptoms.

Other than feeling tired and unmotivated without much gusto to carry on any further, you also experience certain aches and pains. You will get a loss of appetite. I have experienced stomach aches for no reason. I also had frequent headaches.

2. Frequent Illnesses

Okay, so this is a separate symptom altogether from the ones mentioned in item number 1 above. Remember that burnout is often related to long-term exposure to stress. When that happens, your immune system suffers.

The body becomes weak and eventually susceptible to many common illnesses. If you're under constant stress for a prolonged period of time, then you will usually get flu-like symptoms, cough, cold, and other health conditions as well.

Since you will already experience some changes in your sleep patterns, you may already be going through the first few stages of insomnia. As your condition progresses, you may develop anxiety disorders as well as depression as well.

3. Irritability

Here's a fact—burnouts can cause you to lose control. As the level of your anxiety increases, the more you become irritable. You lose your cool with your kids, your spouse or partner, and your co-workers as well.

You get easily irritated and you lash back at people quite easily. You weren't always that way, but now you have become a hot-headed person. You can't tolerate a lot of things and you tend to snap at other people over the smallest things.

As you go along, you find it more difficult to cope with the usual stressors in life, such as household tasks, caring for your kids, and even work meetings. When something goes wrong or some unplanned thing happens, you get irritated.

4. Escape Fantasies

People experiencing burnout will usually fantasize about going on a solo vacation or running away from their current situation in general. There are also extreme circumstances when they may turn to substance abuse to just numb away any pain they may be experiencing.

5. Isolation

When you are overwhelmed, you will feel isolated. Sometimes this isolation is self-imposed. Burned out people may stay away from people or just stop any form of socializing completely.

They stop confiding with friends and family. This is a critical sign, and when you notice it happening to you, then you must get help immediately.

Causes of Burnouts

It is important that when you notice that you have a burnout that you determine the possible causes with your healthcare provider. The following are some of the factors that can lead to work burnout:

- ***Lack of Work-Life Balance***

When your work takes up a lot of your time, then you are on the verge of a burnout. Remember that human beings aren't one-dimensional creatures. Our life at work is only one facet of the totality of our being.

We all need to have time for something else and other people. We need to spend enough time and energy for our family, friends, and other interests. Lack of work-life balance can easily lead to burnout.

- ***Lack of Social Support***

Feeling isolated at work is a dangerous thing. Combine that with isolation and loneliness in your personal life can add to the stress that you are already feeling. You need to reach out and find friends pretty much everywhere.

Remember that it is not the isolation that gets you. It is the stress that comes from a lonely life that will contribute to your stress levels.

- ***Extremely Monotonous Activity***

Last time I checked, you're not a machine. Look at yourself in the mirror and you will see that on the other side is a human being. You're not built to do the same thing over and over again. It's going to drive you into boredom or even chaos.

I find it very hard to remain focused if I keep repeating the same things over and over again ad infinitum at work. The first thing that will come is fatigue. You get tired of doing the same routine.

It will eventually lead to burnout. That means we should find time to break the monotony of our lives in order to derive more meaning into what we do for a living.

- ***Problematic Workplace Dynamics***

I never encountered any office bullies in my life, but I have been bullied at school, so I guess I know how it would feel like. But there have been people in the office that have undermined my work, and that felt almost like I was getting bullied.

I have also had a boss micromanage everything, and that can also contribute to dysfunctional workplace dynamics.

- ***Unclear Job Expectations***

When the degree of authority that you are given (or someone who is supposed to be your superior is given), then you will feel uncomfortable at work. You won't know what is appropriate and what is expected of you or your co-workers performance-wise.

- ***Lack of Control***

When you feel like you have no control over your tasks, or your ability to influence certain decisions, then that might trigger feelings of insecurity.

Having no control over things like your workload, your work schedule, the assignments that you have to work on, and the unavailability of the resources that you need to fulfill your job can produce a lot of anxiety and thus contribute a lot to a possible burnout.

Burnout Prevention

Once you have identified one or two of the symptoms mentioned earlier, you should act promptly. Here are some of the expert tips that I have found useful when it comes to burnout prevention.

Increase Self-Efficacy

"Self-efficacy" is a technical term, and it simply means having that firm belief that you can accomplish things.

Experts also call it a "perceived capability"[59]. When you set these goals, they should be ones that are meaningful to you.

Experts have observed that the people who believe that they can achieve things tend to experience less stress. When people believe that they can overcome problems, then they find inner strength to overcome stressful situations.

According to Albert Bandura, the one who formulated this theory, there are four sources that drive this firm belief in oneself. They include the following:

1. Mastery experiences
2. Verbal persuasion
3. Psychological and emotional states
4. Vicarious experiences

You can use these factors to improve your state or level of self-efficacy.

Mastery Experiences

So, what are mastery experiences? A mastery experience is an experience where you take on a new challenge and then you succeed in it. This can be applied when learning a new skill or achieving a certain goal.

We improve our performance one step at a time, and we gain increased confidence as we master small steps toward a much larger goal. So, how do you do this?

1. Find a task that you find challenging (e.g., increasing sales, creating a marketing strategy, ask someone out on a date, complete your research on a given deadline, etc.)
2. Outline smaller tasks that will help you complete that task (e.g., design ads, send a text message, engage in small talk, etc.)
3. Do one small task at a time until you have accomplished every single one of them. Observe how you feel after accomplishing each task. Know that you can do it if you try.
4. After successfully accomplishing a task, perform a self-evaluation session. Find some quiet time—maybe 10 to 15 minutes—take the time to celebrate what you have accomplished. You can get a drink or maybe have a favorite dessert; any treat will be great. And then while you're at it ask yourself, "I can do this, so what else can I do?"
5. Move on to the next mini-task until you have accomplished the main task. Don't forget to reward yourself at the end.

So, what if you encounter failure? The solution is to sit down and also do a self-evaluation. This time you will determine the factors that brought about your failure. Think about things that you would have done differently.

After that, determine your next course of action or an alternative action. And then go out and do it.

Vicarious Experiences

This is the second most powerful way to increase your self-efficacy. The word "vicarious" sort of sounds quite religious, but it means something very simple. What this means is that you should observe someone else who has already accomplished that thing you want to accomplish.

What you are looking for is someone to "model" how the task can be accomplished. For instance, if you don't feel confident about selling (you believe yourself to be a bad salesperson), then find someone good at it.

Observe how it is done. Bandura says that seeing someone succeed is rather infectious. If they can do it, then that means you can do it as well.

The person who will serve as your model doesn't have to be a co-worker, supervisor, or even your boss. It can be a grandparent, your siblings, an aunt, teachers, your coach, a local celebrity, or any mentor.

What matters is that you can vicariously envision yourself as succeeding using the method that they used to succeed.

Verbal Persuasion

There are some big reasons why people look for motivational speakers. People attend self-improvement seminars and mastery classes conducted by charismatic experts for a reason.

Motivational talks and even that little pep talk that you have with a close friend can help to raise your spirits and reduce stress. It has the same effect as a talk between a parent and a child. That trust and confidence communicated from a trusted person (e.g., the parent) provides solace and motivation for the recipient (e.g., the child).

Psychological and Emotional States

Your emotional state and psychological condition can also be a source of strength and provide you a big boost to one's self-efficacy. It should be obvious that you can't have a positive assessment of your own capability to accomplish anything if you're suffering from depression and/or anxiety.

It won't be realistic to presume that you can get your tasks done if you are currently suffering from a medical condition. A lot of times, when people get over poor psychological and emotional states, they bounce back and take on life with much-needed gusto. They see things as a new chance at life.

Chapter 6 – Discipline Tactics of Navy SEALs and the Spartans

A lot of soldiers and former service members have written entire books on how the Navy SEALs, the Spartans, or other figures that enforce discipline among their numbers. Examples of such authors include Mark Grant, former SEAL Jocko Willink, and Jason Lopez. This chapter goes over ideas and insights that these authors and others like them have shared.

Success = Discipline

Discipline is a necessity, especially when your life is on the line. Self-discipline is on the same level of importance as mental toughness, resilience, and hard work when the safety and fate of a nation is in your hands.

Well, you don't have to enter into military service in order to learn about their methods. You can learn from these authors themselves and pick up lessons from their personal experiences.

When you're a soldier, you embrace pain and hardship as if they were your life and joy. You try to excel and do your best because you know that if you fail hundreds, if not thousands, of lives are at stake.

Military Secrets

Here are some of the rules of thumb and guiding principles that the Navy SEALs and other military service members live by in order to maintain self-control, willpower, and self-discipline.

Don't Quit

Don't quit? Easier said than done, right? This is more of a motto for service members. When faced with challenges, they don't quit. They look at the challenge and act as if they have no other choice but to go forward.

Next time you are faced with seemingly insurmountable odds, think back on the SEALs and how they sacrifice and push forward despite difficulty and pain. Sometimes it takes sheer persistence and determination to see things through.

Always Make Every Goal and Objective a Serious Thing

If you go into the field half-cocked or if you try something and the will is half-baked, then you're bound to fail. According to former Navy SEAL Casey Imafidon, SEALs emphasize only three things when it comes to missions:

1. The objective
2. How to execute it
3. What happens after you have reached that objective

He says that sometimes your success is measured by the level of commitment you give to a specific goal or objective.

Wake Up Early and Win the Morning

We have discussed waking up early in an earlier chapter of this book. There is a reason why military service members are made to wake up early as a matter of routine. Waking up early doesn't only instill a feeling of discipline; it also gives you a lot of opportunities such as:

- Complete all the necessary preparations for that day
- Read a book and prepare your mind
- Meditate
- Exercise
- Gather the necessary intel
- Start your day with better focus and discipline

Jocko Willink also created what he called the 4 AM Club. This is support and a collaboration of a group of people who wake up at 4 in the morning, plan their day well ahead of everyone else, and be better at achieving their goals.

Other than waking up early in the morning, another accompanying or complementing principle that Navy Seals have is called winning the morning.

For military service members, the choice you make every morning is only a simple matter. When the alarm goes off, you have a critical decision to make—do you get up and get your day started, or do you succumb to the comfort of your bed and go back to sleep?

Those who choose to snooze eventually lose, but those who choose to get up win. This simple exercise allows you to overcome a moment of weakness. Overcoming weaknesses eventually become a powerful habit.

Pay Attention to Every Lesson That You Learn

Both the successes and failures that you experience will become your mentors. In many instances, your failures tend to become your biggest and loudest teachers. Navy SEALs are taught leadership principles, and that includes making course corrections quickly.

A quick lesson here is that you shouldn't dwell too much on your failures because it will do nothing for you. Adapt quickly and make adjustments as fast as you can when failure strikes. When there's a lot at stake, there's no time to mull over spilled milk.

Exercise

All soldiers are forced to exercise daily. We all know that there are numerous studies on the benefits of exercise, so there is no need to enumerate every single one of them. One of the most notable benefits of pushing yourself to exercise is that, according to studies, it can increase your emotional and mental resilience [62].

Embrace the Suck

This is military slang that was coined during Operation Iraqi Freedom. So what does it mean? The lesson is powerful here. It implies that you're not the first one to ever experience difficulty and pain, so deal with it. But remember you're not doing it alone.

To embrace the suck means to embrace the situation—to accept that you are really in the current situation you're in. However, that is not a defeatist notion. Sure, you accept the reality of the conditions you're living in now, but you have the power to do something about it.

As soldiers, the Navy Seals have no choice but to go where they are told to go. They do not deny the challenges that they face. This reduces any feelings of discontent among service members.

So, why does the military, including the Spartans, "embrace the suck?" The answer is simple—they do it because it is now a matter of habit. When you rewire your mind and take a more accepting point of view, you will become more aware of your situation and thus will be more likely to spot opportunities to come out victorious.

Mastering the Art of Simplicity

Navy Seals and other military personnel often get told to "cut the crap." It's more than just another military slang or wisecrack. Mark Divine, a former Navy Seal, explains that this principle refers to the art of simplicity.

He says that in order to live with more grit and discipline, we need to learn to live and embrace the art of simplicity. It is quite a liberating concept. We often clutter our lives with lots of gadgets, commitments, unhealthy relationships, and way too many material possessions.

These are things that weigh us down and take away our focus on the things that matter. In effect, the "crap" in our lives distracts us and reduces our effectiveness. We become less disciplined in everything we do because we think of and pay attention to too many things.

In the military, service members live and breathe simplicity. They are given an objective and then they set out to complete the mission and attain the aforementioned objective.

To a soldier, war is nothing but chaos. And so, an objective, a mission, and cutting out the unnecessary things that are in the way help to get rid of the chaos.

Do you want to be more disciplined? Here's what you can do:

1. Decide today to live a simpler life—try a minimalist lifestyle.
2. If you have too many clothes and many of which you never even wear anymore, then get rid of those or give them away to charity.
3. Make an inventory of each room in the house.
4. Start with your bedroom. Find things in there that are just gathering dust, things that you haven't used in the last six to twelve months.
5. Get rid of those or give them away to charity (another option is to collect these items and have a garage sale so you can make some money on the side).
6. Next, go to the living room. Do the same inventory.
7. Make an inventory of every place in your house—especially the garage and your attic. You might be surprised to find that you have been hoarding a lot of stuff that you don't need or use.
8. Clean up these living spaces and put the unused items on sale or give them away to charity (at least you know you're helping other people in the process).
9. Check the emails that you receive. Cancel subscriptions that you don't read or use.
10. Are there people in your life who are nuisances or distractions to you? You have the choice to either put them on your ignore list or just cut ties with them completely. How you do that is all up to you.
11. Are there gym memberships and other subscriptions that you're paying for that you don't really need or rarely use? Get rid of those as well.
12. Is social media taking up too much of your time? You should try uninstalling some of your phone's social media apps.

If you do these things, you live simply and will be adopting a minimalist lifestyle. You will then notice a sense of freedom and clarity, especially after you have removed all the clutter in your home and in your life.

It will be as if you have been renewed. You can now approach your days with better focus and renewed commitment to the things that really matter to you.

In Mark Divine's own words—in the eyes of the Navy Seals, less means more.

You're Never Really Alone

Admiral William McRaven once said that no one wins wars alone. The same is true when we want to win the war against the lack of focus and self-discipline. To have mental toughness, you need to realize that you're not the only one trying to achieve that character trait.

This lesson is usually driven home hard into every Navy Seal. Remember, they are called Navy Seal Teams—there is no room for a one-person army like Rambo or some other fictional war character.

All you need to do is to observe their physical trainings. You will notice that a lot of these trainings involve a degree of strategic teamwork. It's not just teamwork—you're part of a greater whole, and you need to contribute to the strategy that your team will implement to ensure that the mission is a success.

When one person makes a mistake, the entire class gets the brunt of it. However, they're not just on a mission to weed out the weak. The goal is to teach new recruits a lesson. And that lesson is that teamwork is essential to success.

Navy Seals understand this lesson early in training. They understand that they must act as an entire unit and not just individually. That works in military life as well as in life outside of the service.

Here's what you can do:
1. Find support in every endeavor. You can find support groups, clubs, and other organizations. Share your own experiences and be immersed in the experiences of others.
2. The goal is to find likeminded individuals who are willing to encourage you.
3. Find someone, a spouse, a dear friend, a life coach, a therapist, etc. with whom you can confide in. Have regular performance evaluations with that person, whether it is about being more disciplined, gaining more self-control, earning more money, anger management, etc. The goal is to have someone to whom you can report your progress

to. Remember that when effort is measured, then progress increases, and when it is reported and evaluated, then progress multiplies.
4. Reach out to someone and do some good in that person's life. You can volunteer in a soup kitchen or some other cause. This also gets reported back to your friend or confidant. Remember that when people join an endeavor that is something bigger than themselves, their performance tends to increase.

Marianna Pogosyan, a consultant that specializes in cross-cultural transition psychology, and author of the book *Between Cultures,* explains that when people get involved in helping others, they eventually help themselves.

Being in the service of others produces altruistic feelings, but it is more than just that. Studies show that when we go out of our way to help others, it improves our emotional well-being. It improves our ability to empathize with others and increases our capacity to cope with stress.

Our performance and self-control also increase when we focus on tasks that benefit others. Why are Navy Seals more dedicated and more disciplined compared to a lot of people? It is because they understand that what they are doing benefits others.

When the lives of others are at stake, you push yourself to greater heights. Sometimes you find that you can do things better because of this. It eventually gives you a sense of purpose and satisfaction that you can't get anywhere else. It is an act that naturally cycles back to benefit you in the end.

You Need to Challenge Yourself Constantly

Former Navy Seal Cade Courtley explains that you should expect that "you're going to get your ass kicked once in a while" and that is why you should make it a point to constantly challenge yourself.

He says that there is a common factor that is shared by all who succeed at BUDs training. BUDs is short for Basic Underwater Demolition SEAL training. It is a physical and mental training that all candidates go through before they ultimately become part of the Navy Seals.

Courtley explains that this single factor is finding a reason to continue to grow and improve. Challenge yourself constantly and learn to live with true adversity. He observes that the candidates who survive BUDs are those who have lived and survived against adversity their entire lives.

He then makes an interesting analogy. He asks, "Who will you be more prone to trust—someone who inherited millions of dollars or someone who built his financial empire of 10 million dollars at age 45 after going through several bankruptcies to get there?

The more resilient and more disciplined person whom you should emulate is the person who has made all the mistakes and has thrived in adversity. Find a way to challenge yourself, and you will learn to thrive in the same manner.

Did you get promoted a couple of years ago? Did you stop there, and did the drive and ambition die out after you got your pay raise? Challenge yourself to perform better and you will find yourself in a lot of adversity, but that challenge will drive you forward and give you the mental toughness to face even greater difficulties ahead.

Were you able to lose ten pounds in the last two months? But are you at your target weight? If not, then challenge yourself to lose ten more pounds. This will help you become even more disciplined with your workout and stick with your diet plan.

The greater the challenge, the more self-control, grit, and discipline will be required. Beat that, and you will achieve greater levels of self-mastery.

Conclusion

I hope that the lessons here in this book were able to help you understand the logic and science behind self-discipline, motivation, and willpower. It will take a while for practices and lessons like developing and shifting to a new mindset to completely set in.

In your journey to self-mastery, you will be faced with fear, uncertainty, and doubt. I suggest that you try out the habits that have been outlined here from delayed gratification to mindfulness.

Don't stress so much about the outcome, but please learn to enjoy the process. It is not just the end result that brings joy and satisfaction to the soul—the journey itself is something that you should look forward to.

The next step is to practice the principles in this book and get an accountability partner. Find someone who will walk the path to a more self-disciplined life with you. It is never easy, but just like the Spartans of old and the Navy SEALs of today, every task and journey is made easier when you have someone to share it with.

Thank you!

Before you go, I just wanted to say thank you for purchasing my book.

You could have picked from dozens of other books on the same topic but you took a chance and chose this one.

So, a HUGE thanks to you for getting this book and for reading all the way to the end.

Now I wanted to ask you for a small favor. **Could you please consider posting a review on the platform? Reviews are one of the easiest ways to support the work of independent authors.**

This feedback will help me continue to write the type of books that will help you get the results you want. So if you enjoyed it, please let me know!

Lastly, don't forget to grab a copy of your Free Bonus book *"Bulletproof Confidence Checklist."* If you want to learn how to overcome shyness and social anxiety and become more confident, then this book is for you.

Just go to: https://theartofmastery.com/confidence/

CPSIA information can be obtained
at www.ICGtesting.com
Printed in the USA
BVHW082256080421
604477BV00008B/1093